The Vision of Six Sigma

A Roadmap for Breakthrough

Mikel J. Harry, Ph.D.
President & CEO
Six Sigma Academy, Inc.

1994

Sigma Publishing Company
Phoenix, Arizona, USA

Ordering Instructions

"The Vision of Six Sigma:
A Roadmap for Breakthrough"

Mikel J. Harry, Ph.D.

Fax: (602) 921-2954
Call: (602) 921-2852
Write:
Sigma Sigma Academy, Inc.
1501 W. Fountainhead Pkwy., Suite 670
Tempe, Arizona USA 85282

Please Include:
Title of Publication, ISBN#
Your Name, Phone, Fax, Company, Address

Library of Congress Cataloging in Publication Data

Harry, Mikel J.
        The Vision of Six Sigma.

        Includes Bibliography and References
        1. Quality control - Statistical methods. 2. Six Sigma
I. Title

ISBN 0-9643555-2-3
Current Printing (last digit)
1098

Cover Design & Printing By:
TRI STAR PRINTING & VISUAL COMMUNICATIONS
PHOENIX, ARIZONA

To the Memory of Bill Smith

Preface

History of Quality

The need for quality was first recognized after humankind's initial efforts to produce a duplicate of an object. Those initial efforts at object duplication resulted in rather crude copies that were in all probability functional, but rather frail with regard to dimensional stability and applicability of use. Examples of this are clearly seen in arrow flints, stone hammers, and early cooking utensils. Although such efforts at quality control resulted in reproductions which appeared to be relatively similar, there were, however, considerable variations in one or more of the quality characteristics which, in turn, resulted in large differences in performance. In some instances the variations were of enough magnitude to negate any possible use of the reproduction; for example, a weapon made from a stone that was too large or a "food stick" that was too big for the user's mouth.

Over much time, these assertive, if not exasperating, efforts to gain control over the quality of a reproduction gave impetus to the rise of craftsmen. These individuals became quite skilled at duplicating specific types of objects. As demand for their skills increased, craftsmen that produced similar objects slowly banded together to form what became known as guilds. Essentially, guilds allowed craftsmen to further specialize and solidify their skills. Although these craftsmen were highly skilled they still were not capable of duplicating an object accurately enough to create replacement parts in advance of a probable repair. When a repair was necessary, the original object was required. It was not until Eli Whitney conceived the idea of interchangeable parts that this situation was turned around.

Eli Whitney's idea was to have each worker make one specific part, or perform a limited number of operations on a given part to exact specifications so that all of the individual parts would be identical and could be assembled into a product. Although the idea was sound in theory and basically applicable, as evidenced by the production of rifles during that era, it became readily apparent that a human being simply could not produce an "exact" copy of an object. This remained true no matter how skilled the worker was or how simple the part or operation. The recognition of this dilemma led to the development of "tolerances."

The Essence of Six Sigma

Since that time, the need for process control has increased at an astounding rate. The idea of quality control has yielded to the notion of quality assurance. From this perspective, the practice of statistical process control and experimental design has flourished. Yet in spite of these advances, the customers that form the enormous base of today's world market are sending a clear and undeniable message -- produce higher quality products at lower costs with greater responsiveness. Companies are hearing this message and are again rising to the challenge. For many, the stalking of Six Sigma has led to the development of new and exciting approaches for the improvement of business, engineering, and manufacturing, service, and administration performance. The purpose of this book is to present the Six Sigma strategies, tactics, and tools which have been successfully used to achieve a world-class level of business performance.

In essence, Six Sigma advocates that there are strong relationships between product defects and product yield, reliability, costs, cycle time, inventory, schedule, and so on. As the number of defects increase, the number of sigma's decreases. In other words, the larger the sigma value, the better the product quality – and visa versa. Although the ultimate aspiration is zero defects, the threshold of excellence is Six Sigma performance. This target holds for all processes related to the operation of a business.

Interestingly, Six Sigma quality is estimated assuming "typical" shifts and drifts in process centering. In this sense, 99.99966 percent capability at the "part" and "process step" levels is an intermediate target toward the ideal of perfection. This may be illustrated by considering a product that contains 300 unique purchased parts and a related manufacturing process that consists of say, 500 independent operations. A Six Sigma capability at the part and operation level would ensure an aggregate or "rolled" yield of 99.73 percent. This would be to say, out of every 10,000 units of product manufactured, there would be 9,973 units that would be produced completely free of defects.

Aim of the Book

Throughout this book, variation is viewed as the number one enemy of quality, yield, and costs. It must be arrested and ultimately eliminated in order to achieve "best in class." By attacking variation during the design phase, within suppliers' processes, and within our own processes, Six Sigma capability can be achieved. In doing so, the foundation of excellence is laid.

Based on the statistical perspective, the product and process engineering viewpoints are brought into focus by means of analytical examples. Through the discussion and examples, insights are developed as to the objectives of the Six Sigma initiative; enhanced product quality, yield, and cost – all of which, in turn, improve customer satisfaction.

Again, this book has been specifically designed to structure an in-depth overview of the fundamental strategies, tactics, and tools necessary for achieving Six Sigma product designs, manufacturing processes, service quality, and quality of administration. Up front, the basic tenants of Six Sigma will be revealed in a nontechnical manner and then illustrated in more technically oriented discussions. Specifically, the book will explore:

> • *The Driving Need for Six Sigma Quality*
> • *The Fundamental Objective of Six Sigma*
> • *The Customer's Perspective of Six Sigma*
> • *The Basic Tenants of Six Sigma*
> • *Advanced Six Sigma Concepts*
> • *Key Business Conclusions Resulting From Global Benchmarking*
> • *Six Sigma as a Target for Total Quality Management (TQM)*
> • *The Primary Tools for Achieving Six Sigma*
> • *The Impact of Product and Process Complexity on Quality*
> • *The Impact of Six Sigma on Product Reliability*
> • *The Impact of Six Sigma on Manufacturing Cycle-Time*
> • *The Impact of Six Sigma on Inventory*
> • *The Impact of Six Sigma on the Bottom Line*
> • *How to Create and Maintain Six Sigma Product Designs*
> • *How to Create and Maintain Six Sigma Manufacturing Processes*
> • *Strategies and Tactics for Implementing Six Sigma*

In addition, several "real life" case studies from Asea Brown Boveri, Texas Instruments (DSEG), and Motorola Inc. are presented and thoroughly discussed. The case studies are configured to demonstrate many of the how to's, implementation issues, deployment tactics, and lessons learned with respect to Six Sigma. In particular, the cases will highlight the "Six Nuggets of Six Sigma." Those experienced based nuggets are as follows:

1) The same questions most often produces the same actions and, as a consequence, the same result. If we are to break out of this relative stagnation, we must formulate new questions so as to provide new directions and vision. Such action constitutes leadership.

2) We don't know what we don't know and we won't ever know until we measure. As we learn and apply new tools, we will begin to discover new relationships of a technical and/or business nature. The discovery of new relationships creates insight. In turn, insight breeds fresh questions which, in turn, kindles the mind and lays the path for breakthrough and continuous improvement. Naturally, this requires a process focus, or "mind-set" as some would say. This is the fundamental belief which underlies the Six Sigma paradigm -- management of our processes is management of the business.

3) Process capability is the secret of manufacturing success. If we do not know the capability of our processes, we can not design for manufacturability. This would be like trying to bake a good pie without knowing the temperature range of the oven.

4) One of the key performance measures of process capability is Sigma. The sigma scale of measure can be applied to anything which is considered important by the customer or producer. Sigma can be calculated using actual measurements or defect data. The Sigma scale of measure factors out complexity so that homogeneous or heterogeneous comparisons can be made. When this is done, we can directly contrast dissimilar things on a level playing field, so to speak. This is called quantitative benchmarking. By knowing the defect rate of any characteristic, we can use a benchmarking chart to determine the corresponding sigma level of capability. This is because the sigma scale is perfectly correlated to defects. Once the sigma of a process is known, we can readily understand what we do well in addition to what must be improved. In short, the sigma scale is to management as the stopwatch is to racing.

5) Theoretical calculations and massive amounts of data from numerous companies demonstrates that quality is a function of the interaction between the design and its related processes. As the efficacy of interaction increases, so does the quality. As quality improves, costs and cycle-time decrease. A singular focus on the improvement of process capability can typically reduce manufacturing costs by 30% and cut cycle-time in half. An interactive focus can decrease costs by as much as 25% of revenues.

6) The attainment of Six Sigma requires new tools which, in turn, demands the application of new knowledge. To consistently identify new tools, create roadmaps for their use, and ensure the propagation of value added know-how, a supporting infrastructure must be put in place. Such an infrastructure consists of Black-Belts. These are the in-house Six Sigma experts who know how to make improvement happen. People can only apply what they know how to do. If the knowledge is insufficient, chances are that the resulting action will be insufficient. In order to improve a process, we must go beyond experience. We must collect data so as to "let the product do the talking."

Special Acknowledgments

The quest for Six Sigma is a step beyond conventional thinking. It provides us a means to look over the horizon -- at new ways of doing things with bold levels of expectation. In this spirit, the author has explored a nonconventional format for structuring and presenting the vision and underlying concepts of Six Sigma. The format is based on the time proven belief that "a picture is worth a thousand words." In this sense, it is a graphic "story board" of ideas, experiences, and practices. It provides the reader with visual cues and, where necessary, reinforces or clarifies those cues with text. From this perspective, it is a "thinking" book versus a "reading" book. The intent is to stimulate additional questions, not just to provide answers and information. Naturally, when such questions are formed and diligently pursued, the result is discovery -- the core of profound knowledge. This represents the difference between understanding something versus knowing it. The richness of a picture far exceeds the limited budget of words.

Reducing the underlying concepts of Six Sigma to pictures initially appeared to be a fairly easy and straight forward task. Little did this author know that such an approach would prove to be so time consuming. The author discovered (first-hand) that while it is true a simple picture is worth a thousand words, it is far easier to just type the thousand words. Of course achieving the aims of this book required the input of many organizations and people.

The author would like to extend many thanks to Asea Brown Boveri, Texas Instruments (DSEG), and Motorola. These fine organizations cheerfully provided much of the information and data to support the aims of this book. Their experiences down the path of Six Sigma should serve as key landmarks in the pursuit of total customer satisfaction. For they have learned that to focus on the customer, is to focus on the business. As a result, these organizations lead the way in quality improvement and business performance.

Naturally, an organization is only as good as its people. With this in mind, the author would like very much to extend a deep sense of gratitude and heart felt appreciation to those individuals who played a key role in the support, creation, review and production of this book. First, the author would like to acknowledge Mr. Robert "Bob" Galvin, former CEO and Chairman-of-the-Board, Motorola Inc. His wisdom, leadership, and words of encouragement shall always be remembered. Truly, no one can give deeper meaning to Six Sigma.

The author would like express a personal thanks to Dr. Thomas Cheek and Mr. Rich Karm at Texas Instruments, DSEG. In the spirit of Texas, they were always eager to listen, share information, try new things, and strive for a "win-win" relationship. These men exemplify the meaning behind the phrases "paradigm shifters" and "change agents." Their willingness to reach-out is remarkable.

A very special recognition to goes to Mr. Kjell Magnusson, Vice-President, Customer Focus, TPT, Asea Brown Boveri. For more than a year now, Kjell has successfully labored to implement Six Sigma within his area of responsibility. During this period of time, Kjell immersed himself into the deepest recesses of Six Sigma. Never before has a senior executive delved so deep into the topic -- from an organizational, operational, and technical point-of-view. As a result, he has had a profound effect on his organization's thinking, culture, and practices in a very short period of time. In every sense, Kjell has practiced quality leadership. Owing to this, Six Sigma has made yet another step forward in refinement -- it is now a "process" for breakthrough. His influence and friendship will be with this author for a lifetime.

On the home front, the author would like to extend a loving note of gratitude to his beautiful bride, Sherry. She provided the emotional electricity necessary to keep the keyboard running. Without her sparkling support and encouragement, this book would not be. Thank-you sweetheart.

Of course, there were many others who provided critical feedback and review. In particular, the author would like to recognize the contribution of all the Six Sigma Black-Belts around the world. Their memos, faxes, correspondence, and discussions have been invaluable. In the final analysis, we must all understand that individuals, such as those acknowledged in this book, serve to the keep the idea alive and the vision in focus.

Mikel J. Harry, Ph.D.
President & CEO
Six Sigma Academy, Inc.

Table of Contents

Chapter

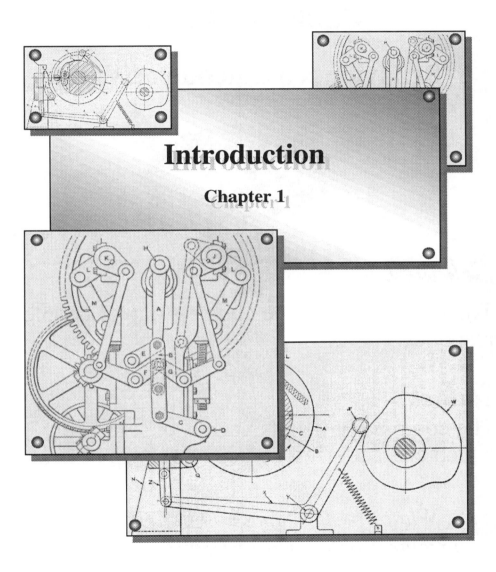

Introduction

Chapter 1

Cutting to the Core

Behavior is a function of Values

$$B = f(V)$$

Behavior

The way in which a person or group of people responds.

Values

The complex of beliefs, ideals, or standards, which characterizes a person or group of people.

. . . What are the "common beliefs" which characterizes your organization ?

Defining Our Values

> **Teamwork**
> **Customers** **Performance**
> **Speed**
> **Integrity** **Innovation**
> **People**

The Values of
AlliedSignal, Inc.

Source: "Total Quality Leadership: A Path To Excellence," AlliedSignal Inc., Morristown NJ.

Exploring Our Values

Describe and prioritize the key values which characterize your organization.

P Priority	Description of Standard
○	
○	
○	
○	
○	
○	
○	
○	
○	
○	

Defining the Ideal Quality Value

1) List the 6 factors which you believe are the major determinants of quality.
2) For each factor, place a rating on the following statements:

M Performance of the listed factor should [   ] be measured.
R The performance measure should [   ] be reported.
R Management should [   ] review the performance reports.
I Improvement actions should [   ] stem from the reviews.

5 = Always
4 = Often
3 = Occasionally
2 = Rarely
1 = Never

Factor	M Measure	R Report	R Review	I Improve	Total
Total					

Defining the Real Quality Value

1) List the 6 factors which you believe are the major determinants of quality.
2) For each factor, place a rating on the following statements:

M	Performance of the listed factor is ⬚ measured in my organization.	5 = Always
R	The performance measure is ⬚ reported in my organization.	4 = Often
R	Management ⬚ reviews the performance reports in my organization.	3 = Occasionally
I	Improvement actions ⬚ stem from the reviews in my organization.	2 = Rarely
		1 = Never

Factor	M Measure	R Report	R Review	I Improve	Total
Total					

The Quality Value Grid

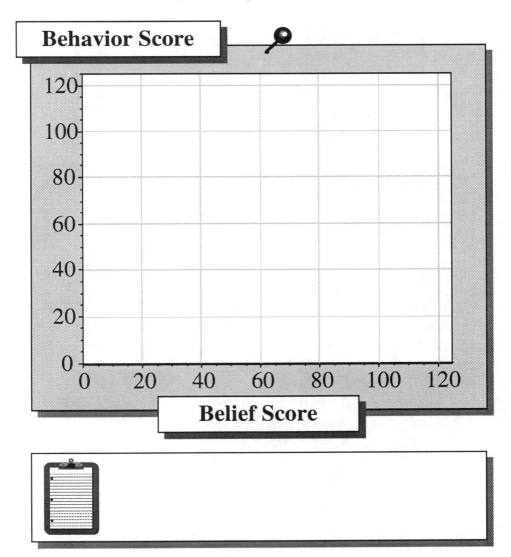

Behavior Score

Belief Score

The Value of Measurement

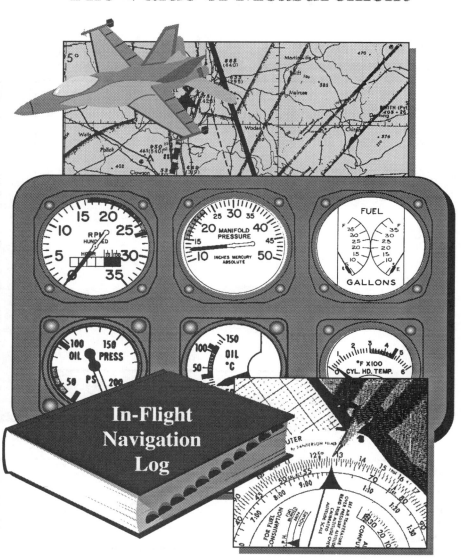

Measurements Get Attention

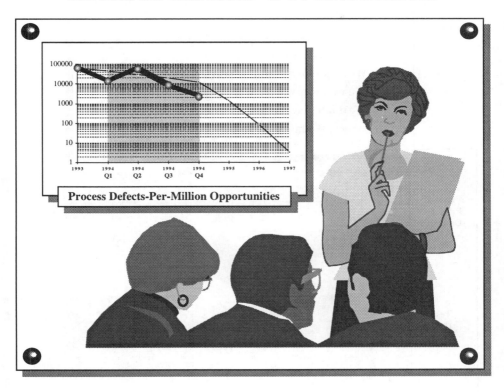

Process Defects-Per-Million Opportunities

- ☯ We don't know what we don't know.

- ☯ If we can't express what we know in the form of numbers, we really don't know much about it.

- ☯ If we don't know much about it, we can't control it.

- ☯ If we can't control it, we are at the mercy of chance.

Performance Metrics Reporting

We don't know what we don't know
We can't act on what we don't know
We won't know until we search
We won't search for what we don't question
We don't question what we don't measure
Hence, We just don't know

Dr. Mikel J. Harry

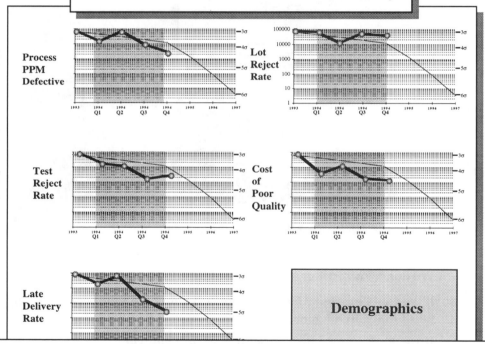

If we know what we should, then we know what to do.

Olle Burtus, ABB Transformers, Sweden

The Need for Knowledge

If we don't know, we can not act
If we can not act, the risk of loss is high
If we do know and act, the risk is managed
If we do know and do not act, we deserve the loss.

Dr. Mikel J. Harry

Therefore, we must conclude:

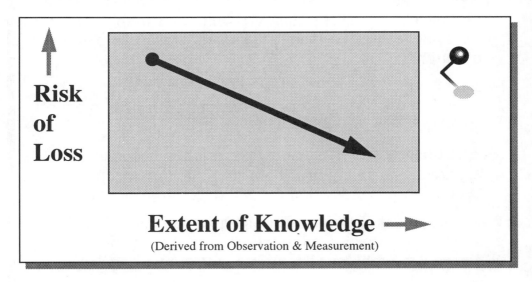

Risk of Loss

Extent of Knowledge ➡
(Derived from Observation & Measurement)

Ignorance is not bliss, it is the food of failure and the breeding ground for loss.

Dr. Mikel J. Harry

The Role of Questions

Questions lead and answers follow. The same questions most often leads to the same answers which, invariably, produces the same result. To change the result, means to change the question.

Management constitutes the leadership element in an organization. When focus is given to the measurement of standards, new questions will continuously arise.

As questions arise, vision emerges, direction becomes apparent, and ambiguity diminishes . In turn, people become organized and mobilized to common action.

When people take common action, the organization's ability to survive and prosper will increase, owing to the discovery of answers to problems; heretofore, not known.

Dr. Mikel J. Harry

Aims of the Discussion

Develop deeper insights into the many facets of Six Sigma. This will be done by discussing the concepts, interrelationships, and principles of Six Sigma. The intent is to further stimulate your questioning process which, in turn, will promote a more intensive pursuit of answers.

* What information do you need to know ?

* What concepts would you like to take back to the job?

* What would you like to see demonstrated?

* What functional areas would you like to see it applied to?

* What would motivate you to embody the principles ?

Questions Most Often Asked

❑ What is Six Sigma and how does it impact the bottom line?

❑ Why should I give Six Sigma serious consideration?

❑ Where and how does Six Sigma fit in my business?

❑ What makes Six Sigma different from other quality programs?

❑ How does Six Sigma help me focus my business operations?

❑ How is Six Sigma used in a low volume environment ?

❑ How does engineering use Six Sigma to improve?

❑ How does manufacturing use Six Sigma to improve quality?

❑ How does nonmanufacturing organizations use Six Sigma?

❑ How does supply management use Six Sigma?

❑ What type of gains can I expect to see if I adopt Six Sigma?

❑ How long does it take to see financial benefits from Six Sigma?

❑ What does it cost to implement Six Sigma?

❑ What resources are required to implement Six Sigma?

❑ What kind of infrastructure is required to support implementation?

❑ What will my business look like after implementing Six Sigma?

❑ What are the implementation shortcuts?

❑ What are my first few steps to get the Six Sigma ball rolling?

The Role of Training

Undoubtedly, the single most important aspect of Six Sigma is people and their knowledge. Without this golden asset, all is for nothing. At the risk of redundancy , you don't know what you don't know, and if you don't know something, nothing will happen. Obviously, the key is knowledge. Successful change and improvement can not occur without it.

Today, the best-in-class companies provide a tremendous amount of training and education to their employees. Many such companies have made significant investments in training, and are discovery the rewards. For example, Motorola Inc. has discovered a 10 to 1 return on their training budget. In fact, they require every employee to receive 40 hours or more of training annually, of which 40% must be in the area of quality.

The Learning Model

- **Lecture**
- **Course Notes**
- **Course Material**
- **Handouts**
- **Examples**
- **Exercises**
- **Case Studies**
- **Self-Review**
- **Step-by-step approach**
- **Video (where appropriate)**
- **Hands-on computations**
- **Computer simulations**
- **Application projects**
- **Participant presentations**

The Keys for Skill Development

- **You must want to do it**
- **You must learn the methods and tools**
- **You must be willing to practice**
- **You must be allowed to practice**
- **You must have adequate resources**
- **You must have adequate coaching**

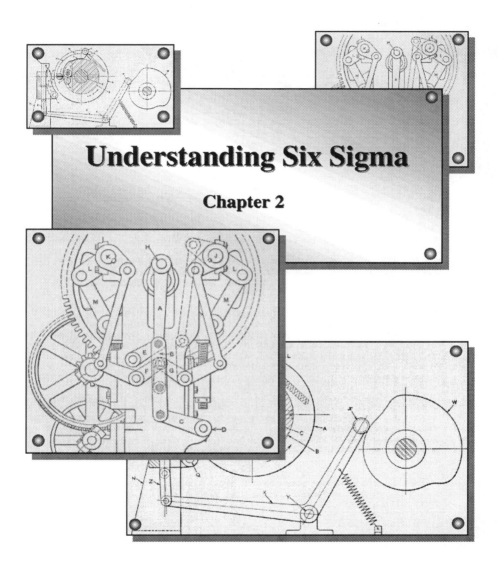

Understanding Six Sigma

Chapter 2

Some Plain Talk About Six Sigma

Mikel J. Harry, Ph.D.
Chief Executive Officer
Six Sigma Academy, Inc.
Phoenix, Arizona

Today, focusing on the customer is absolutely essential. Of course, we all recognize this. But do we really internalize the idea? Do we really believe that such a focus has the potential to drive business growth and impact the level of prosperity which we should come to expect?

Closely linked to the idea of customer satisfaction is the concept of operational excellence -- the kingpin of success. Without a focus on excellence, it becomes easy to accept the position of second or third best. Being the best means embracing change and reaching out for new and higher standards of performance. Only then can one break the chains of complacency and pave the way for breakthrough. The attainment of excellence is no longer a lofty goal or ideal, it is now a fundamental requirement -- the ante for entering the game of business.

As most of us already know, Japan has assumed this perspective and steadily acted upon it. The result of their focus has been staggering, as evidenced by their superb products and services, not to mention their tremendous position in the marketplace. Hence, smart money says we must view the idea of operational excellence as a major force in today's marketplace. For those who might doubt such an assertion, just ask a customer what they think. After all, what the customer thinks provides us with a strong indicator of what will be purchased -- and from whom.

Of course, it is widely recognized that the operational performance of an organization is largely determined by the capability of its processes. Another way of looking at this would be to say that our performance as a company is governed by the quality of our processes -- high quality processes delivers high quality products, at the lowest possible cost, on time. Therefore, a focus on operational excellence (in everything we do) translates to a focus on process quality. Of course, we can not focus on what we do not measure and if we do not measure, we can not improve.

Trying to improve something when you don't have a standard to measure against, is like playing a sports game without knowing the score. Can you imagine setting out on cross-country trip in an automobile without a fuel gauge? Just think of the personal grief, cost, and inconvenience which might result. Would you allow yourself to be placed in such a situation?

As we will discover, the measurement and improvement of our processes is absolutely essential if we are to achieve operational excellence and the ideals of total quality. To do this, we must bear in mind the old axiom -- let the product do the talking. In other words, the quality of our products can tell us how capable our processes really are. To measure product quality is to measure process quality because the two are correlated. It is very important to recognize that the inverse of this also holds true.

Perhaps we should now set the stage for our ensuing discussion by examining what some have called the "chain of causation:"

Our survival is dependent upon growing the business.
Our business growth is largely determined by customer satisfaction.
Customer Satisfaction is governed by quality, price, and delivery.
Quality, price, and delivery is controlled by process capability.
Our process capability is greatly limited by variation.
Process variation leads to an increase in defects, cost, and cycle time.
To eliminate variation, we must apply the right knowledge.
In order to apply the right knowledge, we must first acquire it.
To acquire new knowledge means that we must have the will to survive.

If you can't express something in the form of numbers you don't really know much about it. And if you don't know much about it, you can't control it. And if you can't control it, you're at the mercy of chance. And if you're at the mercy of chance, why bother with it? Hence, we must learn the language of numbers.

Such thinking represents a business philosophy -- a way of guiding our company. From this perspective, we will focus our discussion on an all embracing standard and methodology called "Six Sigma." As we shall see, Six Sigma can be used to measure the quality of our work processes -- in any field, from assembling a motor car to inspiring a classroom full of students.

Over the years, this writer has been asked a great many questions about Six Sigma -- most of which have been quite simple, practical, and straight forward. For the sake of simplicity and reading ease, we shall complement such questions with simple, practical, and straight forward answers. Of course, we recognize that more sophisticated and detailed answers do exist, as many students of Six Sigma will testify. However, there is no point in hooking-up a fire hose when all we want is a glass of water.

QUESTION: What is Six Sigma?

ANSWER: Six Sigma is several things. First, it is a statistical measurement. It tells us how good our products, services, and processes really are. The Six Sigma method allows us to draw comparisons to other similar or dissimilar products, services, and processes. In this manner, we can see how far ahead or behind we are. Most importantly, we can see where we need to go and what we must do to get there. In other words, Six Sigma helps us to establish our course and gauge our pace in the race for total customer satisfaction.

For example, when we say a process is 6 sigma, we are saying it is best-in-class. Such a level of capability will only yield about 3 instances of nonconformance out of every million opportunities for nonconformance. On the other hand, when we say that some other process is 4 sigma, we are saying it is average. This translates to about 6,200 nonconformities-per-million-opportunities for nonconformance. In this sense, the sigma scale of measure provides us with a "goodness micrometer" for gauging the adequacy of our products, services, and processes.

Second, Six Sigma is a business strategy. It can greatly help us gain a competitive edge. The reason for this is very simple -- as you improve the sigma rating of a process, the product quality improves and costs go down. Naturally, the customer becomes more satisfied as a result.

Third, Six Sigma is a philosophy. It is outlook, a way that we perceive and work within the business world around us. Essentially, the philosophy is one of working smarter, not harder. This translates to making fewer and fewer mistakes in everything we do -- from the way we manufacture products to the way we fill out a purchase order. As we discover and neutralize harmful sources of variation, our sigma rating goes up. Again, this means that our process capability improves and the defects (mistakes) go away.

QUESTION: Can the Six Sigma approach be used as a benchmark to measure the capability of any work activity? If so, how does one apply the same system of measurement to, say, manufacturing a transformer or filling out a purchase order?

ANSWER: Yes, the Six Sigma approach allows us to benchmark any work activity. For example, if we were to say that a transformer is 3 sigma, this would characterize the product as having below average quality, because we know (from extensive benchmarking) that the average product, irrespective of complexity, is about four sigma -- with best-in-class at around six sigma.

The same can be said for filling out a purchase order. In this case, the order form itself is a unit of product and the number of boxes to fill in constitutes the number of opportunities for error, where an error is an incorrect or unreadable entry. With this information, the sigma level can be determined.

As you can see, the sigma scale of measure can be universally applied because the common denominator is defects-per-unit, where a unit can be, literally, any kind of task or physical entity -- an hour of classroom instruction, a customer's invoice, a person at a barber shop, a part on a machine, etc. Also recognize that an "opportunity " is anything on, within, or connected to the "unit" which must be right. Thus, an "opportunity for error or defect" is anything which would be considered undesirable.

As should now be apparent, the first step toward improving the sigma capability of a process is defining what the customers' expectations are. Next, you "map" the process by which you get the work done to meet those expectations. This means that you create a "box diagram" of the process flow; i.e., identifying the steps within the process. With this done, you can now affix success criteria to each of the steps.

Next, you would want to record the number of times each of the given success criteria is not met and calculate the total defects-per-unit (TDPU). Following this, the TDPU information is converted to defects-per-opportunity (DPO) which, in turn, is translated into a sigma value (σ). Now, you are ready to make direct comparisons -- even apples and oranges if you want.

Once the comparison is completed, you should ask the following question: "Why is the best-in-class characteristic better than the rest?" If the answer is obvious, then go for it; otherwise, you must track down the sources of variation and then implement a logical scheme of variation reduction. Following this, you should verify the fix and get on to the next big issue. Of course, you would want to keep repeating this cycle until the customer smiles again. When the smiles test reveals the warm glow of lips turned upward, keep doing it because it may not stay that way.

QUESTION: Give an example of how the sigma system could be applied to the activities of a teacher, for instance?

ANSWER: Let us first recognize that a teacher provides a unit of product to their students. Consequently, we could view this as a customer-supplier relationship. Naturally, the delivered product is knowledge. In this case, we would want to measure the quality of the knowledge transfer process because we know that an improvement in the process will translate into improved grades. Thus, the customer sees added value. Of course, the success criteria is given by the traditional grading scale -- be that good or bad, as the case may be.

Based on the grades and the number of steps in the instructional process, we might discover that one of the two teachers is operating a 4 sigma instructional process. This would be to say the 4 sigma teacher will make 6,210 instructional mistakes per million opportunities for process error, on the average. In contrast, we might know the other teacher is 3 sigma. This would translate to 68,807 instructional mistakes per million opportunities for process error. Notice the difference between the two teachers. From the facts, it is obvious - the process of the 4 sigma teacher is over 10 times more error free.

QUESTION: But a teacher can't be only measured against exam results. How does one measure things like enthusiasm, transference of the desire to learn, and so on?

ANSWER: A simple statement explains it all. If you can't express something in the form of numbers, you don't really know much about it. And if you don't know much about it, you can't control it. And if you can't control it, you're at the mercy of chance. and if you're at the mercy of chance, why bother with it?

More directly, a questionnaire can be created to surface subjective ratings. For example, one of the survey items could be worded as follows: My work environment is stimulating. Given this statement, the students would rate their feelings on a one to five scale - strongly agree to strongly disagree.

Yet another statement could be: Do you feel you have a "say" in what goes on in class? Here again, the students would rate the extent to which they agree or disagree with the statement, depending on the number they put after it.

By breaking things into elements, and breaking each element into behavioral questions, people can give a pretty accurate rating. If the scores of several people are grouped together, the results of analysis are even more precise, owing to the law of large numbers. Of course, once you have the numbers, computing the TDPU and DPO is quite easy.

QUESTION: There are other systems for measuring work quality. What makes the Six Sigma approach so good?

ANSWER: First, other systems for measuring quality have traditionally focused on the cost of quality, but with Six Sigma, the belief is that quality is free, in that the more you work towards zero-defect production, the more return on investment you'll have.

Every time you track down a harmful source of variation and eradicate it, you eliminate the related defects, decrease cost, and improve cycle time. Why? Because it takes time and resources to detect, analyze, and fix a defect. In fact, benchmarking has shown that, for the typical 4 sigma company, the cost due to internal and external repair exceeds 10% of revenues. In many cases, it is as high as 30%.

If you are operating on an 8% profit margin, and someone can undercut you by 10% or more, how long will you be in business? Simply stated, a focus on cost-of-quality will lead an organization to the conclusion that to go beyond 4 sigma is not cost effective. Of course, such a perspective is "penny-wise and pound-foolish." Thus, stagnation and complacency sets in and the 4 sigma company will remain just that, average.

Second, the Six Sigma method allows us to reduce things to a common denominator -- defects-per-unit and sigma. In turn, this provides us with a common language and the ability to benchmark ourselves against like products, processes, and practices. Only then can we discover new ways of doing things that helps the business. Of course, the alternative is to wait for people within the company to invent new things -- we must take advantage of the superior practices that already exist. Following this, we can transfer those methods, practices, and technologies back into our business areas. In a nutshell, this is the way of Six Sigma.

QUESTION: What constitutes quality?

ANSWER: Quality is when the customer is totally satisfied. That's the overriding objective. Who is the customer? Someone who buys from us. What is satisfaction? Satisfaction is the extent of certainty which the customer has that their quality, reliability, performance, delivery, and cost standards will be met. How much certainty is needed? Until exceptional quality becomes an everyday expectation in the eyes of the customer -- until near-perfection is a habit on our part. Here again, this translates to operational excellence.

QUESTION: It's interesting that the criterion for measuring quality is the customer, not the thing itself. Can more be said about this?

ANSWER: We're talking quality control versus quality assurance. Quality control is *a posteriori* (after the fact). It's like a boat. You can steer a boat by looking at the wake - that's 'control' and it results after the fact - or you can steer by looking ahead - that's 'assurance' and constitutes what will happen if we keep going in same direction.

In the process of benchmarking, we discovered a typical company is around four sigma, a world class company is at six sigma. Based on such information, things become crystal clear - to compete in a world market, companies have to move toward a 6 sigma level of operational performance. But here again, you don't know what you don't know. If you are not measuring your performance on a level playing field, you don't know how you compare to those around you or rest of the world. Let's face it, if you don't know how you compare, it is easier and less costly to be complacent.

QUESTION: How big a difference, in practical terms, is there between 3 and 6 sigma?

ANSWER: Three sigma would be equivalent to one misspelled work per 15 pages of text. Six sigma would be equivalent to one misspelled word per 300,000 pages, quite a difference indeed. Now, let's put this in real world terms. Some corporations are already running at six sigma. It is self-evident they're going to perform better over the long haul. For example, several of the prestigious Japanese companies (which are doing so well in the world marketplace) are currently running at or near the 6 sigma level.

QUESTION: Many companies have been benchmarked against the 6 sigma standard, is there much difference between nations?

ANSWER: Within the US and Europe, we most often observe a 4 sigma level of operational performance, but in Japan, the attainment of 6 sigma is not uncommon.

In some areas we already have a high level of quality. The airline fatality rate is about 6.5 sigma, but airline baggage handling is about 4 sigma. Both of those areas have processes attached to them. So why is there a difference between the way your baggage is handled versus the way your life is handled? The answer is self-evident. There's a certain amount of tolerance which management has in regard to quality. If peoples' lives are at stake, you can well bet the quality will be there, but if its just a suitcase, there is less focus. After all, a suitcase is relatively cheap and can easily be replaced -- so goes the reasoning.

When a company has its great awakening, when it realizes it is a 3 to 4 sigma organization, and has to move to six sigma, it will improve the processes by which it does its work. It all goes back to that spelling analogy. If you have to improve your quality from one misspelled word per page to one error in 300,000 pages, it won't help much to just polish up what you're doing already. You need breakthrough thinking, new paradigms, to achieve a significant improvement in process capability. In short, you must change the process. Of course, this assumes that we are first willing to change the way we think. Only then will the "do" side of things change.

QUESTION: So, how does an organization put into practice the Six Sigma paradigm?

ANSWER: When an organization asks people for a 10-20 percent improvement in process capability, that's what they give. When the bar is raised to a ten-fold improvement, or even hundred-fold improvement, there are often a lot of bewildered people. Comments of, "That's impossible!" But when two or three business units achieve the quantum improvement, other managers tend to visit those facilities, study them, and transfer the beneficial practices, methods, and technology back to their own workplace.

Organizations can achieve a hundred-fold improvement and it can be done so long as they focus on the process by which they do work and maintain a never ending focus on total quality. This is the path to total customer satisfaction and business prosperity.

QUESTION: It clearly isn't enough just to urge employees to drastic levels of improvement. You have to examine the process by which you work, then involve the staff in finding out how the existing process is failing, and how it can be improved. Is this correct?

ANSWER: That's right. Empowered people (with the necessary mind tools and leadership) have the control they need to improve the way they work. Interaction, participatory management practices, the notion of empowerment, an emphasis on cycle time, and significantly higher levels of expectation in terms of process performance. These are the keys to competitiveness in the world market.

QUESTION: Can equally significant improvements be made in non-manufacturing areas?

ANSWER: Six sigma is applicable in everything we do. It can be used for such diverse tasks as cutting down on the time it takes to process a patent or decrease the cycle time of designs. In addition, Six Sigma is employed to improve the cost of those designs and concurrently enhance manufacturability.

QUESTION: What is meant by that?

ANSWER: Simple. By configuring designs to be tolerant of manufacturing and material variations, we know they can be easily manufactured when it comes time to go into production. Of course, at the same time, the products will be less costly to produce because the designs will be able to utilize less expensive components and material.

QUESTION: That's very interesting. When we talk of the quality of a product, most people assume this means higher quality components, more time spent on welding, or whatever. Does this mean an organization can make a component cheaper and please the customer more?

ANSWER: Yes. Interestingly, the first reaction most companies have when trying to increase their sigma rating is to go out and beat up on suppliers, strive for better and better components, or inspect more. Sooner or later, these companies realize that 6 sigma won't result from a sole focus on suppliers or by better inspection and sorting. They can not get there by "tightening up the tolerances." As a consequence of such revelations, they slowly begin to focus on the capability of the related processes - of all types - everything they do. When breakthrough happens, the success story spreads like a forest fire in high winds.

The Many Facets of Six Sigma

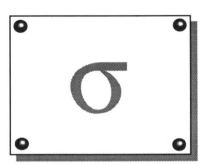

- **Metric**
- **Benchmark**
- **Vision**
- **Philosophy**
- **Method**
- **Tool**
- **Symbol**
- **Goal**
- **Value**

Sigma is a letter in the Greek alphabet.

The term "sigma" is used to designate the distribution or spread about the mean (average) of any process or procedure.

For a business or manufacturing process, the sigma value is a metric that indicates how well that process is performing. The higher the sigma value, the better. Sigma measures the capability of the process to perform defect-free-work. A defect is anything that results in customer dissatisfaction.

With six sigma, the common measurement index is 'defects-per-unit," where a unit can be virtually anything -- a component, piece of material, line of code, administrative form, time frame, distance, etc.

The sigma value indicates how often defects are likely to occur. The higher the sigma value, the less likely a process will produce defects. As sigma increases, costs go down, cycle time goes down, and customer satisfaction goes up.

Six Sigma as a Philosophy

We are in business to make money
We make money by satisfying needs
We are able to satisfy needs by doing
Every need/do pair is an interaction
The aim of customer focus is on improving need/do interactions
Repetition of the same action constitutes a process
Improvement our business means improvement of our processes
Customers need products/services on-time, with zero defects, at the lowest cost
Suppliers create processes to generate needed products
As process capability improves, the product quality increases
As quality increases, costs and cycle-time go down
The attributes of customer satisfaction must be measured if they are to be improved
To improve means we must be able to predict and prevent, not detect and react
Prediction is correlated to certainty
Maximization of certainty is dependent upon the measurement of process capability
Process capability is best understood and reported using statistics
Statistics is dependent upon data
Data must be collected in the process according to a plan
Statistics is used to convert raw data into meaningful summary information
Statistical information is used to report on, improve, and control the process
The basis of statistics is the mean and standard deviation
The mean reports on process centering
The standard deviation reports the extent of variation or "scatter" about the mean
By combining the mean and standard deviation, the "sigma" of a process can be calculated
The "sigma" of a process tells us how capable it is
The process sigma can be used to compare similar or dissimilar processes
Such comparison of processes is called benchmarking
Benchmarking is a competitive tool used to uncover what we do well and not so good
Once basic competencies and deficiencies are know, corrective action can be taken
Corrective action leads to the reduction of defects, cycle-time, and cost
The reduction of defects, cycle-time, and cost leads to improved customer satisfaction
As customer satisfaction improves, the likelihood of doing business increases
As business increases, we (as individuals) grow and prosper

The Classical View of Performance

Practical Meaning of "99% Good"

- ☛ **20,000** lost articles of mail per hour
- ☛ **Unsafe drinking water almost 15 minutes each day**
- ☛ **5,000** incorrect surgical operations per week
- ☛ **2** short or long landings at most major airports each day
- ☛ **200,000** wrong drug prescriptions each year
- ☛ **No electricity for almost 7 hours each month**

	Long-Term Yield	
3σ Capability	93.32%	**Historical Standard**

	Long-Term Yield	
4σ Capability	99.38%	**Current Standard**

	Long-Term Yield	
6σ Capability	99.99966%	**New Standard**

Understanding the Differences

3σ Capability	Historical Standard

4σ Capability	Current Standard

6σ Capability	New Standard

SIGMA	AREA	SPELLING	MONEY	TIME	DISTANCE
3σ	Floor space of a small hardware store	1.5 misspelled words per page in a book	$2.7 million indebtedness per $1 billion in assets	3 1/2 months per century	Coast-to-coast trip
4σ	Floor space of a typical living room	1 misspelled word per 30 pages in a book	$63,000 indebtedness per $1 billion in assets	2 1/2 days per century	45 minutes of freeway driving (in any direction)
5σ	Size of the bottom of your telephone	1 misspelled word in a set of encyclopedias	$570 indebtedness per $1 billion in assets	30 minutes per century	A trip to the local gas station
6σ	Size of a typical diamond	1 misspelled word in all of the books contained in a small library	$2 indebtedness per $1 billion in assets	6 seconds per century	4 steps in any directions

Six Sigma as a Goal

(Distribution Shifted ± 1.5σ)

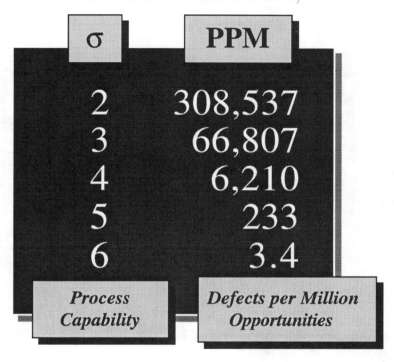

σ	PPM
2	308,537
3	66,807
4	6,210
5	233
6	3.4

Process Capability

Defects per Million Opportunities

Sigma is a statistical unit of measure which reflects process capability. The sigma scale of measure is perfectly correlated to such characteristics as defects-per-unit, parts-per million defective, and the probability of a failure/error

The Magnitude of Difference

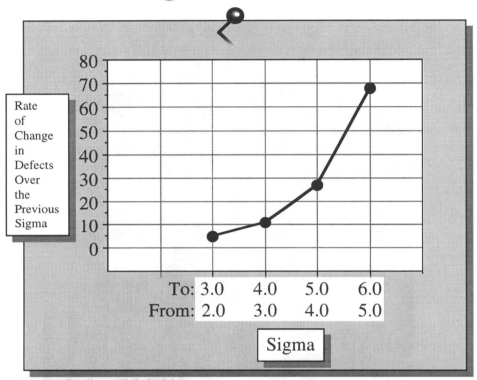

To:	3.0	4.0	5.0	6.0
From:	2.0	3.0	4.0	5.0

Sigma

Rate of Change in Defects Over the Previous Sigma

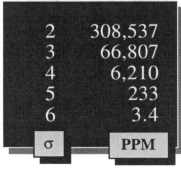

σ	PPM
2	308,537
3	66,807
4	6,210
5	233
6	3.4

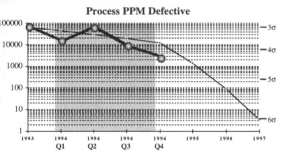

Process PPM Defective

Understanding the Difference

Suppose a process produced 294,118 units of product. If the process capability was 4σ, then the defects produced could be represented by the matrix of dots given below. If the capability was 6σ, only one dot would appear in the entire matrix. How big would this matrix be if the process capability was 3σ?

4σ Capability: Defect Dots = 1849
6σ Capability: Defect Dots = 1

Understanding the Shift Factor

σ	PPM
2	308,537
3	66,807
4	6,210
5	233
6	3.4

To compensate for the inevitable consequences associated with process centering errors, the distribution mean is off-set by 1.5 standard deviations. This adjustment provides a more realistic idea of what the process capability will be over a many cycles of manufacturing.

Primary Sources of Variation

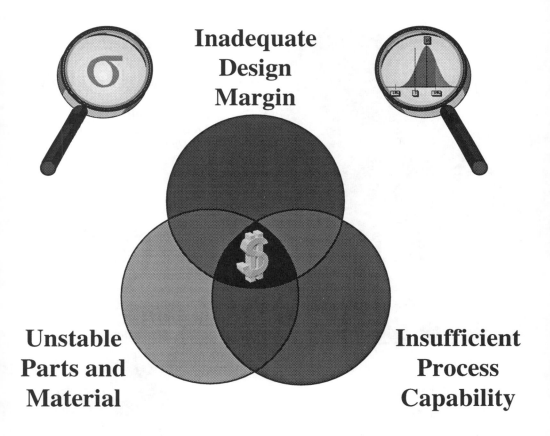

Inadequate
Design
Margin

Unstable
Parts and
Material

Insufficient
Process
Capability

Region of Six Sigma Synergy

Harvesting the Fruit of Six Sigma

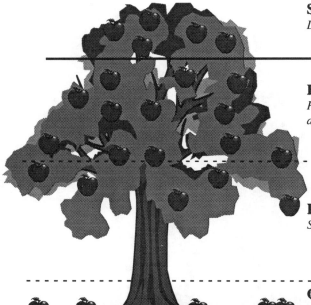

Sweet Fruit
Design for Manufacturability

Process Entitlement

Bulk of Fruit
Process Characterization and Optimization

Low Hanging Fruit
Seven Basic Tools

Ground Fruit
Logic and Intuition

We don't know what we don't know
We can't act on what we don't know
We won't know until we search
We won't search for what we don't question
We don't question what we don't measure
Hence, We just don't know

The Components of Breakthrough

Process Characterization is concerned with the identification and benchmarking of key product characteristics. By way of a gap analysis, common success factors are identified .

Process Optimization is aimed at the identification and containment of those process variables which exert undue influence over the key product characteristics.

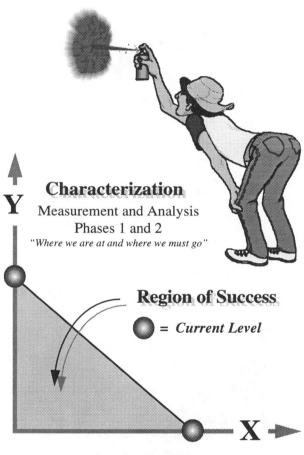

Y

Characterization
Measurement and Analysis
Phases 1 and 2
"Where we are at and where we must go"

Region of Success

= *Current Level*

X

Optimization
Improvement and Control
Phases 3 and 4
"What action we must take to get and stay there"

The Application Roadmap

A Six Sigma Black Belt leads a Customer Focus Team through each of the breakthrough phases with respect to their "line of sight" process.

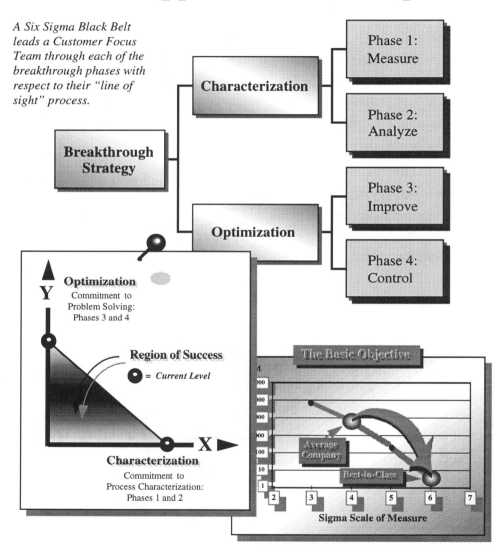

Breakthrough Strategy

Characterization

Optimization

Phase 1: Measure

Phase 2: Analyze

Phase 3: Improve

Phase 4: Control

Optimization
Commitment to Problem Solving: Phases 3 and 4

Region of Success
● = *Current Level*

Characterization
Commitment to Process Characterization: Phases 1 and 2

Y

X

The Basic Objective

Average Company

Best-in-Class

Sigma Scale of Measure

The Application Tactics

Factory XYZ	Measure	Analyze	Improve	Control
Plan				
Tools				
Procedures				
Training				
Application				
Review				

Who   Where
What   Why
When   How

Foundation of the Tools

Data is derived from objects, situations, or phenomenon in the form of measurements.

Data is used to classify, describe, improve, or control objects, situations, or phenomenon.

Levels of Analysis:

1. We only use experience, not data.

2. We collect data, but just look at the numbers.

3. We group the data so as to form charts and graphs.

4. We use census data with descriptive statistics.

5. We use sample data with descriptive statistics.

6. We use sample data with inferential statistics.

Cost, likelihood of improvement, ability to generalize, depth of understanding, quality of knowledge and complexity increases as the level of analysis increases. So how far should we go with this stuff? "After all, I just want to lower my costs, please the customer some more . . . you know, so I can stay in business and all that stuff." Why is there such a strong emphasis on data? "I mean, I've been successful so far and we don't take a lot of measurements!" Why should I start now?

Six Sigma as a Benchmark

Which Process is Performing the Best ?

Issue	Process A		Process B	
	Before	After	Before	After
Yield	95%	96%	85%	87%
DPU	.0513	.0408	.1625	.1393
Steps	83	83	286	286
Step DPU	.0006	.0005	.0006	.0005
Step Yield	.9994	.9995	.9994	.9995
Sigma	4.73	4.80	4.75	4.80

Six Sigma as a Value

What does a Six Sigma organization look like?

Focus

Issue	Classical	Six Sigma
Analytical Perspective	Point Estimate	Variability
Management	Cost & Time	Quality & Time
Manufacturability	Trial & Error	Robust Design
Tolerancing	Worst Case	Root-Sum-of-Squares
Variable Search	One-Factor-at-a-Time	Design of Experiments
Process Adjustment	Tweeking	SPC Charts
Problems	Fixing	Preventing
Problem Solving	Expert Based	System Based
Analysis	Experience	Data
Focus	Product	Process
Behavior	Reactive	Proactive
Suppliers	Cost	Relative Capability
Reasoning	Experience Based	Statistically Based
Outlook	Short-Term	Long-Term
Decision Making	Intuition	Probability
Approach	Symptomatic	Problematic
Design	Performance	Producibility
Aim	Company	Customer
Organization	Authority	Learning
Training	Luxury	Necessity
Chain-of-Command	Heirarchy	Empowered Teams
Direction	Seat-of-Pants	Benchmarking & Metrics
Goal Setting	Realistic Perception	Reach-Out & Stretch
People	Cost	Asset
Control	Centralized	Localized
Improvement	Automation	Optimization

Periods of Implementation

Period	Motorola	Texas Instr.	ABB
1 Enlightenment	1985	1991	1993
2 Acceptance	1986	1992	1994
3 Tools	1987	1993	1995
4 Deployment	1988	1994	1996
5 Results	1989	1995	1997
6 Renewal	1990	1996	1998

The Chemistry of Six Sigma

6σ

A means to link values with actions which, in turn,
sets improvement in motion.

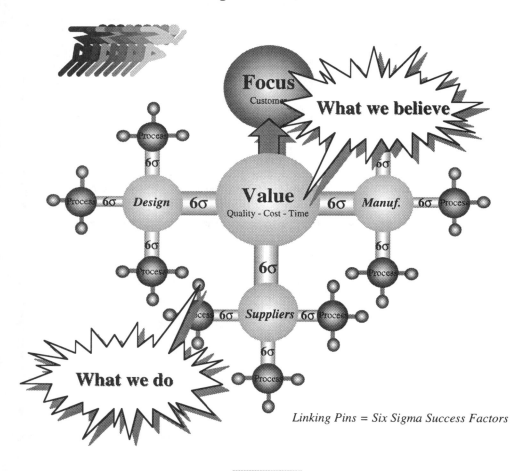

Linking Pins = Six Sigma Success Factors

The Six Sigma Success Factors

Six Sigma Champions

Business Metrics

Common Process Metrics

Benchmarking

Stretch-Goals

Breakthrough Strategy

Six Sigma Black-Belts

Success Stories

Experiment Design & SPC

Quality and Time Focus

Design-for-Manufacturability Methods

Quality Policy and Deployment

Quality Council and Associate Membership

Empowered High-Performance Work Teams

Six Sigma and the Organization

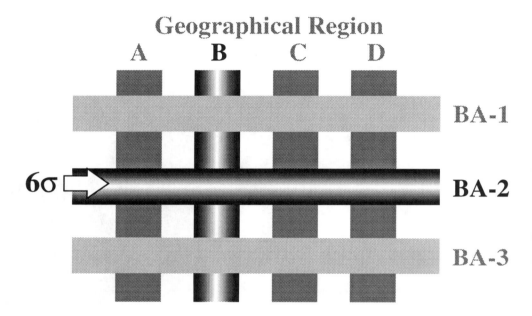

Six Sigma must be **pulled** when implementing across a Business Area, or "common product"

Six Sigma must be **pushed** when implementing in a Geographical Region.

Six Sigma should be used as a **strategy** for increasing customer focus which, in turn, drives the need for Six Sigma.

Structural Role of Six Sigma

Six Sigma is a means to realize the philosophy and values associated with Total Quality Management (TQM)

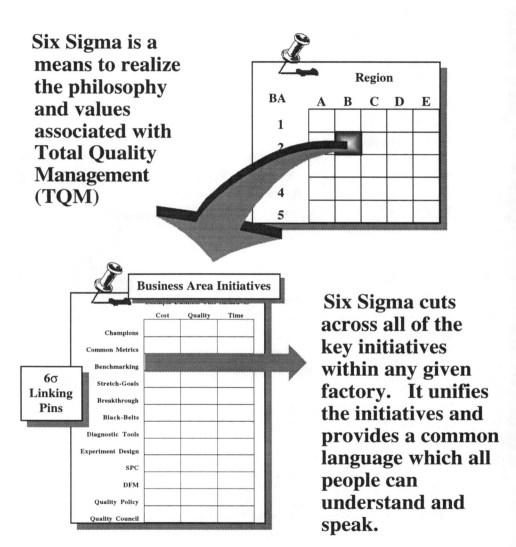

Six Sigma cuts across all of the key initiatives within any given factory. It unifies the initiatives and provides a common language which all people can understand and speak.

Six Sigma Executive Briefing

The Six Sigma Executive Briefing has been specifically designed for executives, managers, and supporting staff personnel. The briefing is 8 hours in duration and will provide an in-depth overview of the fundamental strategies, tactics, and tools necessary for achieving Six Sigma product designs, manufacturing pro cesses, service quality, quality of administration. Specifically, participants of the Six Sigma Executive Briefing will discover:

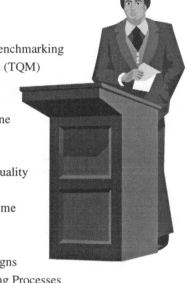

The Driving Need for Six Sigma Quality

The Fundamental Objective of Six Sigma

The Basic Tenants of Six Sigma Quality

Key Business Conclusions Resulting From Global Benchmarking

Six Sigma as a Target for Total Quality Management (TQM)

The Primary Tools for Achieving Six Sigma

The Customer's Perspective of Six Sigma

The Financial Impact of Six Sigma on the Bottom Line

Strategies and Tactics for Implementing Six Sigma

Advanced Six Sigma Concepts

The Impact of Product and Process Complexity on Quality

The Impact of Six Sigma on Product Reliability

The Impact of Six Sigma on Manufacturing Cycle-Time

The Impact of Six Sigma on Inventory

Developing Six Sigma Suppliers

How to Create and Maintain Six Sigma Product Designs

How to Create and Maintain Six Sigma Manufacturing Processes

How to Create and Maintain Six Sigma Services

In addition, several "real life" case studies will be presented and thoroughly discussed. The cases are configured to clearly illustrate many of the "how to's" with respect to selected Six Sigma implementation strategies and application practices. In particular, the cases will highlight the results which were achieved and how the Six Sigma practices were embodied and institutionalized within the organization.

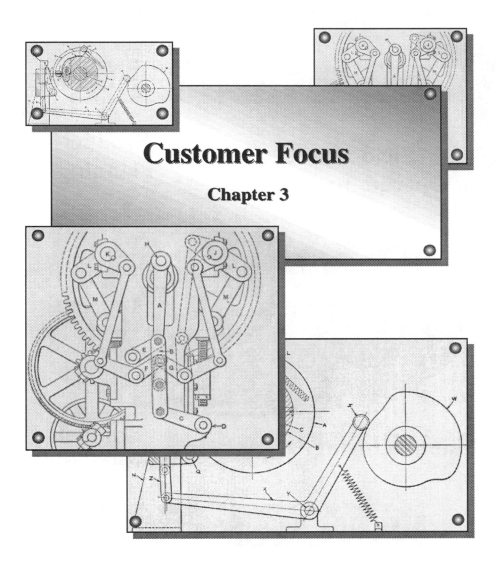

Customer Focus

Chapter 3

Customer-to-Customer Circle

Customer Satisfaction

Field Operations

Product Planning

Manufacturing

Product Development

Quality, Cost, & Delivery

The Customer Supplier Relationship

Deriving value from the Need - Do interaction

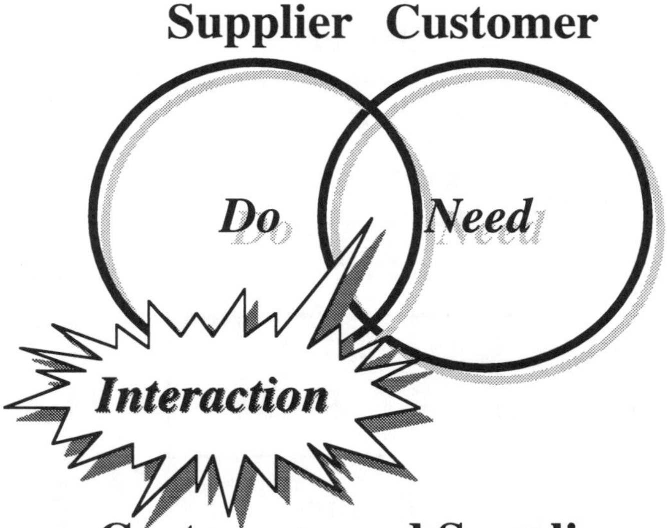

Supplier Customer

Do Need

Interaction

Customers and Suppliers
Exchange Value
through a
Need-Do Interaction.

*The task for both customer and supplier is to
maximize the value derived from this interaction.*

3 . 3

Maximizing the Interaction

Supplier

Customer

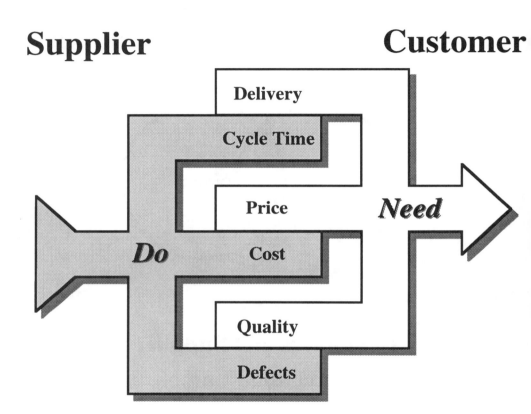

Supplier strives for performance on *Cycle Time, Cost and Defects* to meet Customers' increasing expectations on *Delivery, Price and Quality.*

Definition of Customer Satisfaction

cus'tom•er, *n* [O Fr. *coustumier*, L.L. *custumarius*, custom.]

1. a person who buys, especially one who buy regularly.
2. a person with whom one has to deal

sat•is•fac'tion, *n* [O Fr., from L.*satisfaction* (-onis), from *satisfactus*, pp. of *satisfacere*, to satisfy.]

1. to gratify fully the wants or desires of; to supply to the full extent.
2. to free from doubt, suspense, or uncertainty; to give full assurance to.
3. to comply with (rules or standards).

Embedded within these definitions are two key ideas. First, the notion that the **customer** is a person, not an organization, corporation, etc. Second, the idea that satisfaction is the extent of **certainty** a person [customer] has that the standards will be met. Naturally, this would imply that as certainty increases, the likelihood of satisfaction would likewise increase.

Establishing the Focus

Quality

Performance to the standard expected by the customer.

Customer

Anyone internal or external to the organization who comes in contact with the product or output of my work.

Anyone whose success or satisfaction depends on my actions.

Source: "Total Quality Leadership: A Path To Excellence," AlliedSignal Inc., Morristown NJ.

The Gap in Perspectives

What Makes a Good Coffee Service?

Supplier Perspective (Hotel)	Customer Perspective (Conference Attendees)
➲ Good Hot Coffee	➲ Good Hot Coffee
➲ Clean China	➲ Fast Line, Especially for Refills
➲ Clean Linen	➲ Close to High-Capacity Restrooms
➲ Attractive Display	➲ Close to Telephones
➲ Extras - Snacks	➲ Room to Chat

. . . So why do such differences in perspective exist ?

Barry Bebb & Associates
World Class by Design Conference
November 1993
Buffalo, New York

The Role of Measurement

☞ If we cannot express what we know in the form of numbers, we really don't know much about it.

☞ If we don't know much about it, we cannot control it.

☞ If we cannot control it, we are at the mercy of chance.

Certainty	+ Uncertainty	=	100%
Known	+ Unknown	=	100%
Belief	+ Disbelief	=	100%
Confidence	+ Risk	=	100%
Yield	+ Defect Rate	=	100%

The Focus of Six Sigma

To get results, should we focus our behavior on the Y or X ?

■ Y	■ $X_1 \ldots X_N$
■ **Dependent**	■ **Independent**
■ **Output**	■ **Input-Process**
■ **Effect**	■ **Cause**
■ **Symptom**	■ **Problem**
■ **Monitor**	■ **Control**

If we are so good at X, why do we constantly test and inspect Y?

Achieving Operational Excellence

The Chain of Causation

Our survival is dependent upon growing the business.

Our business growth is largely determined by customer satisfaction.

Customer Satisfaction is governed by quality, price, and delivery.

Quality, price, and delivery is controlled by process capability.

Our process capability is greatly limited by variation.

Process variation leads to an increase in defects, cost, and cycle time.

To eliminate variation, we must apply the right knowledge.

In order to apply the right knowledge, we must first acquire it.

To acquire new knowledge means that we must have the will to survive.

A Model for Success

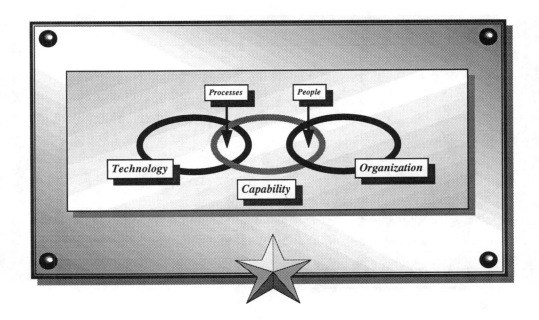

The Fundamental Logic

- Business survival is dependent upon how well we satisfy the customer
- Customer satisfaction is a function of quality, price, and delivery
- Quality, cost, and prompt delivery is dependent upon process capability
- Process capability is dependent upon the knowledge of our people
- Knowledge can be successfully organized and transferred
- The type of knowledge people pursue depends on the where they are being lead
- The direction people are being lead is established by management

. . . What implications does this hold for Customer Focus ?

The Customer Focus Initiative

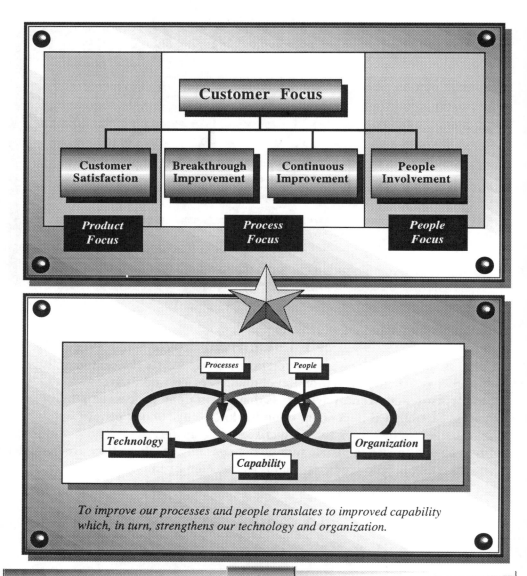

To improve our processes and people translates to improved capability which, in turn, strengthens our technology and organization.

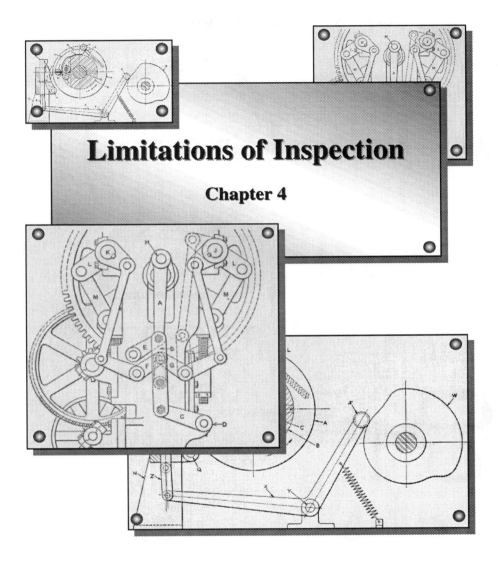

Limitations of Inspection

Chapter 4

Getting to Six Sigma

How far can  **inspection** get us ?

(Distribution Shifted ± 1.5σ)

σ	PPM
2	308,537
3	66,807
4	6,210
5	233
6	3.4

The Inspection Exercise

Task: Count the number of times the 6th letter of the alphabet appears in the following text.

The Necessity of Training Farm Hands for First

Class Farms in the Fatherly Handling of Farm Live

Stock is Foremost in the Eyes of Farm Owners.

Since the Forefathers of the Farm Owners Trained

the Farm Hands for First Class Farms in the

Fatherly Handling of Farm Live Stock, the Farm

Owners Feel they should carry on with the Family

Tradition of Training Farm Hands of First Class

Farmers in the Fatherly Handling of Farm Live

Stock Because they Believe it is the Basis of Good

Fundamental Farm Management.

4.3

Results of the Exercise

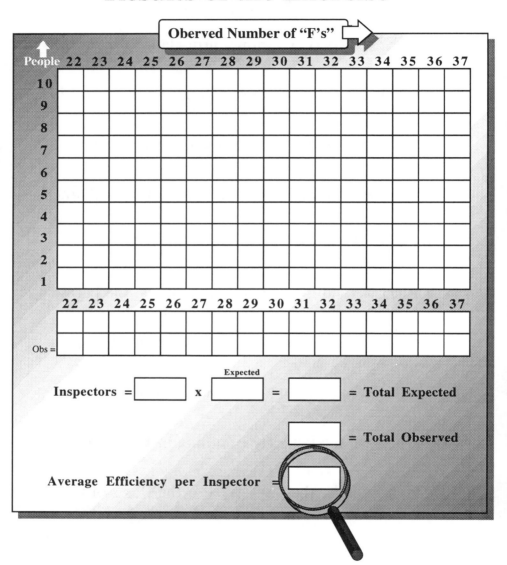

Oberved Number of "F's"

People	22	23	24	25	26	27	28	29	30	31	32	33	34	35	36	37
10																
9																
8																
7																
6																
5																
4																
3																
2																
1																

	22	23	24	25	26	27	28	29	30	31	32	33	34	35	36	37
Obs =																

Inspectors = [ ] x [Expected] = [ ] = Total Expected

[ ] = Total Observed

Average Efficiency per Inspector = [ ]

The Impact of Added Inspection

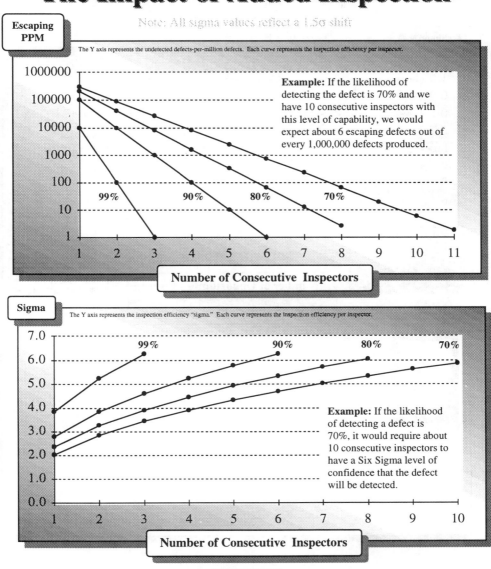

Note: All sigma values reflect a 1.5σ shift

Escaping PPM

The Y axis represents the undetected defects-per-million defects. Each curve represents the inspection efficiency per inspector.

1000000
100000
10000
1000
100
10
1

Example: If the likelihood of detecting the defect is 70% and we have 10 consecutive inspectors with this level of capability, we would expect about 6 escaping defects out of every 1,000,000 defects produced.

99%   90%   80%   70%

1 2 3 4 5 6 7 8 9 10 11

Number of Consecutive Inspectors

Sigma

The Y axis represents the inspection efficiency "sigma." Each curve represents the inspection efficiency per inspector.

99%   90%   80%   70%

7.0
6.0
5.0
4.0
3.0
2.0
1.0
0.0

Example: If the likelihood of detecting a defect is 70%, it would require about 10 consecutive inspectors to have a Six Sigma level of confidence that the defect will be detected.

1 2 3 4 5 6 7 8 9 10

Number of Consecutive Inspectors

Impact of Complexity on Inspection

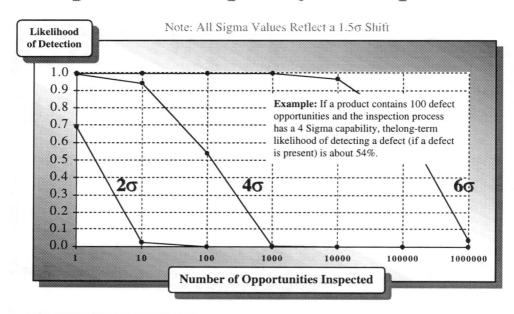

Note: All Sigma Values Reflect a 1.5σ Shift

Likelihood of Detection

Example: If a product contains 100 defect opportunities and the inspection process has a 4 Sigma capability, the long-term likelihood of detecting a defect (if a defect is present) is about 54%.

2σ   4σ   6σ

Number of Opportunities Inspected

4 . 6

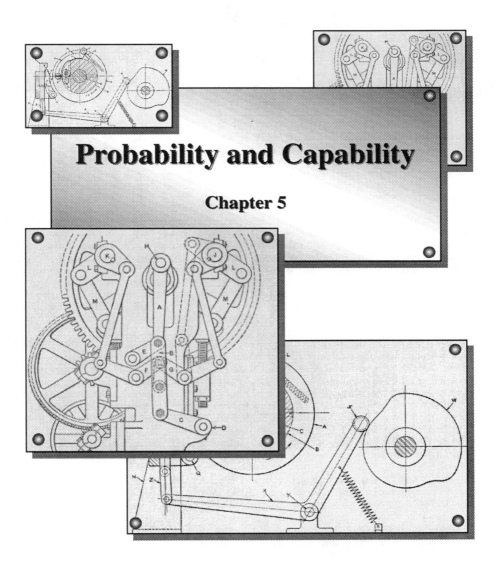

Probability and Capability

Chapter 5

The Probability Game

Since the issue of capability involves the notions of manufacturing confidence and risk, it is reasonable to assert that the concepts underlying probability should serve as the foundation of any measurement scheme. To illustrate why this is so, let us consider an analogous example.

For the moment, we shall hypothesize a pair of "manufacturing dice" and a customer requirement that only allows those combinations that yield a 3, 4, 5, ..., or 11. In this instance, a 2 or 12 represents a nonconformance to standard, or as some would say, a quality defect. Thus, we may ask the question: "To what extent will the customer be satisfied?" In the language of statistics, the question would be, "What is the probability of not rolling a 2 or 12?" In order to answer the latter question, we must apply some fundamental probability theory.

In statistical notation, the likelihood of some event A may be given by $P(A)$. If some event A is independent of some other event, say B, the probability of both A and B occurring is $P(A \text{ and } B) = P(A) \times P(B)$. In other words, the joint probability of A and B is multiplicative by nature. Since a single die has six sides, the random chance probability that any given side will be face up is $1/6 = .1667$ because (a) only one side can be up at any given time, (b) there are a total of six possibilities, and (c) each of the six possibilities has the same probability of occurrence. Of course, all of this assumes the die is unbiased. Extending this reasoning to a pair of dice, we may say that the probability of rolling any given combination would be $.1667 \times .1667 = .0278$, or 2.78 percent.

Because the occurrence of a 2 or 12 cannot happen concurrently, we say that the two outcomes are mutually exclusive of each other. This is to say that a 2 and 12 cannot occur at the same time; i.e., they are restricted from occurring together. Hence, the events of concern are mutually exclusive. Any time that two events (say, A and B) are mutually exclusive, the probability of event A or B occurring may be given by summing their individual probabilities: e.g., $P(A \text{ or } B) = P(A) + P(B)$. Since there is only one way to form a 2 and only one way to create a 12, the probability of not meeting the customer's standard, with respect to our manufacturing example, would be $.0278 + .0278 = .0556$, or 5.56 percent. This represents the risk of nonconformance. This may be directly verified by studying the exhaustive combinations given by a pair of dice.

Given the risk of nonconformance, with respect to our dice example, we may intuitively reason that the probability of yielding a 3, 4, 5, ..., or 11 may be calculated as $1 - .0556 = .9444$. Thus, expected yield may be given by $P(Y) = 1 - [P(A) + P(B)]$. Hence, we may now say that the likelihood of customer satisfaction is 94.44 percent. The uninformed reader is highly encouraged to gain additional knowledge concerning probability theory via almost any introductory textbook on mathematical statistics. Such knowledge is essential in order to progress beyond the elementary mathematical constructs presented in this book.

The Customer Requirements

What is the process capability?

What is the probability of meeting the requirements?

Is capability and probability related?

Suppose a certain customer permits only those combinations which yield 3, 4, 5, . . . , or 11.

Computing the Risks

	1	2	3	4	5	6
1	2	3	4	5	6	7
2	3	4	5	6	7	8
3	4	5	6	7	8	9
4	5	6	7	8	9	10
5	6	7	8	9	10	11
6	7	8	9	10	11	12

Ways to form a "2" ☐ in ☐ = ☐

Ways to form a "12" ☐ in ☐ = ☐

Probability of Defect ➡ ☐

Deeper Insight Into Probability

Die 1	Die 2	Probability
1	4	.0278
2	3	.0278
3	2	.0278
4	1	.0278
	Total	.1111

What is the probability of rolling a "5" using a fair pair of dice?

	1	2	3	4	5	6
1	.0278	.0278	.0278	.0278	.0278	.0278
2	.0278	.0278	.0278	.0278	.0278	.0278
3	.0278	.0278	.0278	.0278	.0278	.0278
4	.0278	.0278	.0278	.0278	.0278	.0278
5	.0278	.0278	.0278	.0278	.0278	.0278
6	.0278	.0278	.0278	.0278	.0278	.0278

5 . 5

Establishing the Odds

Value	Combinations	Probability
2	1	.0278
3	2	.0556
4	3	.0833
5	4	.1111
6	5	.1389
7	6	.1667
8	5	.1389
9	4	.1111
10	3	.0833
11	2	.0556
12	1	.0278
Total	36	1.0000

Probability of any given value on Die 1 $\longrightarrow$ = 1/6 = .1667
Probability of any given value on Die 2 $\longrightarrow$ = 1/6 = .1667
Probability of any given combination = 1/6 x 1/6 = 1/36 = .0278

Graphing the Results

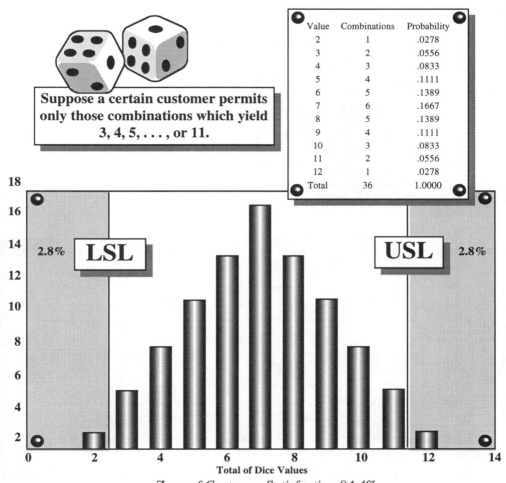

Suppose a certain customer permits only those combinations which yield 3, 4, 5, . . . , or 11.

Value	Combinations	Probability
2	1	.0278
3	2	.0556
4	3	.0833
5	4	.1111
6	5	.1389
7	6	.1667
8	5	.1389
9	4	.1111
10	3	.0833
11	2	.0556
12	1	.0278
Total	36	1.0000

2.8%   LSL   USL   2.8%

Total of Dice Values

Zone of Customer Satisfaction 94.4%

. . .Hence, the probability of Customer Satisfaction is 94.4 %

Gaining Deeper Insights

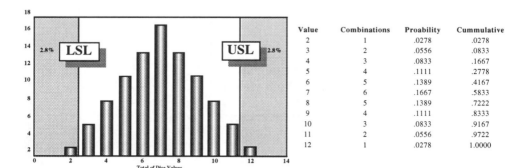

Value	Combinations	Proability	Cummulative
2	1	.0278	.0278
3	2	.0556	.0833
4	3	.0833	.1667
5	4	.1111	.2778
6	5	.1389	.4167
7	6	.1667	.5833
8	5	.1389	.7222
9	4	.1111	.8333
10	3	.0833	.9167
11	2	.0556	.9722
12	1	.0278	1.0000

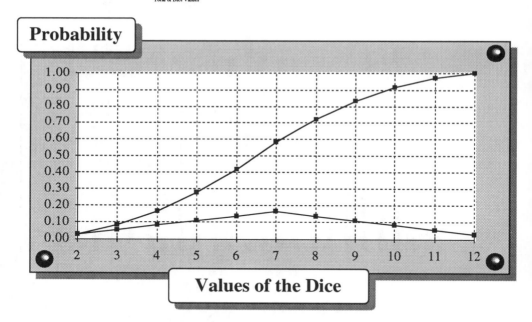

Probability

Values of the Dice

Comments on the Nature of Data

☆Two kinds of data can be used for measuring process capability. Data which characterizes a product or process feature in terms of its size, weight, volts. This type of data is said to be continuous by nature. In other words, the measurement scale can be meaningfully divided into finer and finer increments of precision. To apply the normal distribution, one must necessarily use continuous data.

☆Another way to look at the data is to merely count the frequency of occurrence: e.g., the number of times something happens or fails to happen. Notice that such data is not capable of being meaningfully subdivided into more precise increments and, therefore, is said to be discrete by nature. The Poisson and binomial models are used in connection with this type of data.

☆The validity of inferences made from discrete data are highly dependent upon the number of observations. In other words, the sample size required to characterize a discrete product or process feature is much larger than that required when continuous data is used.

Application of the Concepts

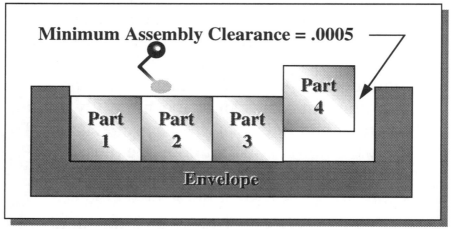

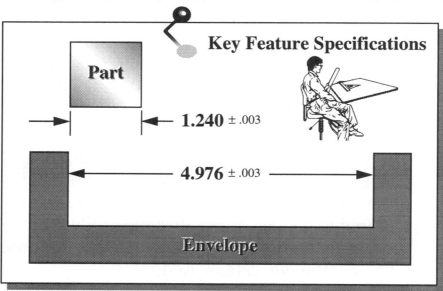

The Manufacturing Process

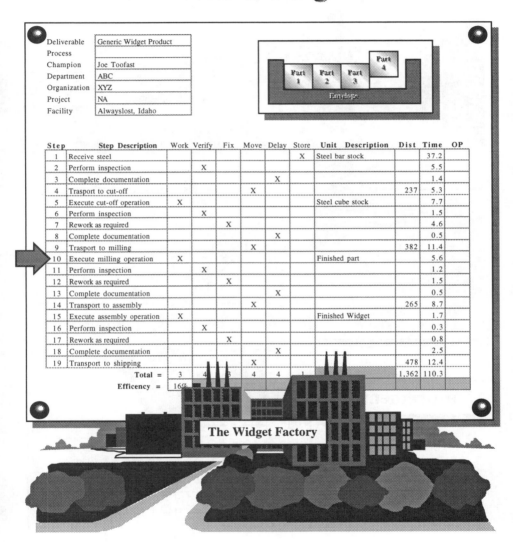

Deliverable	Generic Widget Product
Process	
Champion	Joe Toofast
Department	ABC
Organization	XYZ
Project	NA
Facility	Alwayslost, Idaho

Step	Step Description	Work	Verify	Fix	Move	Delay	Store	Unit Description	Dist	Time	OP
1	Receive steel						X	Steel bar stock		37.2	
2	Perform inspection		X							5.5	
3	Complete documentation					X				1.4	
4	Trasport to cut-off				X				237	5.3	
5	Execute cut-off operation	X						Steel cube stock		7.7	
6	Perform inspection		X							1.5	
7	Rework as required			X						4.6	
8	Complete documentation					X				0.5	
9	Trasport to milling				X				382	11.4	
10	Execute milling operation	X						Finished part		5.6	
11	Perform inspection		X							1.2	
12	Rework as required			X						1.5	
13	Complete documentation					X				0.5	
14	Transport to assembly				X				265	8.7	
15	Execute assembly operation	X						Finished Widget		1.7	
16	Perform inspection		X							0.3	
17	Rework as required			X						0.8	
18	Complete documentation					X				2.5	
19	Transport to shipping				X				478	12.4	
	Total =	3	4	3	4	4	1		1,362	110.3	
	Efficency =	16%									

The Widget Factory

5.11

The Milling Operation

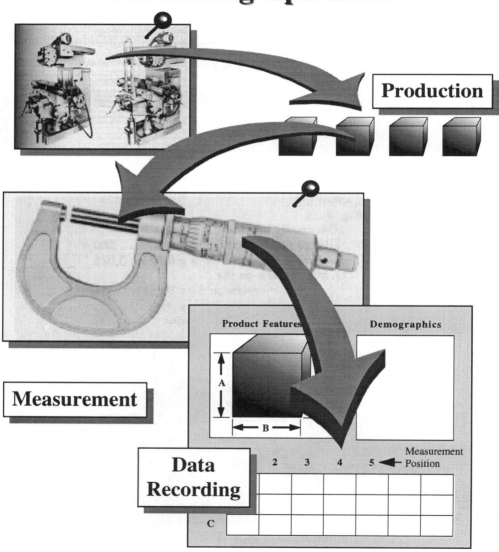

Production

Measurement

Product Features

Demographics

A

B

Data
Recording

2   3   4   5 ← Measurement Position

C

Establishing Process Capability

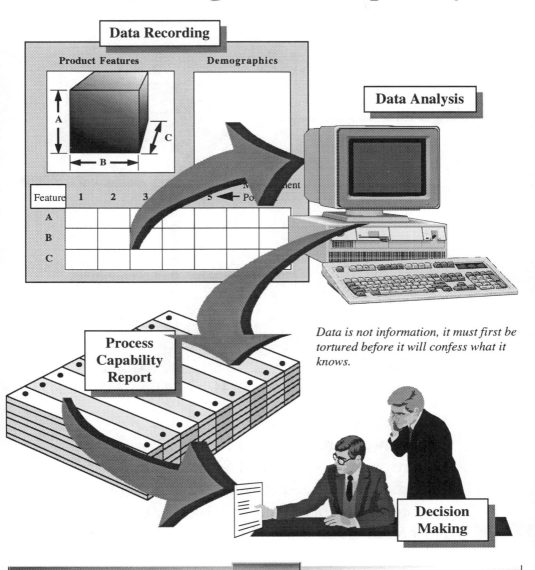

Data Recording

Product Features

Demographics

Data Analysis

Feature	1	2	3		5
A					
B					
C					

Process Capability Report

Data is not information, it must first be tortured before it will confess what it knows.

Decision Making

Understanding the Histogram

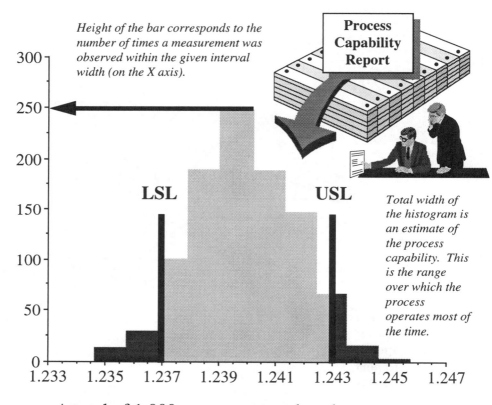

Height of the bar corresponds to the number of times a measurement was observed within the given interval width (on the X axis).

Process Capability Report

LSL　　　　　　　　**USL**

Total width of the histogram is an estimate of the process capability. This is the range over which the process operates most of the time.

A total of 1,000 parts were produced.
22 parts were greater than the USL.
31 parts were less than the LSL.
53 parts were rejected of which 12 were scraped.
The probability of defect is 53/1000 =.053
The process yield is 1 -.053 = .947, or 94.7%

The Nature of Process Variation

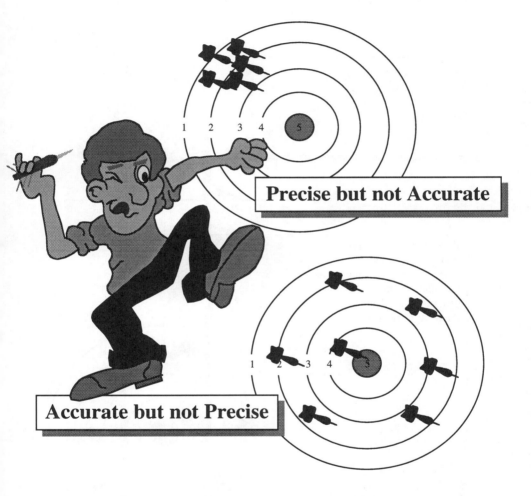

Precise but not Accurate

Accurate but not Precise

. . . So how does this principle
translate into the real world?

Understanding Process Precision

Manufacturing Distribution of the Widget Part

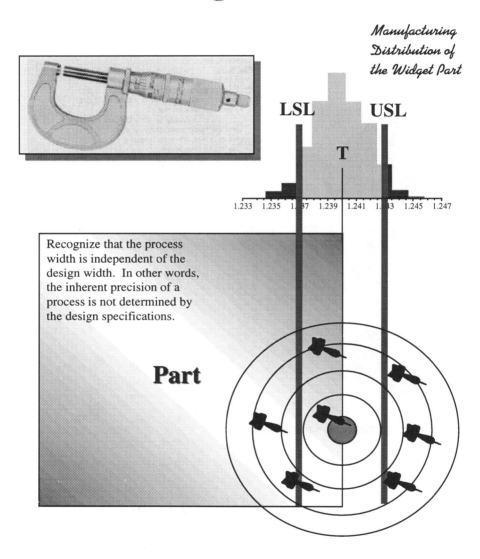

LSL   USL

T

1.233   1.235   1.237   1.239   1.241   1.243   1.245   1.247

Recognize that the process width is independent of the design width. In other words, the inherent precision of a process is not determined by the design specifications.

Part

Understanding Process Accuracy

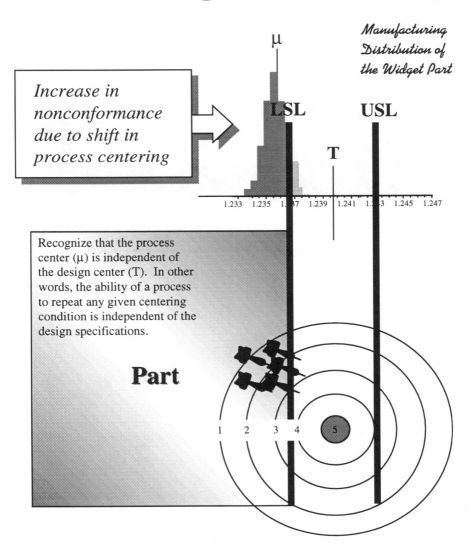

Manufacturing Distribution of the Widget Part

μ

LSL   USL

T

Increase in nonconformance due to shift in process centering

1.233 1.235 1.237 1.239 1.241 1.243 1.245 1.247

Recognize that the process center (μ) is independent of the design center (T). In other words, the ability of a process to repeat any given centering condition is independent of the design specifications.

Part

1   2   3   4   5

Other Histogram Applications

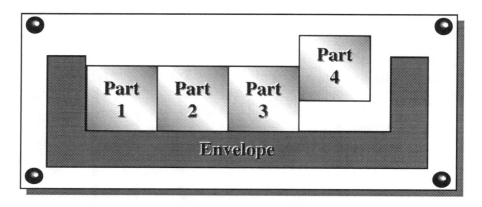

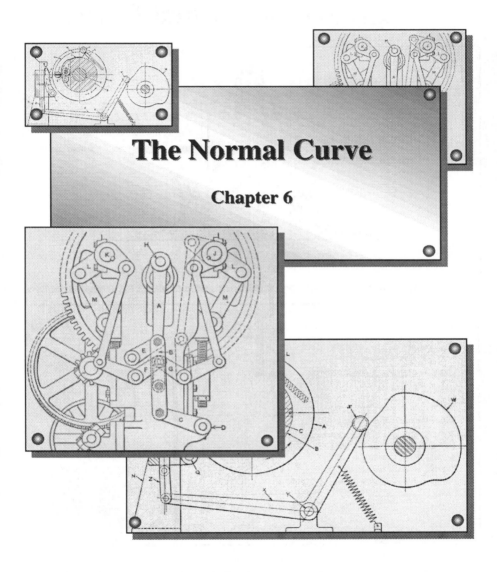

The Normal Curve

Chapter 6

Forming the Normal Curve

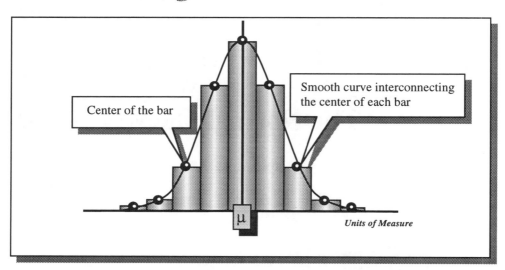

Center of the bar

Smooth curve interconnecting the center of each bar

μ

Units of Measure

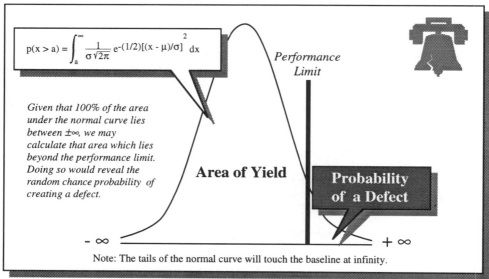

$$p(x > a) = \int_a^\infty \frac{1}{\sigma\sqrt{2\pi}} e^{-(1/2)[(x - \mu)/\sigma]^2} dx$$

Performance Limit

Given that 100% of the area under the normal curve lies between ±∞, we may calculate that area which lies beyond the performance limit. Doing so would reveal the random chance probability of creating a defect.

Area of Yield

Probability of a Defect

- ∞

+ ∞

Note: The tails of the normal curve will touch the baseline at infinity.

The Normal Curve and Capability

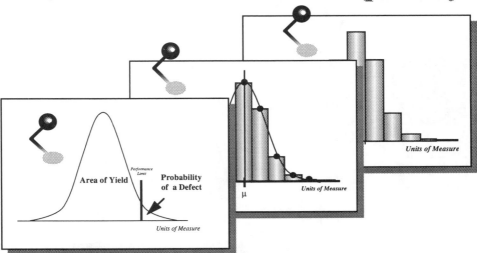

Area of Yield

Performance Limit

Probability of a Defect

Units of Measure

μ   *Units of Measure*

Units of Measure

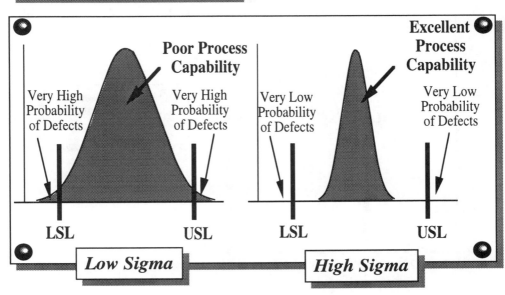

Poor Process Capability

Excellent Process Capability

Very High Probability of Defects

Very High Probability of Defects

Very Low Probability of Defects

Very Low Probability of Defects

LSL

USL

LSL

USL

Low Sigma

High Sigma

Application to the Widget Example

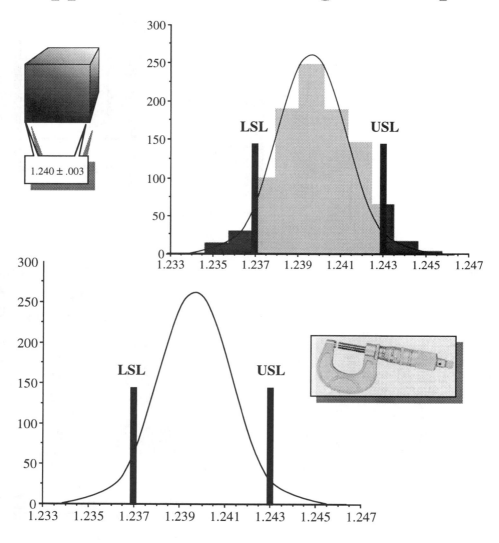

Improving Process Capability

$$Y = f (X_1 \ldots X_N)$$

The variation inherent to any dependent variable (Y) is determined by the variations inherent to each of the independent variables.

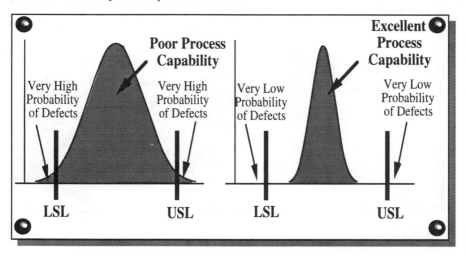

Process Capability and Defects

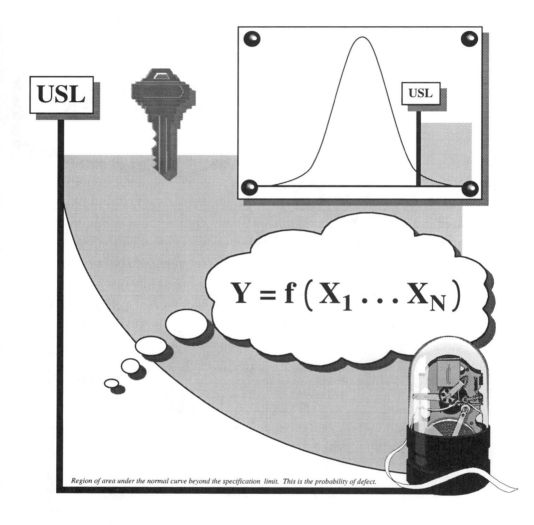

USL

$$Y = f (X_1 \ldots X_N)$$

Region of area under the normal curve beyond the specification limit. This is the probability of defect.

Visualizing the Process Dynamics

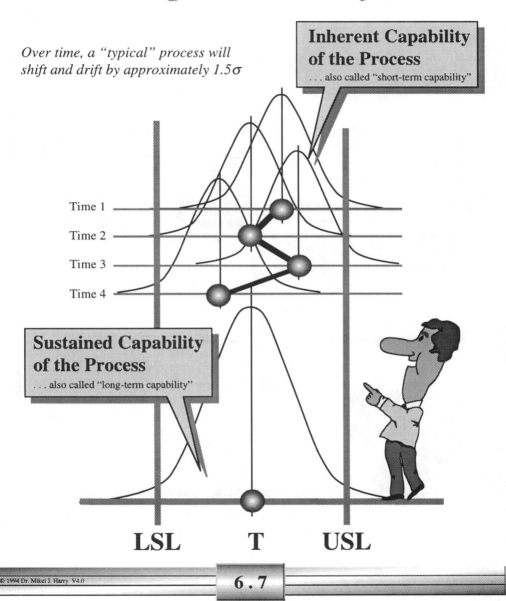

Over time, a "typical" process will shift and drift by approximately 1.5σ

Inherent Capability of the Process
. . . also called "short-term capability"

Time 1

Time 2

Time 3

Time 4

Sustained Capability of the Process
. . . also called "long-term capability"

LSL   T   USL

Improving Process Capability

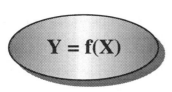

Y = f(X)

- Y is the dependent variable
- X is the independent variable
- The value of Y waits upon X
- X is independent of Y

The dependent variable is sometimes refered to as the "response" variable.

The indpendent variables are often collectively refered to as the "underlying cause system" or "underlying system of causation."

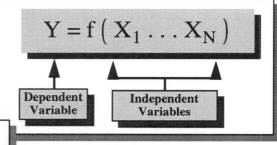

$$Y = f(X_1 \ldots X_N)$$

Dependent Variable	Independent Variables

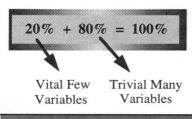

$$20\% + 80\% = 100\%$$

Vital Few Variables   Trivial Many Variables

The "vital few" variables are also called "leverage" variables because they exert a disproportionately large influence on the dependent variable.

$$\Delta Y = \sqrt{X_1^2 + X_2^2}$$

$\sqrt{4+1} = 4.12$	$\sqrt{4+1} = 4.12$
$\sqrt{4+0} = 4.00$	$\sqrt{3+1} = 3.16$
$\Delta = 0.12$	$\Delta = 0.96$

Conclusion: We gain 8 times the Reduction in Y by Changing X1 versus X2; therefore, X1 has leverage.

The Focus of Improvement

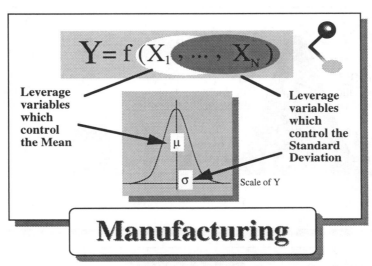

$$Y = f(X_1, \ldots, X_N)$$

Leverage variables which control the Mean

Leverage variables which control the Standard Deviation

μ

σ   Scale of Y

Manufacturing

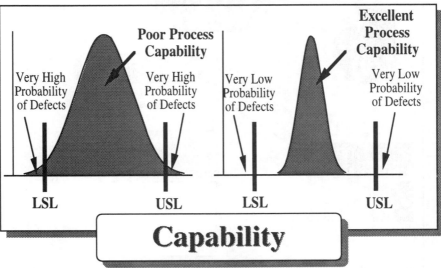

Poor Process Capability

Excellent Process Capability

Very High Probability of Defects

Very High Probability of Defects

Very Low Probability of Defects

Very Low Probability of Defects

LSL   USL   LSL   USL

Capability

Additional Applications

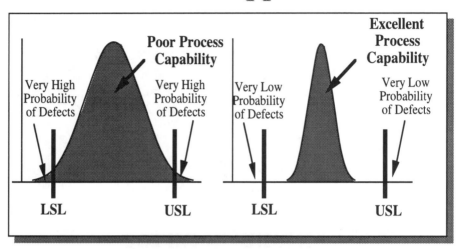

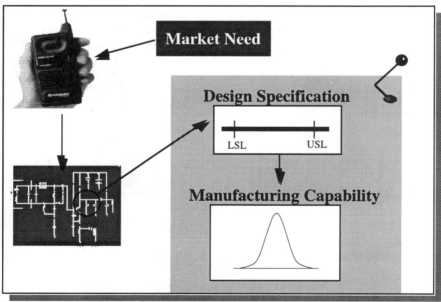

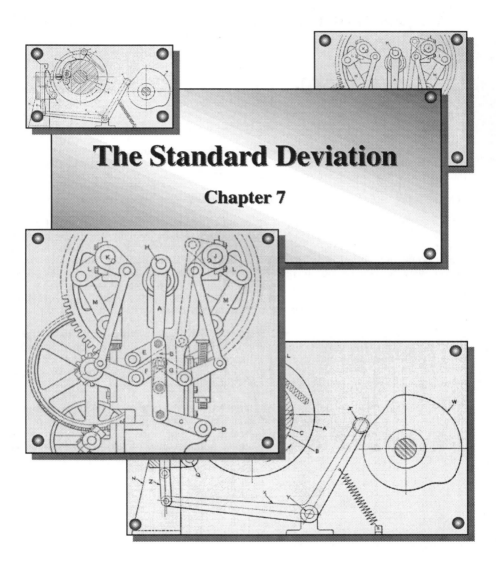

The Standard Deviation

Chapter 7

Purposes of the Standard Deviation

If we accept the fact that variation exists, then we must also recognize that variation in data is nothing more than some form of dispersion or scatter. Expressed differently, continuous data often disperses or spreads out relative to a particular location on some scale of measure or, as one might say, "it is scattered about the average." What this means is that the individual observations (measurements) tend to be "sprinkled" around the balance point of the data.

To illustrate, let us suppose that we were holding a funnel full of sand directly over a large piece of white paper. If we were to project a line from the center of the funnel to the paper, the point at which the line intersects the paper can be thought of as point of contact or a center point. Let us further suppose that we were to allow the sand to pour out of the funnel onto the paper while holding the funnel perfectly steady. What would happen?

As we might expect, the grains of sand would be scattered all over the piece of paper; however, the grains would tend to be most concentrated at the center point. If enough sand were to be released from the funnel, we would expect to see a pile start to form about the center point. In addition, we would also expect to see fewer grains of sand as we move farther away from the peak of the pile - assuming that the person holding the funnel did not shift it to a new center point on the paper. In this analogy, the center of the sand pile would be the arithmetic average, or balance point. But how can we describe the dispersion of the individual grains of sand? How can we express the scatter we see?

One way of expressing the degree of scatter we see would be to measure the distance between the two outermost grains of sand. This is most often called the range. One problem with using the range to express dispersion is that it does not use the additional information that all of the other individual grains of sand could give us, nor does it give us information that is relative to the center point of the pile.

In order to make the individual grains of sand relative to the total width and center point of the pile, we would need to devise an index which takes advantage of the information related to each grain of sand. As previously indicated, one such index is called the standard deviation. This particular index is a summary number that conveys to us the relative distance any particular observation is from the arithmetic balance point of its distribution.

Properties of the Mean

Let us now consider several statistical properties of the mean. First, the mean is very responsive to every value in the data set from which it was computed. When we say that it is "responsive," we are saying that its numerical value is sensitive to the values of the other numbers. That is, if any of the other numbers were to change in magnitude, then the mean would also be affected to some degree. The larger the change, the more the mean will change.

Along these same lines is the second property of the mean - its sensitivity to extreme values. For instance, if we had two small numbers (say, 2 and 4), it is readily apparent that the mean would be 3. Now, let us add a third number (say, 6). Given this, the new average would be 4. This would represent a location change of 1 unit in the mean (from 3 to 4). However, if that third number had been 21, the mean would now be 9. As you can see, this would represent a location change of 6 units. In the first set of three numbers (2, 4, and 6) there was only a 1.33-fold change in the average; however, in the second set of three numbers (2, 4, and 21), there was a 3-fold change in the location. This would tend to tell us that the arithmetic mean is very sensitive to any unbalanced change in the data, as well as extreme values.

In the instance of our widget example, if more were to be produced, say three more, it is possible that the mean (μ) would change in value. Should this happen, we could say the mean shifted to some higher or lower level. In other words, if the cause system (X1...XN) underlying Y were to change, we would see some degree of change in the population or "universe" average (μ). In short, if the cause system were to be suddenly altered, μ would "shift" its location.

Yet another property of the mean would be its ability to resist the influence of sampling fluctuations. This particular property is extremely important whenever random sampling is performed and the assumption of normality is reasonable. For example, let us suppose that we were randomly to draw 100 samples of size 5 from a normally distributed population. If we were to determine the mean, median, and mode for each of the 100 samples and then compare how much each measure of central tendency changed from sample to sample, we would find that the arithmetic average (mean) would be the most resilient to fluctuation.

In general, this holds true for most of the different types of distributions that are commonly used in statistical work. Given these, as well as other properties, the mean is perhaps the most useful measure of central tendency - hence its wide application, reputation, and use in the 6σ quality philosophy.

Properties of the Standard Deviation

Yet another way to describe the nature of the standard deviation is by its unique properties. First, much like the mean, it is very sensitive or responsive to the position of every value in a distribution. If a single value out of a reasonably large distribution of values is shifted to an extreme position, the standard deviation will change noticeably. Expressed differently, the standard deviation is not robust against extreme values. As a result of this property, the standard deviation may not be the best choice among measures of variability when the distribution is markedly skewed or extreme values are present. Of course, mathematical transformers can sometimes be employed to rectify the undesirable situations. [5]

When the deviations are calculated from the arithmetic average, the sum of squares (SS) is smaller than if another measure of central tendency had been used (e.g., mode, median, etc.). Given this, we have yet another way to describe the arithmetic average (mean): that point which minimizes the sum of squares. Another property of the standard deviation would be its resistance to sampling fluctuations. That is to say, the standard deviation does not change a whole lot, as compared to other measures of variability, given normal fluctuations in repeated random samples.

Still another characteristic would be its similarity to the mean in that it is "kind of like" the average of all of the squared deviations. In this respect, it is highly sensitive to extreme values and location. Like the mean, it is used in many descriptive and inferential statistics. In addition, it is probably the most used measure of variability (indicator of dispersion or "scatter").

The Range Method

Because this particular method of computing the sample standard deviation is based on the sample ranges, it is sometimes referred to as the "range method." In general, the range method should be used when rational subgrouping serves as the basis of the sampling scheme. In general, the deviation method should be employed when it is not possible to define rational subgroups. The notion of a "rational subgroup" will be presented in great detail later in the discussion. For the moment, we need only recognize that it is related to a sampling technique designed to limit systematic variations within the sample.

Computing the sample standard deviation via the range method is a relatively easy task. First, the range (R) of each subgroup (G1, ..., G6) must be determined. This may be done by subtracting the minimum value (Xmin) in a particular subgroup - say, Gj - from the maximum value (Xmax) contained within Gj. This may be expressed as

$$Rj = Xmax—Xmin$$

Eq. (1)

Next, we need to find the average range ($\overline{R}$). In the context of Eq. (1), the average range may be given by

$$\overline{R} = \sum_{j=1}^{N} R_j /N$$

Eq. (2)

where Rj is the range of the jth subgroup (Gj) and N is the total number of subgroups. Once the average range ($\overline{R}$) has been computed, the sample standard deviation may be calculated by dividing the average range ($\overline{R}$) by the appropriate constant (d2*) listed in table 1. This operation may be expressed as

$$S = \overline{R}/d2*$$

Eq. (3)

where d2* = 2.353 for the case when there are N = 6 subgroups, under the special condition n = 5. Obviously, if there were more or less subgroups, the value of d2* would be differen

Table 1. Tabulated Values of d2* for a Selected Number of Subgroups (N) of Size n = 5

N	d2*	N	d2*
1	2.474	8	2.346
2	2.405	10	2.342
3	2.379	11	2.339
5	2.358	20	2.334
6	2.353	∞	2.326

The Standard Deviation

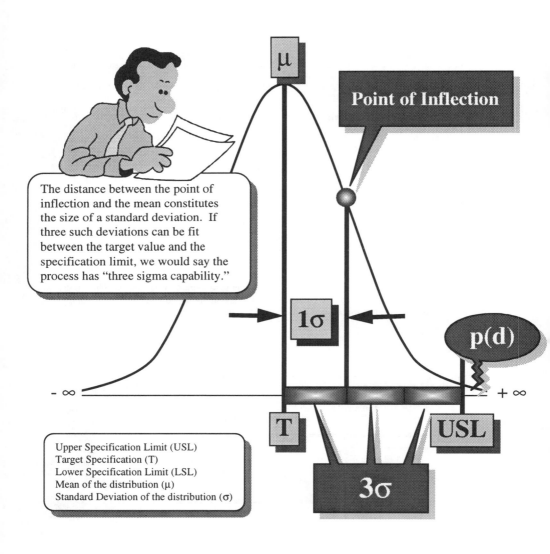

The distance between the point of inflection and the mean constitutes the size of a standard deviation. If three such deviations can be fit between the target value and the specification limit, we would say the process has "three sigma capability."

Point of Inflection

μ

1σ

p(d)

- ∞   + ∞

T

USL

3σ

Upper Specification Limit (USL)
Target Specification (T)
Lower Specification Limit (LSL)
Mean of the distribution (μ)
Standard Deviation of the distribution (σ)

The Computational Equations

Population Mean

$$\mu = \frac{\sum\limits_{i=1}^{N} X_i}{N}$$

Population Standard Deviation

$$\sigma = S = \sqrt{\frac{\sum\limits_{i=1}^{N} (X_i - \mu)^2}{N}}$$

Sample Mean

$$\hat{\mu} = \overline{X} = \frac{\sum\limits_{i=1}^{n} X_i}{n}$$

Sample Standard Deviation

$$\hat{\sigma} = s = \sqrt{\frac{\sum\limits_{i=1}^{n} (X_i - \overline{X})^2}{n-1}}$$

Exercise 1: Standard Deviation

	X	X - $\overline{X}$	$(X - \overline{X})^2$
1			
2			
3			
4			
5			
6			
7			
8			
9			
10			
Σ			
$\overline{X}$			
$\hat{\sigma}^2$			
$\hat{\sigma}$			

$$\overline{X} = \frac{\sum\limits_{i=1}^{n} X_i}{n} \qquad \hat{\sigma} = \sqrt{\frac{\sum\limits_{i=1}^{n} (X_i - \overline{X})^2}{n - 1}}$$

The Quadratic Deviation

Squaring is a means to weight extreme deviations from the natural center of the data.

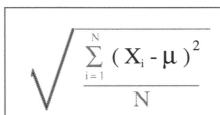

$$\sqrt{\dfrac{\displaystyle\sum_{i=1}^{N}(X_i - \mu)^2}{N}}$$

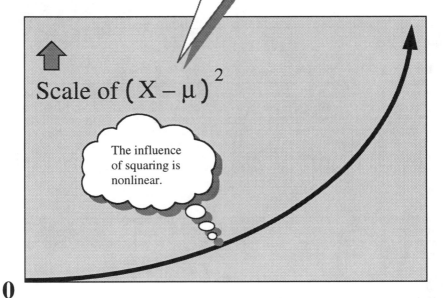

Scale of $(X - \mu)^2$

The influence of squaring is nonlinear.

0

Scale of $(X - \mu)$

Degrees of Freedom

$$\widehat{\sigma} = s = \sqrt{\frac{\sum_{i=1}^{n} (X_i - \overline{X})^2}{n - 1}}$$

The use of n–1 is a mathematical device employed for the purposes of deriving an unbiased estimator of the population standard deviation. In the given context, n–1 is referred to as "degrees of freedom." When the total sums-of-squared deviations is given and the pair-wise deviation contrasts are made for n observations, the last contrast is fixed; hence, there are n–1 degrees of freedom from which to accumulate the total. More specifically, degrees of freedom may be defined as (n–1) independent contrasts out of n observations. For example, in a sample with n = 5, measurements X1, X2, X3, X4, and X5, are made. The independent contrasts are X1, - X2, X2 - X3, X3 - X4, and X4 - X5. The additional contrast, X1 - X5, is not independent since its value is known from

$$(X1 - X2) + (X2 - X3) + (X3 - X4) + (X4 - X5) = X1 - X5$$

Therefore, for a sample of n = 5, there are four (n–1) independent contrasts or "degrees of freedom." In this instance, all but one of the contrasts are free to vary in magnitude, given that the total is fixed. Thus, when n is large, the degree of bias is small; therefore, there is little need for such a corrective device.

Influence of Sample Size

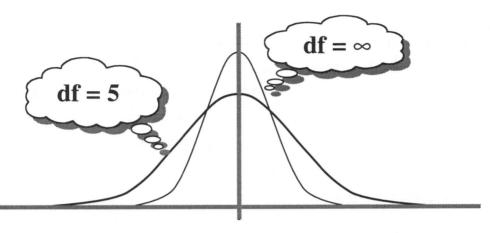

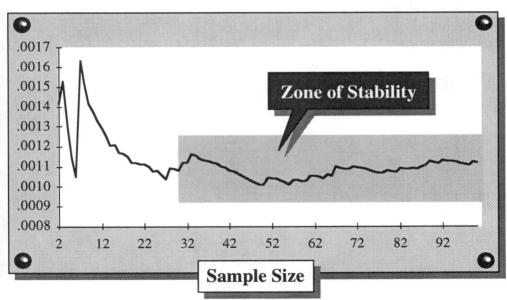

Illustration 1a

A certain engineer made some measurements on the product characteristic called "Y." A single measurement was taken every hour on the hour. Using the measurements gathered between 8:00 AM and 12:00 PM, the engineer prepared to compute the standard deviation.

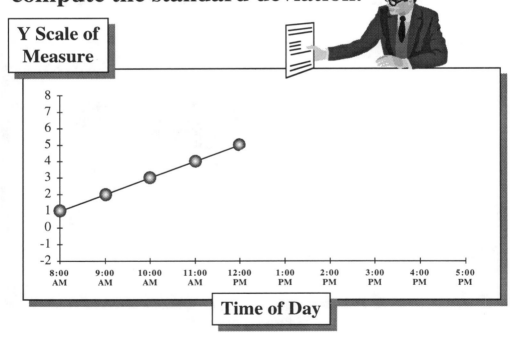

Illustration 1b

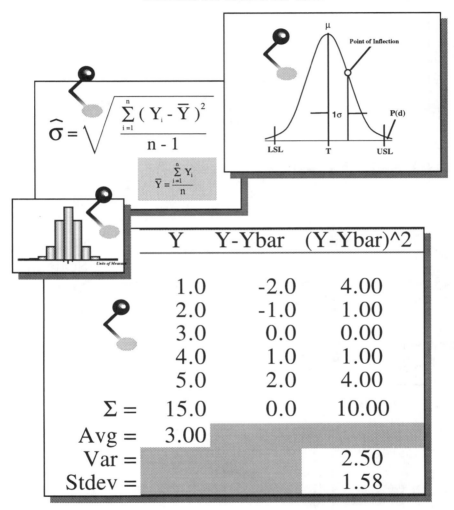

$$\widehat{\sigma} = \sqrt{\frac{\sum\limits_{i=1}^{n}(Y_i - \overline{Y})^2}{n-1}}$$

$$\overline{Y} = \frac{\sum\limits_{i=1}^{n} Y_i}{n}$$

Y	Y-Ybar	(Y-Ybar)^2
1.0	-2.0	4.00
2.0	-1.0	1.00
3.0	0.0	0.00
4.0	1.0	1.00
5.0	2.0	4.00
Σ = 15.0	0.0	10.00
Avg = 3.00		
Var =		2.50
Stdev =		1.58

. . . *So what does 1.58 mean?*

Illustration 1c

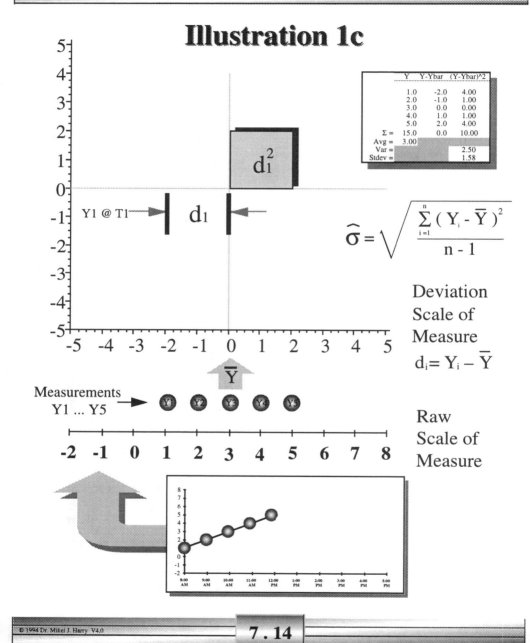

Y	Y-Ybar	(Y-Ybar)^2
1.0	-2.0	4.00
2.0	-1.0	1.00
3.0	0.0	0.00
4.0	1.0	1.00
5.0	2.0	4.00
Σ = 15.0	0.0	10.00
Avg = 3.00		
Var =		2.50
Stdev =		1.58

$$\widehat{\sigma} = \sqrt{\dfrac{\displaystyle\sum_{i=1}^{n}(Y_i - \overline{Y})^2}{n-1}}$$

Deviation Scale of Measure

$$d_i = Y_i - \overline{Y}$$

Measurements Y1 ... Y5

Raw Scale of Measure

Illustration 1d

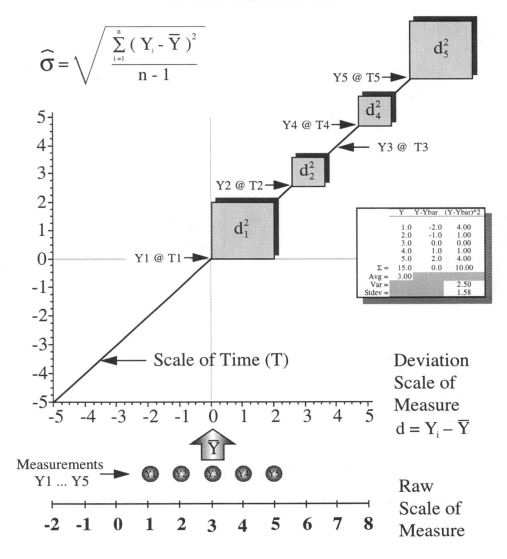

$$\widehat{\sigma} = \sqrt{\frac{\sum\limits_{i=1}^{n} (Y_i - \overline{Y})^2}{n - 1}}$$

Y	Y-Ybar	(Y-Ybar)^2
1.0	-2.0	4.00
2.0	-1.0	1.00
3.0	0.0	0.00
4.0	1.0	1.00
5.0	2.0	4.00
Σ = 15.0	0.0	10.00
Avg = 3.00		
Var =		2.50
Stdev =		1.58

Y5 @ T5

Y4 @ T4

Y3 @ T3

Y2 @ T2

Y1 @ T1

d_5^2

d_4^2

d_2^2

d_1^2

Scale of Time (T)

Deviation
Scale of
Measure
$d = Y_i - \overline{Y}$

Measurements
Y1 ... Y5

$\overline{Y}$

Raw
Scale of
Measure

Illustration 1e

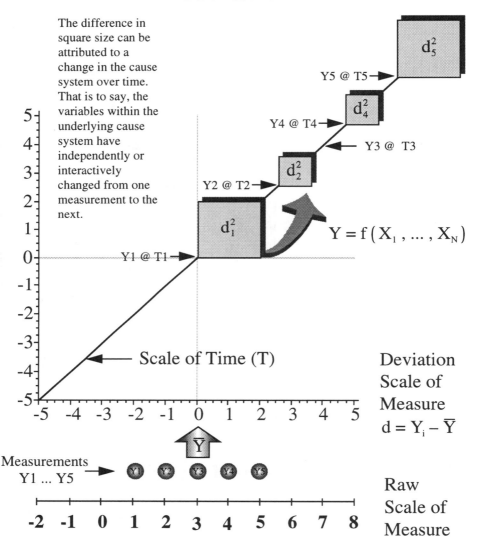

The difference in square size can be attributed to a change in the cause system over time. That is to say, the variables within the underlying cause system have independently or interactively changed from one measurement to the next.

$$Y = f(X_1, \ldots, X_N)$$

Scale of Time (T)

Deviation Scale of Measure
$$d = Y_i - \overline{Y}$$

Measurements Y1 ... Y5

Raw Scale of Measure

7 . 16

Illustration 1f

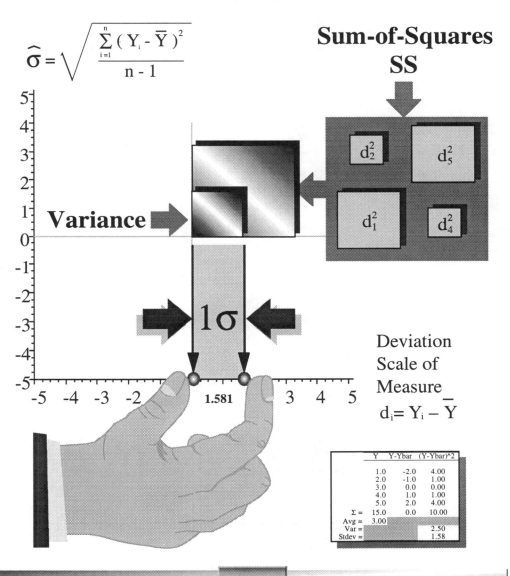

$$\widehat{\sigma} = \sqrt{\frac{\sum_{i=1}^{n}(Y_i - \overline{Y})^2}{n-1}}$$

Sum-of-Squares SS

d_2^2 d_5^2

d_1^2 d_4^2

Variance

1σ

1.581

Deviation Scale of Measure

$d_i = Y_i - \overline{Y}$

	Y	Y-Ybar	(Y-Ybar)^2
	1.0	-2.0	4.00
	2.0	-1.0	1.00
	3.0	0.0	0.00
	4.0	1.0	1.00
	5.0	2.0	4.00
Σ =	15.0	0.0	10.00
Avg =	3.00		
Var =			2.50
Stdev =			1.58

Calculating By Hand

Variable X measurements:

75	80	75	65	70
85	70	70	85	70
60	80	80	80	65
80	75	75	70	85
70	75	75	75	85
80	55	70	70	85
65	70	80	75	65
75	85	90	80	65
70	75	75	80	80
75	95	90	60	65

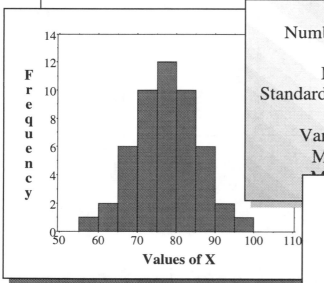

Number of Cases = 50
Mean = 75
Median = 75
Standard Deviation = 8.3299
Range = 40
Variance = 69.388
Minimum = 55

$$\widehat{\sigma} = \sqrt{\frac{\sum\limits_{i=1}^{n} (X_i - \overline{X})^2}{n - 1}}$$

$$\overline{X} = \frac{\sum\limits_{i=1}^{n} X_i}{n}$$

Calculating By Computer - 1a

General Rule: Always graph the data prior to performing a statistical analysis.

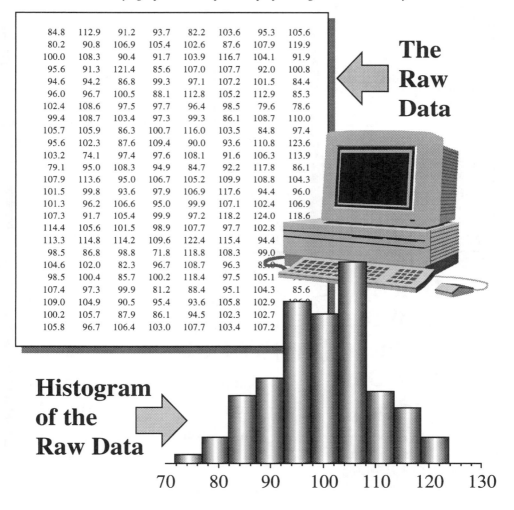

84.8	112.9	91.2	93.7	82.2	103.6	95.3	105.6
80.2	90.8	106.9	105.4	102.6	87.6	107.9	119.9
100.0	108.3	90.4	91.7	103.9	116.7	104.1	91.9
95.6	91.3	121.4	85.6	107.0	107.7	92.0	100.8
94.6	94.2	86.8	99.3	97.1	107.2	101.5	84.4
96.0	96.7	100.5	88.1	112.8	105.2	112.9	85.3
102.4	108.6	97.5	97.7	96.4	98.5	79.6	78.6
99.4	108.7	103.4	97.3	99.3	86.1	108.7	110.0
105.7	105.9	86.3	100.7	116.0	103.5	84.8	97.4
95.6	102.3	87.6	109.4	90.0	93.6	110.8	123.6
103.2	74.1	97.4	97.6	108.1	91.6	106.3	113.9
79.1	95.0	108.3	94.9	84.7	92.2	117.8	86.1
107.9	113.6	95.0	106.7	105.2	109.9	108.8	104.3
101.5	99.8	93.6	97.9	106.9	117.6	94.4	96.0
101.3	96.2	106.6	95.0	99.9	107.1	102.4	106.9
107.3	91.7	105.4	99.9	97.2	118.2	124.0	118.6
114.4	105.6	101.5	98.9	107.7	97.7	102.8	
113.3	114.8	114.2	109.6	122.4	115.4	94.4	
98.5	86.8	98.8	71.8	118.8	108.3	99.0	
104.6	102.0	82.3	96.7	108.7	96.3	85.0	
98.5	100.4	85.7	100.2	118.4	97.5	105.1	
107.4	97.3	99.9	81.2	88.4	95.1	104.3	85.6
109.0	104.9	90.5	95.4	93.6	105.8	102.9	106.0
100.2	105.7	87.9	86.1	94.5	102.3	102.7	
105.8	96.7	106.4	103.0	107.7	103.4	107.2	

The Raw Data

Histogram of the Raw Data

70   80   90   100   110   120   130

7 . 19

Calculating By Computer - 1b

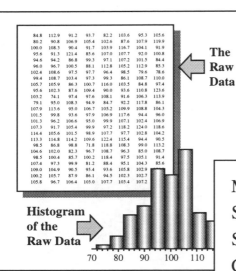

84.8	112.9	91.2	93.7	82.2	103.6	95.3	105.6
80.2	90.8	106.9	105.4	102.6	87.6	107.9	119.9
100.0	108.3	90.4	91.7	103.9	116.7	104.1	91.9
95.6	91.3	121.4	85.6	107.0	107.7	92.0	100.8
94.6	94.2	86.8	99.3	97.1	107.2	101.5	84.4
96.0	96.7	100.5	88.1	112.8	105.2	112.9	85.3
102.4	108.6	97.5	97.7	96.4	98.5	79.6	78.6
99.4	108.7	103.4	97.3	99.3	86.1	108.7	110.0
105.7	105.9	86.3	100.7	116.0	103.5	84.8	97.4
95.6	102.3	87.6	109.4	90.0	93.6	110.8	123.6
103.2	74.1	97.4	97.6	108.1	91.6	106.3	113.9
79.1	95.0	108.3	94.9	84.7	92.2	117.8	86.1
107.9	113.6	95.0	106.7	105.2	109.9	108.8	104.3
101.5	99.8	93.6	97.9	106.9	117.6	94.4	96.0
101.3	96.2	106.6	95.0	99.9	107.1	102.4	106.9
107.3	91.7	105.4	99.9	97.2	118.2	124.0	118.6
114.4	105.6	101.5	98.9	107.7	97.7	102.8	104.2
113.3	114.8	114.2	109.6	122.4	115.4	94.4	90.5
98.5	86.8	98.8	71.8	118.8	108.3	99.0	113.2
104.6	102.0	82.3	96.7	108.7	96.3	85.0	108.7
98.5	100.4	85.7	100.2	118.4	97.5	105.1	91.4
107.4	97.3	99.9	81.2	88.4	95.1	104.3	85.6
109.0	104.9	90.5	95.4	93.6	105.8	102.9	
100.2	105.7	87.9	86.1	94.5	102.3	102.7	
105.8	96.7	106.4	103.0	107.7	103.4	107.2	

The Raw Data

$$\widehat{\sigma} = \sqrt{\frac{\sum\limits_{i=1}^{n} (X_i - \overline{X})^2}{n-1}}$$

$$\overline{X} = \frac{\sum\limits_{i=1}^{n} X_i}{n}$$

Histogram of the Raw Data

70	80	90	100	110

Descriptive Statistics for the Raw Data

Mean	100.30
Std. Dev.	10.01
Std. Error	.71
Count	200
Minimum	71.75
Maximum	123.99
Variance	100.18
Coef. Var.	9.98E-2
Range	52.23
Sum	20060.33
Sum Squares	2032020.74
Median	100.45

The Widget Example Data

g	X1	X2	X3	X4	X5
1	1.242	1.239	1.239	1.242	1.240
2	1.240	1.241	1.240	1.239	1.242
3	1.239	1.239	1.239	1.239	1.240
4	1.241	1.240	1.240	1.240	1.241
5	1.240	1.241	1.240	1.238	1.241
6	1.241	1.240	1.240	1.240	1.239
7	1.237	1.240	1.240	1.237	1.238
8	1.240	1.242	1.240	1.240	1.238
9	1.240	1.239	1.240	1.239	1.242
10	1.239	1.239	1.241	1.239	1.240
11	1.239	1.238	1.242	1.238	1.240
12	1.239	1.241	1.239	1.239	1.242
13	1.239	1.242	1.239	1.239	
14	1.240	1.239	1.240	1.239	
15	1.241	1.240	1.240	1.240	
16	1.240	1.239	1.240	1.240	
17	1.241	1.239	1.238	1.240	
18	1.239	1.239	1.241	1.241	1.239
19	1.240	1.239	1.240	1.238	1.242
20	1.241	1.240	1.241	1.239	1.240

1.240 ± .003

Dimension
"B"

Sampling Strategy: 5 consecutive parts were selected every hour. Each group (g) of parts was labeled and set aside for careful measurement of dimension "B." The location of each measurement was arbitrarily chosen by the inspector.

The Widget Part Analysis

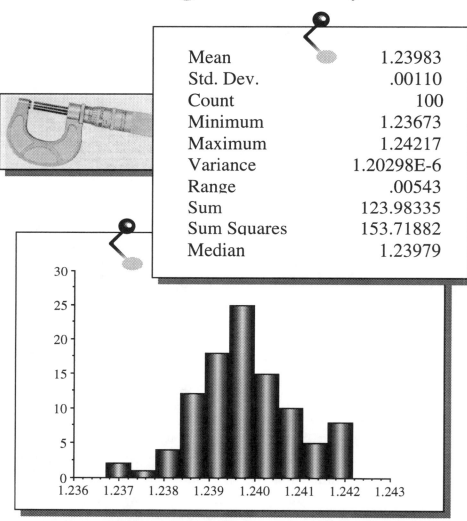

Mean	1.23983
Std. Dev.	.00110
Count	100
Minimum	1.23673
Maximum	1.24217
Variance	1.20298E-6
Range	.00543
Sum	123.98335
Sum Squares	153.71882
Median	1.23979

General Rule: Always graph the data prior to any form of analysis.

The Range and Standard Deviation

g	X1	X2	X3	X4	X5
1	1.242	1.239	1.239	1.242	1.240
2	1.240	1.241	1.240	1.239	1.242
3	1.239	1.239	1.239	1.239	1.240
4	1.241	1.240	1.240	1.240	1.241
5	1.240	1.241	1.240	1.238	1.241
6	1.241	1.240	1.240	1.240	1.239
7	1.237	1.240	1.240	1.237	1.238
8	1.240	1.242	1.240	1.240	1.238
9	1.240	1.239	1.240	1.239	1.242
10	1.239	1.239	1.241	1.239	1.240
11	1.239	1.238	1.242	1.238	1.240
12	1.239	1.241	1.239	1.239	1.242
13	1.239	1.242	1.239	1.239	1.240
14	1.240	1.239	1.240	1.239	1.241
15	1.241	1.240	1.240	1.240	1.240
16	1.240	1.239	1.240	1.240	1.240
17	1.241	1.239	1.238	1.240	1.240
18	1.239	1.239	1.241	1.241	1.239
19	1.240	1.239	1.240	1.238	1.242
20	1.241	1.240	1.241	1.239	1.240

Range	Stdev
.0030	.0015
.0030	.0011
.0010	.0004
.0010	.0005
.0030	.0012
.0020	.0007
.0030	.0015
.0040	.0014
.0030	.0012
.0020	.0009
.0040	.0017
.0030	.0014
.0030	.0013
.0020	.0008
.0010	.0004
.0010	.0004
.0030	.0011
.0020	.0011
.0040	.0015
.0020	.0008

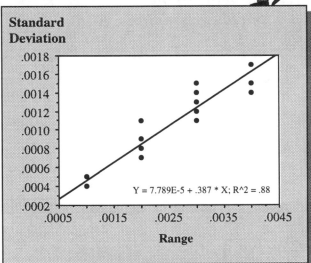

Standard Deviation

$Y = 7.789\text{E-}5 + .387 * X; R^2 = .88$

Range

The Dynamic Range Exercise

Range

					Row Range
1	2	3	4	5	4
1	2	3	4	5	4
1	2	3	4	5	4
1	2	3	4	5	4
1	2	3	4	5	4
		Overall Range =			4

Stdev

					Row Stdev
1	2	3	4	5	1.58
1	2	3	4	5	1.58
1	2	3	4	5	1.58
1	2	3	4	5	1.58
1	2	3	4	5	1.58
		Overall Stdev =			1.44

So what is causing the difference between the upper and lower graphs?

					Row Range
1	2	3	4	5	4
2	3	4	5	6	4
3	4	5	6	7	4
4	5	6	7	8	4
5	6	7	8	9	4
		Overall Range =			8

					Row Stdev
1	2	3	4	5	1.58
2	3	4	5	6	1.58
3	4	5	6	7	1.58
4	5	6	7	8	1.58
5	6	7	8	9	1.58
		Overall Stdev =			2.04

. . . What Conclusions Can We Draw?

Visualizing the Process Dynamics

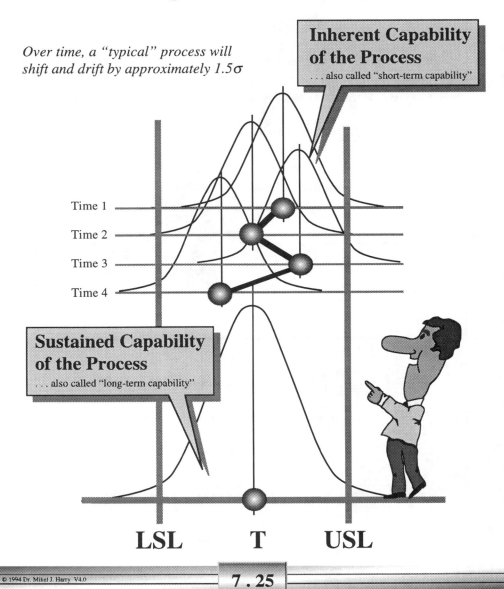

Over time, a "typical" process will shift and drift by approximately 1.5σ

Inherent Capability of the Process
. . . also called "short-term capability"

Time 1
Time 2
Time 3
Time 4

Sustained Capability of the Process
. . . also called "long-term capability"

LSL   T   USL

The Idea of Rational Subgroups

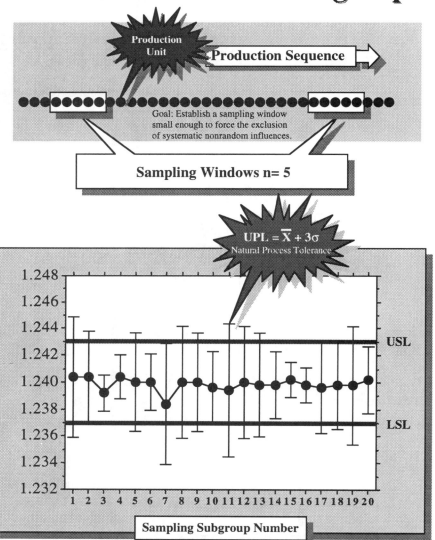

Production Unit

Production Sequence

Goal: Establish a sampling window small enough to force the exclusion of systematic nonrandom influences.

Sampling Windows n= 5

$$UPL = \overline{X} + 3\sigma$$
Natural Process Tolerance

USL

LSL

Sampling Subgroup Number

The Components of Variation

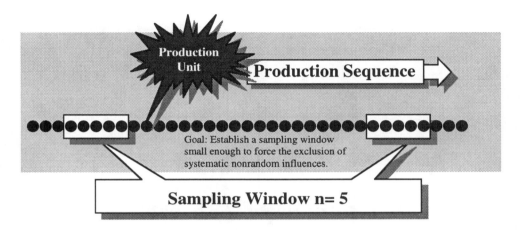

Production Unit

Production Sequence

Goal: Establish a sampling window small enough to force the exclusion of systematic nonrandom influences.

Sampling Window n= 5

SS$_T$ **SS$_B$** **SS$_W$**

$$\sum_{j=1}^{g}\sum_{i=1}^{n}\left(X_{ij}-\overline{\overline{X}}\right)^2 = n\sum_{j=1}^{g}\left(\overline{X}_j-\overline{\overline{X}}\right)^2 + \sum_{j=1}^{g}\sum_{i=1}^{n}\left(X_{ij}-\overline{X}_j\right)^2$$

Total **Between** **Within**

Sustained Reproducibility *Instantaneous Reproducibility*

Capability **Accuracy** **Precision**

Visualizing the Components

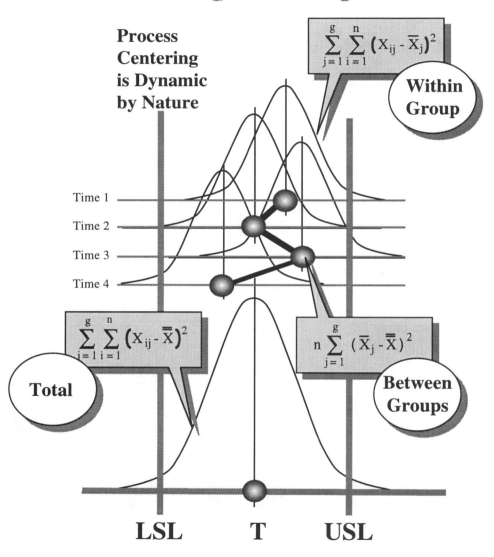

Process Centering is Dynamic by Nature

$$\sum_{j=1}^{g} \sum_{i=1}^{n} (x_{ij} - \overline{x}_j)^2$$

Within Group

Time 1
Time 2
Time 3
Time 4

$$\sum_{j=1}^{g} \sum_{i=1}^{n} (x_{ij} - \overline{\overline{x}})^2$$

$$n \sum_{j=1}^{g} (\overline{x}_j - \overline{\overline{x}})^2$$

Total

Between Groups

LSL   T   USL

Widget Characterization - 1a

Report Name	Example Application		Reporting Period		
Organization			Baseline		
Project			Improvement		
Department			Unit Definition		
Deliverable			Characteristic	Width Dimension	
Deliverable			Units of Measure	Inches	
Process			Upper Specification	1.243	
Operation			Target Value	1.240	
Machine ID			Lower Specification	1.237	
			Subgroup Size (n)	5	

The case-wise analysis sets $\mu = T$ so as to artificially center the process

Subgroup Analysis

Short-Term Capability (Case Analysis)

g	μ	σ	Z.LSL	Z.USL	P.LSL	P.USL	P.TOT	DPMO	Z.B
1	1.2400	0.00	-1.978	1.978	2.40E-02	2.40E-02	4.79E-02	47,913	1.666
2	1.2400	0.00	-2.631	2.631	4.25E-03	4.25E-03	8.51E-03	8,509	2.387
3	1.2400	0.00	-6.708	6.708	1.73E-11	1.73E-11	3.45E-11	0	6.522
4	1.2400	0.00	-5.477	5.477	2.41E-08	2.41E-08	4.81E-08	0	5.333
5	1.2400	0.00	-2.449	2.449	7.15E-03	7.15E-03	1.43E-02	14,306	2.189
6	1.2400	0.00	4.243	4.243	1.11E-05	1.11E-05	2.23E-05	22	4.083
7	1.2400						4.79E-02	47,913	1.666
8	1.2400						3.39E-02	33,895	1.827
9	1.2400						1.43E-02	14,306	2.189
10	1.2400						7.96E-04	796	3.158
11	1.2400						7.30E-02	72,998	1.454
12	1.2400						3.39E-02	33,895	1.827
13	1.2400	0.00	-2.301	2.301	1.07E-02	1.07E-02	2.14E-02	21,398	2.026
14	1.2400	0.00	-3.586	3.586	1.68E-04	1.68E-04	3.36E-04	336	3.401
15	1.2400	0.00	-6.708	6.708	1.73E-11	1.73E-11	3.45E-11	0	6.522
16	1.2400	0.00	-6.708	6.708	1.73E-11	1.73E-11	3.45E-11	0	6.522
17	1.2400	0.00	-2.631	2.631	4.25E-03	4.25E-03	8.51E-03	8,509	2.387
18	1.2400	0.00	-2.739	2.739	3.08E-03	3.08E-03	6.17E-03	6,170	2.503
19	1.2400	0.00	-2.023	2.023	2.16E-02	2.16E-02	4.31E-02	43,115	1.716
20	1.2400	0.00	-3.586	3.586	1.68E-04	1.68E-04	3.36E-04	336	3.401

$$\hat{\sigma} = s = \sqrt{\frac{\sum_{i=1}^{n} (X_i - \overline{X}_j)^2}{n - 1}}$$

Format L2

Widget Characterization - 1b

Short-Term Capability (Cumm Analysis)

g	μ	SS	σ	Z.LSL	Z.USL	P.LSL				
1	1.2400	.000009	.00152	-1.978	1.978	2.40E-02				
2	1.24	.000014	.00134	-2.236	2.236	1.27E-02				
3	1.240	.000015	.00113	-2.666	2.666	3.84E-03				
4	1.2400	.000016	.00101	-2.963	2.963	1.52E-03				
5	1.2400	.00022	.00106	-2.835	2.835	2.29E-03				
6					75	1.46E-03	1.46E-03	2.93E-03	2,927	2.756
7					39	3.08E-03	3.08E-03	6.17E-03	6,170	2.503
8					31	4.25E-03	4.25E-03	8.51E-03	8,509	2.387
9					09	4.54E-03	4.54E-03	9.08E-03	9,081	2.363
10	1.2400	.000051	.00113	-2.802	2.862	3.88E-03	3.88E-03	7.77E-03	7,766	2.420
11	1.2400	.000062					03	1.15E-02	11,495	2.274
12	1.2400	.000070					03	1.30E-02	12,983	2.227
13	1.2400	.000077					03	1.36E-02	13,566	2.210
14	1.2400	.000080					03	1.19E-02	11,860	2.262
15	1.2400	.000080					03	9.55E-03	9,553	2.344
16	1.2400	.000081	.00113	663	2.663	3.87E-03	3.87E-03	7.74E-03	7,736	2.422
17	1.2400	.000086	.0011	2.661	2.661	3.89E-03	3.89E-03	7.78E-03	7,780	2.419
18	1.2400	.000091	.0011	-2.666	2.666	3.84E-03	3.84E-03	7.69E-03	7,686	2.424
19	1.2400	.000100	.001	-2.615	2.615	4.46E-03	4.46E-03	8.91E-03	8,914	2.370
20	1.2400	.000103	.0011	-2.646	2.646	4.07E-03	4.07E-03	8.13E-03	8,133	2.403

Cumulative Short-Term Analysis

The short-term analysis sets μ = T so as to artificially center the process

$$\hat{\sigma}_W = \sqrt{\frac{SS_W}{g\,(n-1)}}$$

Widget Characterization - 1c

Long-Term Capability (Cumm Analysis)

g	μ	SS	σ	Z.LSL	Z.USL	P.LSL	P.USL				ift
1	1.240	.000009	.00152	-2.242	1.7?	1.25E-02	4.32E-0?				4
2	1.2404	.000014	.00126	-2.688	2.055	3.59E-03	1.99E-0?				2
3	1.2400	.000020	.00120	-2.510	2.510	6.04E-03	6.04E-0?				9
4	1.2401	.00022	.00107	-2.894	2.707	1.90E-03	3.39E-0?				7
5	1.2401	.0028?	.00108	-2.860	2.711	2.12E-03	3.35E-03				1
6	1.					1.26E-03	1.92E-03	3.18E-03	3,179	2.729	0.027
7	1.					1.04E-02	4.80E-03	1.52E-02	15,236	2.164	0.338
8	1.					1.03E-02	5.25E-03	1.56E-02	15,552	2.156	0.231
9	1.					9.26E-03	5.03E-03	1.43E-02	14,289	2.190	0.173
10	1.239?	.00000?	.00118			8.24E-03	3.81E-03	1.21E-02	12,050	2.256	0.164
11	1.2398	.000081	.001??	2.380	2.616	1.10E-02	4.45E-03	1.55E-02	15,487	2.158	0.116
12	1.2398	.000089	.0					1.57E-02	15,678	2.153	0.074
13	1.2398	.000096	.0					1.53E-02	15,305	2.163	0.048
14	1.2398	.000099	.0					1.31E-02	13,123	2.223	0.039
15	1.2398	.000100	.0					1.06E-02	10,593	2.305	0.039
16	1.2398	.000101	.00113	?11	2.799	6.02E-03	2.57E-03	8.59E-03	8,588	2.383	0.038
17	1.2398	.000106	.00113	.509	2.823	6.05E-03	2.38E-03	8.43E-03	8,427	2.390	0.029
18	1.2398	.000111	.0011?	2.525	2.843	5.78E-03	2.23E-03	8.01E-03	8,010	2.409	0.015
19	1.2398	.000120	.0011?	-2.497	2.814	6.26E-03	2.45E-03	8.70E-03	8,704	2.378	-0.009
20	1.2398	.000123	.00112	-2.543	2.830	5.49E-03	2.33E-03	7.82E-03	7,817	2.418	-0.014

Cumulative Long-Term Analysis

$$\bar{\bar{X}} = \frac{\sum_{j=1}^{g}\sum_{i=1}^{n} X_{ij}}{ng}$$

$$\hat{\sigma}_T = \sqrt{\frac{SS_T}{ng-1}}$$

Widget Characterization - 1d

Analyzing the Sum-of-Squares . . .

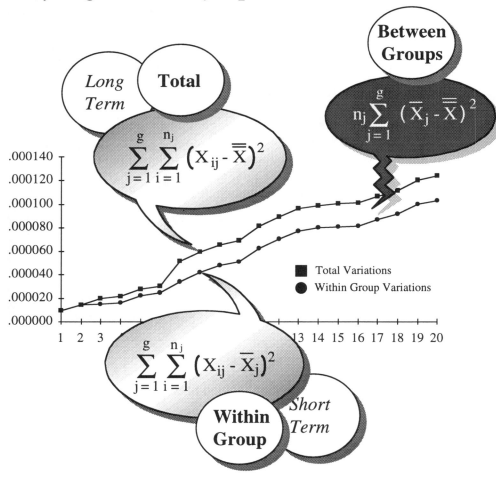

Widget Characterization - 1e

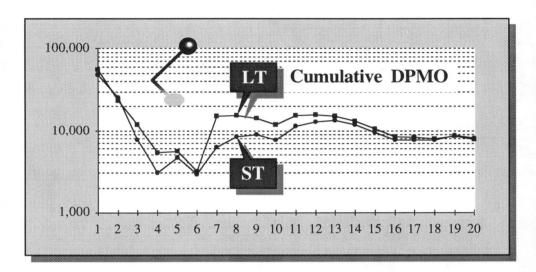

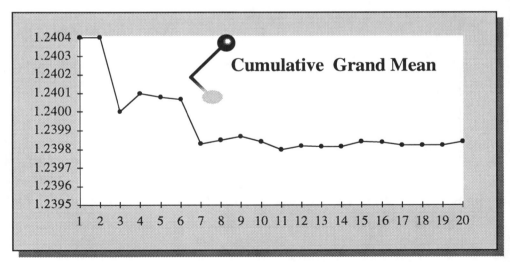

Widget Characterization - 1f

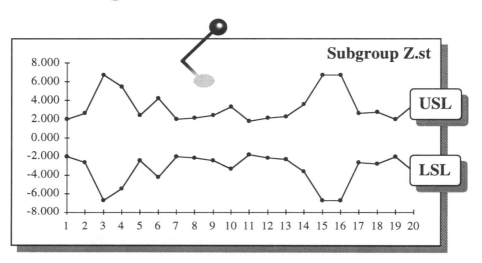

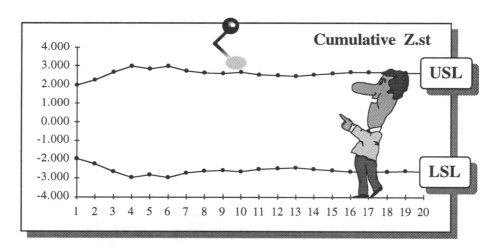

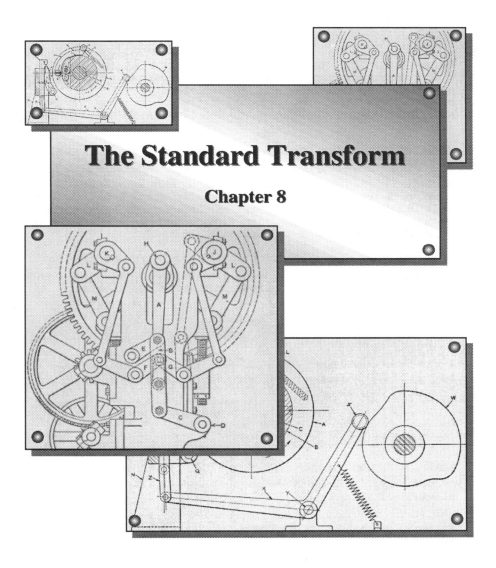

The Standard Transform

Chapter 8

The Standard Transform

In many instances, we need to be able to compute the probability of exceeding a given design constraint without the aid of an illustration, or the complexity of mathematical integration. In such instances, we need only employ what is known as the "standard Z transform." Notice that it is also referred to as the "standard normal deviate." The reader should be aware that both usages will be employed in subsequent discussions and illustrations.

Essentially, the standard transform, or "Z" scale of measure, transforms a set of data such that the mean is always equal to zero ($\mu = 0$) and the standard deviation is always equal to one ($\sigma = 1.0$). Of course, the use of such a transformation assumes that the underlying distribution is normal. Statistically speaking, this would be to say $Z \sim NID$ (0, 1). In addition, the raw units of measure (e.g., inches as related to our widget example) are eliminated, or lost, by virtue of the transformation process. That is to say, the Z measurement scale is without units.

To illustrate how the standard transform is used, let's suppose we wanted to know how many σ are equivalent to 1.242 inches. To get the answer, we must transform the measurement of interest into a Z value by applying the following equation:

$$Z = \frac{(X - \mu)}{\sigma}$$

Eq. (1)

This particular equation is for population values. If a sample is used, then substitute $\overline{x}$ for μ and s for σ. Substituting the values of our known population parameters into the equation, we would have:

$$Z = \frac{1.242 - 1.240}{.001}$$

Eq. (2)

Making the necessary calculations reveals $Z = 2.000$. This tells us that the length measurement of 1.242 lies 2σ to the right of μ. It would be to the right because the Z equivalent of 1.242 in. is positive. If Z were a negative number, say -2.000, then the corresponding product measurement value would lie to the left of μ. We shall see later why the standard transform is so important, but for now, let's just recognize that it's an invaluable tool.

Using Z as a Measure of Capability

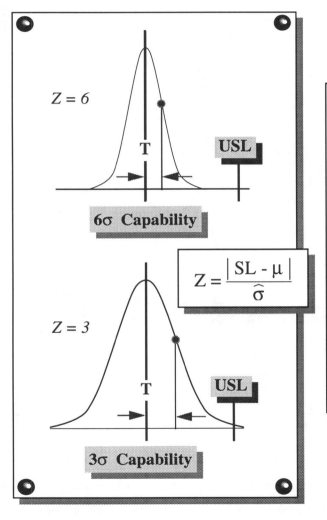

$Z = 6$

T

USL

6σ Capability

$$Z = \frac{|\,SL - \mu\,|}{\widehat{\sigma}}$$

$Z = 3$

T

USL

3σ Capability

As variation decreases, capability increases and, as a consequence, the standard deviation (σ) gets smaller which, in turn, decreases the probability of a defect.

σ

Z

The Standard Normal Deviate

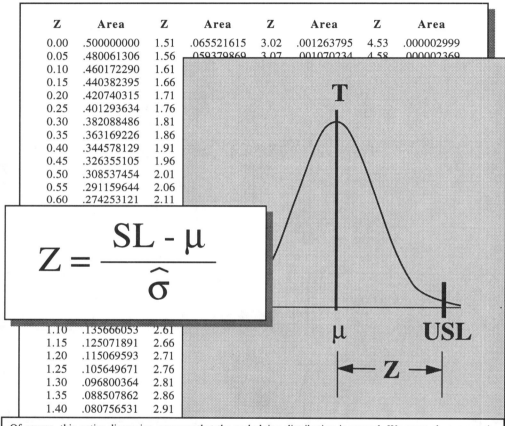

Z	Area	Z	Area	Z	Area	Z	Area
0.00	.500000000	1.51	.065521615	3.02	.001263795	4.53	.000002999
0.05	.480061306	1.56	.059379869	3.07	.001070234	4.58	.000002369
0.10	.460172290	1.61					
0.15	.440382395	1.66					
0.20	.420740315	1.71					
0.25	.401293634	1.76					
0.30	.382088486	1.81					
0.35	.363169226	1.86					
0.40	.344578129	1.91					
0.45	.326355105	1.96					
0.50	.308537454	2.01					
0.55	.291159644	2.06					
0.60	.274253121	2.11					

$$Z = \frac{SL - \mu}{\hat{\sigma}}$$

Z	Area	Z
1.10	.135666053	2.61
1.15	.125071891	2.66
1.20	.115069593	2.71
1.25	.105649671	2.76
1.30	.096800364	2.81
1.35	.088507862	2.86
1.40	.080756531	2.91

Of course, this entire discussion assumes that the underlying distribution is normal. We must always remain cognizant of the fact that whenever a table of normal area is used to establish a rate of nonconformance, and the actual distribution is markedly skewed (i.e., non-normal), the likelihood of grossly distorted estimates is quite high. To avoid such distortion, it is often possible to mathematically transform the raw data. If the transformation is done correctly, the data are artificially forced to a state of normality. Only then can reliable estimates of nonconformance be rendered. Even then, one must always check to be sure that the transformed data retains correlation to the raw data. If not, resultant estimates could be highly misleading.

The Standard Normal Deviate

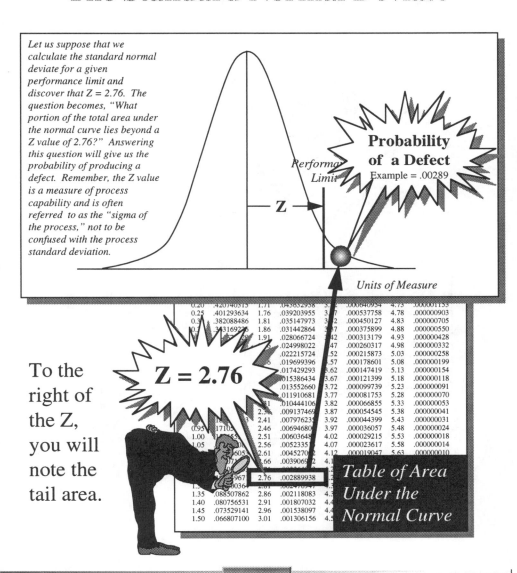

Let us suppose that we calculate the standard normal deviate for a given performance limit and discover that Z = 2.76. The question becomes, "What portion of the total area under the normal curve lies beyond a Z value of 2.76?" Answering this question will give us the probability of producing a defect. Remember, the Z value is a measure of process capability and is often referred to as the "sigma of the process," not to be confused with the process standard deviation.

Probability of a Defect
Example = .00289

Performance Limit

Z →

Units of Measure

To the right of the Z, you will note the tail area.

Z = 2.76

Table of Area Under the Normal Curve

0.20	.420740315	1.71	.043632958		.000640954	4.73	.000001153
0.25	.401293634	1.76	.039203955		.000537758	4.78	.000000903
0.3	.382088486	1.81	.035147973		.000450127	4.83	.000000705
0.3	.343169226	1.86	.031442864		.000375899	4.88	.000000550
		1.91	.028066724		.000313179	4.93	.000000428
			.024998022		.000260317	4.98	.000000332
			.022215724	.52	.000215873	5.03	.000000258
		6	.019699396	.57	.000178601	5.08	.000000199
			.017429293	.62	.000147419	5.13	.000000154
			.015386434	3.67	.000121399	5.18	.000000118
			.013552660	3.72	.000099739	5.23	.000000091
			.011910681	3.77	.000081753	5.28	.000000070
			.010444106	3.82	.000066855	5.33	.000000053
		2.5	.009137469	3.87	.000054545	5.38	.000000041
		2.41	.007976235	3.92	.000044399	5.43	.000000031
0.95	.171	2.46	.006946800	3.97	.000036057	5.48	.000000024
1.00		2.51	.006036480	4.02	.000029215	5.53	.000000018
1.05	605	2.56	.0052335	4.07	.000023617	5.58	.000000014
		2.61	.0045270	4.12	.000019047	5.63	.000000010
		.66	.0039069	4.1			
	967	2.76	.002889938				
	0364	2.81	.002470947				
1.35	.088507862	2.86	.002118083	4.5			
1.40	.080756531	2.91	.001807032	4.4			
1.45	.073529141	2.96	.001538097	4.4			
1.50	.066807100	3.01	.001306156	4.5			

The Universal Equation for Z

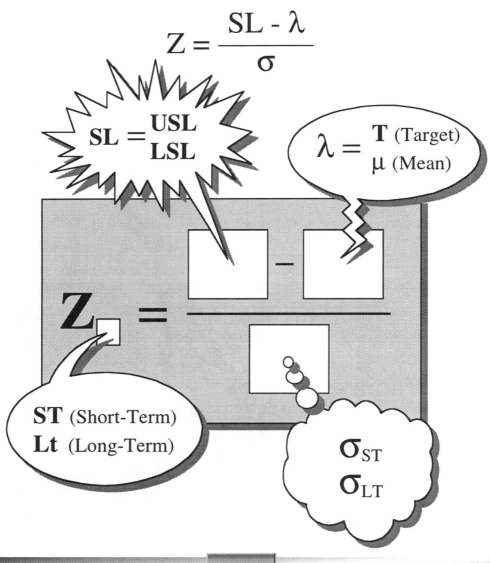

Selecting an Appropriate Z

 Eq. 8.1 $Z = \dfrac{SL - T}{\hat{\sigma}_{st}}$

This Z value is designated as Z.st. It describes how precise the process is at any given moment in time. For this reason, it is referred to as "instantaneous capability." It is also called "short-term capability." In context of the Six Sigma Program, it is the value used when referring to the "SIGMA" of a process. It represents the true potential of the process technology to meet the given performance specification(s); i.e., what the process can do if everything is controlled to such an extent that only background (white) noise is present. It reflects the process capability under the assumption of random variation and does not give consideration to the process center. This metric assumes the data were gathered in accordance to the principals and spirit of a "rational sampling" plan. For a unilateral tolerance with no target Eq. 2 should be used.

Eq. 8.3 $Z = \dfrac{SL - T}{\sigma_{lt}}$

This Z value is designated as Z.lt.d. It is a measure of long-term process capability. It reflects the influence of white noise, as well as the dynamic variations due to nonrandom process centering error; i.e., shifts and drifts in the process mean across sampling subgroups. It assumes that the errors in process centering are dynamic and will eventually average out (over a great many cycles) to the target specification. In context of the Six Sigma Program, it is not often used, except in some design engineering applications. This metric assumes the data were gathered in accordance to the principals and spirit of a "rational sampling" plan. For a unilateral tolerance with no target value, this equation can not be used. In such an event, Eq. 4 should be employed to estimate long-term process capability.

Eq. 8.2 $Z = \dfrac{SL - \hat{\mu}}{\hat{\sigma}_{st}}$

This Z value is designated as Z.lt. It is a measure of long-term capability and, when used properly, reflects process accuracy when compared to Z.st; e.g., Z.st - Z.lt = Z.shift. Expressed differently, it reflects how well the process remains centered over time. Of course, it ignores any nonrandom process centering errors which may occur between sampling intervals. This metric assumes the data were gathered in accordance to the principals and spirit of a "rational sampling" plan. However, in the instance of a unilateral tolerance with no target specification, the given Z value will reflect only short-term capability. In this circumstance, the mean becomes the target. Consequently, it will produce the same result as Eq. 1; therefore, it should be designated as Z.st and so interpreted.

 Eq. 8.4 $Z = \dfrac{SL - \hat{\mu}}{\hat{\sigma}_{lt}}$

This Z value is designated as Z.lt.s. It describes the sustained reproducibility of a process. Because of this, it is also called "long-term capability." In context of the Six Sigma Program, it is the value used to estimate the long-term process "PPM." It reflects the influence of white noise, dynamic nonrandom process centering error, and any static off-set present in the process mean. From this perspective, it considers all of the "vital few" sources of manufacturing error. It is a measure of how well the process is controlled (over many cycles) when compared to Z.st. This metric assumes the data were gathered in accordance to the principals and spirit of a "rational sampling" plan. This equation is applicable to all types of tolerances.

The Widget Example Data

g	X1	X2	X3	X4	X5
1	1.242	1.239	1.239	1.242	1.240
2	1.240	1.241	1.240	1.239	1.242
3	1.239	1.239	1.239	1.239	1.240
4	1.241	1.240	1.240	1.240	1.241
5	1.240	1.241	1.240	1.238	1.241
6	1.241	1.240	1.240	1.240	1.239
7	1.237	1.240	1.240	1.237	1.238
8	1.240	1.242	1.240	1.240	1.238
9	1.240	1.239	1.240	1.239	1.242
10	1.239	1.239	1.241	1.239	1.240
11	1.239	1.238	1.242	1.238	1.240
12	1.239	1.241	1.239	1.239	1.242
13	1.239	1.242	1.239	1.239	1.240
14	1.240	1.239	1.240	1.239	1.241
15	1.241	1.240	1.240	1.240	1.240
16	1.240	1.239	1.240	1.240	1.240
17	1.241	1.239	1.238	1.240	1.240
18	1.239	1.239	1.241	1.241	1.239
19	1.240	1.239	1.240	1.238	1.242
20	1.241	1.240	1.241	1.239	1.240

Sampling Strategy: 5 consecutive parts were selected every hour (X_1, ... , X_N). Each group (g) of parts was labeled and set aside for careful measurement of dimension "B." The location of measurement was arbitrarily chosen by the inspector.

Widget Characterization - 2a

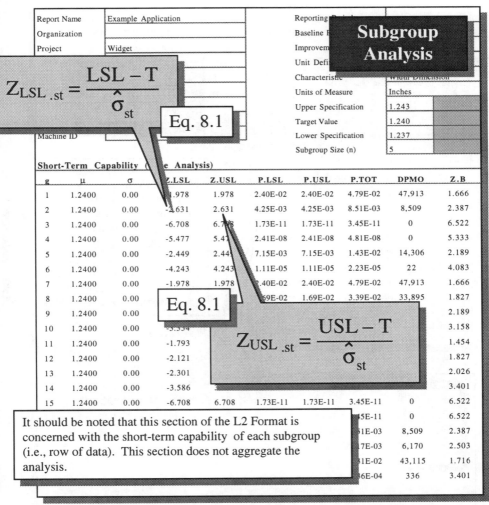

Report Name	Example Application
Organization	
Project	Widget

Subgroup Analysis

Reporting	
Baseline	
Improvem	
Unit Defi	
Characteristic	Width Dimension
Units of Measure	Inches
Upper Specification	1.243
Target Value	1.240
Lower Specification	1.237
Subgroup Size (n)	5

$$Z_{LSL\ .st} = \frac{LSL - T}{\hat{\sigma}_{st}}$$

Eq. 8.1

Machine ID

Short-Term Capability (e Analysis)

g	μ	σ	Z.LSL	Z.USL	P.LSL	P.USL	P.TOT	DPMO	Z.B
1	1.2400	0.00	1.978	1.978	2.40E-02	2.40E-02	4.79E-02	47,913	1.666
2	1.2400	0.00	2.631	2.631	4.25E-03	4.25E-03	8.51E-03	8,509	2.387
3	1.2400	0.00	-6.708	6.708	1.73E-11	1.73E-11	3.45E-11	0	6.522
4	1.2400	0.00	-5.477	5.47	2.41E-08	2.41E-08	4.81E-08	0	5.333
5	1.2400	0.00	-2.449	2.44	7.15E-03	7.15E-03	1.43E-02	14,306	2.189
6	1.2400	0.00	-4.243	4.243	1.11E-05	1.11E-05	2.23E-05	22	4.083
7	1.2400	0.00	-1.978	1.978	2.40E-02	2.40E-02	4.79E-02	47,913	1.666
8	1.2400	0.00			69E-02	1.69E-02	3.39E-02	33,895	1.827
9	1.2400	0.00							2.189
10	1.2400	0.00	-3.534						3.158
11	1.2400	0.00	-1.793						1.454
12	1.2400	0.00	-2.121						1.827
13	1.2400	0.00	-2.301						2.026
14	1.2400	0.00	-3.586						3.401
15	1.2400	0.00	-6.708	6.708	1.73E-11	1.73E-11	3.45E-11	0	6.522
							45E-11	0	6.522
							51E-03	8,509	2.387
							17E-03	6,170	2.503
							31E-02	43,115	1.716
							56E-04	336	3.401

Eq. 8.1

$$Z_{USL\ .st} = \frac{USL - T}{\hat{\sigma}_{st}}$$

It should be noted that this section of the L2 Format is concerned with the short-term capability of each subgroup (i.e., row of data). This section does not aggregate the analysis.

Format L2

Widget Characterization - 2b

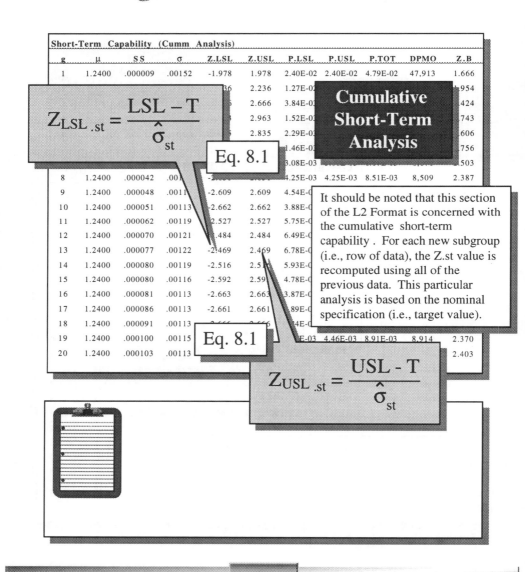

Short-Term Capability (Cumm Analysis)

g	μ	SS	σ	Z.LSL	Z.USL	P.LSL	P.USL	P.TOT	DPMO	Z.B
1	1.2400	.000009	.00152	-1.978	1.978	2.40E-02	2.40E-02	4.79E-02	47,913	1.666
				6	2.236	1.27E-0				954
					2.666	3.84E-0				424
					2.963	1.52E-0				743
					2.835	2.29E-0				606
						1.46E-0				756
						3.08E-03				503
8	1.2400	.000042	.00			4.25E-03	4.25E-03	8.51E-03	8,509	2.387
9	1.2400	.000048	.0011	-2.609	2.609	4.54E-0				
10	1.2400	.000051	.00113	-2.662	2.662	3.88E-0				
11	1.2400	.000062	.00119	2.527	2.527	5.75E-0				
12	1.2400	.000070	.00121	.484	2.484	6.49E-0				
13	1.2400	.000077	.00122	-2.469	2.469	6.78E-0				
14	1.2400	.000080	.00119	-2.516	2.5	5.93E-0				
15	1.2400	.000080	.00116	-2.592	2.59	4.78E-0				
16	1.2400	.000081	.00113	-2.663	2.663	3.87E-0				
17	1.2400	.000086	.00113	-2.661	2.661	89E-0				
18	1.2400	.000091	.00113			4E-0				
19	1.2400	.000100	.00115			E-03	4.46E-03	8.91E-03	8,914	2.370
20	1.2400	.000103	.00113							2.403

$$Z_{LSL\ .st} = \frac{LSL - T}{\hat{\sigma}_{st}}$$

Eq. 8.1

Cumulative Short-Term Analysis

It should be noted that this section of the L2 Format is concerned with the cumulative short-term capability . For each new subgroup (i.e., row of data), the Z.st value is recomputed using all of the previous data. This particular analysis is based on the nominal specification (i.e., target value).

Eq. 8.1

$$Z_{USL\ .st} = \frac{USL - T}{\hat{\sigma}_{st}}$$

Widget Characterization - 2c

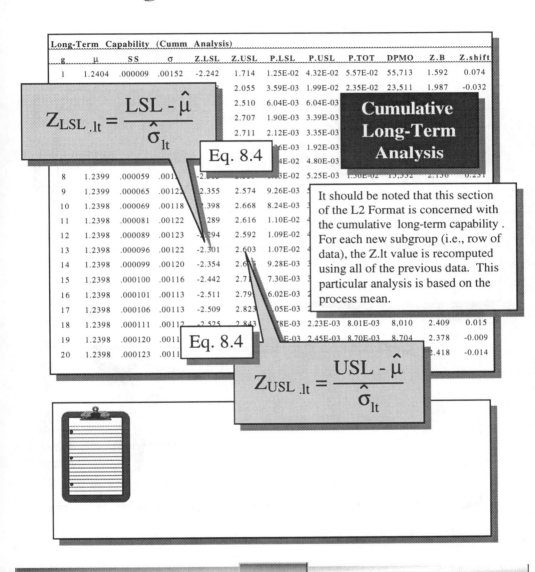

Long-Term Capability (Cumm Analysis)

g	μ	SS	σ	Z.LSL	Z.USL	P.LSL	P.USL	P.TOT	DPMO	Z.B	Z.shift
1	1.2404	.000009	.00152	-2.242	1.714	1.25E-02	4.32E-02	5.57E-02	55,713	1.592	0.074
					2.055	3.59E-03	1.99E-02	2.35E-02	23,511	1.987	-0.032
					2.510	6.04E-03	6.04E-03				
					2.707	1.90E-03	3.39E-03				
					2.711	2.12E-03	3.35E-03				
							1.92E-03				
							4.80E-02				
8	1.2399	.000059	.001				5.25E-03	1.56E-02	15,552	2.150	0.251
9	1.2399	.000065	.00122	2.355	2.574	9.26E-03					
10	1.2398	.000069	.00118	.398	2.668	8.24E-03					
11	1.2398	.000081	.00122	289	2.616	1.10E-02					
12	1.2398	.000089	.00123	294	2.592	1.09E-02					
13	1.2398	.000096	.00122	-2.301	2.603	1.07E-02					
14	1.2398	.000099	.00120	-2.354	2.6	9.28E-03					
15	1.2398	.000100	.00116	-2.442	2.7	7.30E-03					
16	1.2398	.000101	.00113	-2.511	2.79	6.02E-03					
17	1.2398	.000106	.00113	-2.509	2.823	05E-03					
18	1.2398	.000111	.00112	-2.525	2.843	8E-03	2.23E-03	8.01E-03	8,010	2.409	0.015
19	1.2398	.000120	.0011		E-03	2.45E-03	8.70E-03	8,704		2.378	-0.009
20	1.2398	.000123	.0011						2.418		-0.014

$$Z_{LSL \ .lt} = \frac{LSL - \hat{\mu}}{\hat{\sigma}_{lt}}$$

Eq. 8.4

Cumulative Long-Term Analysis

It should be noted that this section of the L2 Format is concerned with the cumulative long-term capability . For each new subgroup (i.e., row of data), the Z.lt value is recomputed using all of the previous data. This particular analysis is based on the process mean.

Eq. 8.4

$$Z_{USL \ .lt} = \frac{USL - \hat{\mu}}{\hat{\sigma}_{lt}}$$

Widget Characterization - 2d

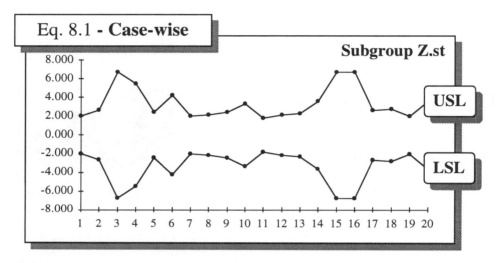

Eq. 8.1 - Case-wise

Subgroup Z.st

USL

LSL

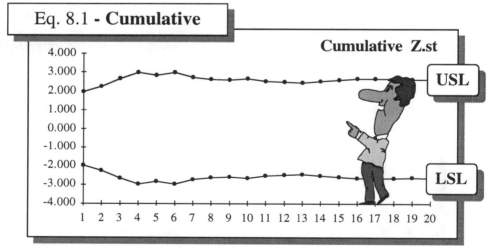

Eq. 8.1 - Cumulative

Cumulative Z.st

USL

LSL

Widget Characterization - 2e

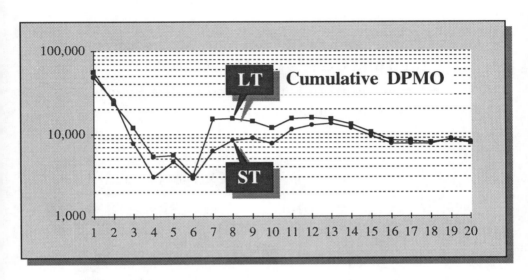

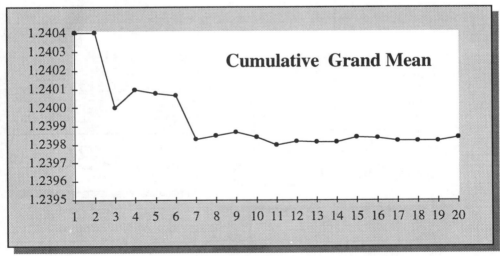

Process Capability Ratios

➤ The greater the design margin, the lower the Total Defects Per Unit (TDU).

➤ Design margin is measured by the Process Capability Index (Cp)

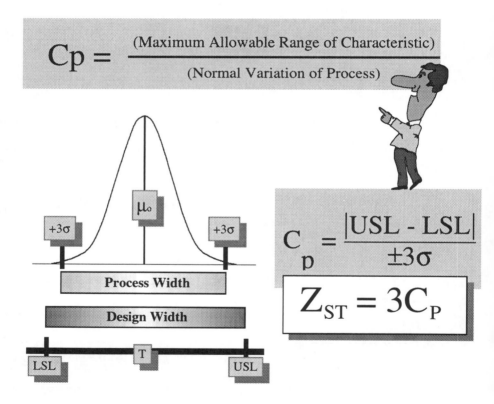

$$Cp = \frac{\text{(Maximum Allowable Range of Characteristic)}}{\text{(Normal Variation of Process)}}$$

$$C_p = \frac{|USL - LSL|}{\pm 3\sigma}$$

$$Z_{ST} = 3C_P$$

+3σ   μ₀   +3σ

Process Width

Design Width

LSL   T   USL

Process Capability Ratios

$$Cpk = Cp (1 - k)$$

Where k1 is the percentage of the tolerance zone
consumed by the static mean shift

$$k = \frac{|T - \mu|}{(USL - LSL)/2}$$

Example: Cp = 2 , k = .25

$$Cpk = 2 (1 - .25) = 1.5$$

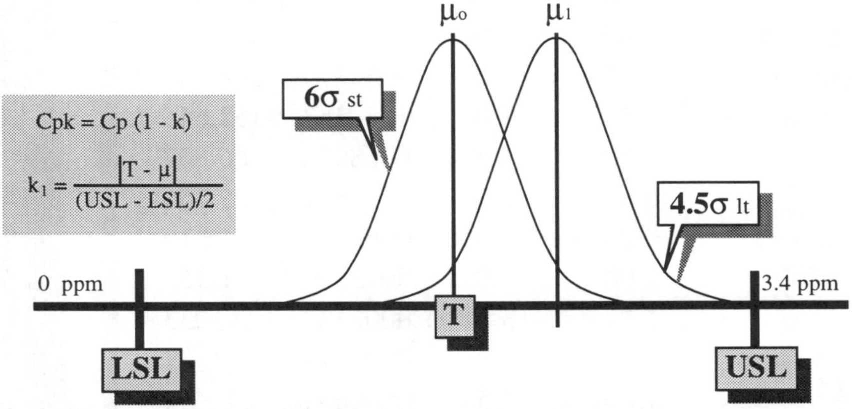

μ_o μ_1

Cpk = Cp (1 - k)

$$k_1 = \frac{|T - \mu|}{(USL - LSL)/2}$$

6σ st

4.5σ lt

0 ppm

T

3.4 ppm

LSL

USL

Indices of Process Capability

Eq. 8.1

	Cp	Z.st	DPO	PPM
	0.50	1.5	.0668072	66,807
	0.67	2.0	.0227501	22,750
	0.83	2.5	.0062097	6,210
	1.00	3.0	.0013500	1,350
	1.17	3.5	.0002327	233
	1.33	4.0	.0000317	32
	1.50	4.5	.0000034	3.4
	1.67	5.0	.0000003	.3
	1.83	5.5	.0000000	.02
	2.00	6.0	.0000000	.001

Short-Term Capability

Note: The short-term capability assumes the process mean is centered on the target specification.

Eq. 8.2

	Cpk	Z.lt	DPO	PPM
	0.00	0.0	.5000000	500,000
	0.17	0.5	.3085375	308,538
	0.33	1.0	.1586553	158,655
	0.50	1.5	.0668072	66,807
	0.67	2.0	.0227501	22,750
	0.83	2.5	.0062097	6,210
	1.00	3.0	.0013500	1,350
	1.17	3.5	.0002327	233
	1.33	4.0	.0000317	32
	1.50	4.5	.0000034	3.4

Long-Term Capability

Note: The long-term capability assumes the process mean is shifted from the target specification by 1.5σ.

Area Under the Normal Curve

Z	Area	Z	Area	Z	Area	Z	Area
0.00	.500000000	0.31	.378280378	0.62	.267628915	0.93	.176185648
0.01	.496010676	0.32	.374484058	0.63	.264347322	0.94	.173608881
0.02	.492021745	0.33	.370699868	0.64	.261086339	0.95	.171056222
0.03	.488033608	0.34	.366928146	0.65	.257846158	0.96	.168527698
0.04	.484046662	0.35	.363169226	0.66	.254626970	0.97	.166023330
0.05	.480061306	0.36	.359423441	0.67	.251428959	0.98	.163543138
0.06	.476077938	0.37	.355691117	0.68	.248252302	0.99	.161087131
0.07	.472096957	0.38	.351972578	0.69	.245097172	1.00	.158655319
0.08	.468118758	0.39	.348268143	0.70	.241963737	1.01	.156247703
0.09	.464143737	0.40	.344578129	0.71	.238852160	1.02	.153864282
0.10	.460172290	0.41	.340902845	0.72	.235762595	1.03	.151505047
0.11	.456204810	0.42	.337242600	0.73	.232695195	1.04	.149169987
0.12	.452241690	0.43	.333597697	0.74	.229650105	1.05	.146859086
0.13	.448283321	0.44	.329968434	0.75	.226627465	1.06	.144572322
0.14	.444330093	0.45	.326355105	0.76	.223627409	1.07	.142309669
0.15	.440382395	0.46	.322758000	0.77	.220650066	1.08	.140071097
0.16	.436440613	0.47	.319177404	0.78	.217695561	1.09	.137856572
0.17	.432505132	0.48	.315613598	0.79	.214764010	1.10	.135666053
0.18	.428576335	0.49	.312066857	0.80	.211855526	1.11	.133499498
0.19	.424654603	0.50	.308537454	0.81	.208970217	1.12	.131356858
0.20	.420740315	0.51	.305025654	0.82	.206108183	1.13	.129238082
0.21	.416833847	0.52	.301531718	0.83	.203269522	1.14	.127143113
0.22	.412935575	0.53	.298055905	0.84	.200454323	1.15	.125071891
0.23	.409045869	0.54	.294598464	0.85	.197662672	1.16	.123024352
0.24	.405165100	0.55	.291159644	0.86	.194894649	1.17	.121000426
0.25	.401293634	0.56	.287739685	0.87	.192150328	1.18	.119000043
0.26	.397431834	0.57	.284338824	0.88	.189429778	1.19	.117023125
0.27	.393580063	0.58	.280957293	0.89	.186733064	1.20	.115069593
0.28	.389738679	0.59	.277595318	0.90	.184060243	1.21	.113139364
0.29	.385908035	0.60	.274253121	0.91	.181411369	1.22	.111232349
0.30	.382088486	0.61	.270930916	0.92	.178786490	1.23	.109348459

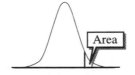

Area Under the Normal Curve

Z	Area	Z	Area	Z	Area	Z	Area
1.24	.107487599	1.55	.060570681	1.86	.031442864	2.17	.015003519
1.25	.105649671	1.56	.059379869	1.87	.030742014	2.18	.014628823
1.26	.103834574	1.57	.058207490	1.88	.030054147	2.19	.014262206
1.27	.102042204	1.58	.057053373	1.89	.029379092	2.20	.013903531
1.28	.100272453	1.59	.055917348	1.90	.028716674	2.21	.013552660
1.29	.098525211	1.60	.054799243	1.91	.028066724	2.22	.013209458
1.30	.096800364	1.61	.053698886	1.92	.027429070	2.23	.012873791
1.31	.095097795	1.62	.052616103	1.93	.026803541	2.24	.012545527
1.32	.093417384	1.63	.051550719	1.94	.026189969	2.25	.012224533
1.33	.091759009	1.64	.050502560	1.95	.025588185	2.26	.011910681
1.34	.090122544	1.65	.049471451	1.96	.024998022	2.27	.011603842
1.35	.088507862	1.66	.048457216	1.97	.024419313	2.28	.011303889
1.36	.086914832	1.67	.047459678	1.98	.023851893	2.29	.011010698
1.37	.085343321	1.68	.046478660	1.99	.023295597	2.30	.010724144
1.38	.083793192	1.69	.045513986	2.00	.022750262	2.31	.010444106
1.39	.082264309	1.70	.044565478	2.01	.022215724	2.32	.010170462
1.40	.080756531	1.71	.043632958	2.02	.021691823	2.33	.009903094
1.41	.079269714	1.72	.042716249	2.03	.021178399	2.34	.009641883
1.42	.077803715	1.73	.041815172	2.04	.020675291	2.35	.009386713
1.43	.076358386	1.74	.040929549	2.05	.020182343	2.36	.009137469
1.44	.074933578	1.75	.040059203	2.06	.019699396	2.37	.008894039
1.45	.073529141	1.76	.039203955	2.07	.019226296	2.38	.008656310
1.46	.072144921	1.77	.038363628	2.08	.018762889	2.39	.008424172
1.47	.070780764	1.78	.037538044	2.09	.018309020	2.40	.008197516
1.48	.069436514	1.79	.036727024	2.10	.017864539	2.41	.007976235
1.49	.068112013	1.80	.035930393	2.11	.017429293	2.42	.007760223
1.50	.066807100	1.81	.035147973	2.12	.017003135	2.43	.007549376
1.51	.065521615	1.82	.034379586	2.13	.016585916	2.44	.007343590
1.52	.064255396	1.83	.033625058	2.14	.016177490	2.45	.007142765
1.53	.063008277	1.84	.032884212	2.15	.015777711	2.46	.006946800
1.54	.061780094	1.85	.032156872	2.16	.015386434	2.47	.006755597

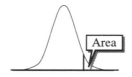

Area Under the Normal Curve

Z	Area	Z	Area	Z	Area	Z	Area
2.48	.006569059	2.79	.002635273	3.10	.000967555	3.41	.000324885
2.49	.006387090	2.80	.002555001	3.11	.000935392	3.42	.000313179
2.50	.006209596	2.81	.002476947	3.12	.000904215	3.43	.000301867
2.51	.006036485	2.82	.002401055	3.13	.000873995	3.44	.000290937
2.52	.005867664	2.83	.002327274	3.14	.000844707	3.45	.000280376
2.53	.005703044	2.84	.002255552	3.15	.000816324	3.46	.000270173
2.54	.005542538	2.85	.002185838	3.16	.000788822	3.47	.000260317
2.55	.005386056	2.86	.002118083	3.17	.000762175	3.48	.000250797
2.56	.005233515	2.87	.002052239	3.18	.000736360	3.49	.000241603
2.57	.005084829	2.88	.001988258	3.19	.000711352	3.50	.000232725
2.58	.004939916	2.89	.001926093	3.20	.000687130	3.51	.000224151
2.59	.004798693	2.90	.001865699	3.21	.000663671	3.52	.000215873
2.60	.004661082	2.91	.001807032	3.22	.000640954	3.53	.000207882
2.61	.004527002	2.92	.001750048	3.23	.000618956	3.54	.000200168
2.62	.004396376	2.93	.001694703	3.24	.000597657	3.55	.000192722
2.63	.004269129	2.94	.001640957	3.25	.000577038	3.56	.000185536
2.64	.004145185	2.95	.001588769	3.26	.000557078	3.57	.000178601
2.65	.004024470	2.96	.001538097	3.27	.000537758	3.58	.000171909
2.66	.003906912	2.97	.001488904	3.28	.000519060	3.59	.000165452
2.67	.003792440	2.98	.001441150	3.29	.000500965	3.60	.000159224
2.68	.003680984	2.99	.001394798	3.30	.000483456	3.61	.000153215
2.69	.003572475	3.00	.001349813	3.31	.000466516	3.62	.000147419
2.70	.003466847	3.01	.001306156	3.32	.000450127	3.63	.000141830
2.71	.003364033	3.02	.001263795	3.33	.000434273	3.64	.000136440
2.72	.003263967	3.03	.001222694	3.34	.000418939	3.65	.000131242
2.73	.003166587	3.04	.001182819	3.35	.000404108	3.66	.000126230
2.74	.003071829	3.05	.001144139	3.36	.000389767	3.67	.000121399
2.75	.002979633	3.06	.001106621	3.37	.000375899	3.68	.000116742
2.76	.002889938	3.07	.001070234	3.38	.000362490	3.69	.000112252
2.77	.002802684	3.08	.001034947	3.39	.000349527	3.70	.000107926
2.78	.002717815	3.09	.001000730	3.40	.000336997	3.71	.000103756

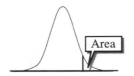

Area Under the Normal Curve

Z	Area	Z	Area	Z	Area	Z	Area
3.72	.000099739	4.03	.000028003	4.34	.000007198	4.65	.000001697
3.73	.000095868	4.04	.000026839	4.35	.000006879	4.66	.000001617
3.74	.000092138	4.05	.000025721	4.36	.000006574	4.67	.000001541
3.75	.000088546	4.06	.000024648	4.37	.000006282	4.68	.000001469
3.76	.000085086	4.07	.000023617	4.38	.000006002	4.69	.000001399
3.77	.000081753	4.08	.000022627	4.39	.000005734	4.70	.000001333
3.78	.000078543	4.09	.000021676	4.40	.000005478	4.71	.000001270
3.79	.000075453	4.10	.000020764	4.41	.000005233	4.72	.000001210
3.80	.000072477	4.11	.000019888	4.42	.000004998	4.73	.000001153
3.81	.000069613	4.12	.000019047	4.43	.000004773	4.74	.000001098
3.82	.000066855	4.13	.000018241	4.44	.000004558	4.75	.000001046
3.83	.000064201	4.14	.000017466	4.45	.000004353	4.76	.000000996
3.84	.000061646	4.15	.000016723	4.46	.000004156	4.77	.000000948
3.85	.000059187	4.16	.000016011	4.47	.000003968	4.78	.000000903
3.86	.000056822	4.17	.000015327	4.48	.000003787	4.79	.000000859
3.87	.000054545	4.18	.000014671	4.49	.000003615	4.80	.000000818
3.88	.000052355	4.19	.000014042	4.50	.000003451	4.81	.000000779
3.89	.000050249	4.20	.000013439	4.51	.000003293	4.82	.000000741
3.90	.000048222	4.21	.000012860	4.52	.000003143	4.83	.000000705
3.91	.000046273	4.22	.000012305	4.53	.000002999	4.84	.000000671
3.92	.000044399	4.23	.000011773	4.54	.000002861	4.85	.000000639
3.93	.000042597	4.24	.000011263	4.55	.000002730	4.86	.000000608
3.94	.000040864	4.25	.000010774	4.56	.000002604	4.87	.000000578
3.95	.000039198	4.26	.000010306	4.57	.000002484	4.88	.000000550
3.96	.000037596	4.27	.000009857	4.58	.000002369	4.89	.000000523
3.97	.000036057	4.28	.000009426	4.59	.000002259	4.90	.000000498
3.98	.000034577	4.29	.000009014	4.60	.000002154	4.91	.000000473
3.99	.000033155	4.30	.000008619	4.61	.000002054	4.92	.000000450
4.00	.000031789	4.31	.000008240	4.62	.000001959	4.93	.000000428
4.01	.000030476	4.32	.000007878	4.63	.000001867	4.94	.000000407
4.02	.000029215	4.33	.000007530	4.64	.000001780	4.95	.000000387

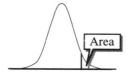

Area Under the Normal Curve

Z	Area	Z	Area	Z	Area	Z	Area
4.96	.000000368	5.27	.000000074	5.58	.000000014	5.89	.0000000024
4.97	.000000350	5.28	.000000070	5.59	.000000013	5.90	.0000000022
4.98	.000000332	5.29	.000000066	5.60	.000000012	5.91	.0000000021
4.99	.000000316	5.30	.000000063	5.61	.000000012	5.92	.0000000020
5.00	.000000300	5.31	.000000059	5.62	.000000011	5.93	.0000000019
5.01	.000000285	5.32	.000000056	5.63	.000000010	5.94	.0000000018
5.02	.000000271	5.33	.000000053	5.64	.0000000098	5.95	.0000000017
5.03	.000000258	5.34	.000000051	5.65	.0000000092	5.96	.0000000016
5.04	.000000245	5.35	.000000048	5.66	.0000000087	5.97	.0000000015
5.05	.000000232	5.36	.000000045	5.67	.0000000083	5.98	.0000000014
5.06	.000000221	5.37	.000000043	5.68	.0000000078	5.99	.0000000013
5.07	.000000210	5.38	.000000041	5.69	.0000000074	6.00	.0000000012
5.08	.000000199	5.39	.000000039	5.70	.0000000070		
5.09	.000000189	5.40	.000000037	5.71	.0000000066		
5.10	.000000180	5.41	.000000035	5.72	.0000000062		
5.11	.000000171	5.42	.000000033	5.73	.0000000059		
5.12	.000000162	5.43	.000000031	5.74	.0000000056		
5.13	.000000154	5.44	.000000029	5.75	.0000000053		
5.14	.000000146	5.45	.000000028	5.76	.0000000050		
5.15	.000000138	5.46	.000000026	5.77	.0000000047		
5.16	.000000131	5.47	.000000025	5.78	.0000000044		
5.17	.000000125	5.48	.000000024	5.79	.0000000042		
5.18	.000000118	5.49	.000000022	5.80	.0000000040		
5.19	.000000112	5.50	.000000021	5.81	.0000000037		
5.20	.000000107	5.51	.000000020	5.82	.0000000035		
5.21	.000000101	5.52	.000000019	5.83	.0000000033		
5.22	.000000096	5.53	.000000018	5.84	.0000000031		
5.23	.000000091	5.54	.000000017	5.85	.0000000030		
5.24	.000000086	5.55	.000000016	5.86	.0000000028		
5.25	.000000082	5.56	.000000015	5.87	.0000000027		
5.26	.000000078	5.57	.000000014	5.88	.0000000025		

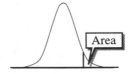

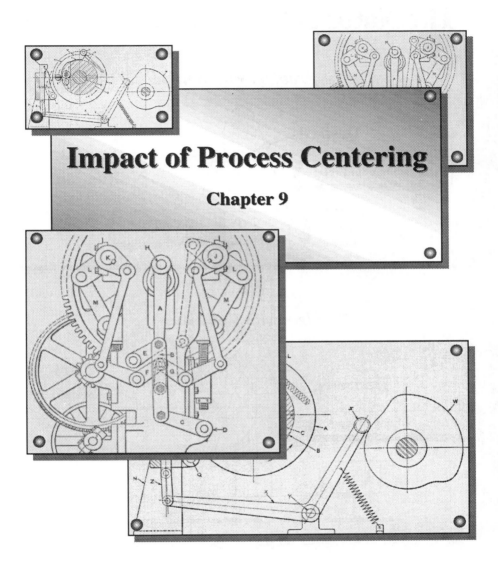

Impact of Process Centering

Chapter 9

The Nature of Statistical Problems

Problem with Spread

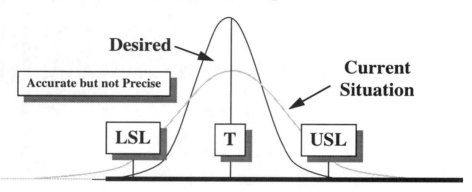

Problem with Centering

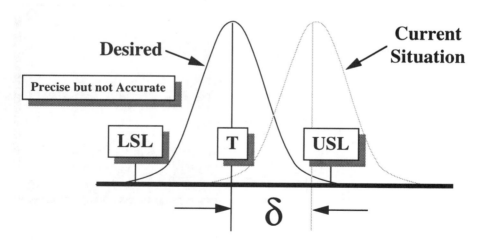

Process Centering and Capability

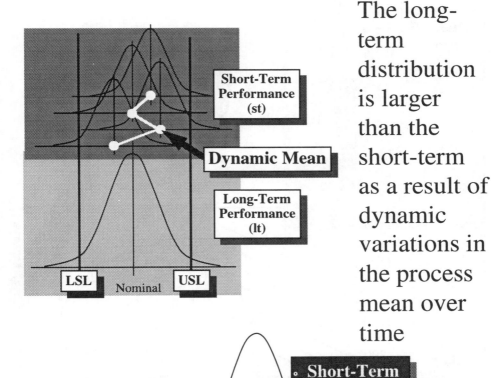

The long-term distribution is larger than the short-term as a result of dynamic variations in the process mean over time

9 . 3

Deeper Insight Into Shifts and Drifts

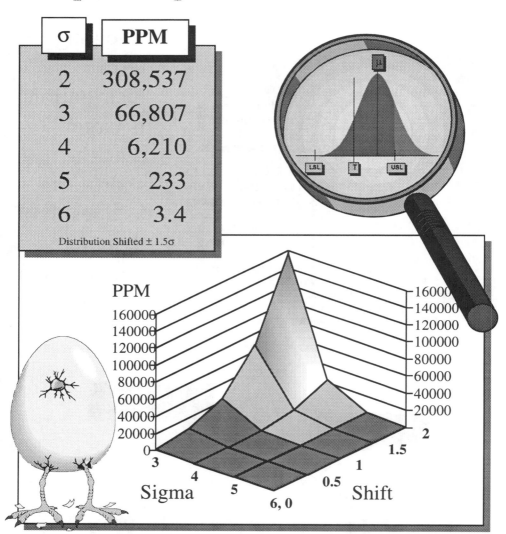

σ	PPM
2	308,537
3	66,807
4	6,210
5	233
6	3.4

Distribution Shifted ± 1.5σ

Influence of the 1.5σ Shift

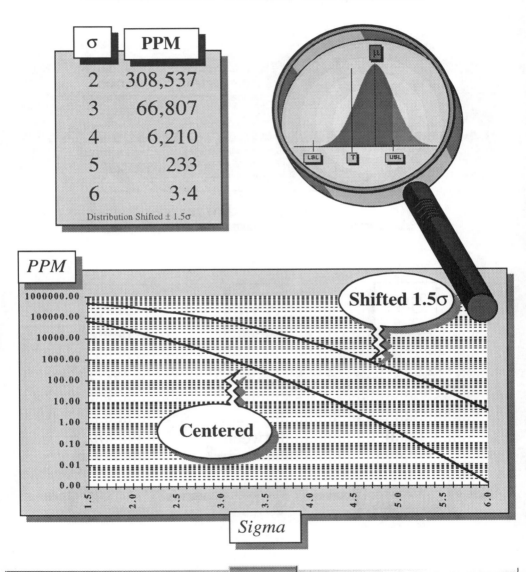

σ	PPM
2	308,537
3	66,807
4	6,210
5	233
6	3.4

Distribution Shifted ± 1.5σ

Shifted 1.5σ

Centered

PPM

Sigma

The Components of Variation

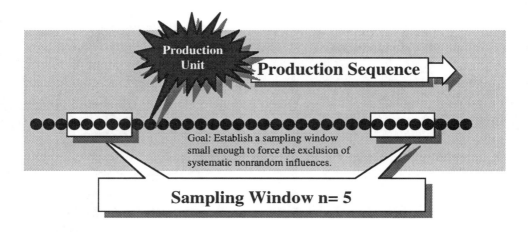

Production Unit **Production Sequence**

Goal: Establish a sampling window small enough to force the exclusion of systematic nonrandom influences.

Sampling Window n= 5

SS$_T$ **SS$_B$** **SS$_W$**

$$\sum_{j=1}^{g}\sum_{i=1}^{n}(X_{ij}-\bar{\bar{X}})^2 = n\sum_{j=1}^{g}(\bar{X}_j-\bar{\bar{X}})^2 + \sum_{j=1}^{g}\sum_{i=1}^{n}(X_{ij}-\bar{X}_j)^2$$

Total   **Between**   **Within**

Sustained Reproducibility   *Instantaneous Reproducibility*

Capability   **Accuracy**   **Precision**

Visualizing the Components

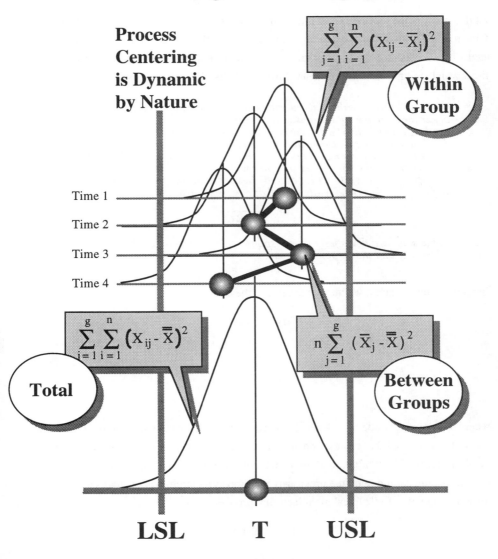

Process Centering is Dynamic by Nature

$$\sum_{j=1}^{g} \sum_{i=1}^{n} (X_{ij} - \overline{X}_j)^2$$

Within Group

Time 1
Time 2
Time 3
Time 4

$$\sum_{j=1}^{g} \sum_{i=1}^{n} (X_{ij} - \overline{\overline{X}})^2$$

$$n \sum_{j=1}^{g} (\overline{X}_j - \overline{\overline{X}})^2$$

Total

Between Groups

LSL   T   USL

The Basis for Research

At this point in the discussion we must turn our attention to the research of Bender (1975), Gilson (1951), and Evans (1975). In essence, their work focused on the problems associated with establishing engineering tolerances in light of nonrandom manufacturing variations which assume the form of mean shifts and drifts. In synopsis, Evans pointed out that

> *... shifts and drifts in the mean of the distribution of a component occur for a number of reasons ... for example, tool wear is one source of a gradual [nonrandom] drift... which can cause [nonrandom] shifts in the distribution. Except in special cases, it is almost impossible to predict quantitatively the changes in the distribution of a component value which will occur, but the knowledge that they will occur enables us to cope with the difficulty. A solution proposed by Bender ... allows for [nonrandom] shifts and drifts. Bender suggests that one should use*

$$V = 1.5 \ \sqrt{VAR \ (X)}$$

> *as the standard deviation of the response ... [so as] to relate the component tolerances and the response tolerance.*

In view of this research, we may generalize to the case

$$\sigma_T^2 = (c\sigma_W)^2$$

or

$$c = \frac{\sigma_T}{\sigma_W}$$

where c is the magnitude of inflation imposed upon the instantaneous reproducibility. In short, it may be said that c is a compensatory constant used to correct the sustained reproducibility for the effect of nonrandom manufacturing errors which perturbs the process center. Again, calling upon the previously mentioned research, we would discover that the general range of c, for "typical manufacturing processes," may be given as

$$1.4 \leq c \leq 1.8 \ .$$

Analysis of Shifts and Drifts

If σ^2_T and σ^2_W can be estimated using a rational sampling strategy we may express c as

$$\hat{c} = \frac{\sqrt{\dfrac{SS_T}{ng-1}}}{\sqrt{\dfrac{SS_W}{g(n-1)}}}$$

By virtue of the additive properties of independent variances, it can be shown that

$$\hat{c}^2 = \frac{\dfrac{SS_B + SS_W}{ng-1}}{\dfrac{SS_W}{g(n-1)}} = \frac{SS_B + SS_W}{SS_W} \cdot \frac{g(n-1)}{ng-1}$$

By simple rearrangement, the average quadratic mean deviation is given as

$$\frac{\displaystyle\sum_{j=1}^{g} \left(\overline{X}_j - \overline{\overline{X}} \right)^2}{g} = \hat{\sigma}^2_W \frac{\hat{c}^2(ng-1) - g(n-1)}{ng}$$

So the "typical" dynamic mean shift which can be expressed as

$$\delta\sigma_W = \sqrt{\frac{\displaystyle\sum_{j=1}^{g} \left(\overline{X}_j - \overline{\overline{X}} \right)^2}{g}} = \hat{\sigma}_W \sqrt{\left[\frac{\hat{c}^2(ng-1) - g(n-1)}{ng}\right]}$$

By standardizing, we observe that

$$Z_{Shift.Typ} = \sqrt{\left[\frac{\hat{c}^2(ng-1) - g(n-1)}{ng}\right]}$$

Results for Typical Sampling Plans

In the spirit of establishing a standard mean shift correction, let us consider the general range of conventional rational sampling practices given by the combinations

$$4 \leq n \leq 6$$

and

$$25 \leq g \leq 100.$$

Perhaps the most commonly employed combination is that of n=5 and g=50. Under this combination, the total sample size is ng=250. Such a sample size has been recommended by other authors writing on the topic of process capability studies.

For the case c=1.8 and a common rational sampling strategy (n=5 and g=50), we compute Z_{Shift} =1.49. Hence, the establishment of δ=1.5σ as the typical mean shift correction for Motorola's Six Sigma initiative is justified.

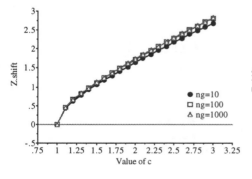
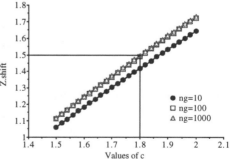

Generalizing the Correction

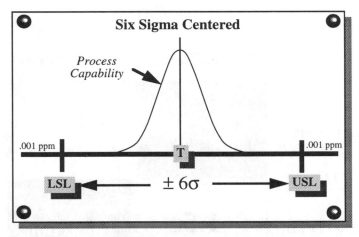

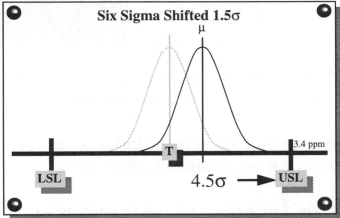

The 1.5σ shift is used as a compensatory off-set in the mean to generally account for dynamic nonrandom variations in process centering. It represents the average amount of change in a typical process over many cycles of that process.

Creating a Truth Table

FROM

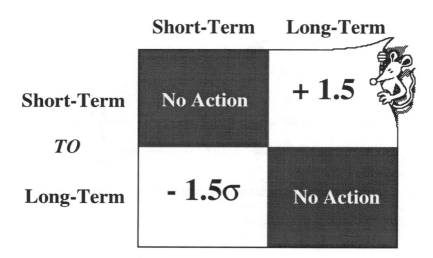

Short-term data is free of assignable causes, thus it represents the effect of random causes only.

Long-term data reflects the influence of random causes as well as assignable phenomena.

If the yield or defect data were gathered over many intervals of production, consider the situation to be long-term; otherwise, assume it to be short-term.

Applying the Truth Table

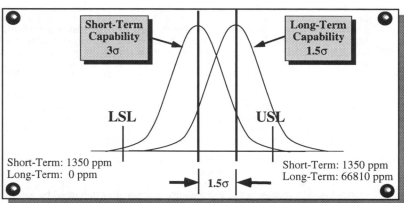

If the initial data was given as 3 σ short-term, the conversion to long-term would be

$$3\sigma - 1.5\sigma = 1.5\sigma$$

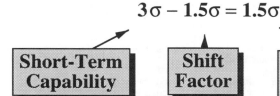

Short-Term Capability   **Shift Factor**   **Long-Term Capability**

The resultant describes the long-term performance of the process, inclusive of assignable causes which impact process centering. The outcome constitutes the sustained reproducibility of the process.

Guidelines for the Correction

Guideline 1: If a metric is computed on the basis of data gathered over many cycles or time intervals, the resultant value should be regarded as a long-term measure of performance. Naturally, the long-term metric must be converted to a probability. Once expressed as a probability, $Z.lt$ value may be established by way of a table of area-under-the-normal-curve, or any acceptable computational device. If we seek to forecast short-term performance ($Z.st$), we must add a shift factor ($Z.shift$) to $Z.lt$ so as to remove time related sources of error which tend to upset process centering. Recognize that the actual value of $Z.shift$ is seldom known in practice; therefore, it may be necessary to apply the accepted convention and set $Z.shift = 1.50$; otherwise, use the actual value. As a consequence of this linear transformation, the final Z value should reflect only random sources of error and, therefore, serve as a projection of short-term performance. Thus, we are able to artificially remove the effect of nonrandom influences (i.e., normal process centering errors) from the analysis via the transform $Z.st = Z.lt + Z.shift$.

Guideline 2: If a metric is computed on the basis of data gathered over a very limited number of cycles or time intervals, the resultant value should be regarded as a short-term measure of performance. Naturally, the short-term metric must be converted to a probability. Once expressed as a probability, $Z.st$ may be established by way of a table of area-under-the-normal-curve, or any acceptable computational device. If we seek to forecast long-term performance, we must subtract $Z.shift$ from $Z.st$ so as to approximate the long-term capability. Recognize that the actual value of $Z.shift$ is seldom known in practice; therefore, it may be necessary to apply the accepted convention and set $Z.shift = 1.50$. If the actual value is known, use it. As a consequence of this linear transformation, the final Z value reflects both random and nonrandom sources of error and, therefore, is a projection of long-term performance. Thus, we are able to artificially induce the effect of nonrandom influences (i.e., normal process centering errors) into the analysis by way of $Z.st - Z.shift = Z.lt$.

Guideline 3: In general, if the originating data is discrete by nature, the resulting Z transform should be regarded as long-term. The logic of this guideline is simple; a fairly large number of cycles or time intervals is often required to generate enough nonconformities from which to generate a relatively stable estimate of Z. Hence, it is reasonable to conclude that both random and nonrandom influences are reflected in such data. In this instance, guideline 1 would be applied.

Guideline 4: In general, if the originating data is continuous by nature and was gathered under the constraint of sequential or random sampling across a very limited number of cycles or time intervals, the resulting Z value should be regarded as short-term. The logic of this guideline is simple; data gathered over a very limited number cycles or time intervals only reflects random influences (white noise) and, as a consequence, tends to exclude nonrandom sources of variation, such as process centering errors.

Guideline 5: Whenever it is desirable to report the corresponding "sigma" of a given performance metric, the short-term Z must be used. For example, let us suppose that we find 6210 ppm defective. In this instance, we must translate 6210 ppm into its corresponding "sigma" value. Doing so reveals $Z.lt = 2.50$. Since the originating data was long-term by nature, guidelines 1 and 3 apply. In this case, $Z.lt + Z.shift = 2.5 + 1.5 = 4.0$. Since no other estimate of $Z.shift$ was available, the convention of 1.5 was employed.

9.14

Insight into the Correction

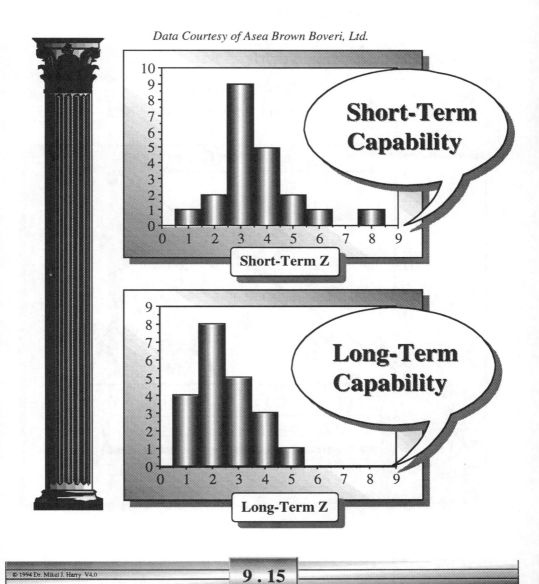

Data Courtesy of Asea Brown Boveri, Ltd.

Studying the Emperical Evidence

Data Courtesy of Asea Brown Boveri, Ltd.

. . . So what does this scattergram have to tell us about mean shifts?

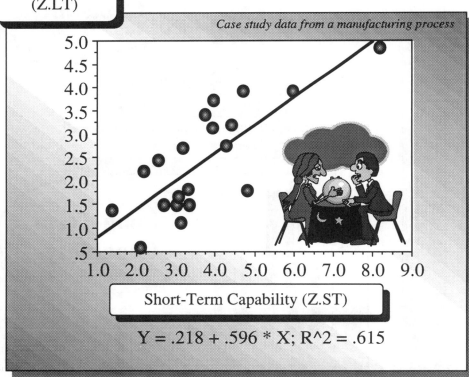

Long-Term Capability (Z.LT)

Case study data from a manufacturing process

Short-Term Capability (Z.ST)

$$Y = .218 + .596 * X; R^2 = .615$$

Some Major Conclusions

Data Courtesy of Asea Brown Boveri, Ltd.

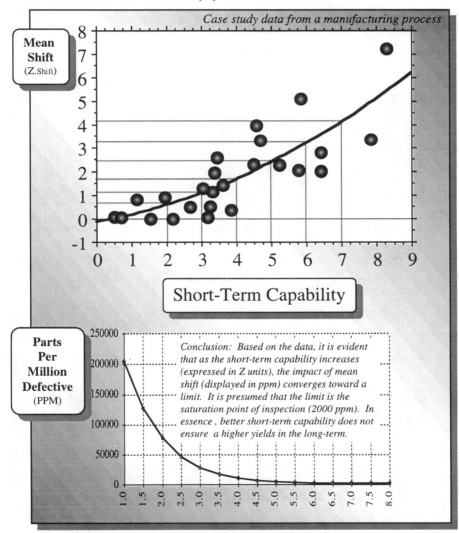

Case study data from a manufacturing process

Mean Shift (Z.Shift)

Short-Term Capability

Parts Per Million Defective (PPM)

Conclusion: Based on the data, it is evident that as the short-term capability increases (expressed in Z units), the impact of mean shift (displayed in ppm) converges toward a limit. It is presumed that the limit is the saturation point of inspection (2000 ppm). In essence , better short-term capability does not ensure a higher yields in the long-term.

Practical Implications: Part A

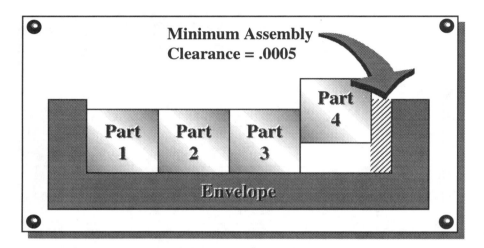

Minimum Assembly
Clearance = .0005

Part 4

Part 1

Part 2

Part 3

Envelope

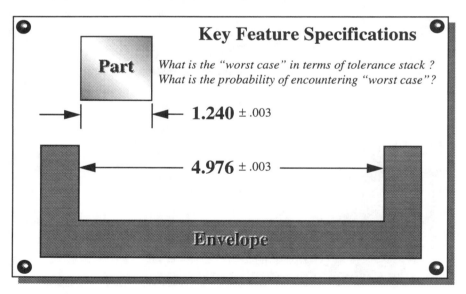

Key Feature Specifications

Part

What is the "worst case" in terms of tolerance stack ?
What is the probability of encountering "worst case"?

1.240 ± .003

4.976 ± .003

Envelope

Practical Implications: Part A

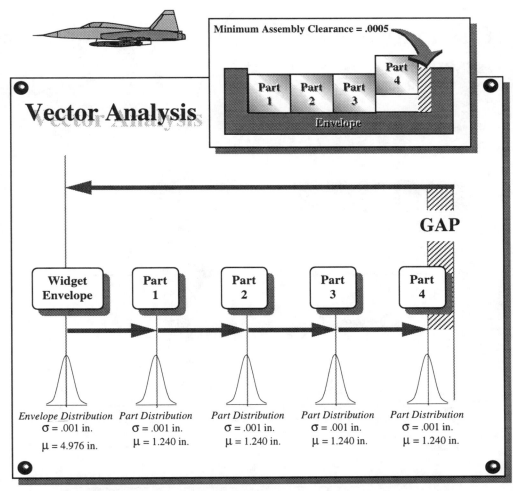

Minimum Assembly Clearance = .0005

Part 1   Part 2   Part 3   Part 4

Envelope

Vector Analysis

GAP

| Widget Envelope | Part 1 | Part 2 | Part 3 | Part 4 |

Envelope Distribution	Part Distribution	Part Distribution	Part Distribution	Part Distribution
σ = .001 in.	σ = .001 in.	σ = .001 in.	σ = .001 in.	σ = .001 in.
μ = 4.976 in.	μ = 1.240 in.	μ = 1.240 in.	μ = 1.240 in.	μ = 1.240 in.

How can the process capability of the envelope and each component be factored into the gap analysis?

Practical Implications: Part B

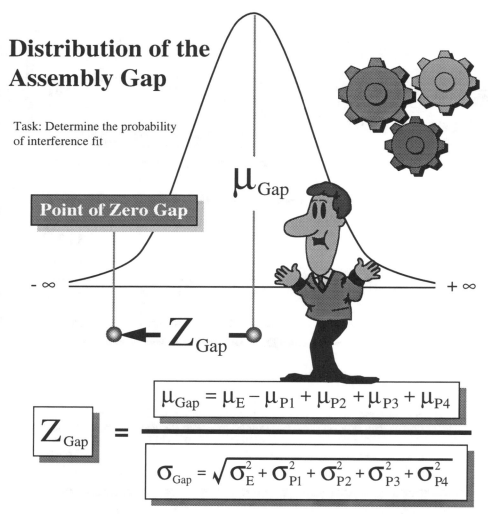

Distribution of the Assembly Gap

Task: Determine the probability
of interference fit

μ_{Gap}

Point of Zero Gap

$- \infty$

$+ \infty$

$\leftarrow Z_{Gap} \rightarrow$

$$Z_{Gap} = \frac{\mu_{Gap} = \mu_E - \mu_{P1} + \mu_{P2} + \mu_{P3} + \mu_{P4}}{\sigma_{Gap} = \sqrt{\sigma_E^2 + \sigma_{P1}^2 + \sigma_{P2}^2 + \sigma_{P3}^2 + \sigma_{P4}^2}}$$

*If we know the "typical" mean off-set for the envelope and each of the parts, how
could this knowledge be used to make the design robust against such shifts and drifts?*

9 . 20

Design for Manufacturability

$$Z_{Gap} = \dfrac{\mu_{Gap} = \mu_E - \mu_{P1} + \mu_{P2} + \mu_{P3} + \mu_{P4}}{\sigma_{Gap} = \sqrt{\sigma_E^2 + \sigma_{P1}^2 + \sigma_{P2}^2 + \sigma_{P3}^2 + \sigma_{P4}^2}}$$

$$V_{Pool} = \sigma_{Gap} \left(Z_{Gap\,;\,Actual} - Z_{Gap\,;\,Need} \right)$$

$$\mu_{Adjusted} = \mu_i + \lambda_i V_{Pool}$$

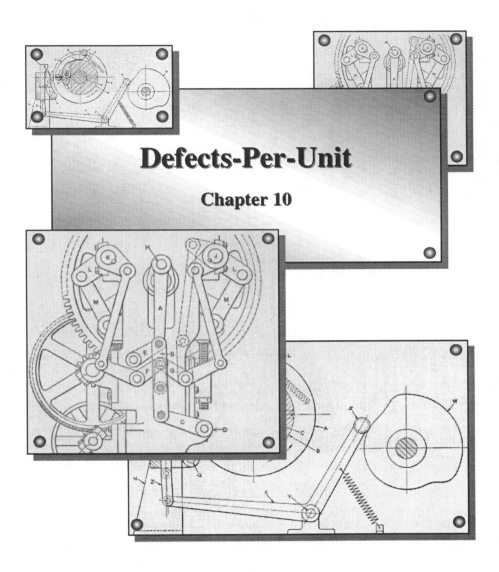

Defects-Per-Unit

Chapter 10

The Defects-Per-Unit Metric

For the sake of discussion, let us suppose that a certain product design may be represented by the area of a rectangle. We shall also postulate that each rectangle contains 10 equal areas of opportunity for nonconformance to standard. Figure 1 illustrates this particular product concept.

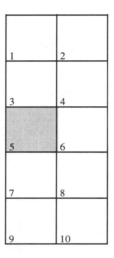

Figure 1. Abstract Unit of Product Consisting of 10 Equal
Areas of Opportunity for Nonconformance

Let us now suppose the quality records related to our example product indicate that, out of the last 1000 units manufactured, 1000 nonconformities were detected. For our example, we would compute

$$dpu = \frac{d}{u}$$

Eq. (1)

where dpu is the defects per unit, d is the frequency or "number" of observed defects, and u is the number of units produced. In this instance, we would determine that dpu = 1000/1000= 1.0.This means that, on the average, each unit of manufactured product will contain 1 such defect. Of course, this assumes the defects are randomly distributed. We must also recognize, however, that within each unit of product there are 10 equal areas of opportunity for nonconformance to standard. Because of this, we may now calculate

10.2

$$dpm = \frac{dpu}{m}$$

Eq. (2)

where dpm defines the defects-per-unit opportunity, and m is the number of independent opportunities for nonconformance per unit. In the instance of our abstract product, m= 10. Because m = 10 is given as a design constant, we may easily demonstrate that the probability of a nonconformance per-unit area of opportunity is (1000/1000)/10 = .10, or 10 percent. Inversely, we may argue that there is a 100(1.00 - 0.10) = 90 percent chance of not encountering a nonconformance with respect to any given unit area of opportunity.

It is very interesting to note that the probability of zero defects, for any given unit of product, would be $.90^{10}$ = .348678, or 34.87 percent. Now, if we increase the number of opportunities for nonconformance such that m = 100, it should be apparent that the probability of nonconformance-per-unit area of opportunity would be 1/100 = .01, or 1 percent. Consequently, the likelihood that any given unit of product will be defect free would be $(1-.01)^{100}$ = $.99^{100}$ = .366032, or 36.60 percent.

At this point, we should consider Table 1. Notice that the table displays the effect of m on the likelihood of zero defects for any given unit of product, given dpu = 1.0. The reader should also notice that as m approaches infinity, the probability that any given unit of product will be defect free approaches e^{dpu}. Further study shows that the probability that any given unit of product will be defect free is approximated by e^{-dpu}. In this case, the probability of zero defects would be $e^{-dpu} = e^{-1}$ = .367879441, or roughly 36.79 percent.

This point will be of immense importance to us in the following discussion concerning the Poisson distribution. As we shall see, this particular distribution is an invaluable tool when assessing process capability.

Table 1. Probability of Zero Defects as m Increases Under the Constraint dpu = 1.0

Number of Areas of Opportunity Per Unit of Product (m)	Confidence That Any Given Area Will Not Contain a Defect* (y)	Probability That Any Given Unit of Product Will Not Contain a Defect γ^m
10	.9	.348678440
100	.99	.36603234 1
1000	.999	.367695425
10000	.9999	.367861050
100000	.99999	.367877601
1000000	.999999	.367879625
10000000	.9999999	.367879459

*Observed dpu = 1.0

Keying off the latter arguments, we may now ask the question, "What is the probability that any given unit of manufactured product will contain two, three, or even more defects?" Well, when the probability of nonconformance per opportunity is less than 10 percent, but the overall likelihood of observing a defect is high, the Poisson distribution can be employed to answer such questions. As may be apparent, these criteria seem applicable to our abstract product example. Given reasonable compliance to the underlying assumptions, we may calculate the probability (Y) by virtue of the Poisson relation. This particular relation is most often expressed as

$$Y = \frac{(np)^r e^{-np}}{r!}$$

Eq. (3)

where n is the total number of independent trials, p is the probability of occurrence, and r is the number of occurrences. Throughout the remainder of this bookl, the term "occurrences" can be used interchangeably with the word "defects." In most instances, the Poisson equation will allow us to avoid the burdensome calculations often associated with the binomial model, as will be discussed in greater detail later on. Such an approximation of the binomial is called "Poisson's Exponential Binomial Limit" or simply, "Poisson's Law." To better relate the Poisson relation to our example, we may rewrite Eq. (3) as

$$Y = \frac{(d/u)^r e^{-d/u}}{r!}$$

Eq. (4)

where d is the number of nonconformities or "defects," and u is the number of units produced. At this point in our discussion, the reader should recognize that d = np. Obviously, normalizing per unit of product reveals that d/u = np/u. Hence, a substitution of terms may be made for the normalized case where u = 1. For the special case of r = 0, Eq. (4) reduces to

$$Y = e^{-d/u}$$

Eq. (5)

Thus, the relation described in Eq. (5) reflects first-time yield (Y_{FT}) for a specified d/u. Obviously, if Y_{FT} is known, or may be rationally postulated, we may solve for d/u by calculating

$$d/u = -\ln (Y_{FT})$$

Eq. (6)

where ln is the natural log. As we shall see, this is also a very useful tool when conducting a producibility analysis. Through the application of Eq. (4), we may create a window from which to view the expected distribution of defects across u number of production units. It would reveal the theoretical number of production units expected to have 0, 1, 2, 3, ..., or more defects. For example, if we were to manufacture, say 1,000 units of product and subsequently discover d/u = 1.0, then we would expect the frequency distribution given in Table 2.

Table 2. Poisson Distribution of Defects Under the Constraint
that m is Large and dpu = 1.0

Number of Defects (r)	Probability of Exactly r Defects* p(r)	Number of Units With Exactly r Defects (u)	Total Number of Defects Contained Within u Units (d)	Expected Number of Escaping Defects** d(I -E)
0	.3679	368	0	0
1	.3679	368	368	4
2	.1839	184	368	4
3	.0613	61	183	2
4	.0153	15	60	0
5	.0031	3	15	0
6	.0005	1	6	0
7	.0001	0	0	0
8	.0000	0	0	0
TOTAL	1.0000	1000	1000	10

* Theoretically, r assumes values to infinity, but beyond r = 8, the resultant probability is so small it is negligible for the case dpu =1.0.
** Assumed test/inspection efficiency (E) = 99%

Should the assumptions surrounding the Poisson model prove to be unreasonable, we may turn to the binomial model. This particular model may be given by

$$Y = \frac{m!}{r!(m-r)!} p^r q^{m-r}$$

Eq. (7)

where p is the constant probability of an event and q = 1 - p. Interestingly, for the special case of r = 0, the binomial model reduces to

$$Y = (1-p)^m$$

Eq. (8)

Because of this special case (i.e., r = 0), we conclude that the probability of zero defects, subject only to the assumptions of the binomial model, may be described by the first time yield (Y_{FT}). For those cases where the underlying assumptions of the Poisson or binomial model cannot be met, the hypergeometric model may be employed. For additional information on this particular model, the reader is directed to the bibliography.

The Two Types of Defect Models

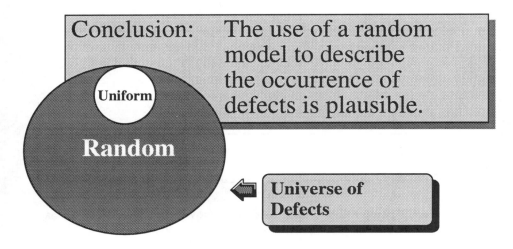

Conclusion: The use of a random model to describe the occurrence of defects is plausible.

Uniform

Random

Universe of Defects

Uniform Defect: *The same type of defect appears within a unit of product; e.g., wrong type of steel.*

Random Defect: *The defects are intermittent and unrelated; e.g., flaw in surface finish.*

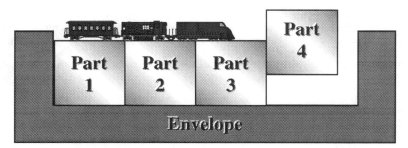

Part 1   Part 2   Part 3   Part 4

Envelope

The Widget Application

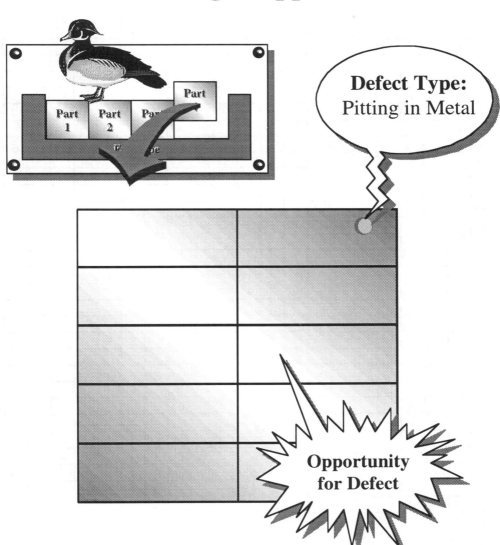

Defect Type:
Pitting in Metal

**Opportunity
for Defect**

The Widget Production

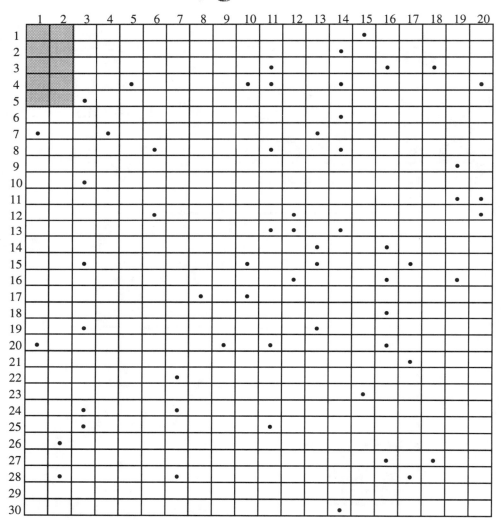

● = Defect   ☐ = Opportunity   ▨ = Unit of Product

10 . 8

Nature of the Problem

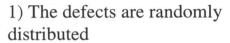

1) The defects are randomly distributed
2) 60 defects were observed out of 60 units produced
3) The defects-per-unit is 1.0
4) There are 10 opportunities for defect per unit of product

Given the facts, what is the likelihood of producing a part with zero defects? In turn, this guarantees no rework or repair.

Defects-per-Opportunity

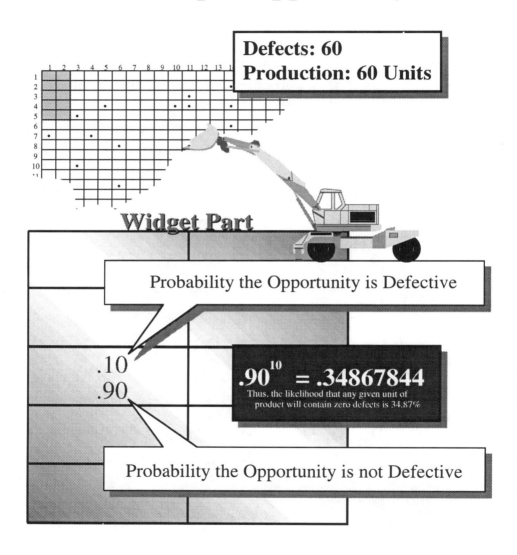

**Defects: 60
Production: 60 Units**

Widget Part

Probability the Opportunity is Defective

.10
.90

$.90^{10} = .34867844$

Thus, the likelihood that any given unit of
product will contain zero defects is 34.87%

Probability the Opportunity is not Defective

Opportunities and DPU

(based on DPU=1.0 example)

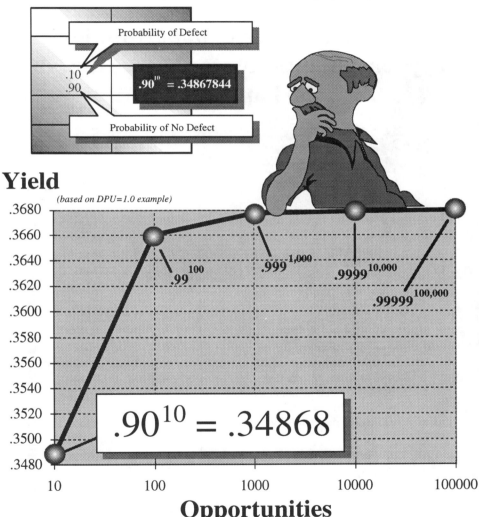

The Poisson as a Defect Model

(based on DPU=1.0 example)

As the number of opportunities approaches infinity we observe that the yield approaches

$$e^{-1} = .36788$$

$$Y = \frac{(d/u)^r e^{-d/u}}{r!}$$

where d/u is the defects-per-unit and r is the number of occurrences . Thus, when r=0, we have the probability of zero defects, or "rolled-throughput yield." Note that this is different from the classical notion of yield; i.e., number of good units divided by the number of units tested/inspected.

$$Y = e^{-d/u}$$

r	p(r)
0	0.3678794412
1	0.3678794412
2	0.1839397206
3	0.0613132402
4	0.0153283100
5	0.0030656620
6	0.0005109437
7	0.0000729920
8	0.0000091240
9	0.0000010138
10	0.0000001014
11	0.0000000092
12	0.0000000008
13	0.0000000001
14	0.0000000000

Notes on the Poisson Approximation

❑ Generalizing from Grant and Leavenworth (1980) we note that the Poisson approximation may be applied when the number of opportunities for nonconformance (n) is large and the probability (p) of an event (r) is small. In fact, as n increases and r decreases, the approximation by the Poisson model improves.

❑ To further extend some of the criteria for applying the Poisson model, Juran (1979) stated that when the sample size is at least 16, the population size is at least 10 times that of the sample, and the probability of an event on each trial is less than 10 percent, the Poisson distribution can be used.

❑ In most industrial applications, the Poisson distribution can be fruitfully applied because the number of defect opportunities is usually quite numerous. Furthermore, the assumption of independence is usually met (in a reasonable way) owing to the nature of manufacturing. These factors, when taken together, set the stage for establishing the Poisson distribution as a viable tool in the quest for Six Sigma.

Analyzing the Poisson Model

r	p(r)	Expected Units	Observed Units	Chi Square
0	.36788	22	20	0.18
1	.36788	22	25	0.41
2	.18394	11	10	0.09
3	.06131	4	5	0.25
4	.01533	1	0	1.00
5	.00307	0	0	0.00
Σ	.99941	60	60	1.93

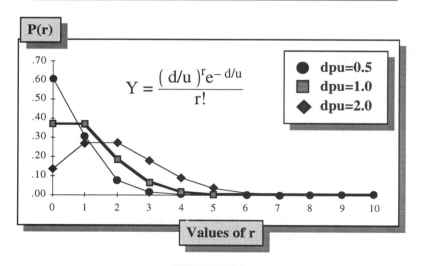

P(r)

$$Y = \frac{(d/u)^r e^{-d/u}}{r!}$$

- ● dpu=0.5
- ■ dpu=1.0
- ◆ dpu=2.0

Values of r

Comparison of Distributions

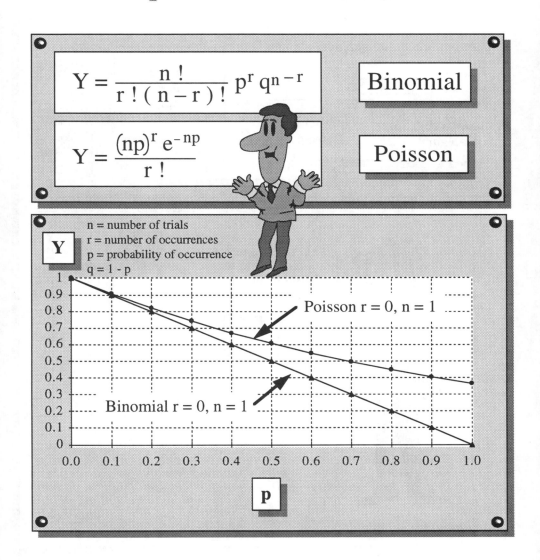

$$Y = \frac{n!}{r!(n-r)!} \, p^r q^{n-r}$$

Binomial

$$Y = \frac{(np)^r e^{-np}}{r!}$$

Poisson

n = number of trials
r = number of occurrences
p = probability of occurrence
q = 1 - p

Y

Poisson r = 0, n = 1

Binomial r = 0, n = 1

p

Application Example 1

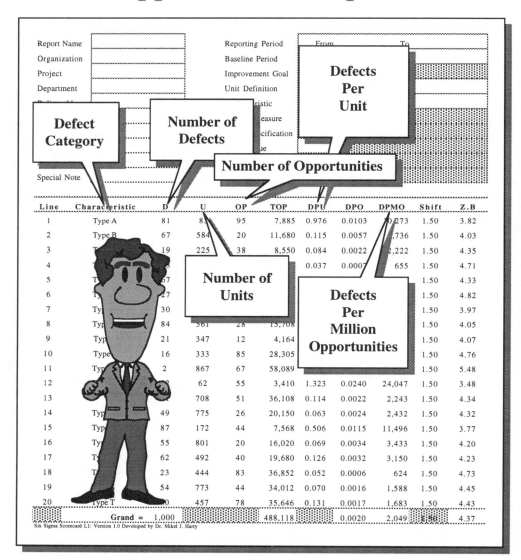

Six Sigma Scorecard L1: Version 1.0 Developed by Dr. Mikel J. Harry

Charting the DPU Metric

Currently, and in the recent past there has been much discussion concerning a quality measure commonly referred to as defects-per-unit or "DPU". The purpose of this paper is to discuss DPU and its implications, not to debate the merits, restrictions, or implications other indices of quality.

Let's clear the air on the mechanics, myths, and misconceptions related to DPU. This particular index (DPU) is nothing more than the total number of defects in a sample (c) divided by the total number of units in the sample (n). Over a period of time, the individual computations (u) are averaged to form a summary figure known as the "average defects per unit" ($\bar{u}$). The computation involves nothing more than simple arithmetic. If one is looking for mathematical mystique or wizzardry, it simply is not there ... just a solid measure of product quality that is clean, simple, and to the point. For example, consider the following information presented in Figure 1.

Sample No.	Total Defects in Sample	Defects per Unit u
1	17	1.7
2	14	1.4
3	6	0.6
4	23	2.3
5	5	0.5
6	7	0.7
7	10	1.0
8	19	1.9
9	29	2.9
10	18	1.8
11	25	2.5
12	5	0.5
13	8	0.8
14	11	1.1
15	18	1.8
16	13	1.3
17	22	2.2
18	6	0.6
19	23	2.3
20	22	2.2
21	9	0.9
22	15	1.5
23	20	2.0
24	6	0.6
25	24	2.4
TOTAL	375	37.5

Figure 1. Example Data for DPU Computation*

*Source: Adapted from Juran, J.M. (1979). Quality Control Handbook (Third Edition). New York: McGraw-Hill Book Company.

By sequentially plotting the individual DPU measurements across time, the "quality behavior" of the product emerges as displayed in Figure 2.

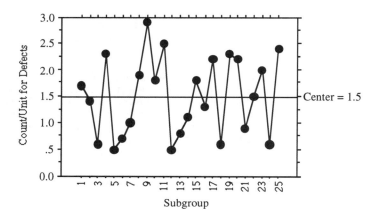

Figure 2. Example Plot of Defects Over Time

If sample number 11 was considered, what should management do? It would appear that some form of action should be taken! Right? ... after all, it is almost the "worst case." What should be the focus of that action ... The process? ... Material? ... People?

Let us now turn our attention to probability. What is the likelihood that observation number 11 could have resulted strictly by chance? If it was not a chance event (e.g., an "assignable" reason exists), then some form of corrective action would be desirable and justified. On the other hand, if it (sample 11) was a chance event, then any action taken to correct the "problem" would not be justified since it was just "random variation" (e.g., the increase in DPU was due to random causes which would not be economical to isolate and remove). In other words, the likelihood of decision error would remain unknown without the knowledge of random chance probability.

Figure 3 presents the same data in the same format but with upper and lower "statistical control limits" added to the graph. The dotted line on the graph indicates the upper and lower "3 sigma limits" of the sampling distribution which, in turn, provides an estimate of the "universe" limits. In other words, the two dotted lines depict the maximum and minimum DPU which could be expected given random variation.

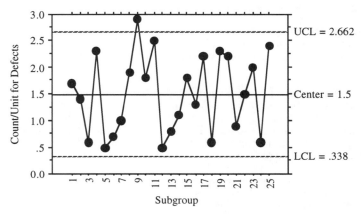

Figure 3. Example Defects per Unit (u) Chart

With this new knowledge (the addition of upper and lower control limits), it is now readily apparent that the DPU associated with sample number 11 was, in all likelihood, due to random variation in one or more of the manufacturing and/or material parameters (assuming no changes in the product design). Furthermore, it is reasonable to assert that it would not be economical to track down and eliminate the source of variation associated with sample number 11 since the variation was of a "random" nature.

The latter conclusion does not appear to hold true for sample number 9. This particular observation is beyond the "3 sigma" high water mark. In other words, there is a very low probability that the variation inherent to sample number 9 could have resulted by chance; therefore, some form of corrective action should be taken. In addition, such action would be initiated with a known degree of "probabilistic confidence" e.g., assurance of not reacting to a "false alarm."

An added feature of the statistical control limits is the ability to make a sound determination as to when the "universe" has shifted to some higher undesirable level or the range has increased. Conversely, it would be nice to know when improvement is nonrandom! Perhaps organizational resources should be expended to isolate these reasons as well as when an "unfavorable out-of-control" situation exists.

The next logical question would be: "Now that I know this stuff, what can I do with it?"...

The following points illustrate the practical utility of DPU charts:

• DPU is additive (assuming the defects are independent). This is important because module DPU's can be summed to create a DPU for the associated assembly. In turn, the assembly DPU's can be merged to create a system DPU ... and so on, all the way to the corporate level.

• The latter point is important because when a higher level (e.g., system, project, division, etc.) u chart displays an "out of control" condition or some nonrandom pattern, the problem can be "source traced" to the lowest levels of manufacture (if it would be necessary to "pareto-ize" that low to isolate the source). This capability serves as the "springboard" for conducting higher resolution statistical work aimed at identifying and removing unwanted sources of costly product and process variation (efficiency is also improved tremendously).

• Inherent simplicity. Unless everyone understands the output, the process is moot! As this writer has heard on several occasions, "If splitting a board is the goal, then why measure it with a micrometer ... just mark it with chalk, and then cut it with a chainsaw." During the initial stages of problem solving, simplicity is the rule. Seven digit precision is not only a burden ... it is too expensive! The more people who understand what is going on, the bigger the bandwagon will be!

• Ease of interpretation. Trends, shifts, cycles, and out-of-control points are readily apparent ... "what you see is what you did!"

• Ease of compilation. Sophisticated forms of data collection and recording are not necessary. Remember, the simpler the system, the greater the likelihood the data will be valid and representative of the universe ... not to mention the fact that the system would be used and appropriately maintained!

• Bonus point ... It doesn't take a "bunch of statistical Ph.D.'s" to make it work!

Now the question becomes: "O.K., I'm sold, but what do I need to do right now to get it off the ground?" Again, the answer is simple and straight forward ...

Step 1: Define what it is you want to know.
Since we want to know how good our quality is in terms of "nonconformance to requirements," then DPU is what we want to know!

Step 2: Determine how you want to see what it is you want to know.
Since DPU is compiled most conveniently in graphical form, then this step is already complete.

Step 3: Identify the type of data it takes to create the defined graph.
Make a list of all possible types of defects (both test and inspect). These categories are the "pigeon holes" that are used to separate the "good guys" from the "bad guys." In all likelihood, all or most of these categories are already defined, so this step is behind us.

Step 4: Identify how the numbers are to be "crunched."
As already indicated, all that is necessary to create and use the u chart is basic arithmetic. Just compute the average DPU and control limits and you are in business. The steps are summarized below:

4a. Compute DPU for each sample.
Note: a sample size of 25 is recommended before the first chart is constructed (the reason for this has to do with the "statistics of the thing").

4b. Compute u bar (average DPU for the sample).

4c. Compute upper and lower control limits.

4d. Construct graph.

4e. Interpret graph.

4f. Take appropriate corrective action as required.

Step 5: Identify where the required type of data can be collected.
Such locations become "monitoring gates." We must all recognize that DPU measures symptoms, not problems. If DPU is high, then this is a symptom of a more intrinsic problem within the "underlying cause system." In this situation, the problem is rooted in the nonrandom variation exhibited by the causal variables ... not the fact that DPU is "going out the roof." It is the causal variables which must be identified with diagnostic and experimentation tools and then controlled across time with statistical process control charts designed for continuous data (e.g., $\overline{X}$ and R charts).

There are no "knobs" to turn which can lower DPU; however, there are "knobs" to turn which controls factors such as wave height, solder flux specific gravity, temperature, etc. Direct control can be exerted over the "knob" variables! DPU is not the resultant measurement ... it is not a variable ... only an index of quality generated by the effects of process, material, design, environmental, and human factors. By systematically "back-tracking" through sub-level DPU charts, one can get very close to the root cause! If the data collection points are not properly established, then the "back-tracking" can lead "up the proverbial creek" ... so great care should be exercised when executing this step ... you know, "no pain, no gain" and all that stuff!

In summary, this writer would like to conclude by saying that virtually all organizations have the talent and resources to take advantage of the DPU concept. As with most things that are worthwhile, they take time and patience. Initially, the DPU method may be somewhat cumbersome. Recognize that transitioning to a "statistical way of doing business "is like" swallowing a bitter pill;" however, like modern medicine, the rewards are great.

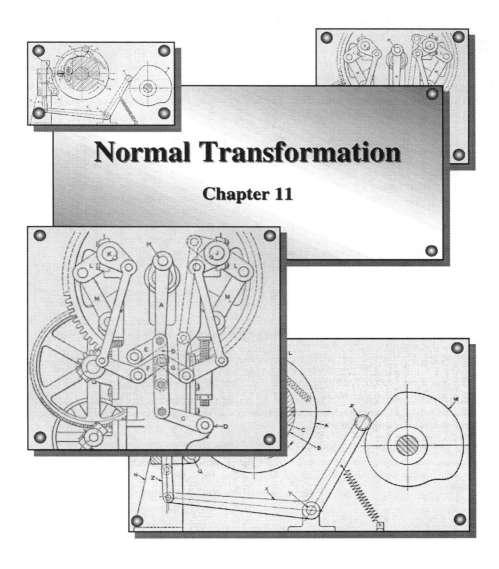

Normal Transformation

Chapter 11

The Reciprocal Nature of Data

We will recall that the normal distribution, as previously discussed, can tell us the number of events to be expected when the distribution parameters are known or estimated. For example, we could determine (from the normal distribution) how many defects to expect within any continuous interval extending from x = a to x = b. Extending this line of reasoning, Taylor (1982) stated that

> *In practice, the observed number [within the interval x = a to x = b] is seldom exactly the expected number. Instead if fluctuates in accordance with the Poisson distribution. In many situations it is reasonable to expect numbers to be distributed approximately according to the Poisson distribution. The approximation is called the Gaussian approximations to the Poisson. It is analogous to the corresponding approximation for the binomial distribution and is useful under the same conditions, namely,*

> *when the parameters involved are large. In fact, it can be proved that as µ -> ∞, the Poisson distribution becomes steadily more symmetrical and approaches the Gauss [normal] distribution with the same mean and standard deviation.*

To illustrate the practical implications of this relation, let us postulate that a given, normally distributed response characteristic (say p1, as related to our widget example) has a capability such that the specification limits are $\mu \pm 3\sigma$. Such a capability would translate to a first-time yield of .9973, or 2700 ppm in terms of a defect rate.

Based on this, we could report the process capability in either form so long as the corresponding distributional assumptions are reasonably adhered to. In this case, we may say that a ppm value of 2700 is directly equivalent, for all practical purposes, to a normal distribution, which is $\pm 3\sigma$ in relation to the bilateral specification limits. As a consequence, it is possible to align the various discrete metrics to those measures of capability based on continuous data, and vice-versa.

Such "metric interconnectivity" will take on immense value and applied meaning in subsequent discussions; however, for now, let us simply recognize the existence of interconnectivity between the Poisson and normal distribution, as well as the binomial model.

The Idea of Data Interchange

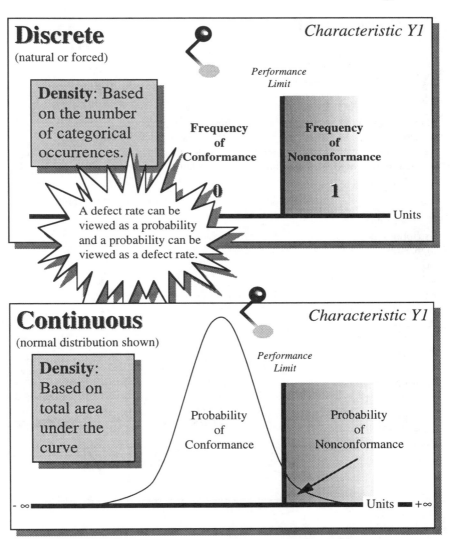

Discrete
(natural or forced)

Characteristic Y1

Density: Based on the number of categorical occurrences.

Performance Limit

Frequency of Conformance

Frequency of Nonconformance

0

1

Units

A defect rate can be viewed as a probability and a probability can be viewed as a defect rate.

Continuous
(normal distribution shown)

Characteristic Y1

Density: Based on total area under the curve

Performance Limit

Probability of Conformance

Probability of Nonconformance

- ∞

Units ■ +∞

11 . 3

Approximating the Normal

The Poisson relation:

$$Y = \frac{(np)^r e^{-np}}{r!}$$

where n is the number of trials, r is the number of occurrences , and p is the probability of occurrence . Thus, when r=0, we have the probability of zero occurrences , or "rolled-throughput yield." Note that this is very different from the classical notion of yield; i.e., number good divided by the total number.

The poisson distribution is an approximation to more exact distributions and applies when the sample size is at least 16, the population is at least 10 times the sample size, and the probability of occurrence p on each trial is less than 10 percent. In practice, these assumptions are often met.

For n = unity and r = 0,

$$Y = e^{-p}$$

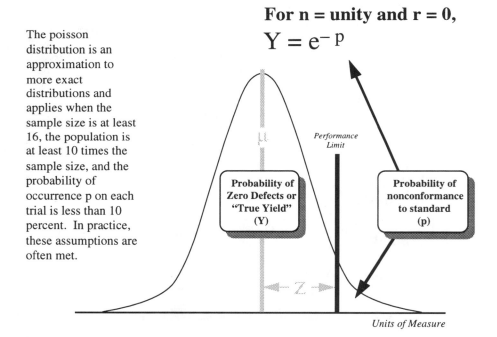

Performance Limit

Probability of Zero Defects or "True Yield" (Y)

Probability of nonconformance to standard (p)

μ

← Z →

Units of Measure

Example Application of the Poisson

A certain engineer observed 1 particular type of defect out of 346 production units. The defects-per-unit was computed as dpu = 1/346 = .00289. Hence,

$$\text{Yield} = Y = e^{-dpu}$$
$$= e^{-.00289}$$
$$= .99711$$

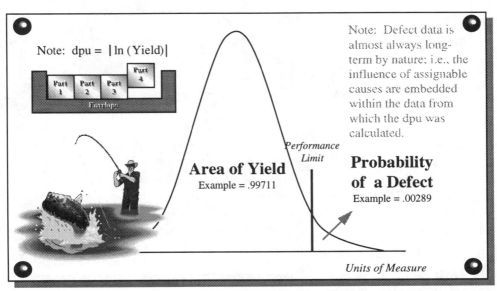

Note: dpu = |ln (Yield)|

Note: Defect data is almost always long-term by nature; i.e., the influence of assignable causes are embedded within the data from which the dpu was calculated.

Performance Limit

Area of Yield
Example = .99711

Probability of a Defect
Example = .00289

Units of Measure

The Normal or "Z" Approximation

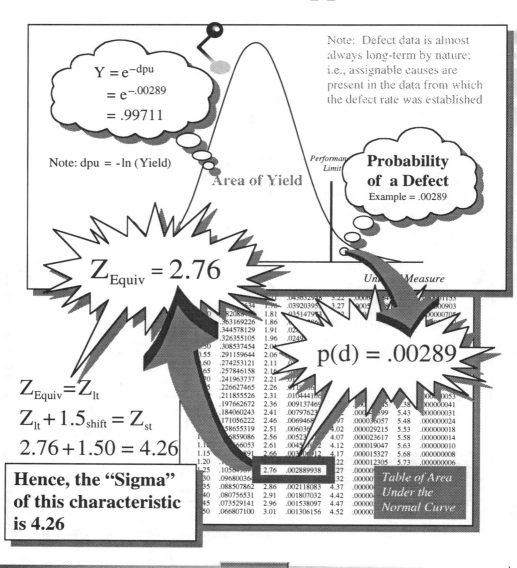

$$Y = e^{-dpu}$$
$$= e^{-.00289}$$
$$= .99711$$

Note: dpu = -ln (Yield)

Note: Defect data is almost always long-term by nature; i.e., assignable causes are present in the data from which the defect rate was established

Area of Yield

Performance Limit

Probability of a Defect
Example = .00289

$$Z_{Equiv} = 2.76$$

Unit of Measure

$$p(d) = .00289$$

$$Z_{Equiv} = Z_{lt}$$
$$Z_{lt} + 1.5_{shift} = Z_{st}$$
$$2.76 + 1.50 = 4.26$$

Hence, the "Sigma" of this characteristic is 4.26

	.043632936	3.22	.0006	.201133
	.03920395	3.27	.0005	.00000903
.32085	1.81	.035147913		.00000705
.363169226	1.86			
.344578129	1.91	.02		
.326355105	1.96	.0249		
.50	.308537454	2.0		
.55	.291159644	2.06		
.60	.274253121	2.11		
.65	.257846158	2.1		
.70	.241963737	2.21	.01	
	.226627465	2.26	.011	
	.211855526	2.31	.010444166	.000 .0053
	.197662672	2.36	.009137469	.000000041
	.184060243	2.41	.00797623	5.43	.000000031
	.171056222	2.46	.0069468	5.48	.000000024
	.58655319	2.51	.006036	4.02	.000029215	5.53	.000000018
1.1	.6859086	2.56	.00523	4.07	.000023617	5.58	.000000014
1.1	.66053	2.61	.0045	4.12	.000019047	5.63	.000000010
1.15	.891	2.66	.003 .12	4.17	.000015327	5.68	.000000008
1.20				.22	.000012305	5.73	.000000006
1.25	.1056	2.76	.002889938	.27	.00000	
.30	.09680036			.32	.00000	**Table of Area**
.35	.088507862	2.86	.002118083	4.37	.00000	**Under the**
.40	.080756531	2.91	.001807032	4.42	.00000	**Normal Curve**
.45	.073529141	2.96	.001538097	4.47	.00000	
.50	.066807100	3.01	.001306156	4.52	.00000	

Comments on the Z Approximation

✔ The rate at which defects are produced must be relatively stable to utilize the Z approximation.

✔ Generally speaking, substantial time must pass to observe a stable rate of defects.

✔ The defect rate will change whenever there is a change in the short-term capability of a process, due to a change in process spread or an alteration of the design limits. In addition, the defect rate will change whenever there is a change in the process mean relative to the design limits.

✔ If, during the course of data collection, a substantial amount of time has elapsed, it is reasonable to assume that the process mean has shifted or drifted over this time interval -- due to changes in material, tool wear, operator differences, etc.

✔ Therefore, if the design and process technology has remained constant over a large interval of time, it is reasonable to assume that the influence of shifts and drifts in μ is fully embodied within the defect data. Hence, the defect data would be considered "long-term" by nature and, as a consequence, reflect random errors within the process as well as nonrandom sources of error.

✔ To assess the short-term capability of a process, it is necessary to remove the nonrandom influences from the data. If the data were based on a simple count of defects, then we must subtract

Using the Sigma Scale of Measure

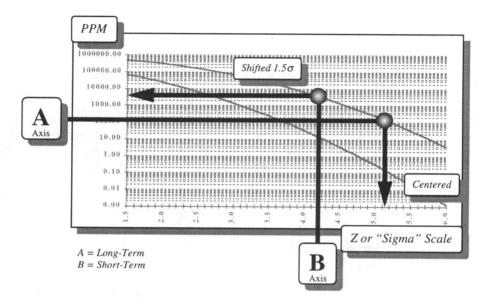

A = Long-Term
B = Short-Term

 If you start with defect data, then compute the PPM per opportunity and enter along the "A" axis. Next, project the "A" value to the "B" axis. The resulting number is an estimate of the short-term Z value, or "sigma" as it is called.

 If you start with a Z or "sigma" value, then enter along "B" axis. Next, project the "B" value to the "A" axis. The resulting number is an estimate of the long-term PPM.

Computing a Probability

It is often the case that we desire to compute the tail area probability associated with a given Z or "sigma" value. Of course, this can be easily accomplished using a standard table of area under the normal curve. However, we can compute the value in an electronic spreadsheet by way of the following equation:

$$\boxed{\text{Eq. 11.1}}$$

$$P = \left[\left(1 + C_1 Z + C_2 Z^2 + \ldots + C_6 Z^6 \right)^{-16} \right] / 2$$

Notes:
1) Z and P are one-tailed
2) Z is the standard normal deviate
3) P is the tail area probability
4) A4 is an arbitrary spreadsheet cell location

Constants

```
=(((((((1+0.049867347*ABS(A4))+
0.0211410061*ABS(A4^2))+
0.0032776263*ABS(A4^3))+
0.0000380036*ABS(A4^4))+
0.0000488906*ABS(A4^5))+
0.000005383*ABS(A4^6))^-16/2)
```

$C1 = 0.0498673470$
$C2 = 0.0211410061$
$C3 = 0.0032776263$
$C4 = 0.0000380036$
$C5 = 0.0000488906$
$C6 = 0.0000053830$

Computing the "Sigma" Value

In many situations, a Z or "sigma" value can be easily ascertained using a standard table of area under the normal curve. However, it is often desirable to directly compute the value in an electronic spreadsheet. This task may be accomplished using the following equation:

$$\boxed{\text{Eq. 11.2}}$$

$$Z = \lambda - \frac{C_1 + C_2\lambda + C_3\lambda^2}{1 + C_4\lambda + C_5\lambda^2 + C_6\lambda^3}$$

$$\lambda = \sqrt{\ln\left(1 / P^2\right)}$$

Notes:
1) Z and P are one-tailed
2) Z is the standard normal deviate
3) P is the tail area probability
4) E8 is an arbitrary spreadsheet cell location

Constants

```
=SQRT(LN(1/(1-E8)^2))-((2.515517
+0.802853*(SQRT(LN(1/(1-E8)^2)))
+0.010328*(SQRT(LN(1/(1-E8)^2)))^2))
/((1+1.432788*(SQRT(LN(1/(1-E8)^2)))
+0.189269*(SQRT(LN(1/(1-E8)^2)))^2
+0.001308*(SQRT(LN(1/(1-E8)^2)))^3))
```

$C1 = 2.515517$
$C2 = 0.802853$
$C3 = 0.010328$
$C4 = 1.432788$
$C5 = 0.189269$
$C6 = 0.000308$

The Sigma Conversion Guidelines

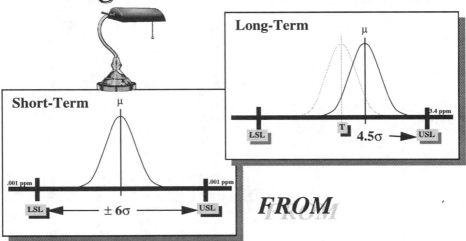

FROM

	Short-Term	Long-Term
Short-Term	No Action	**+ 1.5σ**
Long-Term	**- 1.5σ**	No Action

TO

PPM Conversion Table

Z	PPM	Z	PPM	Z	PPM
0.00	933,193	2.20	241,964	4.40	1,866
0.05	926,471	2.25	226,627	4.45	1,589
0.10	919,243	2.30	211,856	4.50	1,350
0.15	911,492	2.35	197,663	4.55	1,144
0.20	903,199	2.40	184,060	4.60	968
0.25	894,350	2.45	171,056	4.65	816
0.30	884,930	2.50	158,655	4.70	687
0.35	874,928	2.55	146,859	4.75	577
0.40	864,334	2.60	135,666	4.80	483
0.45	853,141	2.65	125,072	4.85	404
0.50	841,345	2.70	115,070	4.90	337
0.55	828,944	2.75	105,650	4.95	280
0.60	815,940	2.80	96,800	5.00	233
0.65	802,338	2.85	88,508	5.05	193
0.70	788,145	2.90	80,757	5.10	159
0.75	773,373	2.95	73,529	5.15	131
0.80	758,036	3.00	66,807	5.20	108
0.85	742,154	3.05	60,571	5.25	89
0.90	274,253	3.10	54,799	5.30	72
0.95	291,160	3.15	49,471	5.35	59
1.00	308,537	3.20	44,565	5.40	48
1.05	326,355	3.25	40,059	5.45	39
1.10	344,578	3.30	35,930	5.50	32
1.15	363,169	3.35	32,157	5.55	26
1.20	382,088	3.40	28,717	5.60	21
1.25	401,294	3.45	25,588	5.65	17
1.30	420,740	3.50	22,750	5.70	13
1.35	440,382	3.55	20,182	5.75	11
1.40	460,172	3.60	17,865	5.80	9
1.45	480,061	3.65	15,778	5.85	7
1.50	500,000	3.70	13,904	5.90	5
1.55	480,061	3.75	12,225	5.95	4
1.60	460,172	3.80	10,724	6.00	3
1.65	440,382	3.85	9,387		
1.70	420,740	3.90	8,198		
1.75	401,294	3.95	7,143		
1.80	382,088	4.00	6,210		
1.85	363,169	4.05	5,386		
1.90	344,578	4.10	4,661		
1.95	326,355	4.15	4,024		
2.00	308,537	4.20	3,467		
2.05	291,160	4.25	2,980		
2.10	274,253	4.30	2,555		
2.15	257,846	4.35	2,186		

Note: This table includes a 1.5σ shift for all listed values of Z.

The Widget Example Data

g	X1	X2	X3	X4	X5
1	1.242	1.239	1.239	1.242	1.240
2	1.240	1.241	1.240	1.239	1.242
3	1.239	1.239	1.239	1.239	1.240
4	1.241	1.240	1.240	1.240	1.241
5	1.240	1.241	1.240	1.238	1.241
6	1.241	1.240	1.240	1.240	1.239
7	1.237	1.240	1.240	1.237	1.238
8	1.240	1.242	1.240	1.240	1.238
9	1.240	1.239	1.240	1.239	1.242
10	1.239	1.239	1.241	1.239	1.240
11	1.239	1.238	1.242	1.238	1.240
12	1.239	1.241	1.239	1.239	1.242
13	1.239	1.242	1.239	1.239	1.240
14	1.240	1.239	1.240	1.239	1.241
15	1.241	1.240	1.240	1.240	1.240
16	1.240	1.239	1.240	1.240	1.240
17	1.241	1.239	1.238	1.240	1.240
18	1.239	1.239	1.241	1.241	1.239
19	1.240	1.239	1.240	1.238	1.242
20	1.241	1.240	1.241	1.239	1.240

Sampling Strategy: 5 consecutive parts were selected every hour (X_1 , ... , X_N). Each group (g) of parts was labeled and set aside for careful measurement of dimension "B." The location of measurement was arbitrarily chosen by the inspector.

Widget Characterization - 2a

Report Name	Example Application
Organization	
Project	Widget
Department	Manufacturing
Deliverable	Part
Deliverable ID	
Process	Milling
Operation	
Machine ID	

Reporting Period
Baseline
Improvement
Unit Definition
Characteristic ... Dimension

Subgroup Analysis

Eq. 11.1

Short-Term Capability (Case Analysis)

g	μ	σ	Z.LSL	Z.USL	P.LSL	P.USL	P.TOT	DPMO	Z.B
1	1.2400	0.00	-1.978	1.978	2.40E-02	2.40E-02	4.79E-02	47,913	1.666
2	1.2400	0.00	-2.631	2.631	4.25E-03	4.25E-03	8.51E-03	8,509	2.387
3	1.2400	0.00	-6.708	6.708	1.73E-11	1.73E-11	3.45E-11	0	6.522
4	1.2400	0.00	-5.477	5.477	2.41E-08	2.41E-08	4.81E-08	0	5.333
5	1.2400	0.00	-2.449	2.449	7.15E-03	7.15E-03	1.43E-02	14,306	2.189
6	1.2400	0.00			1.11E-05	1.11E-05			4.083
7	1.2400	0.00				2.4?E-0?			?.666
8	1.2400	0.00				1.69E-			
9	1.2400	0.0				7.?			
10	1.2400	0.00			E-04	3.98E-			158
11	1.2400	0.00			3.65E-0?	3.65E-02			
				12?	1.69E-02	1.69E-02	3.?E-02	3,895	1.827
				2.301	1.07E-02	1.07E-02	2.14E-02	21,398	2.026
				3.586	1.68E-04	1.68E-04	3.36E-04	33?	3.401
				6.708	1.73E-11	1.73E-11	?E-11		
				6.708	1.73E-11	1.73E-11	?E-11		
				2.631	4.25E				
				2.739					
19	1.2400	0.00	-2.023	2.023					
20	1.2400	0.00	-3.586	3.586				?36	3.401

Eq. 11.1

Eq. 11.2

It should be noted that this section of the L2 Format is concerned with the short-term capability of each subgroup (i.e., row of data). This section does not aggregate the analysis.

$$P_{TOT} = P_{LSL} + P_{USL}$$

$$DPMO = P_{TOT} \times 10^6$$

Format L2

Widget Characterization - 2b

Short-Term Capability (Cumm Analysis)

g	μ	SS	σ	Z.LSL	Z.USL	P.LSL	P.USL	P.TOT	DPMO	Z.B
1	2400	.000009	.00152	-1.978	1.978	2.40E-02	2.40E-02	4.79E-02	47,913	1.666
2	.00	.000014	.00134	-2.236	2.236	1.27E-0				.954
3	1.	.000015	.00113	-2.666	2.666	3.84E-0				424
4	1.2	.000016	.00101	-2. 63	2.963	1.52E-0				743
5	1.24		91	5	2.835	2.29E-0				606
	1					1.46E-0				756
7						E-03				.503
						5E-03	4.25E-03	8.51E-03	8,509	2.387
11						3.88E-0				
						75E-0				
						6.49E-0				
13	1.2			469	2.469	6.78E-0				
14	1.24	.000 80	11	6	2.516	5.93E-0				
15	1.2400	.000080	116	-2.59	2.592	4.78E-0				
16	1.2400	.000081	.00113	-2.663	2.663	3.87E-0				
17	1.2400	.000086	.00113	-2.661	2.661	3.89E-0				
18	1.2400	.000091	.00113	-2.666	2.666	3.84E-0				
19	1.2400	.000100	.00115	-2.615	2.615	4.46E-03	4.46E-03	8.91E-03	8,914	2.370
20	1.2400	.000103	.00113	-2.646	2.646	4.07E-03	4.07E-03	8.13E-03	8,133	2.403

Cumulative Short-Term Analysis

Z.B for the cumulative short-term analysis is computed in the same manner as that given for the case-wise short-term analysis

It should be noted that this section of the L2 Format is concerned with the cumulative short-term capability. For each new subgroup (i.e., row of data), the Z.st value is recomputed using all of the previous data. This particular analysis is based on the nominal specification (i.e., target value).

Widget Characterization - 2c

Long-Term Capability (Cumm Analysis)											
g	μ	SS	σ	Z.LSL	Z.USL	P.LSL	P.USL	P.TOT	DPMO	Z.B	Z.shift
1	.2404	.000009	.00152	-2.242	1.714	1.25E-02	4.32E-02	5.57E-02	55,713	1.592	0.074
2	.404	.000014	.00126	-2.688	2.055	3.59E-03	1.99E-02	2.35E-02	23,511	1.987	-0.032
3	1.?0	.000020	.00120	-2.510	2.510	6.04E-03	6.04E-03				
4	1.?	.00002?	.00107	-2.894	2.707	1.90E-03	3.39E-03				
5	1.2?	.00028	.00108	-?.860	2.711	2.12E-03	3.35E-03				
6	1.24			?.?22	2.890	1.26E-03	1.92E-03				
7						1.04E-02	4.80E-03				
8						?.??E-02	5.25E-03	1.36E-02	13,332	2.136	0.231
							?.26E-03				
							8.24E-03				
							?.??E-02				
							1.09E-02				
13							1.07E-02				
						?.65	?.28E-03				
	1.2?				2.7??	7.30E-03					
16	1.?			11	2.799	6.02E-03					
17	1.2898	.000106	.0113	-2.?9	2.823	6.05E-03					
18	1.2398	.000111	.0112	-2.5?	2.843	5.78E-03	2.23E-03	8.01E-03	8,010	2.409	0.015
19	1.2398	.000120	.00113	-2.497	2.814	6.26E-03	2.45E-03	8.70E-03	8,704	2.378	-0.009
20	1.2398	.000123	.00112	-2.543	2.830	5.49E-03	2.33E-03	7.82E-03	7,817	2.418	-0.014

Cumulative Long-Term Analysis

Z.B for the cumulative long-term analysis is computed in the same manner as that given for the case-wise short-term analysis.

It should be noted that this section of the L2 Format is concerned with the cumulative long-term capability. For each new subgroup (i.e., row of data), the Z.lt value is recomputed using all of the previous data. This particular analysis is based on the process mean.

Application Example 2d

Report Name			Reporting Period		From		To	
Organization			Baseline Period		From		To	
Project								
Department								
Deliverable								
Deliverable ID								
Process								
Step								
Machine ID								
Special Note								

> Remember, defects per opportunity (dpo) is treated as a probability for purposes of applying Eq. 11.1

> Eq. 11.1

> **Defects Per Opportunity**

Line	Characteristic			TOP	DPU	DPO	DPMO	Shift	Z.B
1	Type A		83	95	7,885	0.976	0.0103	10,273	1.50	3.82
2	Type B		584	20	11,680	0.115	0.0057	5,736	1.50	4.03
3		19	225	38	8,550	0.084	0.0022	2,222	1.50	4.35
4			884	57	50,388	0.037	0.0007	655	1.50	4.71
5		57	774	37				2,340	1.50	4.33
6		27	669	91				444	1.50	4.82
7	Ty	30	86	51				6,840	1.50	3.97
8	Typ	84	561	28				5,348	1.50	4.05
9	Typ	21	347	12				5,043	1.50	4.07
10	Type	16	333	85	28,305	0.048	0.0006	565	1.50	4.76
11	Typ	2	867	67	58,089	0.002	0.0000	34	1.50	5.48
12			62	55	3,410	1.323	0.0240	24,047	1.50	3.48
13			708	51	36,108	0.114	0.0022	2,243	1.50	4.34
14	Typ	49	775	26	20,150	0.063	0.0024	2,432	1.50	4.32
15	Typ	87	172	44	7,568	0.506	0.0115	11,496	1.50	3.77
16	Ty	55	801	20	16,020	0.069	0.0034	3,433	1.50	4.20
17	T	62	492	40	19,680	0.126	0.0032	3,150	1.50	4.23
18	T	23	444	83	36,852	0.052	0.0006	624	1.50	4.73
19		54	773	44	34,012	0.070	0.0016	1,588	1.50	4.45
20	Type T		457	78	35,646	0.131	0.0017	1,683	1.50	4.43
	Grand =	1,000			488,118		0.0020	2,049	1.50	4.37

Six Sigma Scorecard L1: Version 1.0 Developed by Dr. Mikel J. Harry

Guidelines for the Mean Shift

Guideline 1: If a metric is computed on the basis of data gathered over many cycles or time intervals, the resultant value should be regarded as a long-term measure of performance. Naturally, the long-term metric must be converted to a probability. Once expressed as a probability, Z.lt value may be established by way of a table of area-under-the-normal-curve, or any acceptable computational device. If we seek to forecast short-term performance (Z.st), we must add a shift factor (Z.shift) to Z.lt so as to remove time related sources of error which tend to upset process centering. Recognize that the actual value of Z.shift is seldom known in practice; therefore, it may be necessary to apply the accepted convention and set Z.shift = 1.50. As a consequence of this linear transformation, the final Z value reflects only random sources of error and, therefore, is a projection of short-term performance. Thus, we are able to artificially remove the effect of nonrandom influences (i.e., normal process centering errors) from the analysis via the transform Z.st = Z.lt + Z.shift.

Guideline 2: If a metric is computed on the basis of data gathered over a very limited number of cycles or time intervals, the resultant value should be regarded as a short-term measure of performance. Naturally, the short-term metric must be converted to a probability. Once expressed as a probability, Z.st may be established by way of a table of area-under-the-normal-curve, or any acceptable computational device. If we seek to forecast long-term performance, we must subtract Z.shift from Z.st so as to approximate the long-term capability. Recognize that the actual value of Z.shift is seldom known in practice; therefore, it may be necessary to apply the accepted convention and set Z.shift = 1.50. As a consequence of this linear transformation, the final Z value reflects both random and nonrandom sources of error and, therefore, is a projection of long-term performance. Thus, we are able to artificially induce the effect of nonrandom influences (i.e., normal process centering errors) into the analysis by way of Z.st - Z.shift = Z.lt

Guideline 3: In general, if the originating data is discrete by nature, the resulting Z transform should be regarded as long-term. The logic of this guideline is simple; a fairly large number of cycles or time intervals is often required to generate enough nonconformities from which to generate a relatively stable estimate of Z. Hence, it is reasonable to conclude that both random and nonrandom influences are reflected in such data. In this instance, guideline 1 would be applied.

Guideline 4: In general, if the originating data is continuous by nature and was gathered under the constraint of sequential or random sampling across a very limited number of cycles or time intervals, the resulting Z value should be regarded as short-term. The logic of this guideline is simple; data gathered over a very limited number cycles or time intervals only reflects random influences (white noise) and, as a consequence, tends to exclude nonrandom sources of variation, such as process centering errors.

Guideline 5: Whenever it is desirable to report the corresponding "sigma" of a given performance metric, the short-term Z must be used. For example, let us suppose that we find 6210 ppm defective. In this instance, we must translate 6210 ppm into its corresponding "sigma" value. Doing so reveals Z.lt = 2.50. Since the originating data was long-term by nature, guidelines 1 and 3 apply. In this case, Z.lt + Z.shift = 2.5 + 1.5 = 4.0. Since no other estimate of Z.shift was available, the convention of 1.5 was employed.

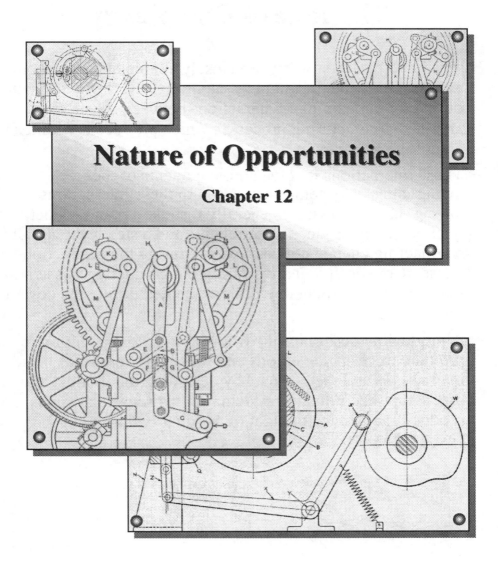

Nature of Opportunities

Chapter 12

The Role of Complexity

➤ Producibility and quality are closely coupled because both are essentially the resultant or integrated effect of a myriad of diverse and complex interactions between the product and the manufacturing processes which produce it within a complex environment.

➤ These interactions involve all components of the manufacturing system. Inattention to these interactions during the design phase generally results in poor product quality, costly production problems, and a steady stream of engineering change notices (ECNs) during the production phase. Conversely, quality during the production phase is the result of a "producible design" created during the design phase.

➤ A producible design results from paying close attention to product/process interactions and seeking to minimize these interactions and their impact by designing the product and process as a coordinated system. In this sense, producibility can be thought of as "quality during the design phase."

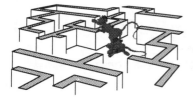

Stoll, H., Kumar, A., and Maas, D. (Date Unknown).
Producibility Measurement: Key to the Design of Producible Products.
Unpublished paper. pp 1-2. Industrial Technology Institute, Ann Arbor,
Michigan.

Dealing with Complexity

"Complexity" is a measure of how complicated something is. From a theoretical perspective, it is doubtful that we will ever be able to quantify this concept in an exacting manner. From a more practical point-of-view, we may say that notion of complexity is closely associated with the number of product and process characteristics.

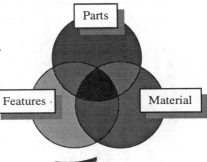

Product

Complexity

If we assume that all characteristics are independent and mutually exclusive, we may say that "complexity" can be reasonably estimated by a simple count.

Process

In terms of quality, each product and process characteristic represents a unique "opportunity" to either add or subtract value.

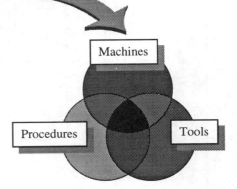

Complexity and Capability

The goal should be to reduce the total number of opportunities and concurrently increase the capability of each opportunity which remains.

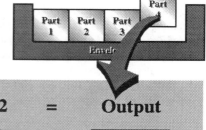

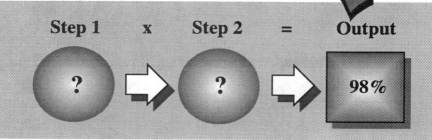

| Step 1 | x | Step 2 | = | Output |

? ➡ ? ➡ **98%**

Sigma Capability (with 1.5s shift)

. . . The following graph displays the Sigma Capability which must be maintained (for X number of process steps) in order to produce 98% of the products defect free.

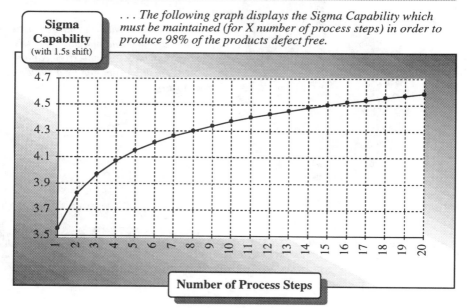

Number of Process Steps

Complexity and Quality

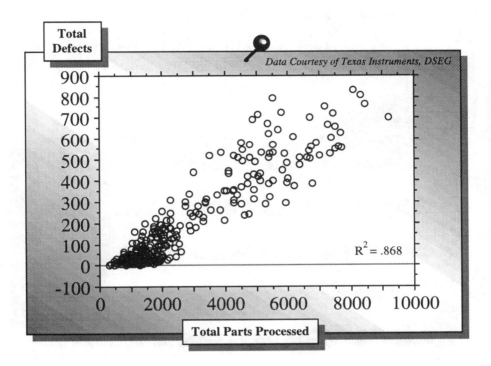

The data suggests that there is a strong correlation between the total number of parts processed and the total number of observed defects. Given the linear nature of this relationship, we may conclude that the process maintains a relatively stable level of capability over time.

The Opportunity Exercise

Part

For the given widget part, identify the product opportunities.

Description of Opportunity	Count

Note: Opportunities must be independent -- one type of opportunity can not cause another type to be nonconforming to its respective standard.

Total =

Example Application Format

Demographics	Project		Document	
	Hardware	A	Design	
	Software		Process	B
	Service		Proceedure	

Level		Description	Legend
Complex	1	NA	F Failure
System	2	Widget Model #7	D Defect
Subsystem	3	Holdit Assembly - ABC	E Error
Component	4	Gotahavit Part #123	A Number Appraised
	5	x	T Total (F+D+E)

Characteristic		F	D	E	A	T
1			6		5	6
2	Finish					
3	Diameter		3		3	3
4	Angle		4		1	4
5	Hardness	1			1	1
6	Stress	1			1	1
7						
8						
9						
10						
11						
12						
13						
14						
15						

Characteristic	F	D	E	A	T
15					
16					
17					
18					
19					
20					
21					
22					
23					
24					
25					
26					
27					
28					
29					
Total	2	13	0	11	15

Comments on Opportunity Counting

Nature of an Opportunity

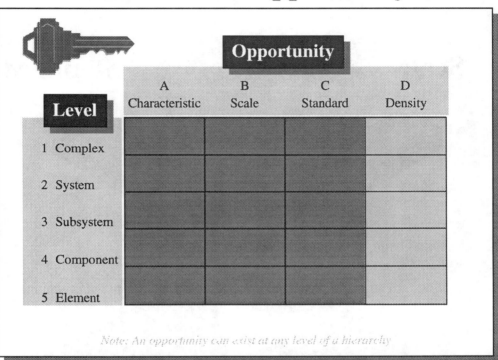

Level	Opportunity			
	A Characteristic	B Scale	C Standard	D Density
1 Complex				
2 System				
3 Subsystem				
4 Component				
5 Element				

Note: An opportunity can exist at any level of a hierarchy

Opportunity: Set of circumstances favorable to an end

Characteristic	Distinguishing attribute, trait, property, or quality.
Scale	Relative basis for measuring a characteristic.
Standard	Criterion state, condition or model circumstance.
Density	Quantity per unit of measure.

The Set of Circumstances

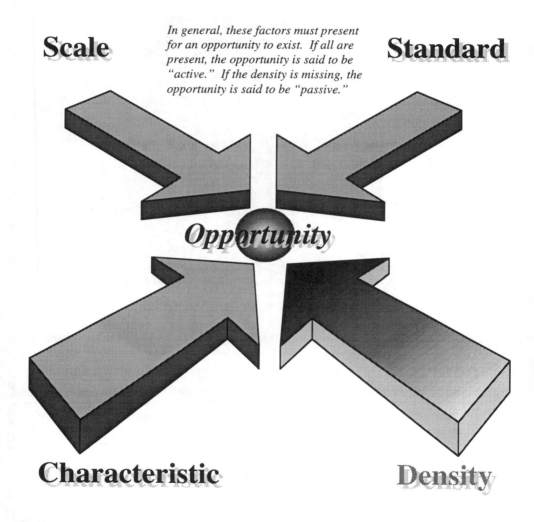

Scale

Standard

In general, these factors must present for an opportunity to exist. If all are present, the opportunity is said to be "active." If the density is missing, the opportunity is said to be "passive."

Opportunity

Characteristic

Density

Measurement Establishes Density

 . . . *Scales of Measure:*

Nominal: Unordered categories which represent membership or non-membership.

Ordinal: Ordered categories with no information about distance between categories.

Interval: Ordered categories with equal distance between categories, but no absolute zero point.

Ratio: Ordered categories with equal distance between categories with an absolute zero point.

Opportunity and Density

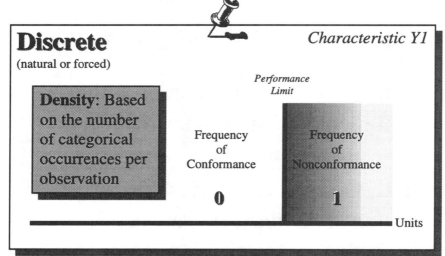

Discrete

(natural or forced)

Characteristic Y1

Density: Based on the number of categorical occurrences per observation

Performance Limit

Frequency of Conformance

Frequency of Nonconformance

0   **1**

Units

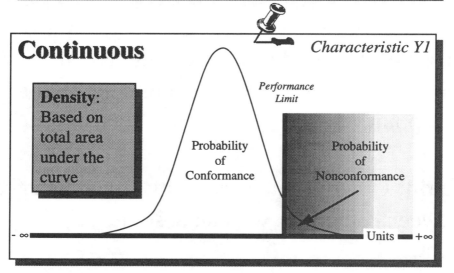

Continuous

Characteristic Y1

Density: Based on total area under the curve

Performance Limit

Probability of Conformance

Probability of Nonconformance

- ∞   Units +∞

The Opportunity Hierarchy

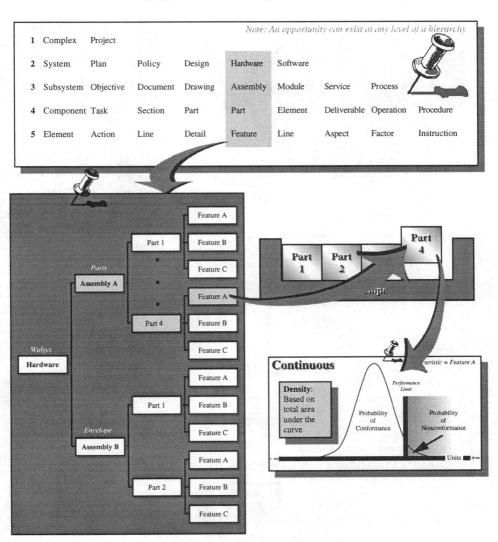

Application to the Widget

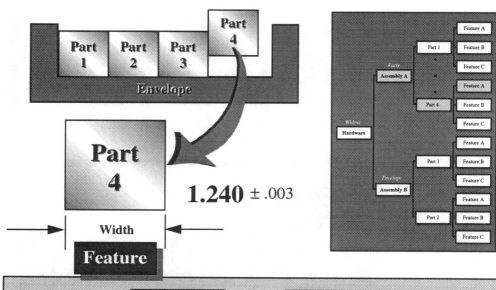

1.240 ± .003

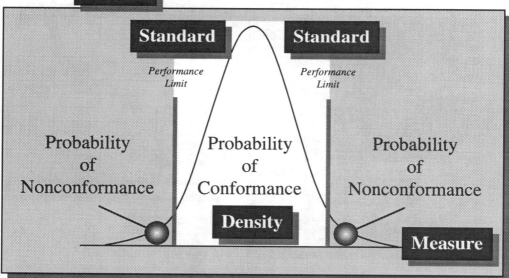

The States of an Opportunity

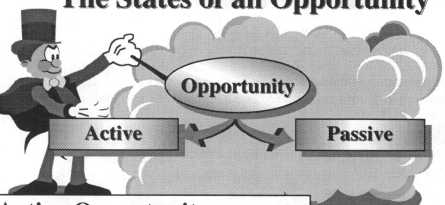

Active Opportunity:
The chance for conformance to standard is assessed.

Passive Opportunity:
The chance for conformance to standard is not assessed.

For a typical product, what proportion of the total opportunities do you suppose are active? If all of the passive opportunities were to become active, do you suppose the "sigma" would change much?

Active and Passive Exercise

Let us suppose that a certain organization determines that process ABC has m = 100,000 opportunities for nonconformance to standard. However, during the normal course of process operation, only 1,000 of these opportunities are assessed and recorded. We will further suppose that TDPU = 10.

General Rule: An opportunity is an opportunity only if it is measured.

What is the defects-per-opportunity and what "sigma" capability should be declared?

If we employ 100,000 opportunities which exist, we compute:

$$DPO = \frac{TDPU}{M} = \frac{10}{100,000} = .0001$$ **Active + Passive**

This converts to 3.72σ. Since the originating data was long-term by nature, we must remove the influence of process shift and drift by adding 1.50σ to the result. Doing so, we discover the short-term opportunity capability is 5.22σ. Such performance is approaching world-class.

If we employ the 1,000 opportunities we assessed , we compute:

$$DPO = \frac{TDPU}{M} = \frac{10}{1,000} = .01$$ **Active Only**

This converts to 2.33σ. After adding 1.5σ to the result, we discover the short-term opportunity capability is 3.83σ. Such performance is slightly below average. Obviously, this is the "true" capability of the process

As we can see, the inclusion of those opportunities which were not assessed makes a big difference in the stated process capability.

The Classes of Nonconformance

Fault: Results when a <u>characteristic</u> does not <u>perform</u> to standard.

Defect: Results when a <u>characteristic</u> does not <u>conform</u> to standard.

Error: Results when an <u>action</u> does not <u>comply</u> with standard.

Note: A failure can only be detected upon the application of energy. The detection of a defect or error is not energy dependent.

The Moving Van Example

	Active	Passive
Fault		
Defect		
Error		

The Basic Model for Failures

A failure at any given level of the opportunity hierarchy can be attributed to the independent or joint occurrence of defects, faults, or errors at one or more of the subordinate levels associated with that hierarchy .

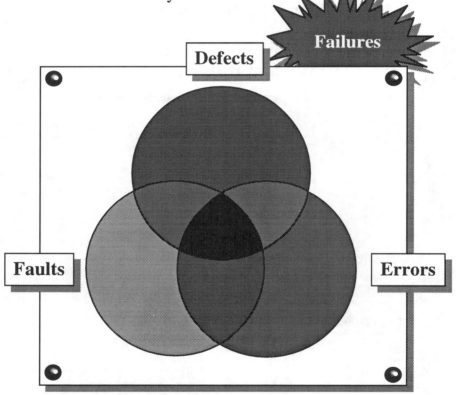

Extending the Basic Model

FPU: Faults per Unit
DPU: Defects per Unit
EPU: Errors per Unit

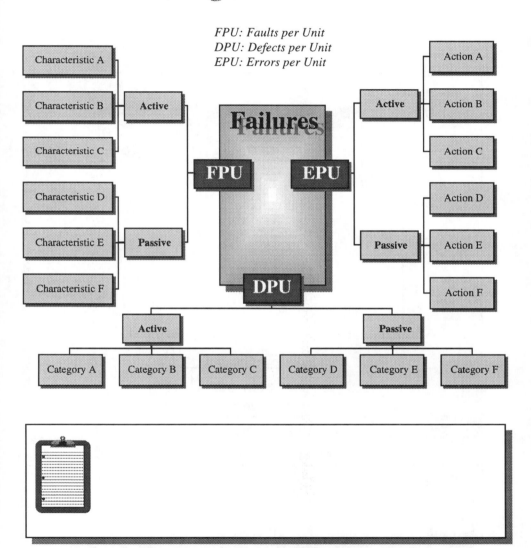

The Impact of DPU

*. . . So why is scatter present in the
yield for a fixed DPU?*

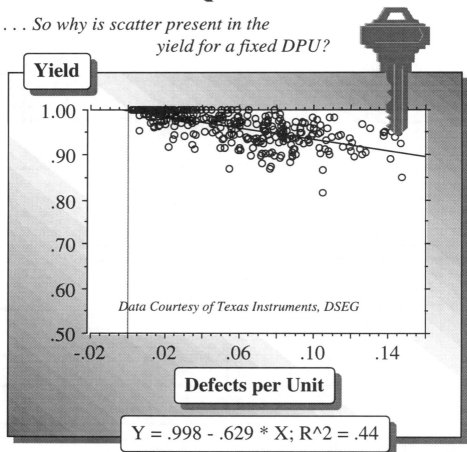

Yield

Data Courtesy of Texas Instruments, DSEG

Defects per Unit

$$Y = .998 - .629 * X; R^2 = .44$$

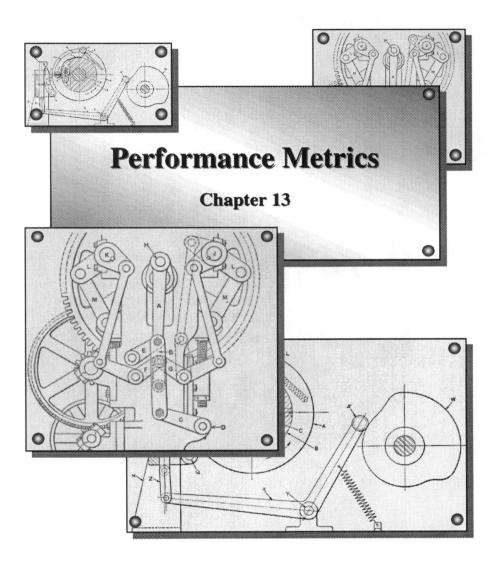

Performance Metrics

Chapter 13

The Need for Performance Metrics

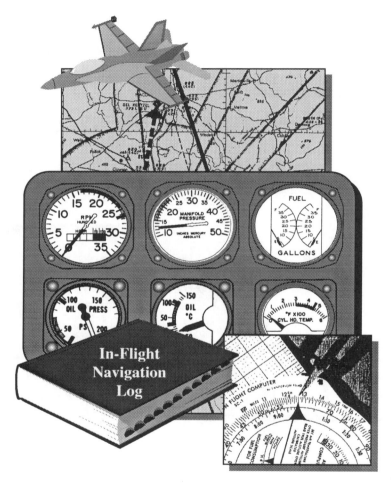

*. . . So what do these things have in common
with business. . . What are the implications?*

Best Quality Management Practice

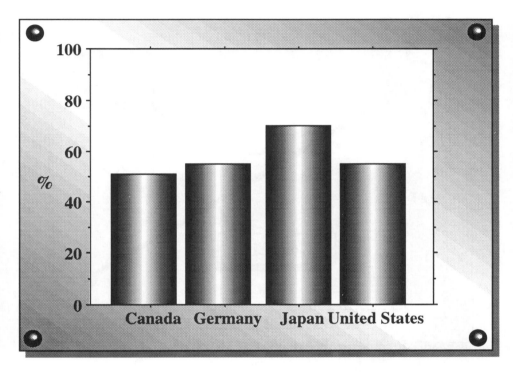

"How often does senior management evaluate information regarding the business consequences of quality performance; that is, gains in market share or profit resulting from quality improvements"

Source: *The Definitive Study of the Best International Quality Management Practices*
Ernst & Young 1991

Nature of Performance Metrics

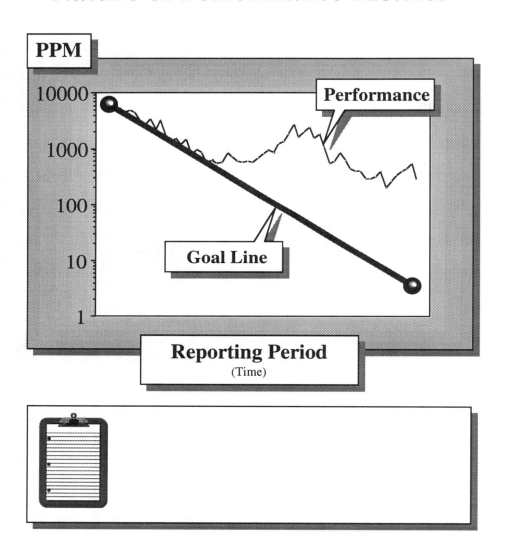

13 . 4

Using the Log Scale for Graphs

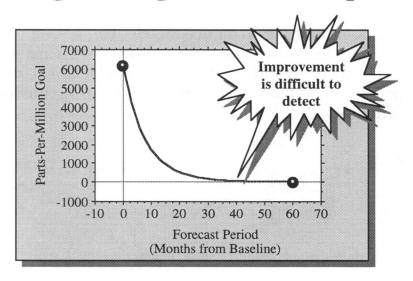

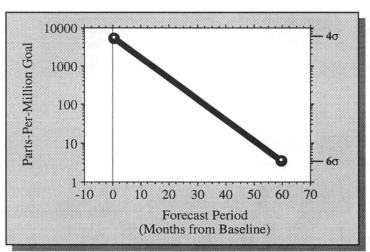

Guiding the Business with Metrics

The benefit of performance metrics can not be understated. Use of metrics is a proven means to guide the basic operations of business. Performance metrics provides feedback and a ensures a focus on business fundamentals.

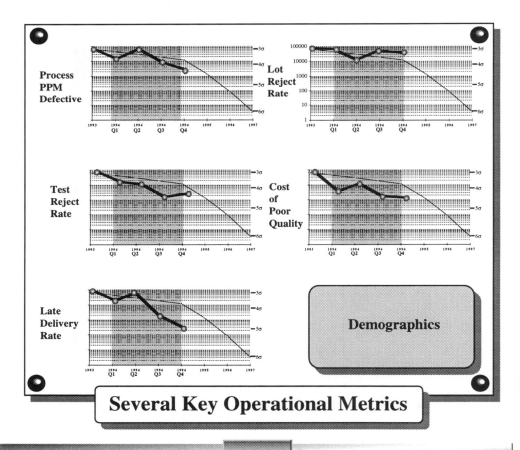

Several Key Operational Metrics

Business Metrics Report Summary

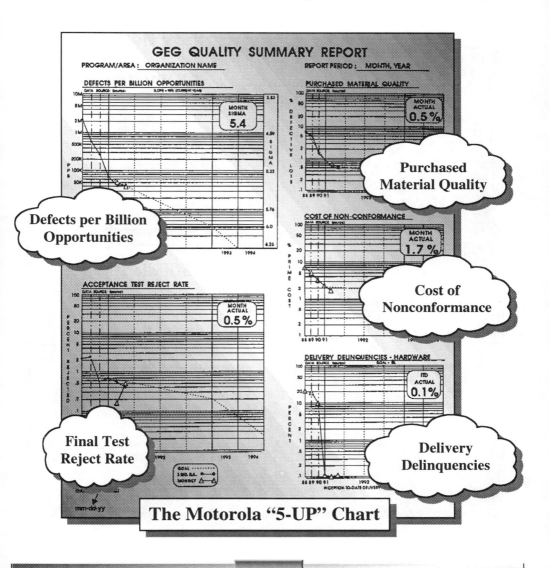

The Motorola "5-UP" Chart

Hierarchical Reporting

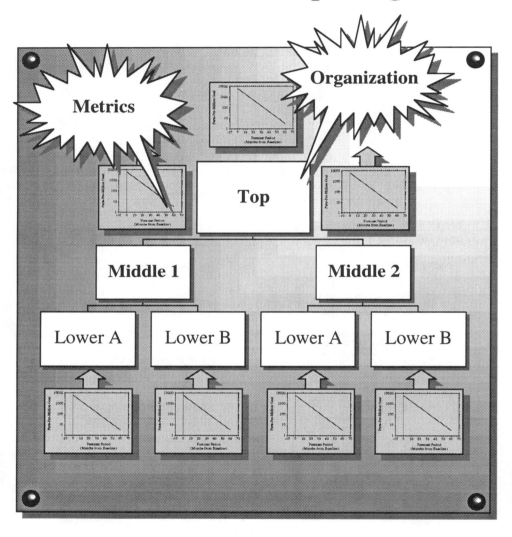

Example Performance Metrics

Motorola Factory

Metrics Report	QSR 5-UP	Goal	Baseline Period
Acceptance/Realiabiltiy Test Rejects	A	68% IPY	1988 average
Cost of Nonconformance	A	25% IPY	1988 average
Cost of Quality		18% IPY	1988 average
Defects per Cost Proposal		68% IPY	1988 average
Defects per Million Opportunities-Assembly		68% IPY	1st & 2nd Q, 1990
Defects per Million Opportunities-Manufacturing		68% IPY	1st & 2nd Q, 1989
Defects per Million Opportunities-Solder		68% IPY	1st & 2nd Q, 1990
Defects per Million Opportunities-Test and Inspection	A	68% IPY	1988 average
Delivery Delinquencies-CDRLs		0 Delinquencies	N/A
Delivery Delinquencies-Hardware	A	0 Delinquencies	N/A
First-Time Test Reject-Subassemblies		25% IPY	1st & 2nd Q, 1989
First-Time Test Reject Rate-Systems		25% IPY	1st & 2nd Q, 1989
Method Bs (QDR)		0 QDRs	N/A
MRB Actions		0 MRB Actions	N/A
MRB Items-Number Processed		0 MRB Items	N/A
Productivity		10% IPY	1st Q of meas.
Purchased Material Quality-Project Responsibility	P	0 Defects	N/A
Purchased Material Quality-QSM Responsibility		0 Defects	N/A
Purchased Material Quality	G	50% IPY	1987 average
Quality Summary Report		N/A	N/A
Software-Total Defect Containment Effectiveness		100% by 1992	1st Q, 1988
Standard Repairs		68%	4th Q, 1989
Technical Documentation Accuracy		68% IPY	4th Q, 1987
Time Card /Time Sheet Accuracy		68% IPY	1987 average
Waivers		0 Waivers	N/A

IPY = Improvement Per Year

N/A = Not Applicable

A = This report is included in the Program, Division, and Group Quality Summary Reports (5-Up)

G = This report is included in the Division and Group Quality Summary Reports (5-Up)

P = This report is included in the Program Quality Summary Report (5-Up)

Example Metrics Reporting

Motorola Factory

Metrics Report	QSR 5-UP	Review	Division Review	Group Review	Corp Review
Acceptance/Realiabiltiy Test Rejects	A	X	X	X	X
Cost of Nonconformance	A	X	X	X	X
Cost of Quality			X	X	
Defects per Cost Proposal			X	X	X
Defects per Million Opportunities-Assembly		X			
Defects per Million Opportunities-Manufacturing		X	X		
Defects per Million Opportunities-Solder		X			
Defects per Million Opportunities-Test and Inspection	A	X	X	X	X
Delivery Delinquencies-CDRLs		X	X	X	X
Delivery Delinquencies-Hardware	A	X	X	X	X
First-Time Test Reject-Subassemblies		X			
First-Time Test Reject Rate-Systems		X			
Method Bs (QDR)				X	X
MRB Actions		X	X	X	
MRB Items-Number Processed		X	X	X	
Productivity		X	X	X	
Purchased Material Quality-Project Responsibility	P	X	X	X	
Purchased Material Quality-QSM Responsibility			X	X	
Purchased Material Quality	G		X	X	X
Quality Summary Report		X	X	X	X
Software-Total Defect Containment Effectiveness		X	X	X	
Standard Repairs		X	X		
Technical Documentation Accuracy			X	X	
Time Card /Time Sheet Accuracy			X	X	X
Waivers		X	X	X	

IPY = Improvement Per Year

N/A = Not Applicable

A = This report is included in the Program, Division, and Group Quality Summary Reports (5-Up)

G = This report is included in the Division and Group Quality Summary Reports (5-Up)

P = This report is included in the Program Quality Summary Report (5-Up)

Note 1. Operations Reviews are not required by the Strategic Electronics Division.

Note 2. Purchased Material Quality-Supplier Responsibility is reported by the Quality Supply Management organization.

Performance Metrics Manual

Standardized documentation and reporting formats is a major key to successful application

Creating Performance Metrics

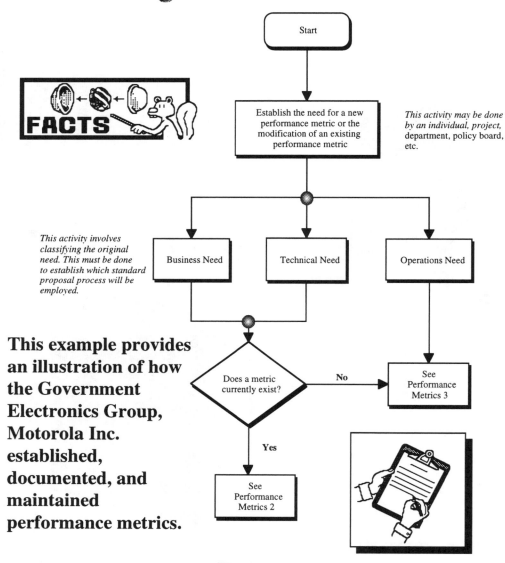

FACTS

Start

Establish the need for a new performance metric or the modification of an existing performance metric

This activity may be done by an individual, project, department, policy board, etc.

This activity involves classifying the original need. This must be done to establish which standard proposal process will be employed.

Business Need

Technical Need

Operations Need

This example provides an illustration of how the Government Electronics Group, Motorola Inc. established, documented, and maintained performance metrics.

Does a metric currently exist?

No → See Performance Metrics 3

Yes

See Performance Metrics 2

Performance Metrics: Option 2

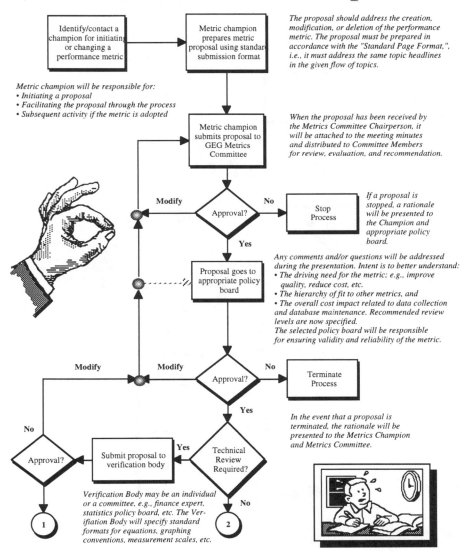

Identify/contact a champion for initiating or changing a performance metric

Metric champion prepares metric proposal using standard submission format

The proposal should address the creation, modification, or deletion of the performance metric. The proposal must be prepared in accordance with the "Standard Page Format,", i.e., it must address the same topic headlines in the given flow of topics.

Metric champion will be responsible for:
* *Initiating a proposal*
* *Facilitating the proposal through the process*
* *Subsequent activity if the metric is adopted*

Metric champion submits proposal to GEG Metrics Committee

When the proposal has been received by the Metrics Committee Chairperson, it will be attached to the meeting minutes and distributed to Committee Members for review, evaluation, and recommendation.

Modify   Approval?   **No**   Stop Process

If a proposal is stopped, a rationale will be presented to the Champion and appropriate policy board.

Yes

Proposal goes to appropriate policy board

Any comments and/or questions will be addressed during the presentation. Intent is to better understand:
* *The driving need for the metric; e.g., improve quality, reduce cost, etc.*
* *The hierarchy of fit to other metrics, and*
* *The overall cost impact related to data collection and database maintenance. Recommended review levels are now specified.*
The selected policy board will be responsible for ensuring validity and reliability of the metric.

Modify   **Modify**   Approval?   **No**   Terminate Process

In the event that a proposal is terminated, the rationale will be presented to the Metrics Champion and Metrics Committee.

Yes

No   Approval?   Submit proposal to verification body   **Yes**   Technical Review Required?

Verification Body may be an individual or a committee, e.g., finance expert, statistics policy board, etc. The Verifiation Body will specify standard formats for equations, graphing conventions, measurement scales, etc.

No

(1)

(2)

Performance Metrics: Options 3

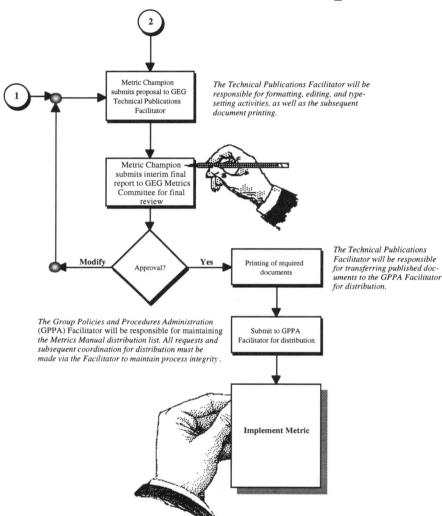

The Technical Publications Facilitator will be responsible for formatting, editing, and type-setting activities, as well as the subsequent document printing.

The Technical Publications Facilitator will be responsible for transferring published documents to the GPPA Facilitator for distribution.

The Group Policies and Procedures Administration (GPPA) Facilitator will be responsible for maintaining the Metrics Manual distribution list. All requests and subsequent coordination for distribution must be made via the Facilitator to maintain process integrity.

Establishing Performance Goals

$$Y_G = B \left(10^{\ \log [(1-R)/12]} \right)^N$$

Y = Goal value for the forecast period
B = Baseline performance for given metric
R = Desired annual improvement rate
N = Number of months since baseline period

B   6,210
R   78.00

N	Y.G	N	Y.G	N	Y.G
0	6209.7				
1	5473.6	21	438.8	41	35.2
2	4824.7	22	386.8	42	31.0
3	4252.8	23	341.0	43	27.3
4	3748.7	24	300.5	44	24.1
5	3304.3	25	264.9	45	21.2
6	2912.6	26	233.5	46	18.7
7	2567.3	27	205.8	47	16.5
8	2263.0	28	181.4	48	14.5
9	1994.7	29	159.9	49	12.8
10	1758.3	30	141.0	50	11.3
11	1549.9	31	124.3	51	10.0
12	1366.1	32	109.5	52	8.8
13	1204.2	33	96.5	53	7.7
14	1061.4	34	85.1	54	6.8
15	935.6	35	75.0	55	6.0
16	824.7	36	66.1	56	5.3
17	726.9	37	58.3	57	4.7
18	640.8	38	51.4	58	4.1
19	564.8	39	45.3	59	3.6
20	497.9	40	39.9	60	3.2

If the baseline capability is 4σ, the corresponding ppm = 6210. Given an improvement rate of 78% per year, the goal for the 60th month would be Y.G = 3.2 ppm, or 6σ.

Annual Rate of Improvement

$$Y_A = 1 - \left(10^{\,\log(C/B)/N}\right)^{12}$$

Y = Improvement rate for the given month
B = Baseline performance for given metric
C = Performance for current month
N = Number of months since baseline period

B	6,210
C	233

N	Y.A	N	Y.A	N	Y.A
1	1.0000	21	0.8469	41	0.6176
2	1.0000	22	0.8333	42	0.6087
3	1.0000	23	0.8198	43	0.6001
4	0.9999	24	0.8064	44	0.5917
5	0.9996	25	0.7933	45	0.5835
6	0.9986	26	0.7804	46	0.5755
7	0.9964	27	0.7677	47	0.5677
8	0.9927	28	0.7553	48	0.5600
9	0.9875	29	0.7431	49	0.5526
10	0.9806	30	0.7312	50	0.5453
11	0.9722	31	0.7195	51	0.5383
12	0.9625	32	0.7082	52	0.5313
13	0.9518	33	0.6971	53	0.5246
14	0.9401	34	0.6862	54	0.5180
15	0.9277	35	0.6757	55	0.5116
16	0.9148	36	0.6654	56	0.5053
17	0.9016	37	0.6553	57	0.4991
18	0.8880	38	0.6455	58	0.4931
19	0.8743	39	0.6360	59	0.4873
20	0.8606	40	0.6267	60	0.4815

If the baseline capability is 4σ, the corresponding ppm = 6210. If after the 60th month ppm = 233, the rate of improvement per year would be Y.A = 48.15%.

Note: In order to achieve a 10X reduction in defects every two years, Y.A = 68.37%. This learning curve is currently employed by Motorola. Thus, the goal is a 100X reduction in defects every 4 years.

Monthly Rate of Improvement

R	Y.M
.00	.00000
.05	.00427
.10	.00874
.15	.01345
.20	.01842
.25	.02369
.30	.02929
.35	.03526
.40	.04168
.45	.04860
.50	.05613
.55	.06438
.60	.07352
.65	.08377
.70	.09546
.75	.10910
.80	.12551
.85	.14623
.90	.17460
.95	.22092

$$Y_M = 1 - \left(10^{\,[\log(1-R)]/12} \right)$$

Y = Monthly rate of improvement
R = Desired annual improvement rate

If the annual improvement rate is 70%, the monthly rate is 10.9%.

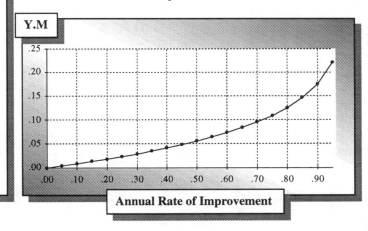

Annual Rate of Improvement

Computing the "Sigma" Value

Short-term data is free of assignable causes, thus it represents the effect of random causes only.

Long-term data reflects the influence of random causes as well as assignable phenomena.

If the yield or defect data were gathered over many intervals of production, consider the situation to be long-term; otherwise, assume it to be short-term.

FROM

	Short-Term	Long-Term
Short-Term	No Action	**+ 1.5σ**
TO		
Long-Term	**- 1.5σ**	No Action

Equations

$$P = \left[\left(1 + C_1 Z + C_2 Z^2 + \ldots + C_6 Z^6 \right)^{-16} \right] / 2$$

Constants

C1 = 0.0498673470
C2 = 0.0211410061
C3 = 0.0032776263
C4 = 0.0000380036
C5 = 0.0000488906
C6 = 0.0000053830

Equations

$$Z = \lambda - \frac{C_1 + C_2 \lambda + C_3 \lambda^2}{1 + C_4 \lambda + C_5 \lambda^2 + C_6 \lambda^3}$$

Notes:
1) Z and P are one-tailed
2) Z is the standard normal deviate
3) P is the tail area probability

$$\lambda = \sqrt{\ln \left(1 / P^2 \right)}$$

Constants

C1 = 2.515517
C2 = 0.802853
C3 = 0.010328
C4 = 1.432788
C5 = 0.189269
C6 = 0.000308

Creating a Benchmarking Chart

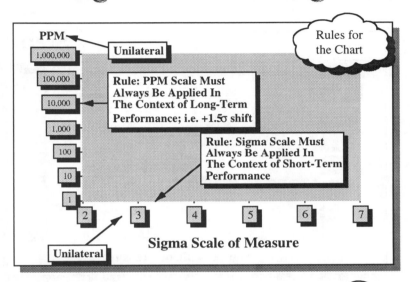

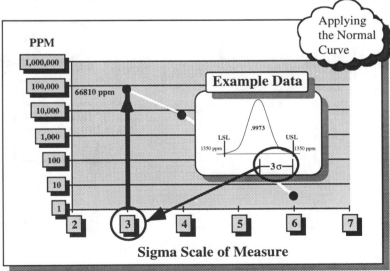

Creating a Benchmarking Chart

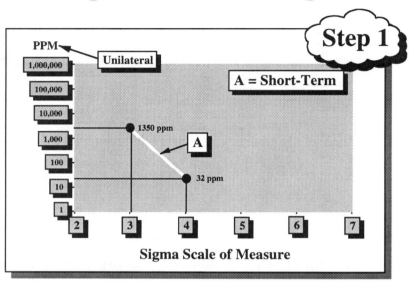

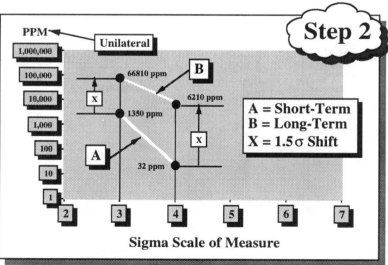

Creating a Benchmarking Chart

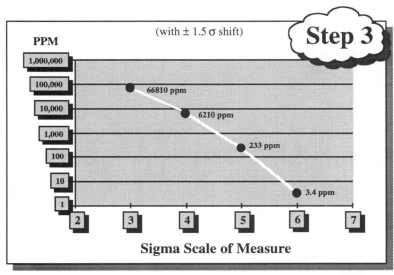

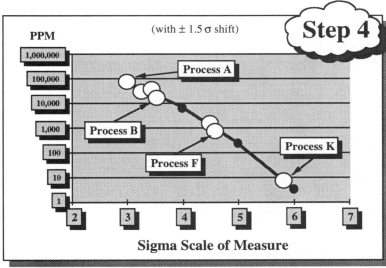

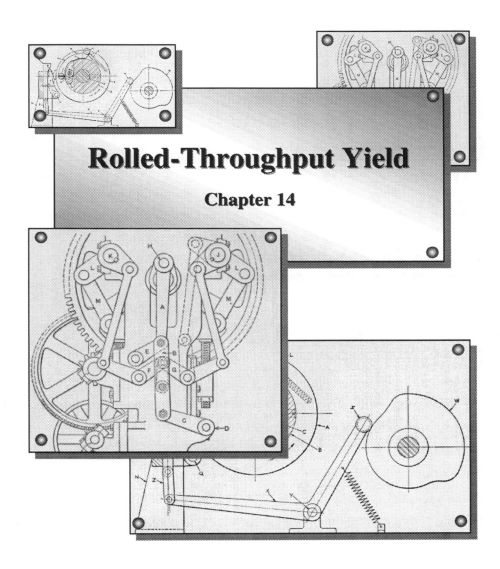

Rolled-Throughput Yield

Chapter 14

The Classical Perspective of Yield

$$Y_{FT} = \frac{S}{U}$$

Where:

$Y_{.FT}$ = First Time Yield
S = Number of Units that Pass
U = Number of Units Tested

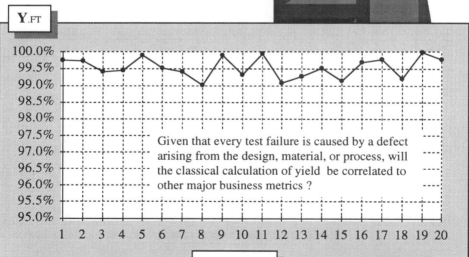

Given that every test failure is caused by a defect arising from the design, material, or process, will the classical calculation of yield be correlated to other major business metrics ?

Time Period

Questioning Basic Beliefs

Data: Jan 92 through Dec 92

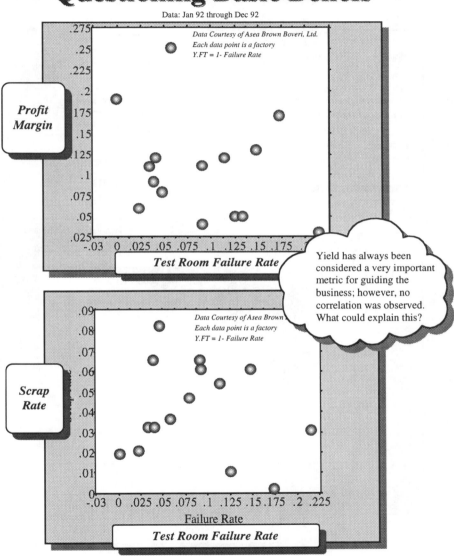

Profit Margin

.275
.25
.225
.2
.175
.15
.125
.1
.075
.05
.025

Data Courtesy of Asea Brown Boveri, Ltd.
Each data point is a factory
Y.FT = 1- Failure Rate

-.03 0 .025 .05 .075 .1 .125 .15 .175

Test Room Failure Rate

Yield has always been considered a very important metric for guiding the business; however, no correlation was observed. What could explain this?

Scrap Rate

.09
.08
.07
.06
.05
.04
.03
.02
.01
0

Data Courtesy of Asea Brown
Each data point is a factory
Y.FT = 1- Failure Rate

-.03 0 .025 .05 .075 .1 .125 .15 .175 .2 .225

Failure Rate

Test Room Failure Rate

14.3

The Dilemma of Classical Yield

. . . Obviously, there is a correlation between process capability and first-time yield. However, if we hold the process capability at a constant level, say 3.2σ, we observe that the first-time yield varies from about 92% to 100%. Why is this so? We also observe that this range decreases as the process capability improves. What is happening to cause this phenomenon?

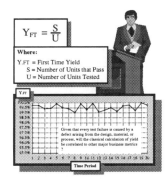

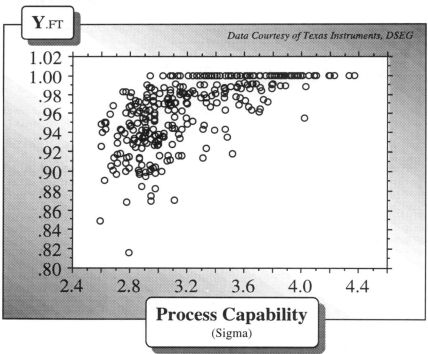

Data Courtesy of Texas Instruments, DSEG

Y.FT

Process Capability
(Sigma)

The Idea of Rolled-Throughput Yield

Suppose we say that there are 5 key characteristics which must be executed (without error) in order to successfully complete the event. In this case, what is the probability of accomplishing the task error free?

	3σ	6σ
Vision	.9973	.999999998
Hole	.9973	.999999998
Ball	.9973	.999999998
Reflexes	.9973	.999999998
Putter	.9973	.999999998
Rolled Yield	.9866	.999999990

Extension of the Application

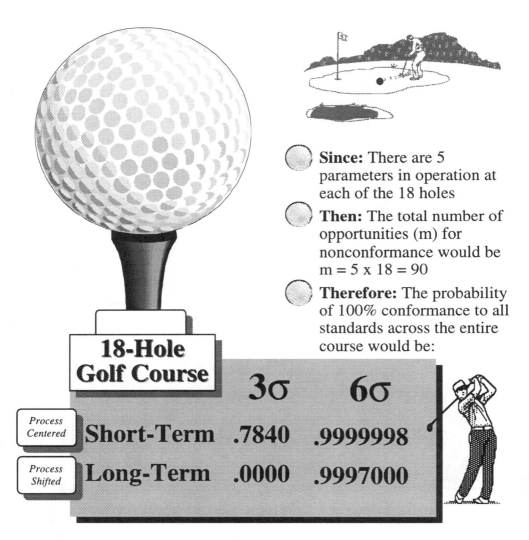

Since: There are 5 parameters in operation at each of the 18 holes

Then: The total number of opportunities (m) for nonconformance would be m = 5 x 18 = 90

Therefore: The probability of 100% conformance to all standards across the entire course would be:

18-Hole Golf Course

		3σ	6σ
Process Centered	**Short-Term**	.7840	.9999998
Process Shifted	**Long-Term**	.0000	.9997000

Comparison of the Yield Models

For Example:

$$Y_{FT} = \frac{S}{U} = \frac{90}{100} = .90, \text{ or } 90\%$$

$$Y_{TP} = e^{-DPU} = e^{-1.0} = .3679, \text{ or } 37\%$$

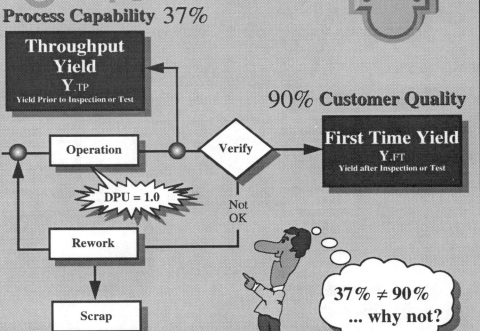

Process Capability 37%

Throughput Yield $Y_{.TP}$
Yield Prior to Inspection or Test

90% **Customer Quality**

First Time Yield $Y_{.FT}$
Yield after Inspection or Test

Operation

Verify

DPU = 1.0

Not OK

Rework

Scrap

37% ≠ 90%
... why not?

The Hidden Operation

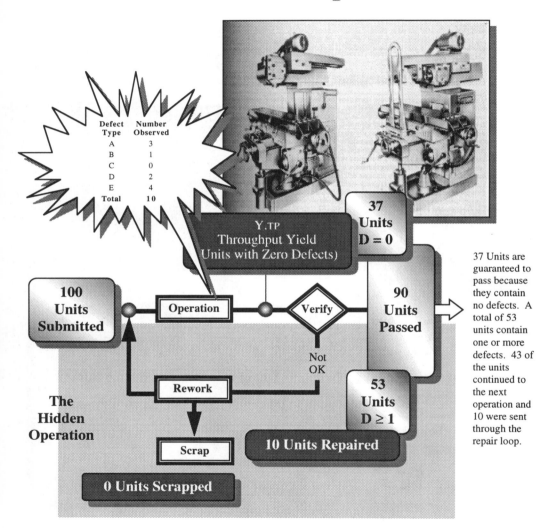

Defect Type	Number Observed
A	3
B	1
C	0
D	2
E	4
Total	**10**

$Y_{.TP}$
Throughput Yield
(Units with Zero Defects)

37 Units D = 0

100 Units Submitted

Operation

Verify

90 Units Passed

Not OK

Rework

The Hidden Operation

Scrap

53 Units D ≥ 1

10 Units Repaired

0 Units Scrapped

37 Units are guaranteed to pass because they contain no defects. A total of 53 units contain one or more defects. 43 of the units continued to the next operation and 10 were sent through the repair loop.

The Root of Defects

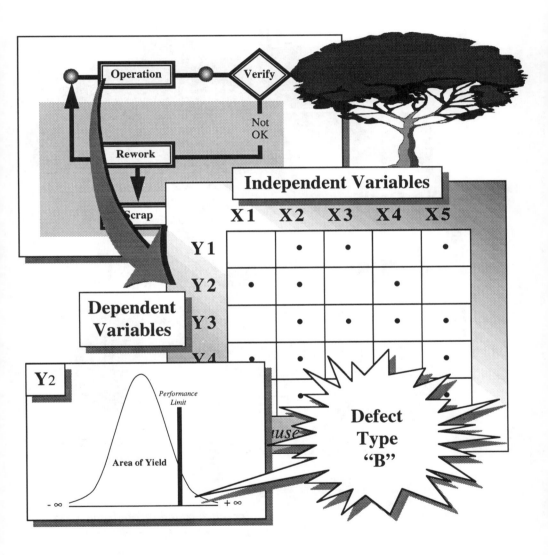

Operation → **Verify**

Not OK

Rework

Scrap

Independent Variables

Dependent Variables

Y2

Performance Limit

Area of Yield

- ∞   + ∞

Defect Type "B"

	X1	X2	X3	X4	X5
Y1		•	•		•
Y2	•	•		•	
Y3		•		•	•
Y4	•	•			•

A New Perspective of the Factory

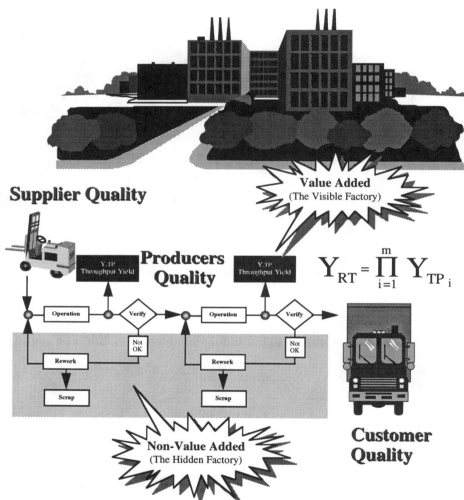

Supplier Quality

Value Added
(The Visible Factory)

Producers Quality

$$Y_{RT} = \prod_{i=1}^{m} Y_{TP_i}$$

Non-Value Added
(The Hidden Factory)

Customer Quality

To decrease defects-per-unit means to increase rolled through-put yield which, in turn, improves product reliability and customer satisfaction.

Extending the Concept

A given process has two operations. Each operation has a first-time yield of 99 percent. The rolled-throughput yield equals:

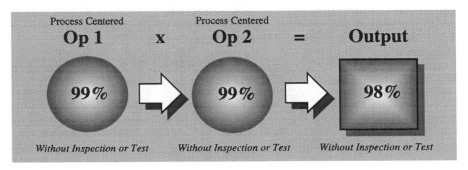

. . . There is an 98% probability that any given unit of product could pass through both operations defect free.

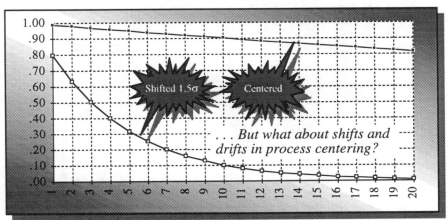

The Impact of Complexity

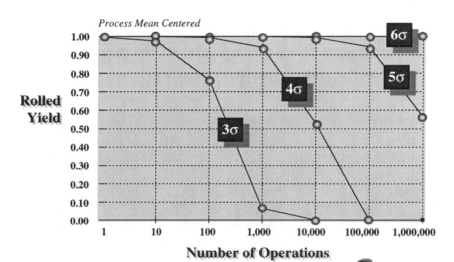

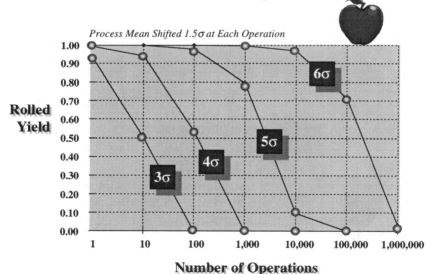

Chocolate Manufacturing Process

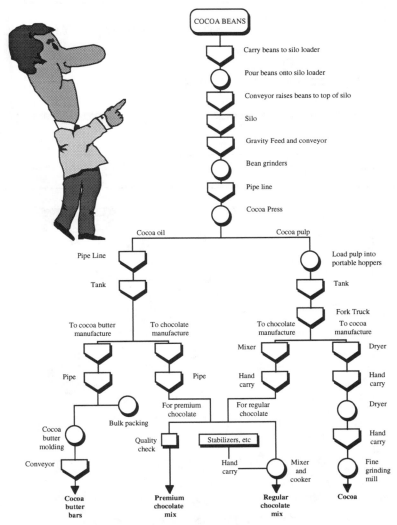

COCOA BEANS

Carry beans to silo loader

Pour beans onto silo loader

Conveyor raises beans to top of silo

Silo

Gravity Feed and conveyor

Bean grinders

Pipe line

Cocoa Press

Cocoa oil

Cocoa pulp

Pipe Line

Load pulp into portable hoppers

Tank

Tank

Fork Truck

To cocoa butter manufacture

To chocolate manufacture

To chocolate manufacture

To cocoa manufacture

Mixer

Dryer

Pipe

Pipe

Hand carry

Hand carry

Cocoa butter molding

Bulk packing

For premium chocolate

For regular chocolate

Dryer

Quality check

Stabilizers, etc

Hand carry

Conveyor

Hand carry

Mixer and cooker

Fine grinding mill

Cocoa butter bars

Premium chocolate mix

Regular chocolate mix

Cocoa

From Edward H. Bowman and Robert B. Fetter, Analysis for Production and Operations Management, 3rd Edition (Homewood, IL : Richard D. Irwin, Inc., 1961), pp. 38-39

Rolled-Throughput Yield Case Study

$$Y_{RT} = e^{-DPU} \quad \text{Rolled-Throughput Yield}$$

$$Y_{FT} = \frac{S}{U} \quad \text{Classical First-Time Yield}$$

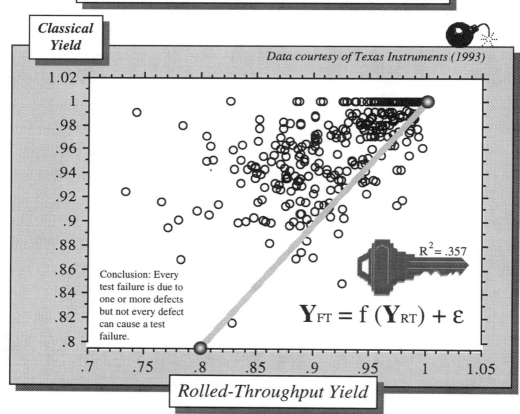

Classical Yield

Data courtesy of Texas Instruments (1993)

Conclusion: Every test failure is due to one or more defects but not every defect can cause a test failure.

$R^2 = .357$

$$Y_{FT} = f\left(Y_{RT}\right) + \varepsilon$$

Rolled-Throughput Yield

14.14

Improving Rolled-Throughput Yield

Which factor(s) should be the central focus of a sustained effort to improve the rolled-throughput yield of a typical manufacturing process?

Experimental Matrix

Complexity	Capability	Control	Rolled-Yield
500	4.0	1.00	.50893
1000	4.0	1.00	.25901
500	5.0	1.00	.98428
1000	5.0	1.00	.96881
500	4.0	1.50	.04440
1000	4.0	1.50	.00197
500	5.0	1.50	.89016
1000	5.0	1.50	.79239

Analysis of Variance Table

Source	df	Sum of Squares	Mean Square	F-Value	P-Value
Complexity	1	.02	.02	1.96	.3949
Capability	1	.99	.99	94.79	.0652
Control	1	.12	.12	11.72	.1809
Complexity * Capability	1	4.01E-3	4.01E-3	.38	.6476
Complexity * Control	1	1.96E-3	1.96E-3	.19	.7404
Capability * Control	1	.03	.03	2.42	.3636
	1	.01	.01		

nt: Rolled-Yield

$Y_{.RT}$

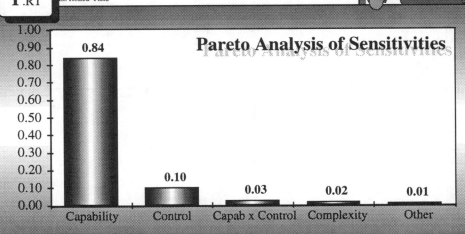

Pareto Analysis of Sensitivities

- Capability: 0.84
- Control: 0.10
- Capab x Control: 0.03
- Complexity: 0.02
- Other: 0.01

Understanding the Factor Effects

The ordinate of each graph corresponds to Rolled-Throughput Yield.

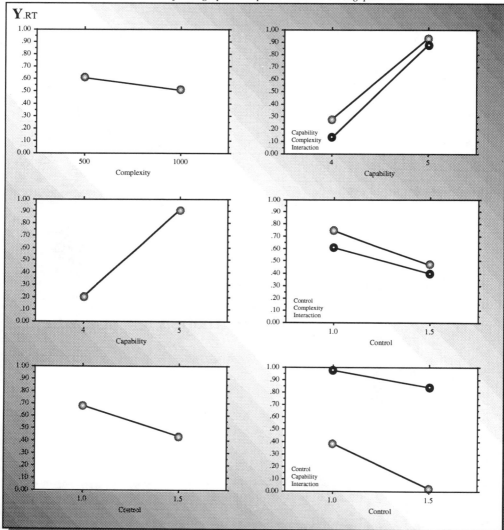

Simulation of a Typical Process

Note: One opportunity per operation

Ops = 1200

Short-Term
Process
Capability

Long-Term
Process
Centering

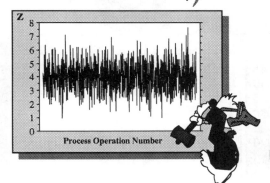

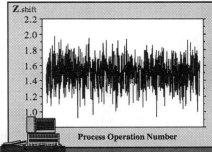

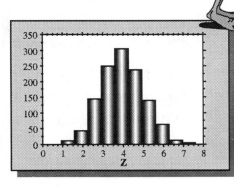

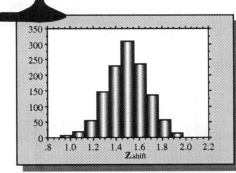

Results of Computer Simulation

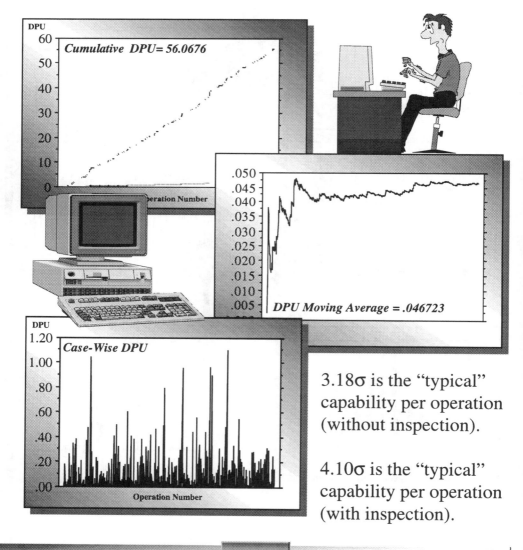

DPU

Cumulative DPU= 56.0676

Operation Number

DPU Moving Average = .046723

DPU

Case-Wise DPU

Operation Number

3.18σ is the "typical" capability per operation (without inspection).

4.10σ is the "typical" capability per operation (with inspection).

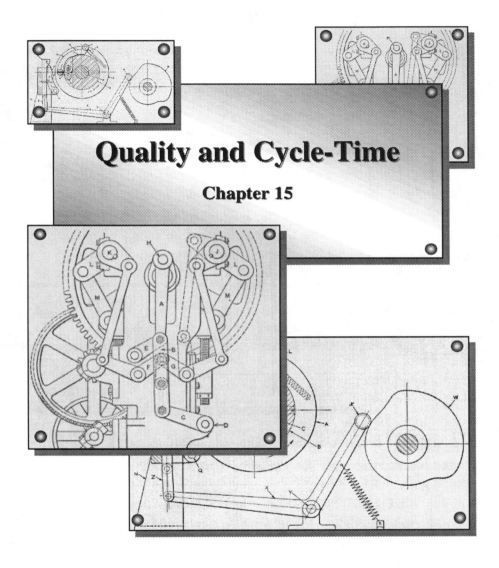

Quality and Cycle-Time

Chapter 15

The States of Cycle Time

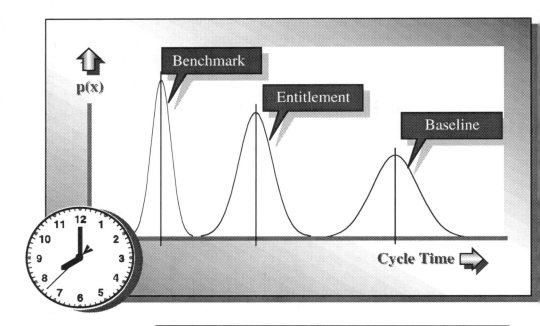

Benchmark: World-Class performance.

Baseline: The current level of performance.

Entitlement: The level of performance a business should be able to achieve given the investments already made.

Process Cycle Time Detractors

How do these things impact cycle time?

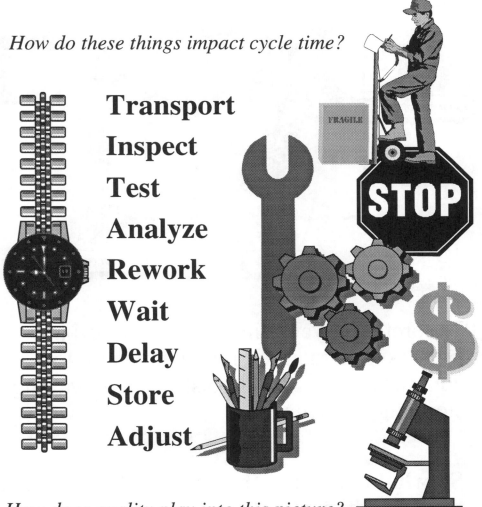

Transport

Inspect

Test

Analyze

Rework

Wait

Delay

Store

Adjust

FRAGILE

STOP

$

How does quality play into this picture?

Unmasking the Hidden Factory

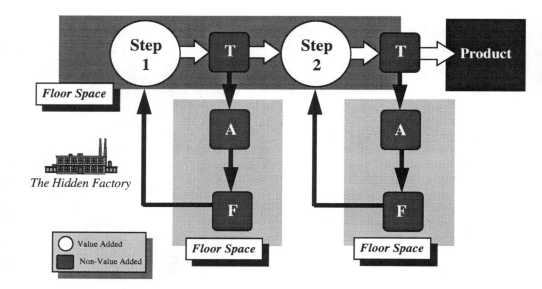

"Theoretical Cycle Time: The back-to-back process time required for a single unit to complete all stages of a task without waiting, stopping, or setups."

Philip R. Thomas, Competitiveness Through
Total Cycle Time. McGraw-Hill (1990)

So what can cause the baseline to be greater than the theoretical ?

How Capability Impacts Cycle-Time

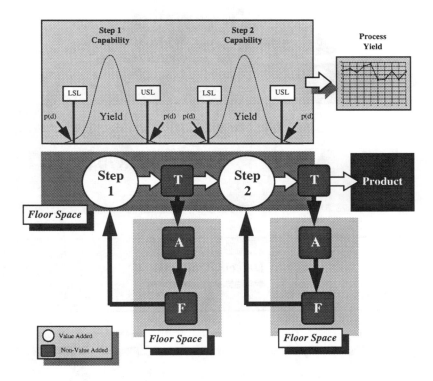

Every time a defect is created during the course of operating a process, it takes additional cycle-time to inspect and/or test (T), analyze (A), and repair/fix (F) the nonconformance. Most generally, this nonvalue added activity also requires capital equipment, material, people, and floor space. Naturally, as the defect rate increases, so does the cost.

Analysis of the Hidden Factory

Rolled-Throughput Yield:

$$Y_{RT} = e^{-DPU} = e^{-1} = .3678794$$

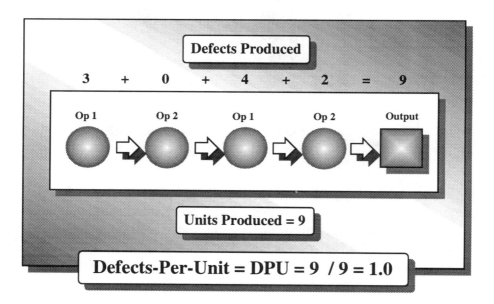

Defects Produced

$$3 \quad + \quad 0 \quad + \quad 4 \quad + \quad 2 \quad = \quad 9$$

Op 1   Op 2   Op 1   Op 2   Output

Units Produced = 9

Defects-Per-Unit = DPU = 9 / 9 = 1.0

Implications of the Hidden Factory

$$1 + \left(1 - e^{-1}\right) = 2 - .3679 = 1.6321$$

1.63 equivalent units must be produced to get out 1 good unit

Every occurrence of a defect within the manufacturing process requires time to verify, analyze, repair and re-verify.

$$T_{actual} = T_{min}\left[1 + \left(1 - e^{-DPU}\right)\right]$$

Average cycle time per unit is directly proportional to the total number of defects per unit.

$$T_{total} = T_{min} + (1)T_{insp} + (1)T_{test} + \left(1 - e^{-DPU}\right)T_{insp} + DPU\left(T_{test} + T_{analy} + T_{repair}\right) + T_{queue}$$

$$\text{Cycle Time}^* = \frac{\text{Work In Process}}{\text{Throughput}}$$

$$\text{WIP} = \text{Cycle Time} * \text{Throughput}$$

Little, J.D.C. (1961). *"A Proof for the Queueing Formula L=lW"* Operations Research. 9, 383-387

Quality and Cycle Time Data

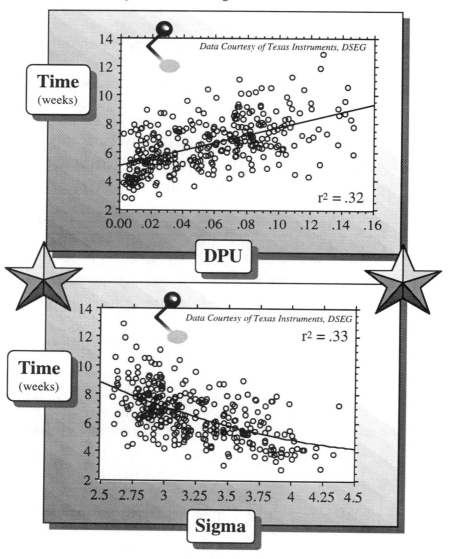

Quality and Cycle Time Data

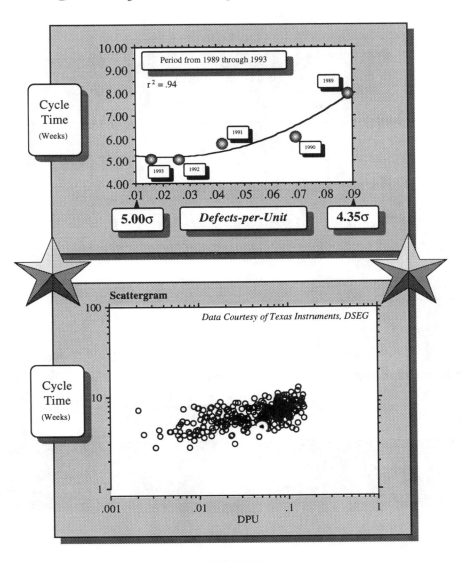

Inventory and Cycle-Time

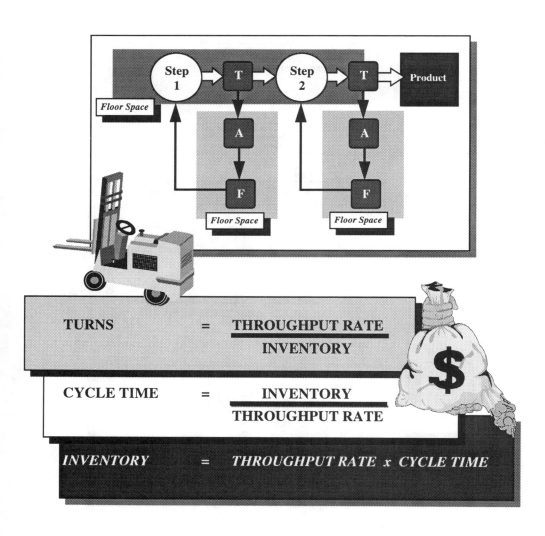

TURNS	=	THROUGHPUT RATE
		INVENTORY

CYCLE TIME	=	INVENTORY
		THROUGHPUT RATE

INVENTORY = *THROUGHPUT RATE x CYCLE TIME*

The Bottom Line Impact

In 1987, Motorola discovered that poor quality accounted for approximately 25% of their annual inventory carrying costs. Since this expense added no value, it was just like taking $250,000,000 and burning it . . . annually.

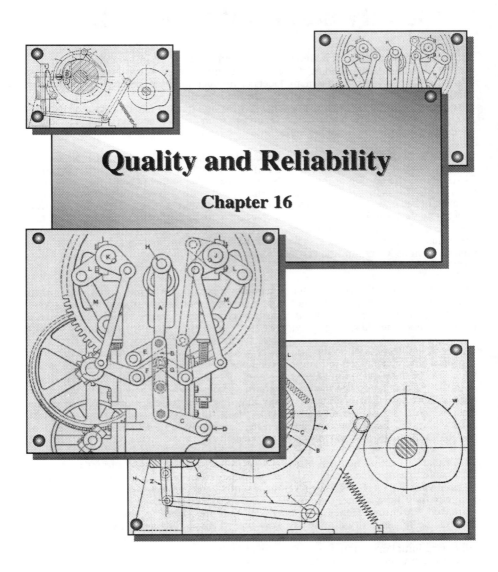

Quality and Reliability

Chapter 16

Quality and Product Reliability

As we know, producibility is inextricably linked to variation in a dynamic, synergistic fashion. From this vantage point, it is easy to see how variation is the principal determinant of product quality. In turn, the many facets of product quality either directly or indirectly contribute to the overall reliability of the end product. As a result of this domino relationship, we may say that the assurance of optimum product reliability is directly tied to an organization's ability to take a design concept from development on through production which, to a large extent, is tied to variation.

In order to better grasp such interconnectivity, let us consider the classical "bathtub" reliability curve. The bathtub curve is formed by the blending of three different curves. First, there is the portion of the bathtub effect that is due to the inherent characteristics of the design. This is to say that the engineering specifications define the performance limits for each of the individual elements that comprise the entire product. Given this, we would expect any design-related stress to be a constant across many units of product. This holds because each and every unit of product is subject to the same "engineering-imposed" performance limits. Therefore, the product failure rate, attributable to the design, would tend to form as a straight line across the graph, thereby forming the floor of the bathtub curve.

The second part of the curve is due to natural "wearout" of the individual elements that comprise the product. As one might expect, a part is more likely to display wear after an extended period of operation than after a short period; hence, the curve moves up across the graph. In short, the old saying "gravity prevails" holds true - all things eventually wear out.

The third and last curve on the graph is related to quality failures. Again, as one would expect, a newly manufactured unit of product is more likely to fail than a unit of product which has been operated for a moderate period of time. This phenomenon is primarily due to those defects that escape the manufacturing process. When a new unit of product fails after a short period of operation, we say that it was an "infant mortality," for obvious reasons. To avoid delivering such units to the customer, we perform what is typically called "burn-in." Each unit of product is tested, or otherwise "functionally exercised" for a period of time to get the "bad guys" out before delivery.

Given that inspection and test efficiency are relatively constant from unit to unit, it is reasonable to assert that escaping defects will increase as manufacturing, component, and material variation increases. Whenever the rate of escaping defects increases, we can expect a higher field failure rate, due to the weakened condition of product as a function of increased variation. Hence, we may say that the need for burn-in increases as manufacturing capability diminishes. However, if the initial capability of the processes, components, and material is high enough to ensure that any given unit of product will not fail during initial operation, there would be little, if any, need for test, inspection, or burn-in. Thus, a product could be manufactured and shipped without unnecessary delay and cost.

Obviously, the production of an exceptionally high quality product under such conditions significantly increases the likelihood of customer satisfaction and simultaneously decreases producer risk. At this point, the reader should fully recognize the synergistic link between process/component/ material variation, design producibility, product reliability, and production costs.

Thus far, we have determined that variation is the primary enemy of customer satisfaction. We have also reasoned that we must describe variation numerically if we are to study and ultimately improve the ease by which products are manufactured. In particular, we must be able to quantitatively assess variation with respect to design margins, material/component specifications, and process control/ capability. Only then can the issue of reliability be addressed in a practical and meaningful way. Again, if the producers cannot express what they know in numbers, control can not be exerted and, if control cannot be realized, the producer and customer are at the mercy of chance.

In light of the latter arguments, it may now be reasoned that the ability to forecast reliability is highly dependent upon a measure of the interplay within and between the design, manufacturing processes, and materiel. In addition, we may also say that the cost-effective optimization of reliability requires that we "design for producibility." This implies that the product designs will be relatively impervious or as some would say, "robust" to natural, unavoidable sources of process, component, and material variation. In turn, this assumes that we have a quantitative knowledge of process, component, and material capabilities.

As may be apparent, this suggests that we design products in the light of that variation which we know is inevitable rather than in the darkness of chance; hence, the need for the various Six Sigma initiatives presented in this book. It should go without saying that the synergistic effects of these initiatives react in such a fashion that the whole is far greater than the sum of the parts - no pun intended.

Understanding Reliability

Reliability is the probability of operating successfully for a predetermined amount of time.

$$P_s = R = e^{-t/\mu} = e^{-t\lambda}$$

Ps = R = probability of failure free operation for a time period equal to or greater than t.

t = a specified period of failure free operation

μ = mean time between failures, or MTBF

λ = failure rate (reciprocal of μ)

Example:

A particular product has demonstrated a MTBF of 8760 hours (1 year). Assuming a constant failure rate, the probability of failure free operation over any 24 hour interval is

$$P_s = R = e^{-24/8670} = .99724$$

MTBF is the average amount of time which elapses between successive failures. It is not the same as "operating life" or "service life" and does not connote overhaul or replacement time. An increase in MTBF does not result in a proportional increase in the probability of survival. Furthermore, the assumption of a constant failure rate is often considered reasonable for a great many applications. See Juran (1979).

Reliability and Confidence

$$P_s = R = e^{-t/\mu} = e^{-t\lambda}$$

Required MTBF	Required Reliability	Sigma Confidence
10	.9048374	2.8
100	.9900498	3.8
1,000	.9990005	4.6
10,000	.9999000	5.2
100,000	.9999900	5.8
1,000,000	.9999990	6.3

Table Includes 1.5σ Shift

This table displays the MTBF required to achieve various levels of reliability in the instance t = 1.0.

Capability and Reliability

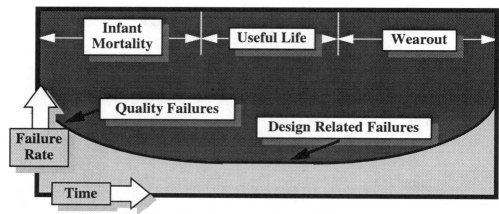

Each phase of reliability has a different "instantaneous failure rate." What could account for the differences?

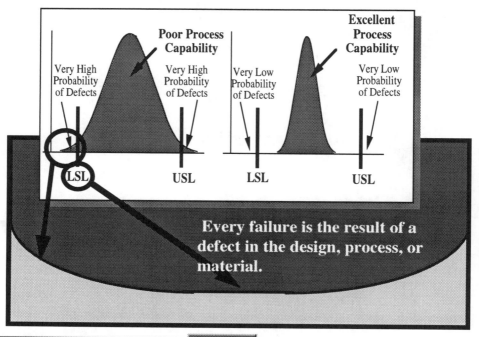

16 . 6

Reliability and Defect Abnormality

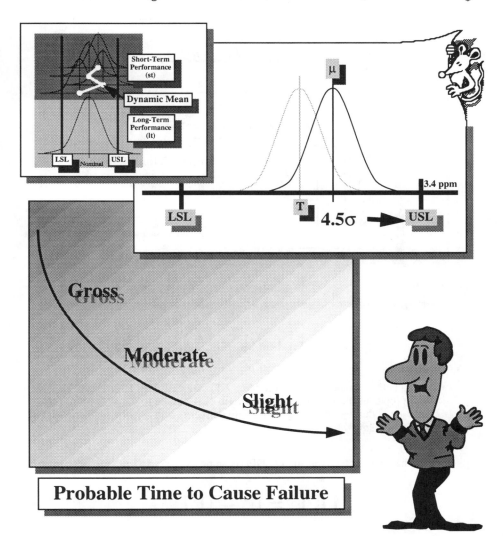

Short-Term Performance (st)

Dynamic Mean

Long-Term Performance (lt)

LSL   Nominal   USL

μ

3.4 ppm

LSL

T   4.5σ →   USL

Gross

Moderate

Slight

Probable Time to Cause Failure

Impact of Latent Defects

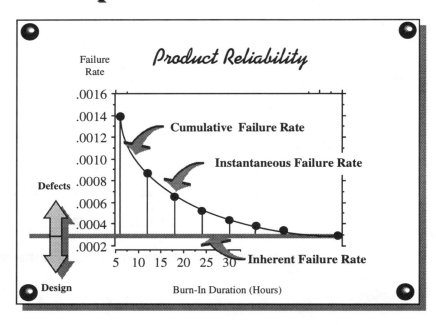

$$\lambda_i = \left[\, 1 + (k - 1)e^{-t/T}\right]\lambda_c$$

where λ_i is the instantaneous failure rate, λ_d is the delivered failure rate, λ_c is the inherent (constant) failure rate, k is the ratio of delivered to inherent failure rate (λ_d / λ_c), t is the real time (beginning with delivery), and T is the time constant of latent defect removal.

Thus, the latent defects-per-unit (LDPU) can be expressed as

$$LDPU = (k - 1)\, T\, \lambda_c$$

Note: The instantaneous failure rate is virtually impossible to measure directly. To overcome this limitation, adjust λ_c, k, and T until the cummulative failure "fits" the observed cummulative failure rate. This procedure may be accomplished using a chi-square goodness-of-fit test.
Reference: *Design for Manufacturability: Course Narrative.* Motorola (1986)

16 . 8

Comments on Latent Defects

❀ No test/inspection is 100% effective in finding defects.

❀ Delivered defects escape the test/inspection process within the factory.

❀ Delivered defects are directly proportional to the total defects found in the entire manufacturing process.

❀ Early life failures are the result of latent defects.

❀ Latent defects are controlled by the manufacturing process.

❀ Latent defects are directly proportional to the total defects found in the entire manufacturing process.

Reference: *Design for Manufacturability: Course Narrative.* Motorola (1986)

Comments on Latent Defects

❁ **A latent defect is some abnormal characteristic which, in all likelihood, will result in a failure.**

❁ **Such failures are dependent upon a) the degree of abnormality, b) the magnitude of applied stress, and c) the duration of applied stress.**

❁ **When corrected, the abnormal characteristic is returned to its normal state; hence, the apparent failure rate decreases.**

❁ **The failure rate continues to decrease until all latent defects have been discovered and corrected .**

Reference: *Design for Manufacturability: Course Narrative.* Motorola (1986)

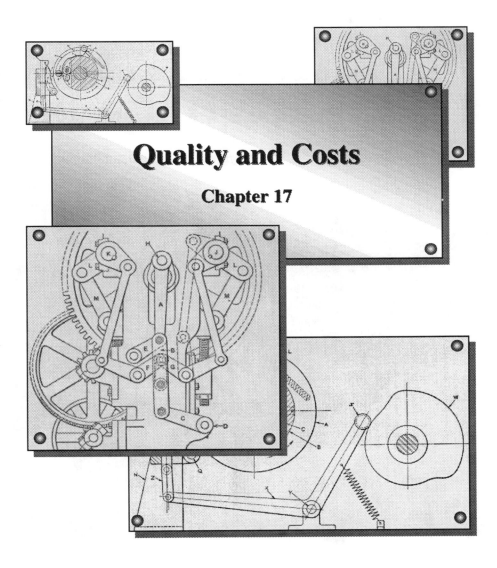

Quality and Costs

Chapter 17

The Proverbial Cash Farm

Six Sigma has shown that the Highest Quality Producer is the Lowest Cost Producer.

Understanding Quality Costs

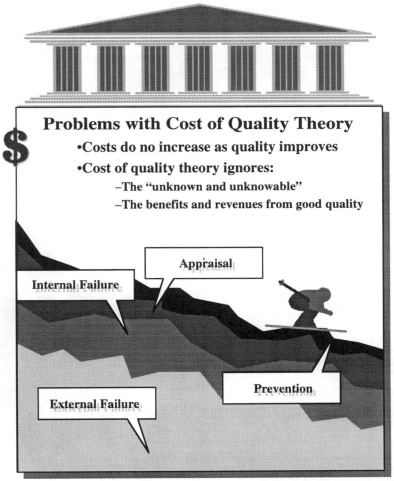

Problems with Cost of Quality Theory
- •Costs do no increase as quality improves
- •Cost of quality theory ignores:
  - –The "unknown and unknowable"
  - –The benefits and revenues from good quality

$

Appraisal

Internal Failure

Prevention

External Failure

Time ⟹

Cost of Quality Categories

	Month Total	Month Percent	Year Total	Year Percent
Prevention Costs				
Quality Administration				
Quality Engineering				
Reliability Engineering				
Training				
Total Prevention				
Appraisal Costs				
Inspection				
Test				
Vendor Control				
Measurement Control				
Materials Consumed				
Quality Audits				
Total Appraisal				
Internal Failure Costs				
Scrap				
Repair and Rework				
Vendor Losses				
Failure Analysis				
Total Internal				
External Failure Costs				
Failures - Manufacturing				
Failures - Engineering				
Failure - Sales				
Warranty Charges				
Failure Analysis				
Total External				
Total Quality Cost				
Bases				
Direct Labor				
Conversion Cost				
Sales				
Ratios				
Internal to Direct				
Internal to Conversion				
Total to Sales				

Adapted From: Juran, J. Quality Control Handbook (1979). 3rd Edition. McGraw-Hill Book Company

Cost of Nonconformance

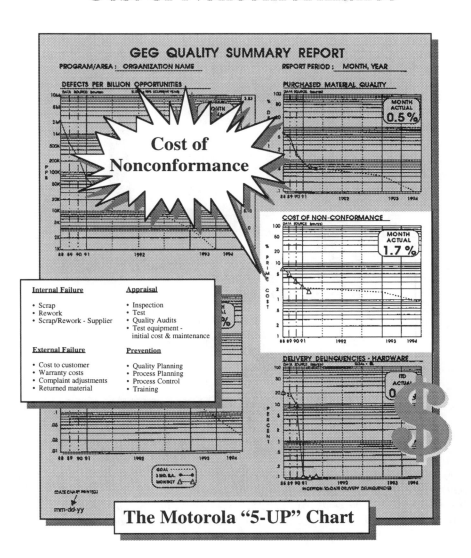

Computing Cost of Quality

$$COQ = \frac{(MS + LS + RC) + (PC + AP)}{TMC}$$

COQ	Cost of Quality
MS	Material Scrap
LS	Labor Scrap
RC	Rework Cost
PC	Prevention Cost
AC	Appraisal Cost

Internal Failure

- Scrap
- Rework
- Scrap/Rework - Supplier

External Failure

- Cost to customer
- Warranty costs
- Complaint adjustments
- Returned material

Appraisal

- Inspection
- Test
- Quality Audits
- Test equipment - initial cost & maintenance

Prevention

- Quality Planning
- Process Planning
- Process Control
- Training

Note: The listed categories provides an understanding of the COQ structure. In general, COQ is comprised of costs due to failure, appraisal, and prevention.

Owing to different methods of cost accounting and organization, there are several ways to compute cost-of-quality. The given example illustrates a typical method. As with most performance metrics, the emphasis should be on the rate of improvement, not the absolute value. This can not be over emphasized. The central problem is not one of identifying what costs should be included, but what costs should be excluded.

Results of Sustained Improvement

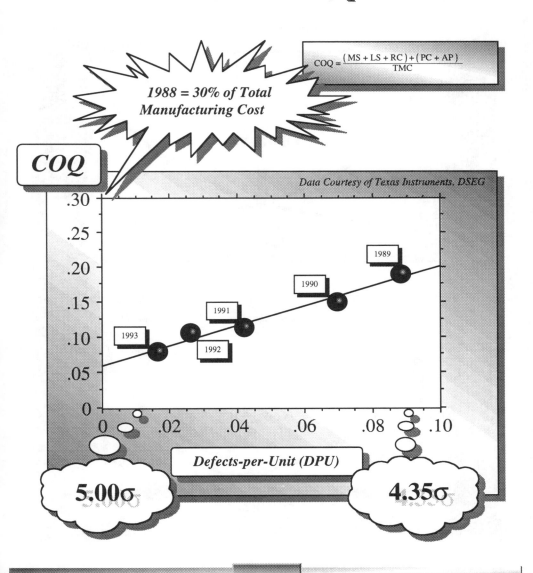

$$COQ = \frac{(MS + LS + RC) + (PC + AP)}{TMC}$$

1988 = 30% of Total Manufacturing Cost

COQ

Data Courtesy of Texas Instruments, DSEG

Defects-per-Unit (DPU)

5.00σ   4.35σ

The Enlightened Perspective

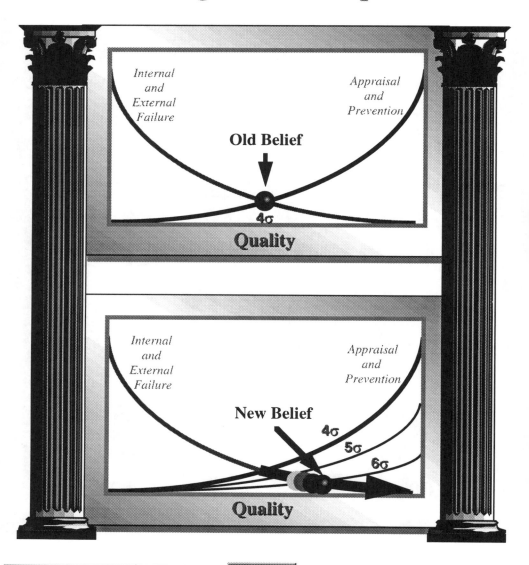

The Cost of Remaining Average

Waste as a proportion of total sales revenue

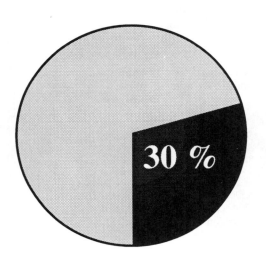

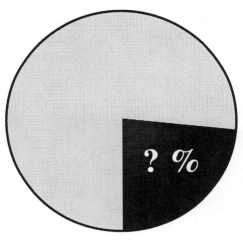

Typical Company   Your Area?

Evolving the Use of Quality Costs

Phase ⇨

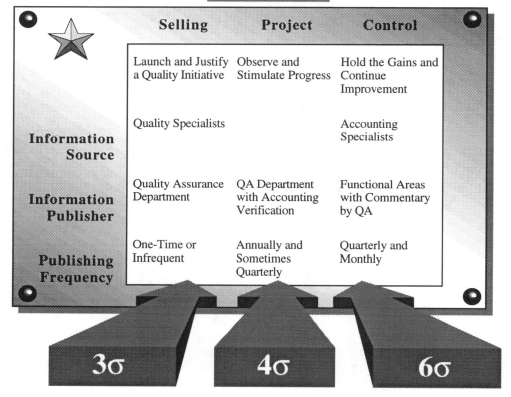

	Selling	Project	Control
	Launch and Justify a Quality Initiative	Observe and Stimulate Progress	Hold the Gains and Continue Improvement
Information Source	Quality Specialists		Accounting Specialists
Information Publisher	Quality Assurance Department	QA Department with Accounting Verification	Functional Areas with Commentary by QA
Publishing Frequency	One-Time or Infrequent	Annually and Sometimes Quarterly	Quarterly and Monthly

3σ   4σ   6σ

Adapted From: Juran, J. Quality Control Handbook (1979). 3rd Edition. McGraw-Hill Book Company

Impact of Variation on Cost

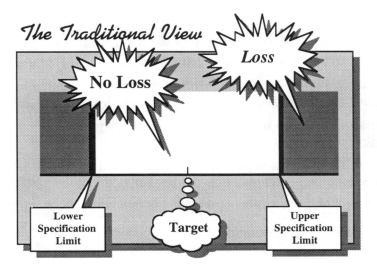

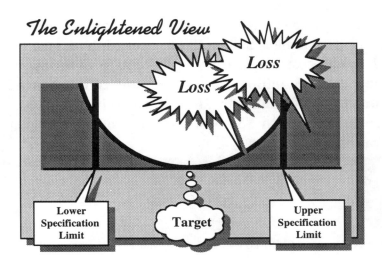

17 . 11

Reasons for Improving Quality

$ Businesses which have achieved significant quality improvement earn 8% higher prices

$ Businesses who achieve a superior quality position are 3X more profitable as those with inferior levels of quality

$ Businesses who improved their quality gained 4% market share per year

$ Each significant positive shift in process capability equates to a 10X improvement in profitability

Facts from the PIMS Data Survey in 1992 and the US Government General Accounting Office Report of 1991

For many companies, cost of quality accounts for more than 40% sales price [1]. Assume that a company's annual operating revenue is $100 million, operating income is $10 million, and cost of quality is equal to 25% of the operating revenue, or $25 million. If this company could reduce its assumed cost of quality by 20%, it would increase its operating income by $5 million, or 50% of the current operation income.

AT&T Cost of Quality Guideline
Published 1990

[1] H. James Harrington. 1987 Poor-Quality Cost. Marcel Dekker, Inc. ASQC Quality Press

Reasons for Improving Quality

For the most part, we have met our goals of 10-times improvement by 1989 and 100-times improvement by 1991. At several Motorola facilities, we even exceeded Six Sigma capability in some products and processes. On average, however, our manufacturing operations are at about 5.4 Sigma capability, or 40 ppm - - somewhat short of our original goal. Nonetheless, we have made very significant progress in improving the quality level of our products and services.

In getting to 5.4 Sigma capability, we have reduced our in-process defect level by 150 times during the five-year period. We have improved the reliability of the products we ship to customers. And, we have saved a significant amount of the cost of manufacturing - - $700 million during 1991 and $2.4 billion since the beginning of our Six Sigma thrust. In addition, we have achieved a number of significant improvements in our administrative functions by applying the Six Sigma methodology there as well.

George Fisher
CEO & Chairman of the Board
Motorola Inc.

Results of Quality Improvement

Six Sigma has shown that the Highest Quality Producer is the Lowest Cost Producer

$

Actual Savings Over

$US 2.2 Billion

1987, 1988, 1989, 1990, 1991

$1 Billion

Savings Potential in non-manufacturing costs

A Focus on Total Defects Per Unit

$ Reduces the *cycle time per unit*

$ Reduces WIP *inventory carrying costs*

$ Reduces *delivered defects*

$ Reduces *early life failure rate*

$ Reduces *defect analysis and repair cost per unit*

. . . Higher Quality, Lower Cost, On Time
. . . Increases *Customer Satisfaction*

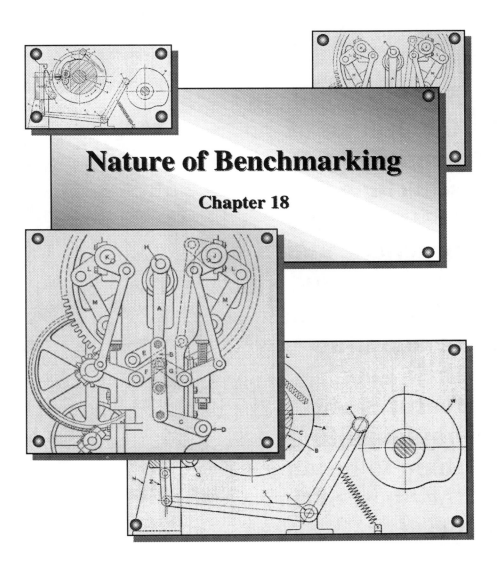

Nature of Benchmarking

Chapter 18

Nature of Benchmarking

Benchmarking is the process of continually searching for the best methods, practices, and processes and either adopting or adapting their good features and implementing them to become the "best of the best"

Types of Benchmarking

Competitive Benchmarking

Product Benchmarking

Process Benchmarking

Best Practices Benchmarking

Strategic Benchmarking

Parameter Benchmarking

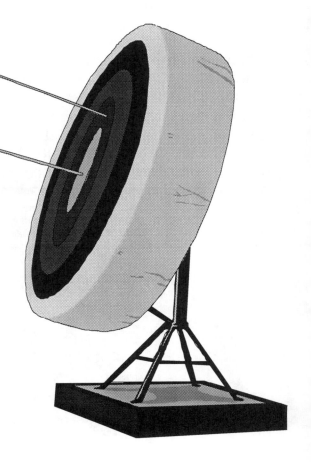

Understanding Benchmarking

Benchmarking is not industrial tourism.

It represents a tool for the identification best practices.
It is an effective TQM approach for guiding improvement.
It is a formalized way to manage change.
It helps determine the most important things to improve.
It helps determine the best approach to use.
It establishes best practices.
It is not a magical solution to problems.
It is not a one time program that's used and then forgotten.
It is not a single person activity that can be done alone.
It is not competitive intelligence or market research.

Benchmarking is not operating in a, "doing business as usual," manner. No matter how big a lead a company has today, doing business as usual can result in a future business decline. Benchmarking is not a task that is delegated to others. It requires commitment and involvement in all phases. It is a "way" of doing business. It is a key part of the breakthrough strategy.

"If I have seen further, it is because I have stood of the shoulders of giants" Sir Isaac Newton

Concept Versus Process

Benchmarking is *simple as a concept* but much more *involved as a process.* The Ultimate payoff is that you can become the best of what you do, and continuously improve upon that superiority.

Benchmarking is a means of identifying best practices and using this knowledge to continuously improve our products, services, and systems so that we increase our capability to provide total customer satisfaction.

Benchmarking ensures that best practices from competitors or best-in-class companies will be identified. These in turn will point the way to needed improvements. It can help locate new techniques and technologies that are used by best-in-class companies, whether they are competitors or non-competitors.

Benchmarking will help a company to realize the value of having a marketing focus rather than strictly an internal one

Benchmarking is a continuous process of measuring products, services, and practices against the toughest competitors and/or those companies renowned as the leaders.

Benchmarking is a process used to identify, establish, and achieve standards of excellence, standards based on the realities of the marketplace. It is a process to be used to manage on a continuous basis.

Benchmarking draws upon the integration of competitive information, practices, and performance into the decision-making and communication functions at all levels of the business.

The Step-Wise Progression

Select Benchmark Topic
Estimate Cost of The Study
Make Decision to Continue
Select Benchmark Team
Train Benchmark Team
Select Key Metrics
Select Survey Type
Develop Questions
Develop Data Collection Devices
Test Data Analysis Methods
Perform Self Analysis
Identify Companies and Contacts
Collect Public Domain Data
Analyze Public Domain Data
Formulate Benchmark Plan
Conduct Benchmark Study
Analyze Information and Data
Conduct Gap Analysis
Develop Recommendations
Develop Implementation Plan
Identify Support Departments
Present Plans to Management
Present to Support Departments
Implement and Monitor Progress
Recalibrate Market

Sources of Information

Library Data Base

Internal Reviews

Internal Publications

Professional Associations

Industry Publications

Special Industry Reports

Functional Trade Publications

Seminars

Industry Data Firms

Industry Experts

University Sources

Company Watches

Newspapers

Advertisements

Newsletters

Original Research

Customer Feedback

Supplier Feedback

Telephone Surveys

Inquiry Service

Networks

Benchmarking Checklist

❏ Why should we use benchmarking?

❏ How will benchmarking improve performance?

❏ What are the objectives of the benchmarking study?

❏ Who will be the stakeholders in the benchmarking study?

❏ Have they been informed about the study and the objectives?

❏ How do you measure your own performance?

❏ Are internal measurements available, or can they be calculated?

❏ Can companies be compared against internal measurements?

❏ Have you studied the performance of your own operations?

❏ What competitors should be studied? Who is the best?

❏ Are direct competitors the most appropriate to be studied?

❏ Are these leaders in unrelated industries?

❏ How can competitive information be obtained?

❏ Would information on other company groups be appropriate?

Host Checklist

❏ **Notify benchmarking champion of the request**

❏ **Request a copy of the questions to be addressed**

❏ **Gather appropriate personnel to answer questions**

❏ **Agree to fully document answers**

❏ **Assign roles and responsibilities during visit**

❏ **Prepare an agenda**

❏ **If time allows, plan tours to enhance understanding**

❏ **Prepare a list of actions items following the session**

❏ **Prepare a final document of the session**

Example Benchmarking Outcome

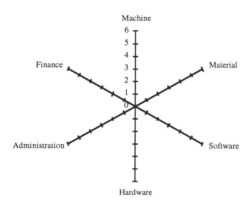

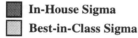

■ **In-House Sigma**
□ **Best-in-Class Sigma**

The example spider charts make use of the "sigma scale of measure." Other metrics may be employed; however, the sigma scale maintains a level-playing-field, so to speak. From this perspective, dissimilar things can be readily compared.

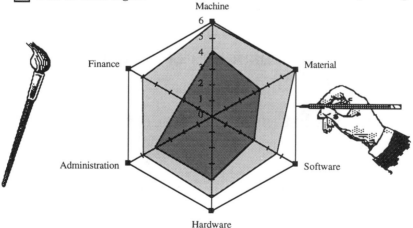

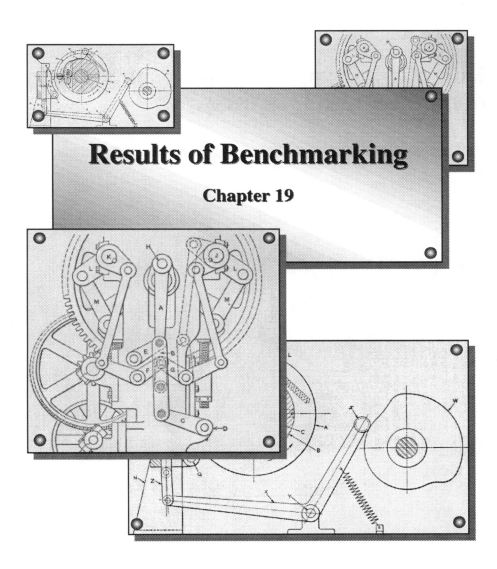

Results of Benchmarking

Chapter 19

World's Best View

How often do you use process simplification to improve business processes?

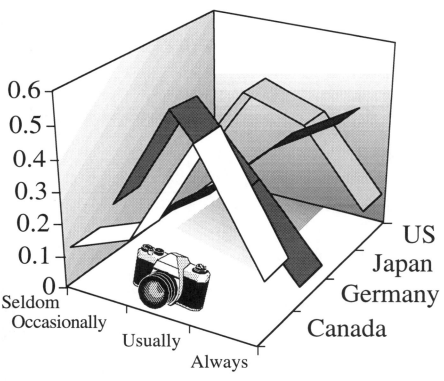

Source of Data Unknown (Observed from Presentation Slides)

A Practical Benchmarking Example
Part A

Process Step	First Yield	Step Sigma	Rolled Yield	Norm Yield	Norm Sigma
1	.9963	4.18	.9963	.9963	4.18
2	.9986	4.50	.9950	.9975	4.30
3	.9999	5.21	.9948	.9983	4.43
4	.9796	3.55	.9746	.9936	3.99
5	.9980	4.37	.9726	.9945	4.04
6	.9993	4.71	.9719	.9953	4.09
7	.9978	4.34	.9697	.9956	4.12
8	.9999	5.14	.9696	.9962	4.16
9	.9886	3.78	.9586	.9953	4.10
10	.9816	3.59	.9410	.9939	4.01
11	.9988	4.53	.9398	.9944	4.03
12	.9947	4.06	.9348	.9944	4.04
13	.9987	4.51	.9336	.9947	4.06
14	.9919	3.90	.9261	.9945	4.04
15	.9968	4.23	.9231	.9947	4.05
16	.9977	4.34	.9210	.9949	4.07
17	.9994	4.72	.9204	.9951	4.09
18	.9986	4.49	.9191	.9953	4.10
19	.9724	3.42	.8937	.9941	4.02
20	.9907	3.85	.8854	.9939	4.01

A Practical Benchmarking Example
Part B

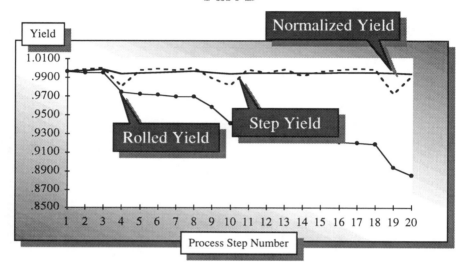

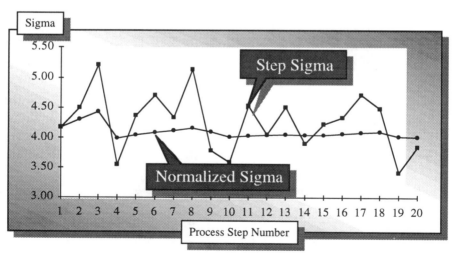

Benchmarking Data: Case 1

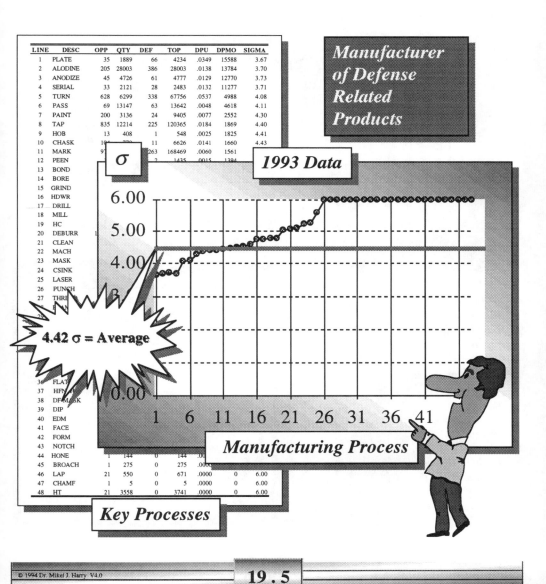

LINE	DESC	OPP	QTY	DEF	TOP	DPU	DPMO	SIGMA
1	PLATE	35	1889	66	4234	.0349	15588	3.67
2	ALODINE	205	28003	386	28003	.0138	13784	3.70
3	ANODIZE	45	4726	61	4777	.0129	12770	3.73
4	SERIAL	33	2121	28	2483	.0132	11277	3.71
5	TURN	628	6299	338	67756	.0537	4988	4.08
6	PASS	69	13147	63	13642	.0048	4618	4.11
7	PAINT	200	3136	24	9405	.0077	2552	4.30
8	TAP	835	12214	225	120365	.0184	1869	4.40
9	HOB	13	408	1	548	.0025	1825	4.41
10	CHASK	10	779	11	6626	.0141	1660	4.43
11	MARK	9		263	168469	.0060	1561	
12	PEEN			2	1435	.0015	1394	
13	BOND							
14	BORE							
15	GRIND							
16	HDWR							
17	DRILL							
18	MILL							
19	HC							
20	DEBURR							
21	CLEAN							
22	MACH							
23	MASK							
24	CSINK							
25	LASER							
26	PUNCH							
27	THRE							
36	FLAT							
37	HF							
38	DFMASK							
39	DIP							
40	EDM							
41	FACE							
42	FORM							
43	NOTCH							
44	HONE	1	144	0	144	.0000		
45	BROACH	1	275	0	275	.0000		
46	LAP	21	550	0	671	.0000	0	6.00
47	CHAMF	1	5	0	5	.0000	0	6.00
48	HT	21	3558	0	3741	.0000	0	6.00

Manufacturer of Defense Related Products

σ

1993 Data

6.00
5.00
4.00

4.42 σ = Average

0.00

1   6   11   16   21   26   31   36   41

Manufacturing Process

Key Processes

19 . 5

Case Study Data

Note: The capability data displayed in the histograms was gathered across more than 30 factories in Germany, Sweden, Italy, and the United States. Consequently, it may be considered representative of the total business.

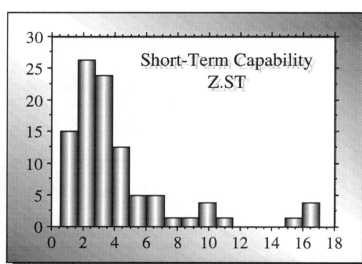

Note: The histograms were based solely on continuous data. All necessary precautions were made to guard against measurement error and other sources of error which might have severely contaminated the data

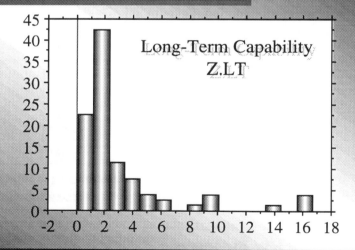

Benchmarking Data: Case 2

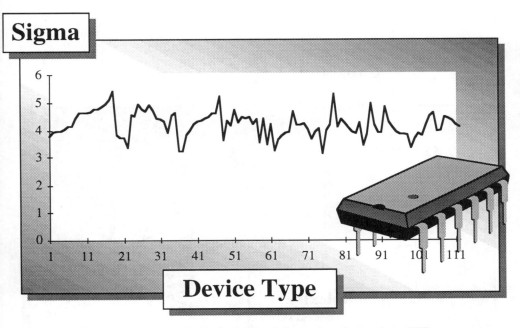

Sigma

Device Type

Source: Reliability and Quality Handbook: Motorola Semiconductor Products Sector (1987)

The Benchmarking Chart

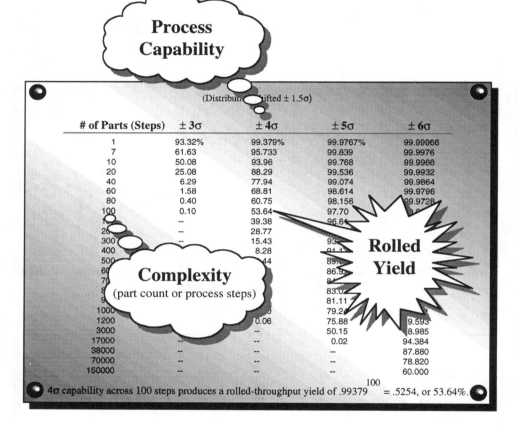

4σ capability across 100 steps produces a rolled-throughput yield of .99379^{100} = .5254, or 53.64%.

If you do what you did, you will get what you got. . . .
So don't ask for what you got, but for what you should get.

Benchmarking Products

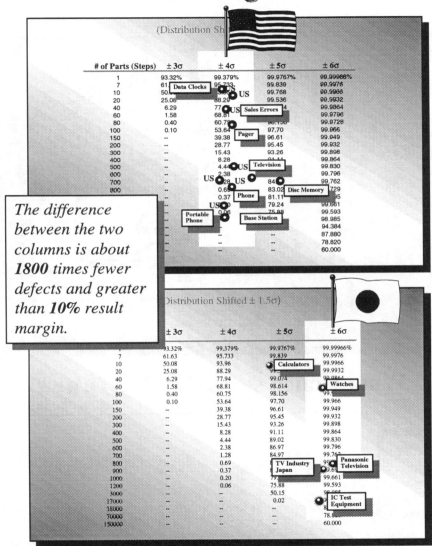

The difference between the two columns is about **1800** times fewer defects and greater than **10%** result margin.

Typical Capability in the US

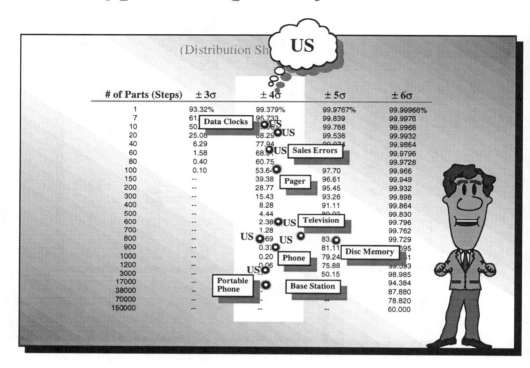

(Distribution Shi... **US**

# of Parts (Steps)	± 3σ	± 4σ	± 5σ	± 6σ
1	93.32%	99.379%	99.9767%	99.99968%
7	61... **Data Clocks**	95.733	99.839	99.9978
10	50... **US**	99.768	99.9966
20	25.06	68.29 **US**	99.536	99.9932
40	6.29	77.94	99.074	99.9864
60	1.58	68.5 **US** **Sales Errors**	99.769	99.9796
80	0.40	60.75	99.7728
100	0.10	53.64	97.70	99.966
150	--	39.38 **Pager**	96.61	99.949
200	--	28.77	95.45	99.932
300	--	15.43	93.26	99.898
400	--	8.28	91.11	99.864
500	--	4.44	99.02	99.830
600	--	2.38 **US** **Television**	99.796
700	--	1.28	99.762
800	**US** .69 **US**	83	99.729
900	--	0.37	81.11 **Disc Memory**	95
1000	--	0.20 **Phone**	79.24	1
1200	--	0.06	75.88	99.593
3000	--	**US**	50.15	98.985
17000	--	**Portable Phone**	**Base Station**	94.384
38000	--			87.880
70000	--			78.820
150000	--	--	--	60.000

What Conclusions Can We Draw?

Typical Capability in Europe

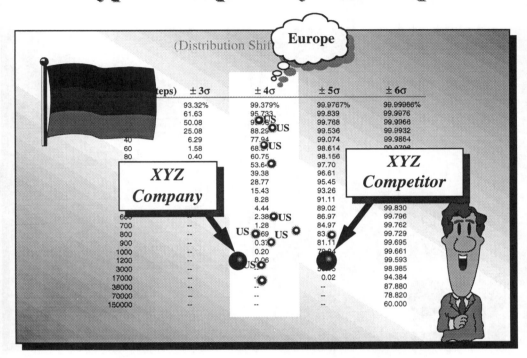

What Conclusions Can We Draw?

Best-in-Class Capability

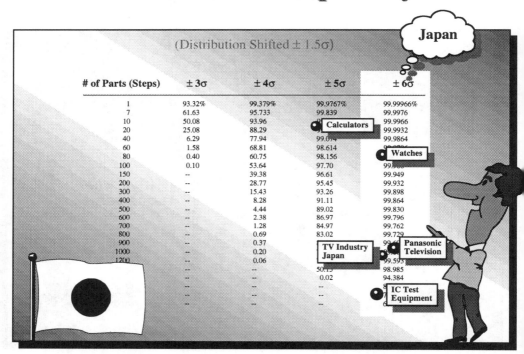

(Distribution Shifted ± 1.5σ)

Japan

# of Parts (Steps)	± 3σ	± 4σ	± 5σ	± 6σ
1	93.32%	99.379%	99.9767%	99.99966%
7	61.63	95.733	99.839	99.9976
10	50.08	93.96		99.9966
20	25.08	88.29		99.9932
40	6.29	77.94	99.0-4	99.9864
60	1.58	68.81	98.614	
80	0.40	60.75	98.156	
100	0.10	53.64	97.70	99.
150	--	39.38	96.61	99.949
200	--	28.77	95.45	99.932
300	--	15.43	93.26	99.898
400	--	8.28	91.11	99.864
500	--	4.44	89.02	99.830
600	--	2.38	86.97	99.796
700	--	1.28	84.97	99.762
800	--	0.69	83.02	99.729
900	--	0.37		99.
1000	--	0.20		99.593
1200	--	0.06		98.985
	--	--	50.15	94.384
	--	--	0.02	
	--	--	--	8
	--	--	--	6

Calculators

Watches

TV Industry
Japan

Panasonic
Television

IC Test
Equipment

What Conclusions Can We Draw?

Macro-Level Benchmarking

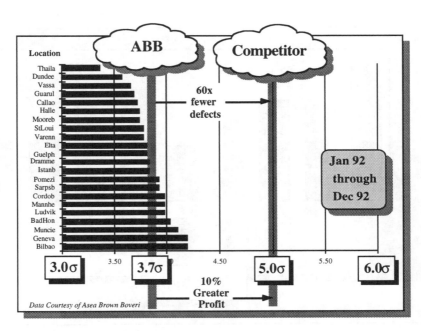

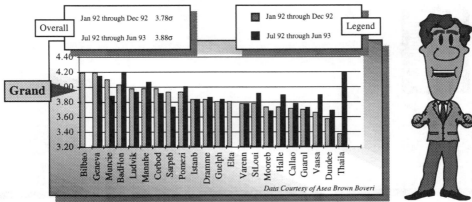

Sigma's for Supplier Performance

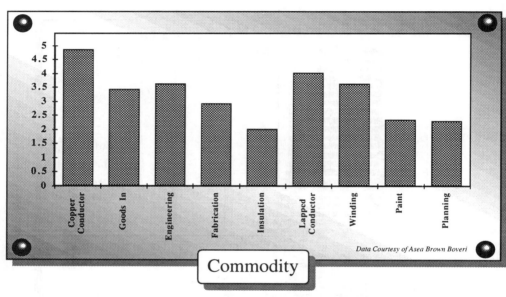

Data Courtesy of Asea Brown Boveri

Commodity

Quality of Engineering Drawings

Report Name												
Organization				Baseline Period	From	Dec'92	To Dec'93					
Project				Improvement Goal	From		To					
Department			*Demographic*	Unit Definition								
Deliverable			*Information*	Characteristic								
Deliverable ID				Units of Measure								
Process				Upper Specification								
Step				Target Value								
Machine ID				Lower Specification								
Special Note				Default Shift	1.50							

Line	Desp.	Contract	Description	D	U	OP	TOP	DPU	DPO	DPMO	Shift	Z.B
1	02-93	910019		2	1	659	659	2	0.0030	3,035	1.50	4.24
2	05-93	910062		8	1	544	544	8	0.0147	14,706	1.50	3.68
3	05-93	910063	*Data Courtesy of Asea Brown Boveri*	5	1	544	544	5	0.0092	9,191	1.50	3.86
4	07-93	910069		5	1	659	659	5	0.0076	7,587	1.50	3.93
5	03-93	910070		14	1	659	659	14	0.0212	21,244	1.50	3.53
6	06-92	910082		1	1	544	544	1	0.0018	1,838	1.50	4.41
7	09-92	910091		1	1	544	544	1	0.0018	1,838	1.50	4.41
8	01-93	910092		1	1	544	544	1	0.0018	1,838	1.50	4.41
9	01-93	910093		1	1	544	544	1	0.0018	1,838	1.50	4.41
10	01-93	910109		4	1	544	544	4	0.0074	7,353	1.50	3.94
11	04-93	920006		17	1	481	481	17	0.0353	35,343	1.50	3.31
12	04-93	920007		1	1	481	481	1	0.0021	2,079	1.50	4.37
13	12-92	920009		1	1	481	481	1	0.0021	2,079	1.50	4.37
14	07-93	920012		8	1	544	544	8	0.0147	14,706	1.50	3.68
15	07-93	920013		6	1	544	544	6	0.0110	11,029	1.50	3.79
16	04-93	920017		19	1	544	544	19	0.0349	34,926	1.50	3.31
17	07-93	920018		10	1	544	544	10	0.0184	18,382	1.50	3.59
18	02-93	920032		6	1	481	481	6	0.0125	12,474	1.50	3.74
19	02-93	920033		0	1	481	481	0	0.0000	0	1.50	6.00
20	04-93	920038		29	1	481	481	29	0.0603	60,291	1.50	3.05
21	12-93	920050		38	1	659	659	38	0.0577	57,663	1.50	3.08
22	09-93	920056		32	1	659	659	32	0.0486	48,558	1.50	3.16
23	09-93	920063		19	1	500	500	19	0.0380	38,000	1.50	3.27
24	09-93	920064		3	1	500	500	3	0.0060	6,000	1.50	4.01
25	02-93	920071		12	1	481	481	12	0.0249	24,948	1.50	3.46
26	06-93	920072		7	1	481	481	7	0.0146	14,553	1.50	3.68
27	09-93	920073		2	1	481	481	2	0.0042	4,158	1.50	4.14
28	03-93	920074		27	1	481	481	27	0.0561	56,133	1.50	3.09
29	03-93	920075		6	1	481	481	6	0.0125	12,474	1.50	3.74
30	05-93	920076		4	1	481	481	4	0.0083	8,316	1.50	3.90
31	11-93	920080		46	1	583	583	46	0.0789	78,902	1.50	2.91
32	11-93	920081		7	1	583	583	7	0.0120	12,007	1.50	3.76
33	11-93	920083		7	1	544	544	7	0.0129	12,868	1.50	3.73
34	10-93	920084		1	1	544	544	1	0.0018	1,838	1.50	4.41
35	06-93	920087		12	1	481	481	12	0.0249	24,948	1.50	3.46
36	11-93	920091		8	1	544	544	8	0.0147	14,706	1.50	3.68
37	12-93	920094		5	1	544	544	5	0.0092	9,191	1.50	3.86
38	02-94	920096		1	1	544	544	1	0.0018	1,838	1.50	4.41
39	09-93	920098		8	1	544	544	8	0.0147	14,706	1.50	3.68
40	11-93	920100		7	1	544	544	7	0.0129	12,868	1.50	3.73
41	07-93	920103		9	1	481	481	9	0.0187	18,711	1.50	3.58
42	11-93	920104		8	1	544	544	8	0.0147	14,706	1.50	3.68
43	11-93	920105		3	1	544	544	3	0.0055	5,515	1.50	4.04
44	11-93	920106		1	1	544	544	1	0.0018	1,838	1.50	4.41
45	05-93	920107		4	1	481	481	4	0.0083	8,316	1.50	3.90
46	09-93	920108		7	1	481	481	7	0.0146	14,553	1.50	3.68
47	05-93	920110		4	1	481	481	4	0.0083	8,316	1.50	3.90
48	11-93	920112		12	1	481	481	12	0.0249	24,948	1.50	3.46
49	07-93	920113		18	1	420	420	18	0.0429	42,857	1.50	3.22
50	10-93	920115		12	1	394	394	12	0.0305	30,457	1.50	3.37
51	10-93	930007		16	1	500	500	16	0.0320	32,000	1.50	3.35
52	10-93	930008		1	1	500	500	1	0.0020	2,000	1.50	4.38
53	11-93	930025		13	1	481	481	13	0.0270	27,027	1.50	3.44
54	10-93	930028		8	1	481	481	8	0.0166	16,632	1.50	3.63
55	10-93	930029		1	1	481	481	1	0.0021	2,079	1.50	4.37
56	10-93	930030		1	1	481	481	1	0.0021	2,079	1.50	4.37
57	11-93	930031		0	1	481	481	0	0.0000	0	1.50	6.00
58	10-93	930038		5	1	481	481	5	0.0104	10,395	1.50	3.81
59	12-93	930043		1	1	481	481	1	0.0021	2,079	1.50	4.37
60	12-93	930044		0	1	481	481	0	0.0000	0	1.50	6.00
61	12-93	930051		13	1	420	420	13	0.0310	30,952	1.50	3.37
62	12-93	930052		2	1	420	420	2	0.0048	4,762	1.50	4.09
63	12-93	930058		2	1	481	481	2	0.0042	4,158	1.50	4.14
			Grand = 532			32,526			0.0164	16,356	1.50	3.64

Overall 3.64σ

19 . 15

Quality of Engineering Drawings

Engineering Drawings

"Sigma" Capability

Data Courtesy of Asea Brown Boveri

Sigma's for Production Planning

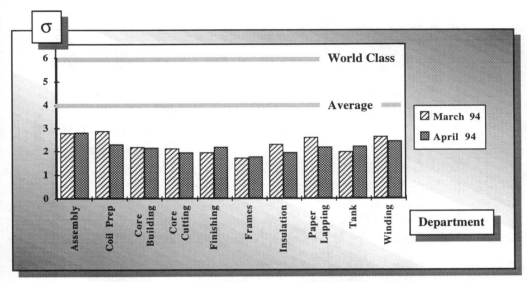

Data Courtesy of Asea Brown Boveri

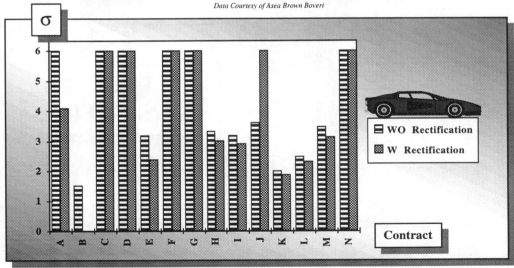

19 . 17

The Engineering Point-of-View

Report Name	Benchmarking		Reporting Period		From	To Dec-93
Organization			Baseline Period		From	To Uncertain
Project			Improvement Goal		Not Specified	
Department			Unit Definition		Not Applicable	
Deliverable			Characteristic		Categories of Error	
Deliverable ID			Units of Measure		Not Applicable	
Process			Upper Specification		NA	**Drawings**
Step			Target Value		NA	
Machine ID			Lower Specification		NA	
Special Note	See Below		Default Shift		1.50	

Note: The data for this study was obtained by a Public Service Organization

Line	Characteristic	D	U	OP	TOP	DPU	DPO	DPMO	Shift	Z.B
1	Drawings - Hopper	56	1	1,740	1,740	56.000	0.0322	32,184	1.50	3.35
2	Drawings - Grid Sheet	10	1	300	300	10.000	0.0333	33,333	1.50	3.33
3	Drawings - Plenum Flr	3	1	1,030	1,030	3.000	0.0029	2,913	1.50	4.26
	Grand =	60			3,070		0.0225	22,4		3.51

Report Name	Benchmarking		Reporting Period		From	
Organization			Baseline Period		From	
Project			Improvement Goal		Not Specified	
Department			Unit Definition		Not Applicable	
Deliverable			Characteristic		Categories of Error	
Deliverable ID			Units of Measure		Not Applicable	
Process			Upper Specification		NA	
Step			Target Value		NA	**Shop Floor**
Machine ID			Lower Specification		NA	
Special Note	See Below		Default Shift		1.50	

Note: The data for this study was obtained by a Public Service Organization

Line	Characteristic	D	U	OP	TOP	DPU	DPO	DPMO	Shift	Z.B
1	Shop - Steel/Bag	28	1	22,050	22,050	28.000	0.0013	1,270	1.50	4.52
2	Shop - Hop Beams	30	1	2,905	2,905	30.000	0.0103	10,327	1.50	3.81
3	Shop - Inlet Damp	2	1	575	575	2.000	0.0035	3,478	1.50	4.20
	Grand =	60			25,530		0.0024	2,350	1.50	4.33

Benchmarking Engineering Factors

A Hopper Drawings

B Grid Sheet Drawings

C Plenum Floor Drawings

D Steel Baghouse & Hopper Access in Shop

E Hopper Beams in Shop

F Inlet Dampers in Shop

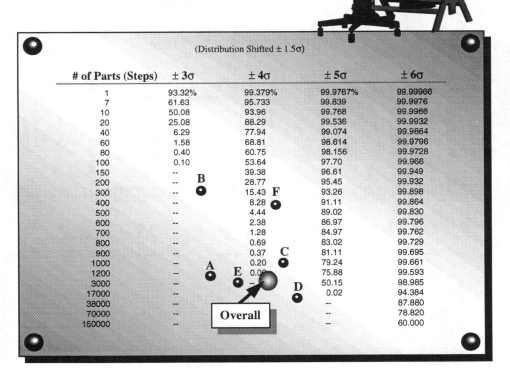

(Distribution Shifted ± 1.5σ)

# of Parts (Steps)	± 3σ	± 4σ	± 5σ	± 6σ
1	93.32%	99.379%	99.9767%	99.99966
7	61.63	95.733	99.839	99.9976
10	50.08	93.96	99.768	99.9966
20	25.08	88.29	99.536	99.9932
40	6.29	77.94	99.074	99.9864
60	1.58	68.81	98.614	99.9796
80	0.40	60.75	98.156	99.9728
100	0.10	53.64	97.70	99.966
150	--	39.38	96.61	99.949
200	--	28.77	95.45	99.932
300	--	15.43	93.26	99.898
400	--	8.28	91.11	99.864
500	--	4.44	89.02	99.830
600	--	2.38	86.97	99.796
700	--	1.28	84.97	99.762
800	--	0.69	83.02	99.729
900	--	0.37	81.11	99.695
1000	--	0.20	79.24	99.661
1200	--	0.09	75.88	99.593
3000	--	--	50.15	98.985
17000	--	--	0.02	94.384
38000	--	--	--	87.880
70000	--	--	--	78.820
150000	--	--	--	60.000

B (at 200, ±4σ)
F (at 300, ±4σ)
C (at 900, ±4σ)
A (at 1200, ±4σ)
E (at 1200, ±4σ)
D (at 3000, ±5σ)
Overall

19.19

Understanding the Difference

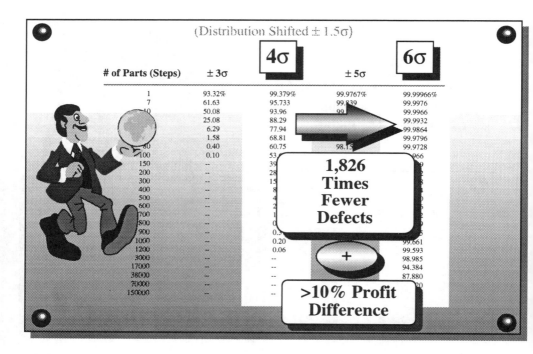

(Distribution Shifted ± 1.5σ)

# of Parts (Steps)	± 3σ	**4σ**	± 5σ	**6σ**
1	93.32%	99.379%	99.9767%	99.99966%
7	61.63	95.733	99.839	99.9976
10	50.08	93.96	99.	99.9966
	25.08	88.29		99.9932
	6.29	77.94		99.9864
	1.58	68.81		99.9796
	0.40	60.75	98.15	99.9728
100	0.10	53.		966
150	--	39		
200	--	28		
300	--	15		
400	--	8		
500	--	4		
600	--	2		
700	--	1		
800	--	0		
900	--	0.		
1000	--	0.20		99.661
1200	--	0.06		99.593
3000	--	--		98.985
17000	--	--		94.384
38000	--	--		87.880
70000	--	--		
150000	--	--		

1,826 Times Fewer Defects

+

>10% Profit Difference

What Questions Should We Ask?

Profile of the Average Company

4σ

- ➲ **Profitable and growing**
- ➲ **Market prices declining**
- ➲ **Competitors increasing**
- ➲ **Has a quality assurance program**
- ➲ **Spending 10-25% of sales dollars on repairing or reworking product before it ships**
- ➲ **Unaware that best in class companies have similar processes that are greater than 100X more defect-free**
- ➲ **Believes that a zero-defects goal is neither realistic nor achievable**
- ➲ **Has 10X the number of suppliers required to run the business**
- ➲ **5-10% of the firm's customers are dissatisfied with product, sales, or service and will not recommend that others purchase products or services**

Key Motorola Benchmarks

Sigma	LMPS	PTSG	GSS	SPS	GEG	AIEG	CDX	UDS	CORP	INT	TOTAL
Mar-88	•	•	3.91	4.31	3.89	3.26	4.20	•	3.99	•	3.98
Dec-88	•	•	3.92	4.45	4.23	4.10	3.84	4.71	4.25	•	4.27
Dec-89	•	•	4.49	4.56	4.54	4.47	3.35	4.90	4.69	•	4.40
Dec-90	•	•	4.41	4.99	5.12	4.69	3.59	4.92	4.95	5.19	4.58
Dec-91	5.10	4.81	4.98	5.09	4.78	4.83	4.70	4.96	5.02	4.92	4.95
Jan-92	5.14	4.56	4.87	5.07	4.94	4.45	3.98	4.91	5.21	6.00	4.79
Feb-92	5.11	4.87	5.05	4.90	4.70	4.69	4.88	5.16	4.46	4.73	4.91
Mar-92	5.24	5.32	5.03	5.17	4.77	4.84	4.91	5.16	4.80	6.00	5.06
Apr-92	5.40	5.19	5.09	5.08	4.72	4.87	5.05	4.91	5.15	4.82	5.08
May-92	5.31	5.17	4.84	4.96	4.78	4.89	4.43	5.01	5.05	4.76	4.94
Jun-92	5.35	5.70	5.15	5.03	4.68	4.93	4.99	5.10	5.07	4.68	5.07
Jul-92	5.41	5.40	5.29	5.06	4.77	4.96	4.93	5.05	5.17	4.65	4.92
Aug-92	5.41	5.46	5.19	4.98	4.80	4.91	5.01	4.98	5.17	4.99	5.11
Sep-92	5.41	5.45	5.33	5.13	5.06	5.04	5.09	5.29	4.92	4.43	5.21
Oct-92	5.54	5.47	5.20	5.10	5.17	4.98	5.06	5.09	5.10	4.79	5.21

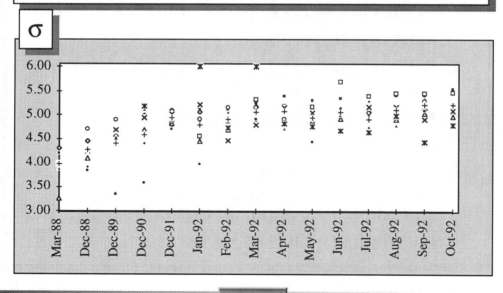

Sales per Employee

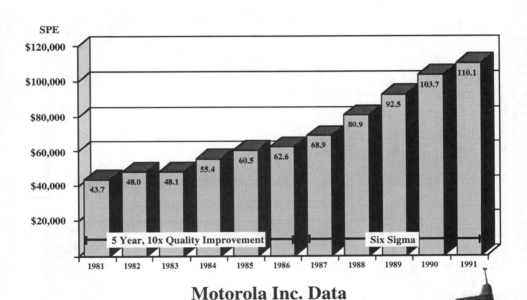

Motorola Inc. Data

What Questions Should We Ask?

Key Motorola Benchmarks

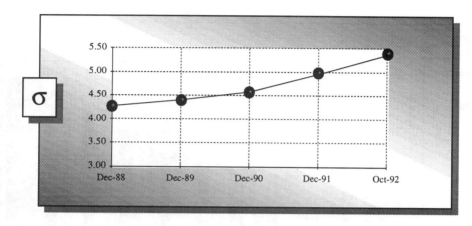

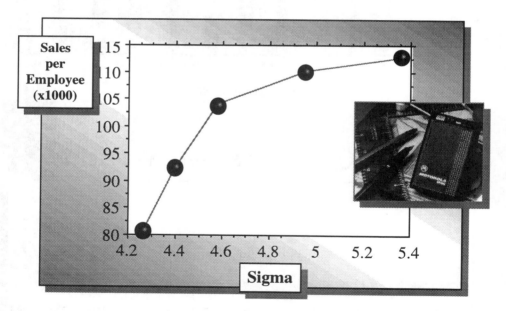

Key Motorola Benchmarks

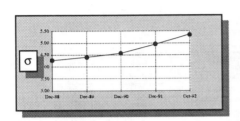

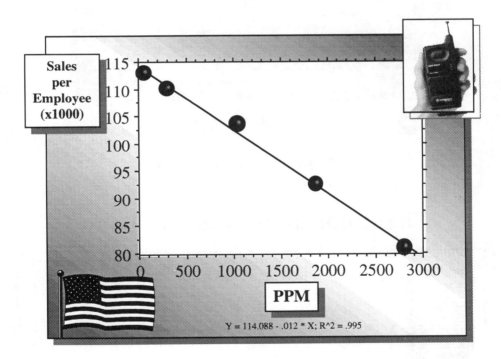

Sales per Employee (x1000)

PPM

$Y = 114.088 - .012 * X; R^2 = .995$

Results of Service Benchmarking

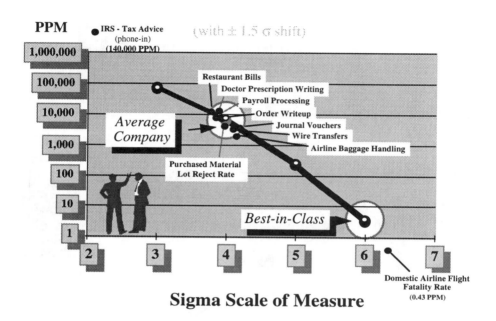

PPM

IRS - Tax Advice
(phone-in)
(140,000 PPM)

(with ± 1.5 σ shift)

1,000,000	
100,000	Restaurant Bills
10,000	Doctor Prescription Writing
	Payroll Processing
1,000	Order Writeup
100	Journal Vouchers
10	Wire Transfers
1	Airline Baggage Handling

Average Company

Purchased Material
Lot Reject Rate

Best-in-Class

2   3   4   5   6   7

Sigma Scale of Measure

Domestic Airline Flight
Fatality Rate
(0.43 PPM)

What Conclusions Can We Draw?

Service Process Benchmarking

Step	Description	Sigma
1	**Customer Access**	
	Speed of answer - facilitator	3.42
	Speed of answer -customer serv	2.77
	Speed of answer - CSR	2.22
	Calls abandoned - Facilitator	3.21
	Calls abandoned - customer service	3.50
	Calls abandoned - CSR	3.42
2	**Collect Customer Details and Requirements**	
	New Serv incorrectly labled intact	2.50
	New Serv incorrectly labled intact	
	Intact incorrectly labled New Serv.	2.56
	Intact incorrectly labled New Serv.	
	Customer Detail discrepancies	2.88
	Customer Detail discrepancies	3.54
	Appointment not made	2.76
	Appointment not made	3.52
	Charges not included	3.39
	Charges not included	1.64
	Scheduling units not correct	3.15
	Charges not quoted by sales	1.75
	Charges not quoted by sales	
	Order incomplete, incorrect or follow-up	4.24
	Order incomplete, incorrect or follow-up	4.24
	Appointment not suitable	2.02
	Appointment not suitable	
	DCRIS order quality -TSR	4.44
	DCRIS order quality -DSR	4.41
	DCRIS order quality - CSR	4.20
	Quoting & charging - CRS	3.16
	Quoting & charging - DSR	3.09
	Quoting & charging - TSR	3.12
	Quoting & charging - S/E	
	Guarantee Errors	4.77
	Gurarantee Errors	5.01
	Number changed	3.42
	Wrong exchange on order	4.94
	Std Address Abbreviations Used	2.27
3	**Assign Plant**	
	Choice of Number Problems	
	Choice of Number Problems	4.50
	Cable Details Correct	
	Cable Details Correct	3.48
	No LIs	2.73
4	**Establish Service in Exchange**	
	Meter Reading	4.42
5	**Connect Facilities in Field**	
	Line work not completed by due date	
	Line work (and other) problems - WR LW ER	2.62
	Line work (and other) problems - WR LW ER	2.79
	Line work (and other) problems - WR LW ER	2.62
	Line work (and other) problems - WR LW ER	2.79
	Appointment met-cons	2.98
	Appointment met - comm	2.42
	RCRD met - In-place	2.47
	RCRD met - In-place	2.80
	FFS dockets signed - techs	2.90
	FFS dockets signed - lines	3.07
	Installer did not explain charges	2.45
	Installer did not explain charges	
	Quoting & charging questionnaire - Controllers	
	Quoting & charging questionnaire - Installers	
	Quoting & charging questionnaire - CED	3.27
6	**Complete Order and Follow Up**	
	Not rung back	2.09

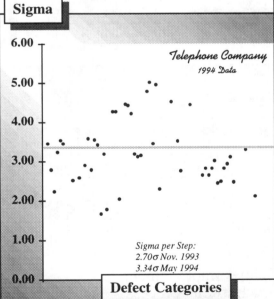

Sigma

Telephone Company
1994 Data

Sigma per Step:
2.70σ Nov. 1993
3.34σ May 1994

Defect Categories

Administration Benchmarking

Row	Demographic	Response
1	System	Claim Payment
2	Process	Claim/Medical
3	Conducted by	M. Harry
4	Date of analysis	8/7/92
5	Approved by	J. Couch
6	Normalized Shift Factor	1.50
7	Unit	Claim
8	Total Annual Volume	35,357,876
9	Total Unit Cost ($)	7.49
10	Total Annual Cost ($)	264,830,491
11	Min Cycle Time (minutes)	4
12	Min Cycle Time (days)	0.01
13	Min Cost per Minute	1.78333
14	Rolled Throughput Yield	.6518114
15	Yield Per Opportunity	.9985046
16	Sigma per Opprotunity	4.469
17	Defect Detection Efficiency	98.00%

Insurance Company

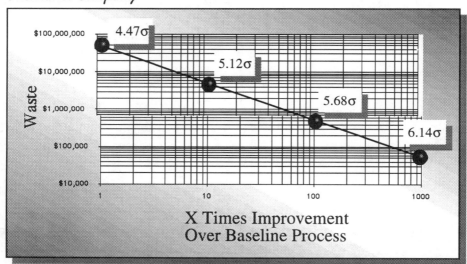

Results of Software Benchmarking

(with ± 1.5 σ shift)

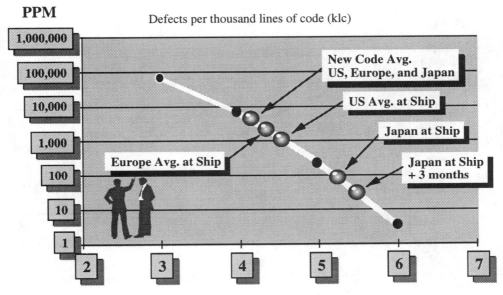

Sigma Scale of Measure

What Conclusions Can We Draw?

Consequences of Being Average

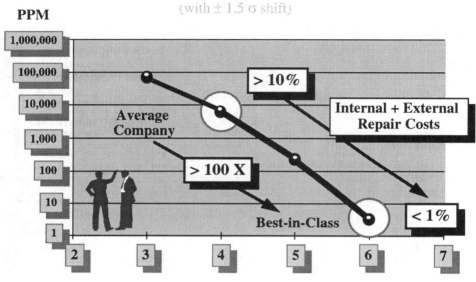

PPM

(with ± 1.5 σ shift)

> 10%

Internal + External Repair Costs

Average Company

> 100 X

Best-in-Class

< 1%

Sigma Scale of Measure

What Questions Should We Ask?

19 . 30

Auto Assembly Plant Quality

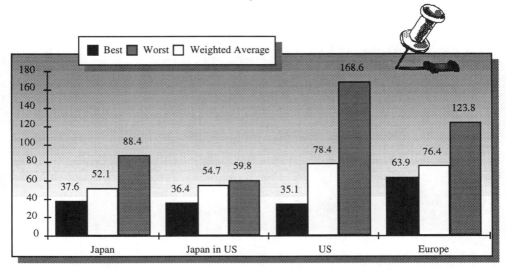

Defects per 100 cars traceable to the assembly plant reported in the first three months of use.

What Conclusions Can We Draw?

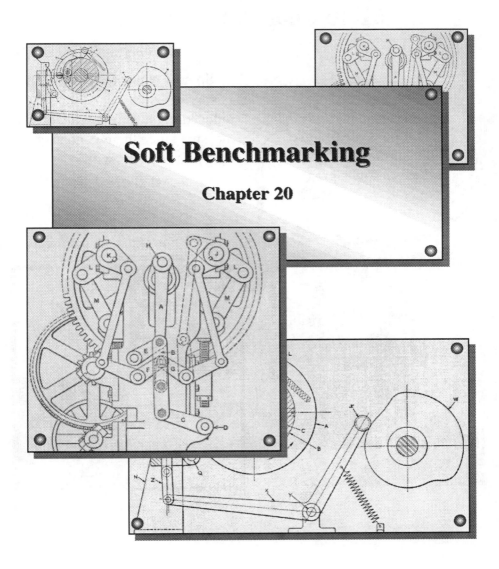

Soft Benchmarking

Chapter 20

The People Dilemma

. . . So how can something such as survey results be reduced to the sigma scale of measure since there is no such thing as a "defect" with respect to a performance score?

. . . Is it possible to have a high sigma person who produces a low sigma product or vice versa ?

Understanding the Problem

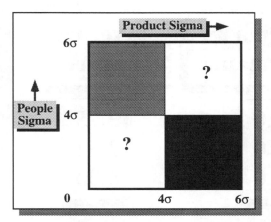

... Is it possible to have a high sigma person who produces a low sigma product or vice versa ?

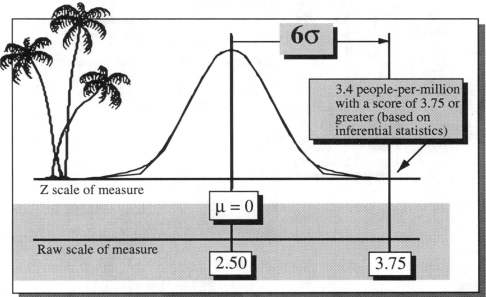

20 . 3

Creating the Transfer Function

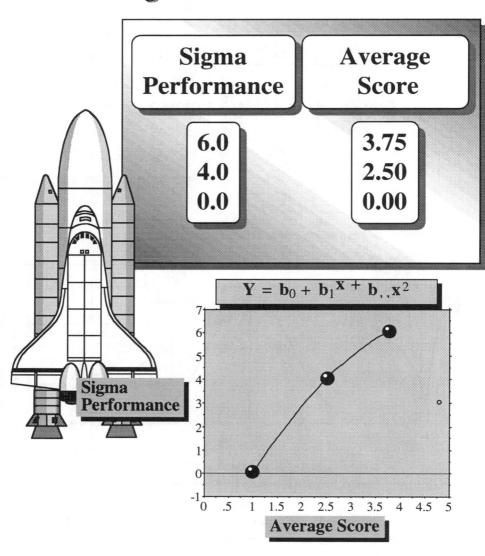

Sigma Performance	Average Score
6.0	3.75
4.0	2.50
0.0	0.00

$$Y = b_0 + b_1 x + b_{,,} x^2$$

Sigma Performance

Average Score

20 . 4

Benchmarking the Results

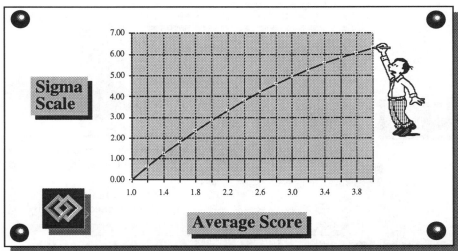

Sigma Scale

Average Score

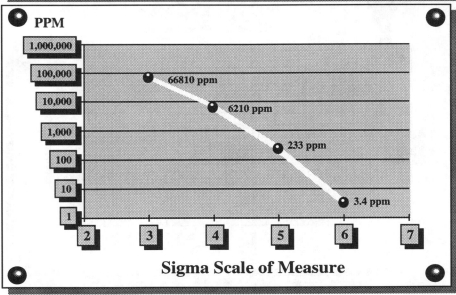

PPM

66810 ppm

6210 ppm

233 ppm

3.4 ppm

Sigma Scale of Measure

Creating the Transfer Functions

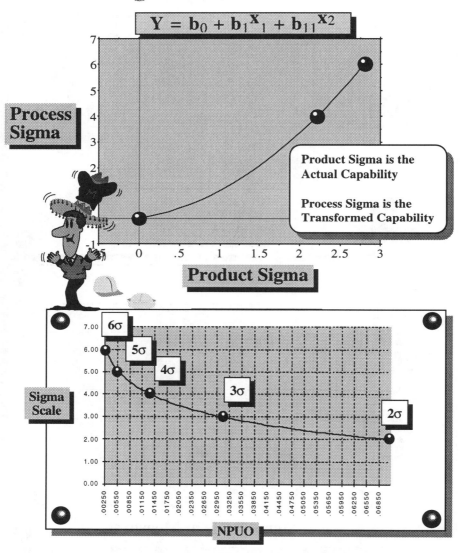

$$Y = b_0 + b_1{}^{X_1} + b_{11}{}^{X_2}$$

Process Sigma

Product Sigma

Product Sigma is the
Actual Capability

Process Sigma is the
Transformed Capability

Sigma Scale

6σ 5σ 4σ 3σ 2σ

NPUO

20 . 6

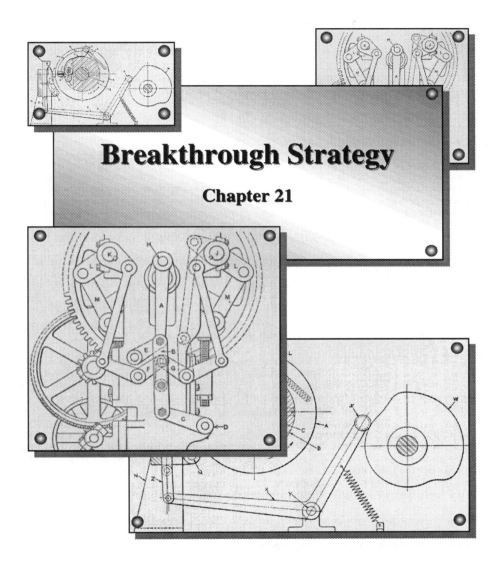

Breakthrough Strategy

Chapter 21

The Breakthrough Strategy

Manufacturing industries are becoming increasingly aware that the practice of Six Sigma has the potential to extend many benefits to the producer, as well as to their prized asset -- their customers. Some of those benefits include, but are not limited to; a) reduced total cost, b) enhanced product quality and reliability, c) lower manufacturing cycle time, and d) fewer design changes after release for production. However, such benefits can only be realized if the product design and manufacturing process can "play" together; i.e., the product and process are optimal relative to each other.

This portion of the book will discuss a methodology to achieve best-in-class products. Supporting this approach is the central belief that the product is a function of the design and the manufacturing process which must produce it. Owing to this reasoning, a focus on process improvement will result in superior product. Herein, the discussion pivots on how to properly characterize and optimize one or more of the product characteristics through the systematic measurement, analysis, improvement, and control of the manufacturing process. When properly done, the approach leads to all of the previously mentioned benefits.

Perhaps the best place to begin this discussion is with a recognition of the need for planning. Intuitively, we all clearly understand why planning is such a vital link in the success chain. However, we often lose sight of this fact as we move toward the threshold of a project. Some may often say, "Well, this project isn't as big as it looks . . . so we really don't need a whole lot to get it off the ground . . . the details can be worked out as we go along!" Obviously, such reasoning seemingly passes the common sense test; however, in many instances, things are not always as they seem.

To illustrate the latter point, let us consider an amphibious military operation. As may be apparent, the objective of such an operation is to put soldiers on a ship, along with the appropriate supplies, and then transport them to a beachhead to confront a resistive force. Given this mission, it becomes crystal clear that logistics plays a major role. After all, we certainly recognize the importance of "beans, bullets, and bandaids" to a soldier.

Without the basic supplies, the mission cannot be achieved, no matter how motivated the troops are; therefore, it makes proper sense to put the high-priority items at the top of the "be-sure-to-put-on-the-ship" list, right? Well, it may seem so, however, we have forgotten to consider the other end of the mission. More specifically, our planning did not consider how the ship would be unloaded once the Commander calls back to the ship and says, "Hey, send the beans, bullets, and band-aids - we're just about out!"

Because the high-priority items were at the top of the ship's manifest, they were the first to be loaded into the ship's hull. Consequently, they were the last to come off. In the case of our example, the commander had to surrender because it took three days to unload the ship and reach the critical supplies. The moral is quite simple - reverse planning has many practical benefits.

In many respects, the construction of a breakthrough strategy is no different than planning a military operation, or any other undertaking, for that matter. The fundamental elements related to the planning process are much the same; i.e., certain strategies, tactics, and tools need to be identified and subsequently organized to successfully achieve a particular goal. For example, let us consider a simple capability study of a certain response characteristic. In this situation, we must "reverse load" the planning. To do this, we must answer the following questions for each phase of the breakthrough strategy:

> Question 1: What do we ultimately want to know?
> Question 2: How do we want to see what we need to know?
> Question 3: What type of analytical tool will best generate what we must see?
> Question 4: What type of data is required of the selected tools?
> Question 5: Where can the specified type of data be gathered?

All too often, the questioning process is turned upside down. In other words, the engineer first says, "Where can I get some data to accomplish the task?" Not so obvious is the fact that whenever a data collection point is fixed, the type of data which can be gathered at that point is also fixed. When this happens, the range of applicable analytical tools is greatly restricted because most statistical devices (i.e., methods and equations) will only work properly with certain types of data.

As now may be apparent, the analytical tool which is used largely controls the type of information which will be extracted from the data. Naturally, this limits the number of ways in which the resultant information can be displayed. Now comes the downside to it all: the latter outcome dictates what the engineer ultimately will know about the response characteristic under investigation - which may or may not be related to the original objectives of the study. Again, the moral is one of reverse planning.

Much too often, well-intentioned engineers call for consultation on how best to analyze a particular set of data only to discover, much to their dismay, that the given data cannot be "crunched" to provide an answer to what they originally wanted to know. Usually, the call for consultation comes just before their "conclusions and recommendations" are to be submitted to management. In such instances, it is quite clear that various links in the "success chain" were very weak or even nonexistent.

Unfortunately, some engineers try to force fit their data into an improper format to comply with their respective submission date. Needless to say, such action can set up a domino chain of decisions that often leads to the loss of precious resources, not to mention the engineer's reputation. The underlying principle at hand is quite simple. Just as a given rifle is designed to accommodate a certain size bullet (or vice-versa), a selected statistic will only work with a certain type of data. Imagine being dropped off on a beachhead, only to discover that your rifle has the wrong kind of bullets. Obviously, the original strategy of a frontal assault would prove unsuccessful under such conditions.

The Driving Need for Breakthrough

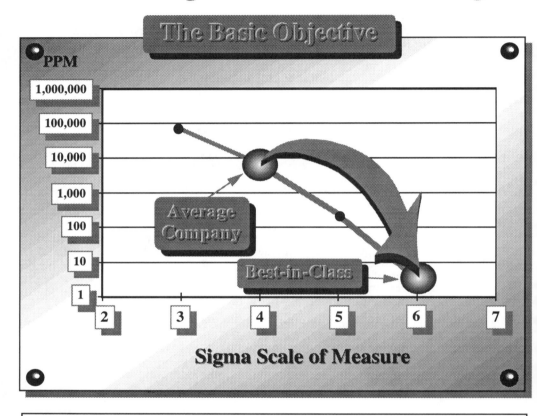

The Basic Objective

PPM

1,000,000	
100,000	
10,000	
1,000	
100	
10	
1	

Average Company

Best-in-Class

2   3   4   5   6   7

Sigma Scale of Measure

So what does it take to make the change?

21 . 4

The Nature of Breakthrough

When the Lord created the world and people to live in it - an enterprise which, according to modern science, took a very long time - I could well imagine that He reasoned with Himself as follows: "If I make everything predictable, these human beings, whom I have endowed with pretty good brains, will undoubtedly learn to predict everything, and they will thereupon have no motive to do anything at all, because they will recognize that the future is totally determined and cannot be influenced by any human action.

On the other hand, if I make everything unpredictable, they will gradually discover that there is no rational basis for any decision whatsoever and, as in the first case, they will thereupon have no motive to do anything at all. Neither scheme would make sense.

I must therefore create a mixture of the two. Let some things be predictable and let others be unpredictable. They will then, amongst many other things, have the very important task of finding out which is which."

E.F. Schumacher
From: Small is Beautiful

The Components of Breakthrough

Process Characterization is concerned with the identification and benchmarking of key product characteristics. By way of a gap analysis, common success factors are identified .

Process Optimization is aimed at the identification and containment of those process variables which exert undue influence over the key product characteristics.

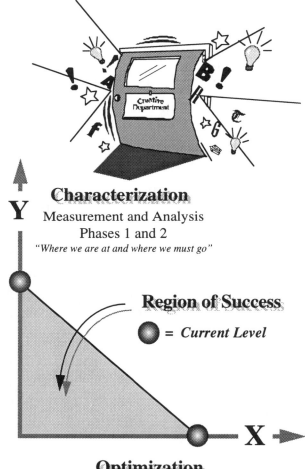

Characterization
Measurement and Analysis
Phases 1 and 2
"Where we are at and where we must go"

Region of Success

● = *Current Level*

Optimization
Improvement and Control
Phases 3 and 4
"What action we must take to get and stay there"

21 . 6

The Breakthrough Phases

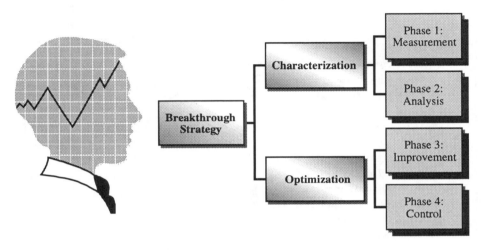

Phase 1 (Measurement). This phase is concerned with selecting one or more product characteristics; i.e., dependent variables, mapping the respective process, making the necessary measurements, recording the results on process "control cards," and estimating the short- and long-term process capability.

Phase 2 (Analysis). This phase entails benchmarking the key product performance metrics. Following this, a gap analysis is often undertaken to identify the common factors of successful performance; i.e., what factors explains best-in-class performance. In some cases, it is necessary to redesign the product and/or process.

Phase 3 (Improvement). This phase is usually initiated by selecting those product performance characteristics which must be improved to achieve the goal. Once this is done, the characteristics are diagnosed to reveal the major sources of variation. Next, the key process variables are identified by way of statistically designed experiments. For each process variable which proves to be leverage in nature, performance specifications are established.

Phase 4 (Control). This phase is related to ensuring that the new process conditions are documented and monitored via statistical process control methods. After a "settling in" period, the process capability would be reassessed. Depending upon the outcomes of such a follow-on analysis, it may be necessary to revisit one or more of the preceding phases.

The Breakthrough Roadmap

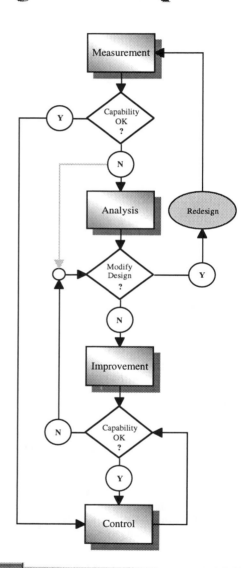

Six Sigma Breakthrough Strategy

Measurement
1. Select Key Product
2. Create Product Tree
3. Define Performance Variables
4. Create Process Map
5. Measure Performance Variables
6. Establish Performance Capability

Analysis
7. Select Performance Variable
8. Benchmark Performance Metric
9. Discover Best-in-Class Performance
10. Conduct Gap Analysis
11. Identify Success Factors
12. Define Performance Goal

Improvement
13. Select Performance Variable
14. Diagnose Variable Performance
15. Propose Causal Variables
16. Confirm Causal Variables
17. Establish Operating Limits
18. Verify Performance Improvement

Control
19. Select Causal Variable
20. Define Control System
21. Validate Control System
22. Implement Control System
23. Audit Control System
24. Monitor Performance Metrics

The Breakthrough Architecture

Six Sigma Breakthrough Strategy

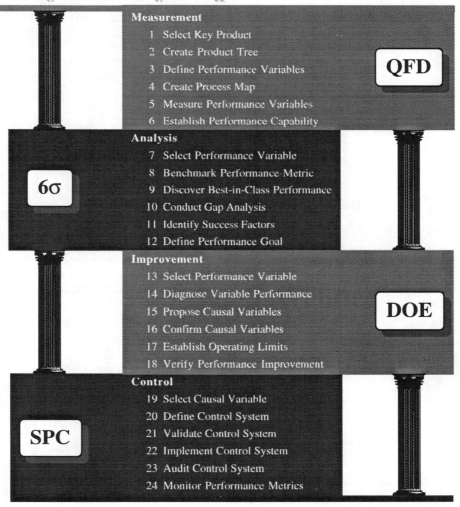

Measurement

1 Select Key Product
2 Create Product Tree
3 Define Performance Variables
4 Create Process Map
5 Measure Performance Variables
6 Establish Performance Capability

QFD

Analysis

7 Select Performance Variable
8 Benchmark Performance Metric
9 Discover Best-in-Class Performance
10 Conduct Gap Analysis
11 Identify Success Factors
12 Define Performance Goal

6σ

Improvement

13 Select Performance Variable
14 Diagnose Variable Performance
15 Propose Causal Variables
16 Confirm Causal Variables
17 Establish Operating Limits
18 Verify Performance Improvement

DOE

Control

19 Select Causal Variable
20 Define Control System
21 Validate Control System
22 Implement Control System
23 Audit Control System
24 Monitor Performance Metrics

SPC

Phase 1: Product Measurement

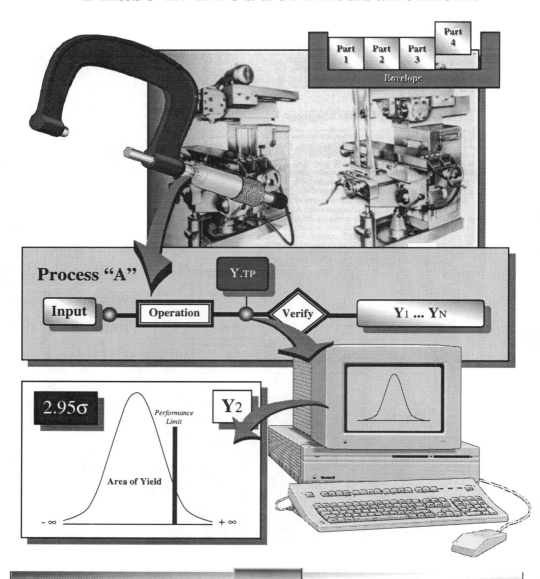

Process "A"

Y.TP

Input — Operation — Verify — Y₁ ... Yₙ

Part 1 | Part 2 | Part 3 | Part 4

Envelope

2.95σ

Performance Limit

Y₂

Area of Yield

- ∞   + ∞

Phase 2: Performance Analysis

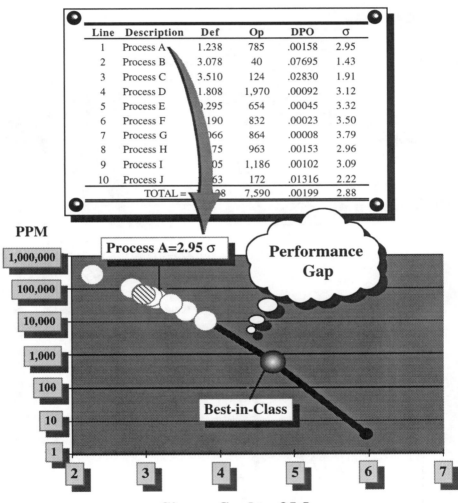

Line	Description	Def	Op	DPO	σ
1	Process A	1.238	785	.00158	2.95
2	Process B	3.078	40	.07695	1.43
3	Process C	3.510	124	.02830	1.91
4	Process D	1.808	1,970	.00092	3.12
5	Process E	.295	654	.00045	3.32
6	Process F	190	832	.00023	3.50
7	Process G	066	864	.00008	3.79
8	Process H	75	963	.00153	2.96
9	Process I	05	1,186	.00102	3.09
10	Process J	63	172	.01316	2.22
	TOTAL =	28	7,590	.00199	2.88

PPM

Process A=2.95 σ

Performance Gap

Best-in-Class

Sigma Scale of Measure

Phase 3: Performance Improvement

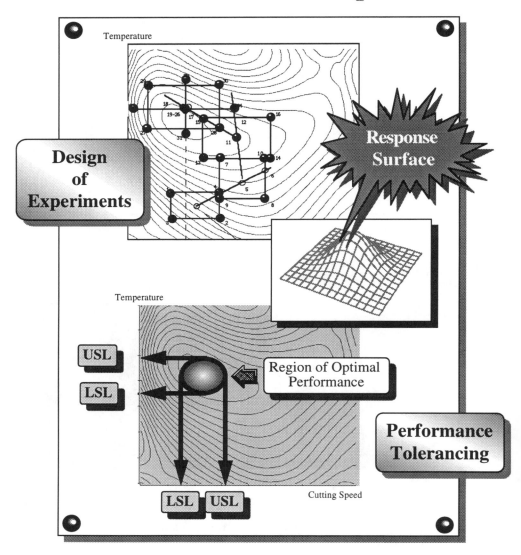

Phase 4: Process Control

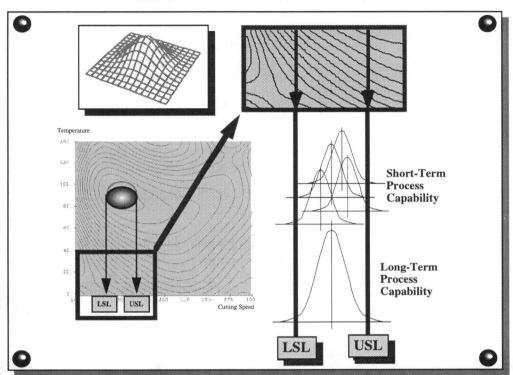

Temperature

Short-Term
Process
Capability

Long-Term
Process
Capability

LSL   USL

LSL   USL

Cutting Speed

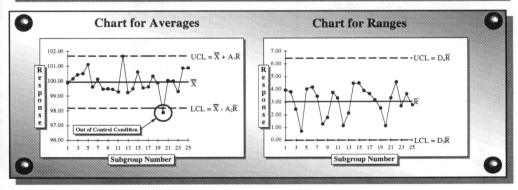

Chart for Averages

$UCL = \overline{X} + A_2\overline{R}$

$\overline{X}$

$LCL = \overline{X} - A_2\overline{R}$

Out of Control Condition

Subgroup Number

Chart for Ranges

$UCL = D_4\overline{R}$

$\overline{R}$

$LCL = D_3\overline{R}$

Subgroup Number

The Planning Questions

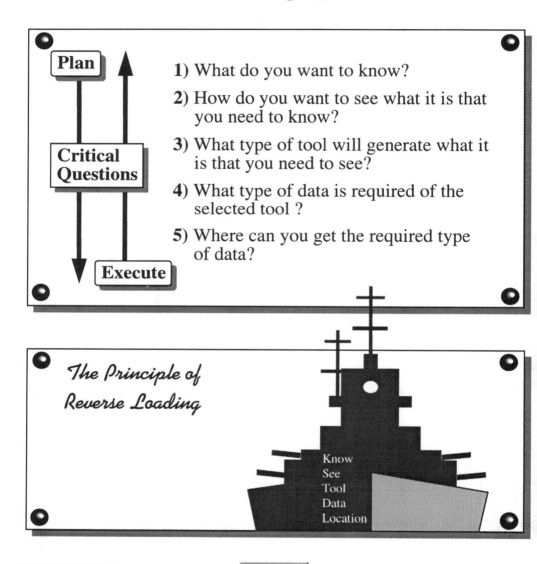

Plan

Critical
Questions

Execute

1) What do you want to know?

2) How do you want to see what it is that you need to know?

3) What type of tool will generate what it is that you need to see?

4) What type of data is required of the selected tool ?

5) Where can you get the required type of data?

The Principle of Reverse Loading

Know
See
Tool
Data
Location

The Planning Format

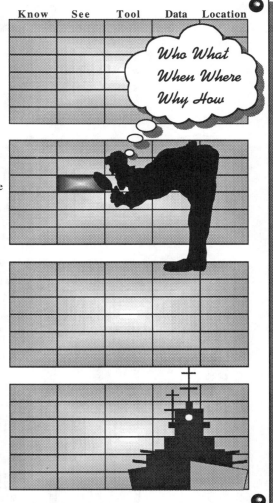

Measurement	Know	See	Tool	Data	Location
1 Select Key Product					
2 Create Product Tree					
3 Define Performance Variables					
4 Create Process Map					
5 Measure Performance Variables					
6 Establish Performance Capability					
Analysis					
7 Select Performance Variable					
8 Benchmark Performance Metric					
9 Discover Best-in-Class Performance					
10 Conduct Gap Analysis					
11 Identify Success Factors					
12 Define Performance Goal					
Improvement					
13 Select Performance Variable					
14 Diagnose Variable Performance					
15 Propose Causal Variables					
16 Confirm Causal Variables					
17 Establish Operating Limits					
18 Verify Performance Improvement					
Control					
19 Select Causal Variable					
20 Define Control System					
21 Validate Control System					
22 Implement Control System					
23 Audit Control System					
24 Monitor Performance Metrics					

Who What When Where Why How

Applying the Planning Principles

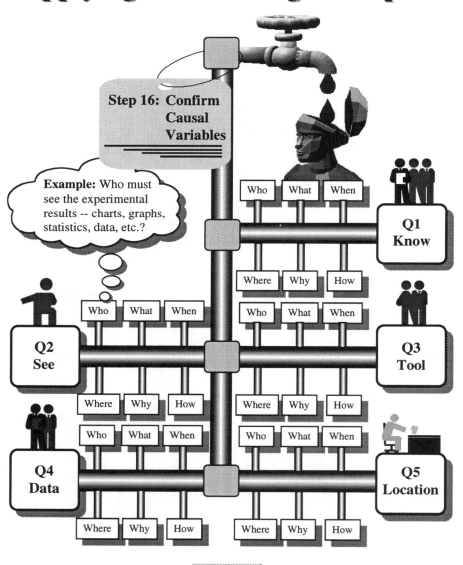

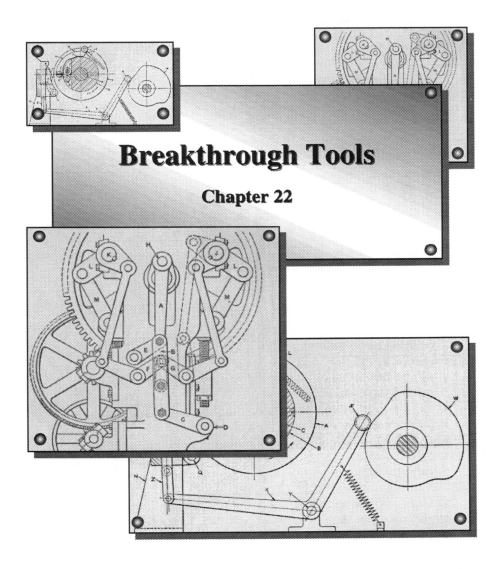

Breakthrough Tools

Chapter 22

The Breakthrough Roadmap

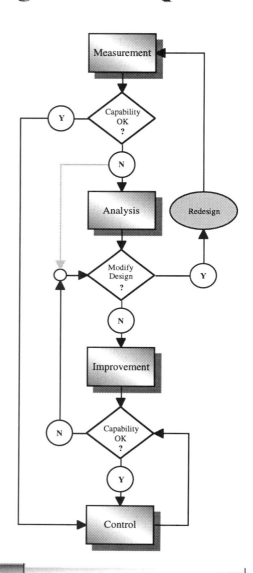

Six Sigma Breakthrough Strateg

Measurement
1 Select Key Product
2 Create Product Tree
3 Define Performance Variables
4 Create Process Map
5 Measure Performance Variables
6 Establish Performance Capability

Analysis
7 Select Performance Variable
8 Benchmark Performance Metric
9 Discover Best-in-Class Performance
10 Conduct Gap Analysis
11 Identify Success Factors
12 Define Performance Goal

Improvement
13 Select Performance Variable
14 Diagnose Variable Performance
15 Propose Causal Variables
16 Confirm Causal Variables
17 Establish Operating Limits
18 Verify Performance Improvement

Control
19 Select Causal Variable
20 Define Control System
21 Validate Control System
22 Implement Control System
23 Audit Control System
24 Monitor Performance Metrics

Classes of Breakthrough Tools

Phase 1:
Measurement

This phase is concerned with selecting one or more product characteristics; i.e., dependent variables, mapping the respective process, making the necessary measurements, recording the results on process "control cards," and estimating the short- and long-term process capability.

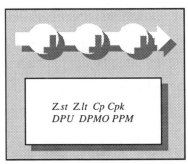

Z.st Z.lt Cp Cpk
DPU DPMO PPM

Planning and Organization

Six Sigma Metrics

Phase 2:
Analysis

This phase entails benchmarking the key product performance metrics. Following this, a gap analysis is often undertaken to identify the common factors of successful performance; i.e., what factors explains best-in-class performance. In some cases, it is necessary to redesign the product and/ or process.

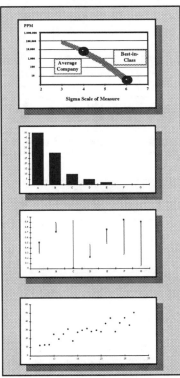

Performance Benchmarking

Gap Analysis

Classes of Breakthrough Tools

Phase 3:

Improvement

This phase is usually initiated by selecting those product performance characteristics which must be improved to achieve the goal. Once this is done, the characteristics are diagnosed to reveal the major sources of variation. Next, the key process variables are identified by way of statistically designed experiments. For each process variable which proves to be leverage in nature, performance specifications are established.

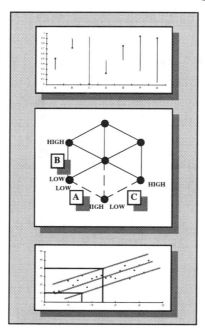

Diagnostic Methods

Design of Experiments

Performance Tolerancing

Phase 4:

Control

This phase is related to ensuring that the new process conditions are documented and monitored via statistical process control methods. After a "settling in" period, the process capability would be reassessed.

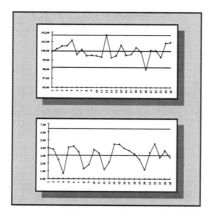

Statistical Process Control

A Sampling of the Black Belt Toolkit

The Top 50 Tools

1	Analysis-of-Covariance	26	Indices of Location
2	Analysis-of-Variance	27	Indices of Process Capability
3	Binomial Distribution	28	Indices of Variability
4	Brainstorming Techniques	29	Line, Bar, Pie Charts
5	Cause and Effect Matrix	30	Mathematical Transformations
6	Check Sheets	31	Median Test
7	Chi-Square Distribution	32	Normal Distribution
8	Chi-Square Test for Goodness-of-Fit	33	Pareto Diagrams and Charts
9	Chi-Square Test of Independence	34	Performance Figures-of-Merit
10	Confidence Intervals	35	Performance Tolerancing
11	Control Cards	36	Poisson Distribution
12	Correlation Methods	37	Positrol Logs
13	Cross Tabulation Tables	38	Pre-control
14	Data Collection Sheets	39	Process Flow Diagrams
15	Exponential Distribution	40	Random Number Generation
16	F Distribution	41	Random Strategy Experiment Designs
17	F Test	42	Regression
18	Failure Mode and Effect Analysis	43	Response Surface Experiment Designs
19	Fishbone Diagrams	44	Root-Sum-of-Squares
20	Force Field Diagrams	45	Sample Size Equations and Tables
21	Fractional Factorial Experiment Designs	46	Statistical Process Control Charts
22	Full Factorial Experiment Designs	47	Statistical Tables
23	Group Screening Experiment Designs	48	t Distribution
24	Histograms	49	t Test
25	Hypothesis Construction	50	Tests for Randomness

The Basic Toolkit for Team Members

Checksheets
Pareto Chart
Run Chart
Histogram
Scatter Diagram

Fishbone
Benchmarking
Brainstorming
Affinity Diagram
Design Matrix
Force Field Analysis

Gantt Chart
Pert Chart
Top Down Map
Wall Map
Product Map

QFD
DOE
DFMA
FMEA
Tree Diagram
Cell Design
Mistake Proof
Why-Why-Why

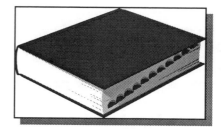

Linking the Tools to the Strategy

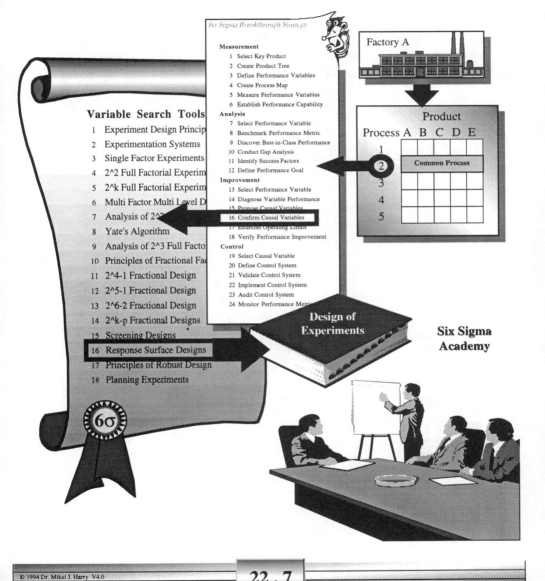

Six Sigma Breakthrough Strategy

Measurement
1 Select Key Product
2 Create Product Tree
3 Define Performance Variables
4 Create Process Map
5 Measure Performance Variables
6 Establish Performance Capability

Analysis
7 Select Performance Variable
8 Benchmark Performance Metric
9 Discover Best-in-Class Performance
10 Conduct Gap Analysis
11 Identify Success Factors
12 Define Performance Goal

Improvement
13 Select Performance Variable
14 Diagnose Variable Performance
15 Propose Causal Variables
16 Confirm Causal Variables
17 Establish Operating Limits
18 Verify Performance Improvement

Control
19 Select Causal Variable
20 Define Control System
21 Validate Control System
22 Implement Control System
23 Audit Control System
24 Monitor Performance Metric

Factory A

Product
Process A B C D E
1
2   Common Process
3
4
5

Variable Search Tools
1 Experiment Design Princip
2 Experimentation Systems
3 Single Factor Experiments
4 2^2 Full Factorial Experim
5 2^k Full Factorial Experim
6 Multi Factor Multi Level D
7 Analysis of 2^
8 Yate's Algorithm
9 Analysis of 2^3 Full Facto
10 Principles of Fractional Fa
11 2^4-1 Fractional Design
12 2^5-1 Fractional Design
13 2^6-2 Fractional Design
14 2^k-p Fractional Designs
15 Screening Designs
16 Response Surface Designs
17 Principles of Robust Design
18 Planning Experiments

Design of
Experiments

**Six Sigma
Academy**

6σ

The Use of Data Control Cards

The scorecards are used by the BATPT to record various measurements related to the top 30 characteristics of a Power Transformer.

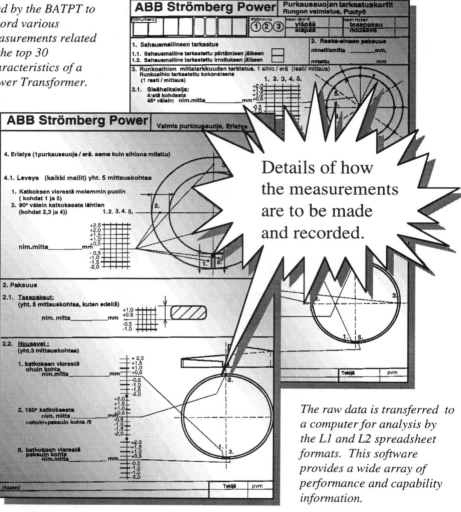

Details of how the measurements are to be made and recorded.

The raw data is transferred to a computer for analysis by the L1 and L2 spreadsheet formats. This software provides a wide array of performance and capability information.

The Use of Electronic Spreadsheets

The Control Cards are used as the source document from which to input data into a standardized electronic spreadsheet.

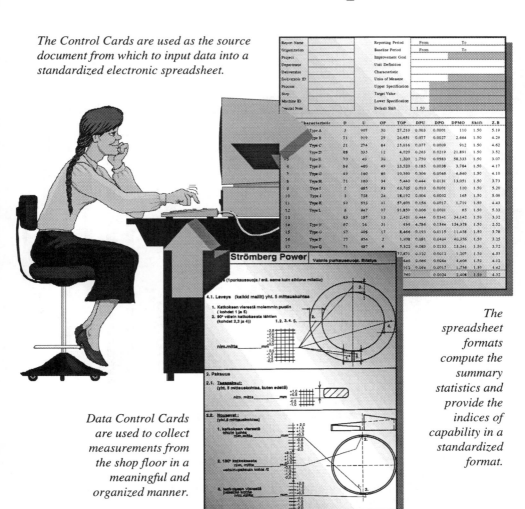

Data Control Cards are used to collect measurements from the shop floor in a meaningful and organized manner.

The spreadsheet formats compute the summary statistics and provide the indices of capability in a standardized format.

The Standard Application Formats

The application formats are spreadsheet "masks" which help the Black-Belt with basic organization and computational tasks during execution of phases 1 and 2 of the breakthrough strategy. The output of one mask serves as the input to another. Essentially, this provides the Black-Belt with an "application cook-book."

The Application Formats

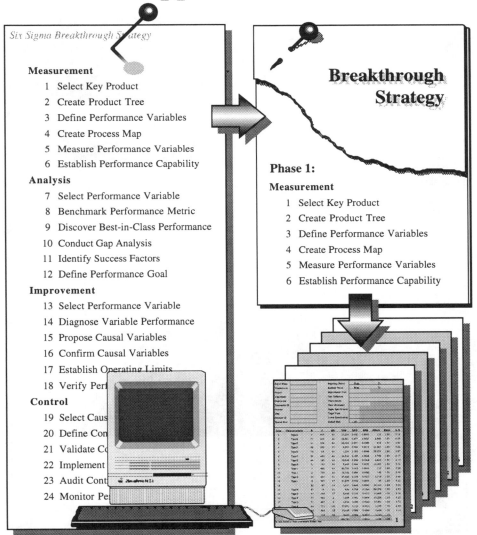

Six Sigma Breakthrough Strategy

Measurement
1 Select Key Product
2 Create Product Tree
3 Define Performance Variables
4 Create Process Map
5 Measure Performance Variables
6 Establish Performance Capability

Analysis
7 Select Performance Variable
8 Benchmark Performance Metric
9 Discover Best-in-Class Performance
10 Conduct Gap Analysis
11 Identify Success Factors
12 Define Performance Goal

Improvement
13 Select Performance Variable
14 Diagnose Variable Performance
15 Propose Causal Variables
16 Confirm Causal Variables
17 Establish Operating Limits
18 Verify Perf

Control
19 Select Caus
20 Define Con
21 Validate Co
22 Implement
23 Audit Cont
24 Monitor Pe

**Breakthrough
Strategy**

Phase 1:

Measurement
1 Select Key Product
2 Create Product Tree
3 Define Performance Variables
4 Create Process Map
5 Measure Performance Variables
6 Establish Performance Capability

Example Application Format

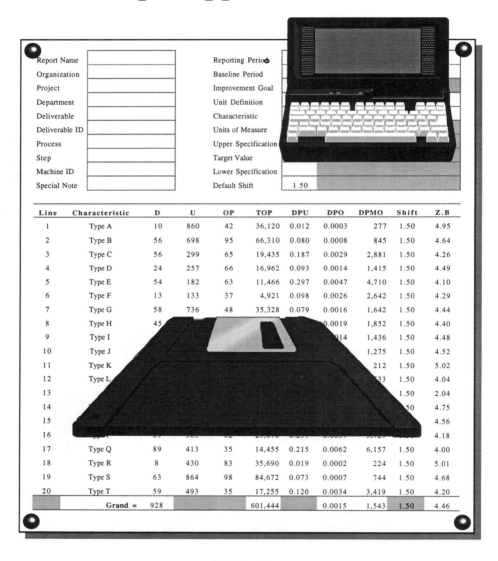

Report Name		Reporting Period	
Organization		Baseline Period	
Project		Improvement Goal	
Department		Unit Definition	
Deliverable		Characteristic	
Deliverable ID		Units of Measure	
Process		Upper Specification	
Step		Target Value	
Machine ID		Lower Specification	
Special Note		Default Shift	1.50

Line	Characteristic	D	U	OP	TOP	DPU	DPO	DPMO	Shift	Z.B
1	Type A	10	860	42	36,120	0.012	0.0003	277	1.50	4.95
2	Type B	56	698	95	66,310	0.080	0.0008	845	1.50	4.64
3	Type C	56	299	65	19,435	0.187	0.0029	2,881	1.50	4.26
4	Type D	24	257	66	16,962	0.093	0.0014	1,415	1.50	4.49
5	Type E	54	182	63	11,466	0.297	0.0047	4,710	1.50	4.10
6	Type F	13	133	37	4,921	0.098	0.0026	2,642	1.50	4.29
7	Type G	58	736	48	35,328	0.079	0.0016	1,642	1.50	4.44
8	Type H	45					0.0019	1,852	1.50	4.40
9	Type I						014	1,436	1.50	4.48
10	Type J							1,275	1.50	4.52
11	Type K							212	1.50	5.02
12	Type L							33	1.50	4.04
13									1.50	2.04
14									50	4.75
15										4.56
16		89	903	62	23,870	0.251	0.0057	5,729		4.18
17	Type Q	89	413	35	14,455	0.215	0.0062	6,157	1.50	4.00
18	Type R	8	430	83	35,690	0.019	0.0002	224	1.50	5.01
19	Type S	63	864	98	84,672	0.073	0.0007	744	1.50	4.68
20	Type T	59	493	35	17,255	0.120	0.0034	3,419	1.50	4.20
	Grand =	928			601,444		0.0015	1,543	1.50	4.46

Example Application Format

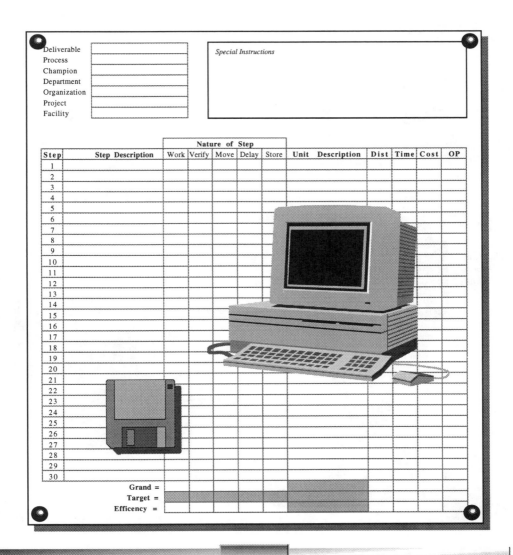

Deliverable
Process
Champion
Department
Organization
Project
Facility

Special Instructions

Step	Step Description	Nature of Step					Unit Description	Dist	Time	Cost	OP
		Work	Verify	Move	Delay	Store					
1											
2											
3											
4											
5											
6											
7											
8											
9											
10											
11											
12											
13											
14											
15											
16											
17											
18											
19											
20											
21											
22											
23											
24											
25											
26											
27											
28											
29											
30											
	Grand =										
	Target =										
	Efficency =										

Phases of Database Implementation

1. *Manual Calculation*

Product Measurements from the Shop Floor are recorded on paper

Calculations are made by hand

Calculations are reviewed as a part of the Black-Belt training

2. *Spreadsheet Calculation*

Product Measurements from the Shop Floor are recorded on Control Cards

Indices of Capability Computed Using L1 and L2 Spreadsheets

Data Storage and Retrieval is Manual

Six Sigma Process Capability Report

Management Begins to Review Six Sigma Report

3. *Statistical Software Calculation*

Product Measurements from the Shop Floor

Computer Data Base and Standardized Statistical Software

Standard Six Sigma Process Capability Report

Management Decisions Based on Standard Six Sigma Report

The Nature of a Database

☺ Solving industrial problems requires the use of data.

☺ A database is a collection of alpha numeric information.

☺ Such information is most often stored on a computer disk for future access.

☺ The information must be structured in a manner that is logical to how it will be accessed and used.

☺ If the structure of the database is inconsistent with respect to how it is used, it must be restructured prior to each use.

☺ After each use, new information is often added to the database.

☺ Each piece of new information must be "labeled " in a consistent manner so that it can be identified.

☺ Databases can be merged together only if they have compatible structures.

☺ To solve common problems, we must have common databases which, in turn, means we must have common structure.

. . . In order to achieve the long-term vision of Six Sigma, we must ensure that the databases we create today are compatible with our needs for tomorrow . Remember, databases tend to become "cast in concrete" once they are designed and implemented.

Characteristics of a Good Database

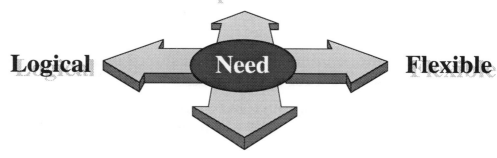

Expandable

Logical   **Need**   **Flexible**

Traceable

Logical: The format anatomy is meaningful to the user.

Expandable: The database can be enlarged without changing the anatomy.

Flexible: Any portion of the anatomy can be manipulated for a specific task.

Traceable: Each piece of data can be skeletonized to its originating source.

Practical Use of the Database

Data is not information ...
It must be tortured to confess

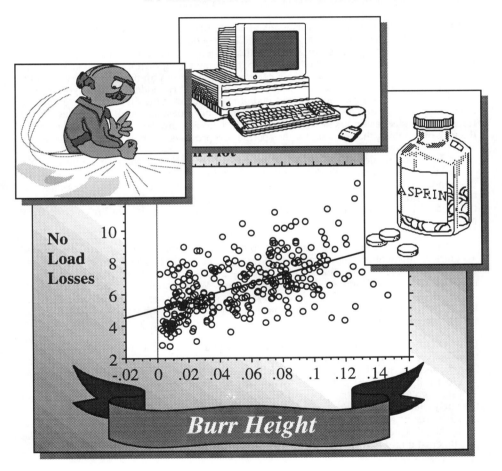

Process Data Gates

As Joe was walking down a dimly lit street in Middletown, USA, he noticed a young man on the opposite side of the street. The young man appeared to be ill, as he was on his knees. Joe thought to himself, "That guy must be awfully sick to be on his hands and knees on this filthy street .. unless ... yes, maybe he has lost something and is looking for it!" Joe, being the good guy he was, walked across the street and asked the young man if he needed help. The young man responded, "I sure could use some ... if you don't mind rolling your sleeves up and getting your clothes soiled a little." Joe then asked, "Why do I need to get down there .. why do I need to do that?" the young man looked up at Joe with a disgusted face and sharply said, "How can you help me from up there ... you see ... I am trying to find a small diamond that I lost out of my ring!" He added, "Unless you have x-ray vision, I don't believe you will spot it six feet in the air in the dim orange glow of this street light ... it is much too dark!" Well, as the story goes, Joe took off his jacket and rolled up the sleeves on his designer shirt, and cautiously dropped to the ground to begin the task of scanning the concrete for the sparkle of a precious stone.

After 30 or 40 minutes of eye-straining, knee-bending work, Joe stood up and proclaims, "You know young man, I don't believe we are going to have much success finding you diamond." "Besides," Joe added, "I don't believe it is here!" The man quickly pointed out to Joe that this was not quite the location where he had lost the diamond. In fact, he then told Joe, "Mister,, I didn't lose it here! ... I never said that! ... only that I'm looking for it here!"

With those words, Joe was not sure what to say. He thought the young man was joking! To clarify the situation, Joe asked, "Did I hear you correctly ... you mean to say that you didn't lose it here?" "Yip, that's right .. .you got it," said the young man. As the anger began to swell in Joe's gut, he sarcastically blurted "Well, if you didn't lose it here, where do you think you lost it?" With a face as straight a mortician, the young man said "Oh! .. I lost it 'bout two blocks south of here near the broken street lamps down by the barber shop!" Joe could hardly believe his ears.

Under his breath, Joe muttered, "This guy is one can short of a six-pack! ... Whew! ... talk about rowing a boat with only one oar in the water ... This guy takes the cake!" After a few seconds passed, Joe said, "Do I dare ask when you lost it ... that is ... let me guess ... you lost it 3 weeks ago! ... Right?" "Well, you see," said the young man, "it was exactly 20 years ago today when the diamond fell out of my ring .. I saw it fall out as I walked past the curly-cue in front of Fred's Barber shop two blocks south of here!" Well, needless to say, Joe was just about ready to tell this guy what he really didn't want to hear! But Joe, being the all-American kind of guy that he was, decided to play it cool! Besides, a fruitcake like this just might pull something funny if you hurt his feelings ... right?"

Just out of sheer curiosity," said Joe, "why are you looking in a section of the street where you know for sure you didn't lose it ... 20 years after the fact?" The young man slowly turned to Joe. His face began changing to a look that would have even made Albert Einstein feel stupid! In the voice of a wise and distinguished university professor, he stated "isn't it intuitively obvious to you my good man ... there's more light here!" As if that by itself wasn't enough to blow Joe away, the young man added "better late than never ... huh?"

Probably by now, you are surely wondering what this story has to do with statistics ... right? Actually it concerns data! How many times have you witnessed people capturing data at a particular point in a manufacturing process where the data is readily available or attainable? You know ... where there's more light! The problem at hand (such as excessive solder shorts) may require data from the supplier, or some other source, which controls the problem but it is being taken at the end of the wave soldering operation, e.g., at the "light source".

By the time the "symptomatic" data is collected "under the light", it is "20 years old". By the time someone tries to back trace the source of some trend, shift, or cycle appearing in the symptomatic data, the controlling variables have been through several generations of additional change. In this situation, the time lag prohibits effective problem solving. In order to achieve real-time problem solving it is necessary to have adequate "light" at the locations where control is actually lost. This is not to say that symptomatic data is not needed, but rather to make the point that it takes more than frequencies and percentages (e.g. categorical data) to control a process. On the other hand, if the problem is too brightly illuminated at the source, (e.g. too much continuous data) we tend to jump with excitement at all of the little "diamond-like" flickers emanating from the sharp angles of granite rocks embedded in the concrete, and the diamond remains lost!

As manufacturing processes grow in sophistication, the need for "designing in street lights" with the proper candlepower becomes increasingly important. Most of the precious gems we lose (e.g., profit loss due to specification nonconformance) could be prevented! To achieve such cost avoidance, a manufacturing process must be "wired" that is to say, an adequate number of "light bulbs" must be present throughout the process in order to maintain constant illumination of the potential location(s) of common problems. In addition, the number and size of "bulbs" establishes such factors as wire size and type. In other words, there is more to consider than just the fact that "light is needed here and there".

The "wiring" of a process for optimum product quality, yield, and cost involves such factors as communication data standardization, training, and management support. If these and other key components are not present, the "bulbs" will not provide adequate intensity, fail to work, or worse yet, "blow-up". Effective problem solving comes to a grinding halt! If a process is to be adequately "wired", careful attention must be given to the formulation of "monitoring" and "control" gates during the design phases of the product and subsequent process.

Process "fuses" (monitoring gates) must be "designed in". When the line current increases to an unacceptable level (e.g., yield characteristics decline), the related portion of the circuit (e.g., process) does not cause the bulb (e.g., product) to "blow up" (e.g., display poor yield/quality/reliability characteristics).

Additional "safety mechanisms" can be built into the system to ensure even higher levels of circuit performance and reliability. One such mechanism is $\overline{X}$ (average) and R (range) charts. If the line current is always kept within certain limits (e.g., leverage variables such as chain speed and oven temperature are maintained within the correct specifications), then the likelihood of "blowing a fuze" is decreased even further. In other words, the likelihood of experiencing erratic yield due to process and material related fluctuations is further minimized.

However, as one wise person once said, "the best laid plans of mice and men ...", in short, Murphy's Law applies! Whenever Murphy strikes, the circuit "goes down", and the light is temporarily extinguished. During this period of time, quality, yield, and profit suffers.

In order to determine the cause of failure, an electrician must be summoned. In turn, this person uses tools to "probe" the circuit for the root cause. In the case of a manufacturing process, the engineer must "probe" with analytical tools such as diagnostic methods and design of experiments. Again, powerful and precise tools can not be effectively used on gross data (e.g., attribute data). Most tools of this nature are designed for continuous data. Furthermore, when "original data" (as distinct from "historical data") has to be gathered, downtime is further extended.

In short, there is a general relationship between product performance indices (e.g., quality, yield, and costs) and analytical resolution (e.g., the type, number, and location of data gates; nature of the statistical tools used at the data gates; and the knowledge level of those individuals wielding the tools).

In summary, if a process is to be adequately controlled, data must be collected. In turn, the data sheds light on the nature of the product. If the light is too dim (e.g., excessive continuous data with too much precision), the potential gains are lost chasing after the "many pieces of sparkling granite". In other words, effective process control is more than just "slapping up control charts"., it is a blending of tools and resources to achieve optimum quality, yield, and profit.

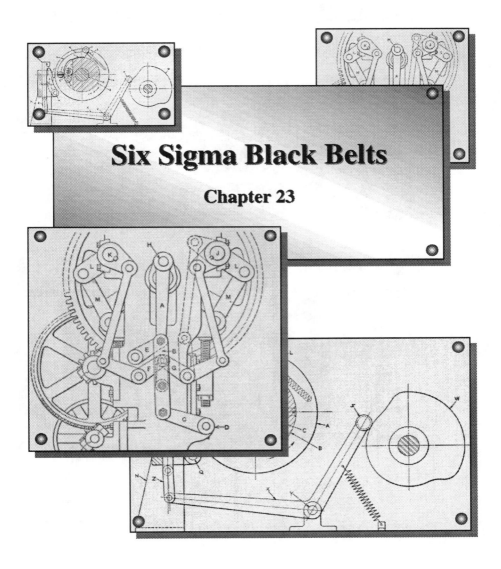

Six Sigma Black Belts

Chapter 23

The AlliedSignal Deployment Plan

Six Sigma Black Belts

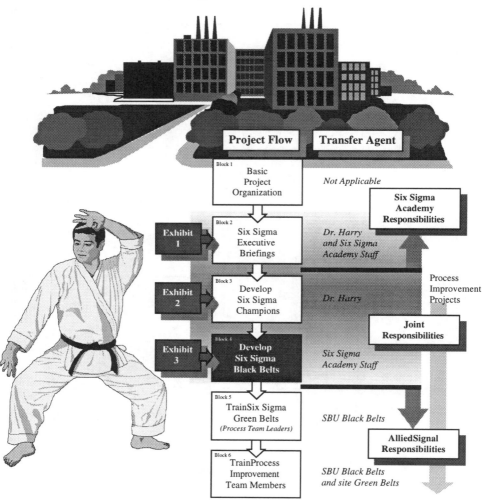

Project Flow	Transfer Agent
Block 1 Basic Project Organization	*Not Applicable*

Six Sigma Academy Responsibilities

Exhibit 1 → **Block 2** Six Sigma Executive Briefings	*Dr. Harry and Six Sigma Academy Staff*

Process Improvement Projects

Exhibit 2 → **Block 3** Develop Six Sigma Champions	*Dr. Harry*

Joint Responsibilities

Exhibit 3 → **Block 4** Develop Six Sigma Black Belts	*Six Sigma Academy Staff*

Block 5 TrainSix Sigma Green Belts *(Process Team Leaders)*	*SBU Black Belts*

AlliedSignal Responsibilities

Block 6 TrainProcess Improvement Team Members	*SBU Black Belts and site Green Belts*

Six Sigma Black Belt Overview

The aim is to create technical leaders, advanced users, and teachers of the Six Sigma tools and methods. These individuals have the potential to produce highly credible break-through success stories and then subsequently transfer those methods, techniques, procedures, and tools to their peers and Customer Focus Teams.

The focus is on developing an in-depth understanding of the Six Sigma philosophy, theory, and application tactics, as well as advanced applications in the areas of descriptive statistics, inferential statistics, nonparametric statistics, quantitative benchmarking, process control techniques, process diagnostic methods, experiment design, as well as organizational/group dynamics and the change process. This knowledge is acquired to facilitate breakthrough improvement in key processes.

The intent is to implant people within the organization who can; a) effectively develop and lead people and teams to improvement, b) work with and advise management on the formulation and subsequent implementation of improvement plans, and c) utilize and disseminate the Six Sigma tools and methods.

The target population for Black-Belt training is characterized by those individuals who are technically oriented, are highly regarded within their respective discipline area or line of work, and are also actively involved in the process of organizational change and development.

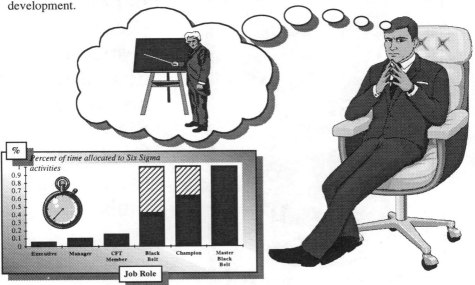

Nature of a Six Sigma Black Belt

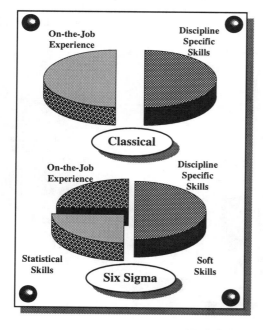

On-the-Job Experience

Discipline Specific Skills

Classical

On-the-Job Experience

Discipline Specific Skills

Statistical Skills

Soft Skills

Six Sigma

Individuals who have the potential to realize a <u>synergistic</u> proficiency between their respective discipline and the Six Sigma strategies, tactics, and tools

Roles of a Six Sigma Black Belt

The Black-Belts are a cadre of individual contributors from various discipline areas which, when adequately trained and technically supported, can serve as change agents, internal consultants, tool mentors, and assist Six Sigma champions. The Black-Belts are the paradigm shifters within an organization. They stimulate management thinking by posing new ways of doing things, challenge conventional wisdom by demonstrating successful application of new methodologies, seek out and pilot new tools, create innovative strategies, and develop others to follow in their footsteps. The Black-Belts can speak the language of management (e.g., money, time, organizational dynamics, etc.) and the language of individual contributors (e.g., implementation details, quality tools, statistical techniques, problem solving methods, etc.) The Black-Belts carry a very high level of peer respect and are clearly seen as leaders -- They manage risk, set direction, and lead the way to breakthrough improvement. In essence, the Black-Belts perform the following tasks:

Mentoring: Cultivate a network of local Six Sigma individuals at the local organization or site.

Teaching: Provide formal training of local personnel in new strategies and tools.

Coaching: Provide one-on-one support to local personnel.

Transferring: Pass on new strategies and tools in the form of training, workshops, case studies, local symposia, etc.

Discovering: Finding application opportunities for Six Sigma strategies and tools, both internal and external (e.g., suppliers and customers).

Identifying: Surfacing business opportunities through partnerships with other organizations.

Influencing: Selling the organization on the use of Six Sigma strategies and tools.

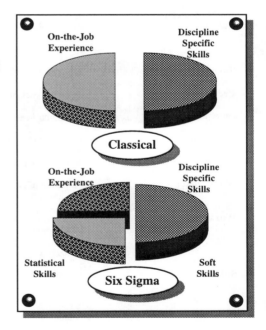

Exhibit 3.0 - Program Description

Six Sigma Black Belt Certification Program

Description: The intent of the *Six Sigma Black Belt Certification Program* is to develop and implant on-site Six Sigma experts within each Strategic Business Unit (SBU) of AlliedSignal Inc. These on-site experts are referred to as "Six Sigma Black Belts." Black Belts have the ability to; a) effectively develop and lead line-of-sight or cross functional process improvement teams, b) work with, mentor, and advise middle management on the formulation and subsequent implementation of process improvement plans, c) utilize and disseminate the Six Sigma tools and methods, and d) network with other Black Belts around the world for the benefit of their SBU. The aim is to produce highly credible breakthrough success stories within their respective SBU using the four-phase Breakthrough Strategy and then transfer the application methods, techniques, procedures, and tools to their peers and process improvement teams.

The central focus of the program is on developing an in-depth understanding of the Six Sigma philosophy, theory, tactics, breakthrough strategy, and application tools. Particular emphasis is placed on the tools of breakthrough -- statistics, quantitative benchmarking, process control techniques, process diagnostic methods, and experiment design. Throughout the certification process, the Black Belt Candidate will discover how the key tools are blended and sequenced to form a scientific and repeatable process for solving critical manufacturing, engineering, service, and administrative problems. The Six Sigma Black Belt Certification is granted after successful completion of the process outlined in Exhibit 3.2.

Target Population:	Experienced SBU engineers and operations personnel.
Prerequisites:	Technical background and leadership ability
Instructor:	Six Sigma Academy Staff (Certified Master Black Belt)
Location:	Established by the Master Black Belt and local Six Sigma Champion
Timing:	As per the master project schedule
Class Size:	Minimum of 20 participants per class Maximum of 30 participants per class
Workbook:	*"The Vision of Six Sigma: A Roadmap for Breakthrough"* *"The Vision of Six Sigma: Tools and Methods for Breakthrough"*
Software:	*"Six Sigma Scorecards: Spreadsheet Applications"*

Exhibit 3.1 - Black Belt Certificate

Six Sigma Black Belt Certification Program

Exhibit 3.2 - Certification Process

Six Sigma Black Belt Certification Program

Description: Prior to initiating the certification process, the SBU Six Sigma Champion identifies 25-30 Black Belt Candidates from within the SBU. The intent is to create a relatively homogeneous group of candidates in terms of the organizational structure and geographic site locations. Following this, the Champion meets with the Master Black Belt so as to coordinate the program delivery. The program delivery is divided into 4 instructional sessions, where each session correlates to one of the four phases contained within the Six Sigma Breakthrough Strategy.

In terms of delivery, each instructional session contains 3 days of classroom activity followed by a 21 day on-the-job (OJT) application experience. During the OJT exercise, the Black Belt Candidates are supported and mentored by a visiting Master Black Belt. Each candidate's OJT results are reviewed and critiqued by the instructor (Master Black Belt), local Six Sigma Champion, and the Candidate's classmates. This is called the "Standard Six Sigma Review." From this perspective, we see that each of the 4 instructional sessions follows the Plan-Train-Apply-Review (PTAR) delivery model.

As should be apparent, the Six Sigma Black Belt Certification Process is founded upon the merits and benefits most commonly associated with a closed-loop feedback system. The terms and definitions related to this process are located in Exhibit 3.3.

	Event	Cycle	Activity Description	Duration
	1	•	Initial Meeting and Planning Session	2 days
1st Month	2	1	Champion Coordination Meeting	1 day
	3	1	Session 1: Black-Belt Training	3 days
	4	1	On-The-Job Application Exercise	21 days
2nd Month	5	2	Champion Coordination Meeting	1 day
	6	2	Standard Six Sigma Review	1 day
	7	2	Session 2: Black-Belt Training	3 days
	8	2	On-The-Job Application Exercise	21 days
3rd Month	9	3	Champion Coordination Meeting	1 day
	10	3	Standard Six Sigma Review	1 day
	11	3	Session 3: Black-Belt Training	3 days
	12	3	On-The-Job Application Exercise	21 days
4th Month	13	4	Champion Coordination Meeting	1 day
	14	4	Standard Six Sigma Review	1 day
	15	4	Session 4: Black-Belt Training	3 days
	17	•	Contingency	6 days

Exhibit 3.3 - Process Definitions

Six Sigma Black Belt Certification Program

Initial Meeting and Planning Session: These two days are utilized by the SBU Champion. The first day is used to mentor the Champion in key deployment issues and/or the various technical aspects of Six Sigma. The second day is used for the purpose of planning, coordinating, and finalizing the various instructional, logistical, and administrative details associated with the ensuing certification process. Of particular importance, the Champion and Master Black Belt have the opportunity to develop a working relationship over the course of these two days prior to launching into a certification cycle.

Champion Coordination Meeting: This is the first active day of a certification cycle. Four such days occur over the certification process. Each of the 4 days is dedicated to the SBU champion and is focused on coordinating the immediate instructional activities at hand, reviewing recent on-site developments/applications, performing technical/deployment mentoring to the Champion, and ensuring any last minute administrative/logistical details are taken care of.

Six Sigma Black Belt Training: Each of the 4 training sessions requires a 3 day period of classroom instruction, for a total of 12 classroom days across the entire certification process. Recognize that each of the 4 training sessions correlates to the 4 phases comprising the Six Sigma Breakthrough Strategy; i.e., Measurement-Analysis-Optimization-Control.

On-The-Job Application Exercise: Following three of the instructional sessions is a time period in which the Black Belt Candidates apply what they have just learned in the classroom. This is called the "On-the-Job Application Exercise," or simply OJT. Each OJT assignment is 21 days in duration. The nature of each of the three OJT assignments (as given to each Black Belt candidate) is established by the Master Black Belt Instructor and are subsequently approved by the SBU Champion prior to the actual assignment. During each OJT period, the Black Belts will be partially supported by on-site consulting services. Such services are provided by the Master Black Belt Instructor and/or a visiting Master Black Belt. The Champion and Master Black Belt will jointly establish the on-site consulting support schedule for each OJT period.

Standard Six Sigma Review: This day is used by the SBU Champion and Master Black Belt Instructor to perform an in-depth review and critique of the OJT assignments given to Black Belt candidates. Each candidate presents the results of his/her exercise to the "class." In this manner, the other candidates are able to see a wide array of applications related to the Six Sigma tools and methods.

Contingency: These days are set aside for any residual training, on-site consulting, and/or support activity which must occur to bring logical closure to the given certification cycle.

Exhibit 3.4 - Program Objectives

Six Sigma Black Belt Certification Program

The purpose of the Six Sigma Black Belt Certification Program is to create a cadre of in-house consultants with the capability to apply and teach Six Sigma, as well as lead Customer Focus Teams to improved process performance. This is accomplished through classroom training, action planning, on-the-job exercises, on-site consultation, and standard application reviews. The overall program goal is to:

Develop key individuals with the fundamental Six Sigma knowledge and skills necessary to implement, sustain, and visibly lead a highly focused Six Sigma initiative within a target business area or unit.

The program goal is realized by progressively weaving the key implementation principles, practices, and tactics within the fabric of the technical material. To accomplish this aim, the instructional material has been decomposed into 4 self-contained training sessions which correlates to the sequence of application. This allows each of the 4 plan-train-apply-review cycles to be executed in a meaningful and consistent manner. The specific objectives for each session are as follows:

Session 1
a) Understand the Basic Concepts of Six Sigma
b) Develop the Language of Six Sigma and Statistics
c) How to Compute and Apply Basic Statistics
d) How to Establish and Benchmark Process Capability

Session 2
a) Understand the Theory of Sampling and Hypothesis Testing
b) How to Apply the Key Statistical Tools for Testing Hypotheses
c) Understand the Elements of Successful Application Planning
d) How to Apply and Manage the Breakthrough Strategy
e) How to Identify and Leverage Dominant Sources of Variation
f) How to Establish Realistic Performance Tolerances

Session 3
a) Understand the Basic Principles of Experimentation
b) How to Design and Execute Multi-Variable Experiments
d) How to Interpret and Communicate the Results of an Experiment
c) How to Plan and Execute a Variable Search Study

Session 4
a) Understand the Basic Concepts of Process Control
b) How to Construct, Use, and Maintain Charts for Variables Data
c) How to Construct, Use, and Maintain Charts for Attribute Data
d) How to Implement and Maintain Precontrol and Positrol Plans
e) How to Plan and Implement Process Control Systems

Exhibit 3.5 - Training Agenda

Six Sigma Black Belt Certification Program

Session	Day	AM	PM
1	1	Core Six Sigma Concepts	Basic Statistics
1	2	Basic Statistics	Basic Statistics
1	3	Advanced Six Sigma Concepts	Advanced Six Sigma Concepts
2	1	Advanced Statistics	Advanced Statistics
2	2	Advanced Statistics	Advanced Statistics
2	3	Breakthrough Strategy	Diagnostic Methods
3	1	Principles of Experiment Design	Full Factorial Designs
3	2	Full Factorial Designs	Full Factorial Designs
3	3	Fractional Factorial Designs	Advanced Topics in Experiment Design
4	1	Foundations of Process Control	Control Charts for Variables
4	2	Control Charts for Variables	Control Charts for Variables
4	3	Control Charts for Attributes	Planning Process Control

Note: The training agenda may vary owing to differences in business environments, people, aims, etc. Such adjustments will be decided upon by the Champion and Master Black-Belt. However, the spirit and intent of this agenda will be maintained at all times so as to ensure the consistency of knowledge. Obviously, this is vital to assure the underlying meaning of certification.

Exhibit 3.6 - Application Links

Six Sigma Black Belt Certification Program

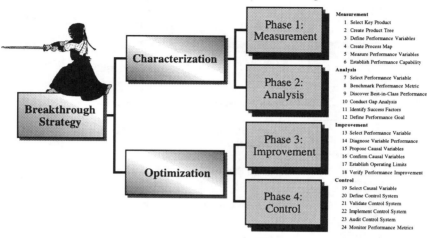

Measurement
1. Select Key Product
2. Create Product Tree
3. Define Performance Variables
4. Create Process Map
5. Measure Performance Variables
6. Establish Performance Capability

Analysis
7. Select Performance Variable
8. Benchmark Performance Metric
9. Discover Best-in-Class Performance
10. Conduct Gap Analysis
11. Identify Success Factors
12. Define Performance Goal

Improvement
13. Select Performance Variable
14. Diagnose Variable Performance
15. Propose Causal Variables
16. Confirm Causal Variables
17. Establish Operating Limits
18. Verify Performance Improvement

Control
19. Select Causal Variable
20. Define Control System
21. Validate Control System
22. Implement Control System
23. Audit Control System
24. Monitor Performance Metrics

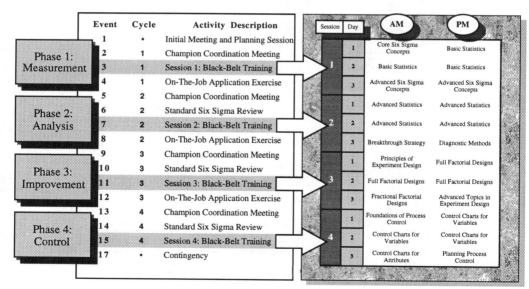

Event	Cycle	Activity Description
1	•	Initial Meeting and Planning Session
2	1	Champion Coordination Meeting
3	1	Session 1: Black-Belt Training
4	1	On-The-Job Application Exercise
5	2	Champion Coordination Meeting
6	2	Standard Six Sigma Review
7	2	Session 2: Black-Belt Training
8	2	On-The-Job Application Exercise
9	3	Champion Coordination Meeting
10	3	Standard Six Sigma Review
11	3	Session 3: Black-Belt Training
12	3	On-The-Job Application Exercise
13	4	Champion Coordination Meeting
14	4	Standard Six Sigma Review
15	4	Session 4: Black-Belt Training
17	•	Contingency

Session	Day	AM	PM
1	1	Core Six Sigma Concepts	Basic Statistics
	2	Basic Statistics	Basic Statistics
	3	Advanced Six Sigma Concepts	Advanced Six Sigma Concepts
2	1	Advanced Statistics	Advanced Statistics
	2	Advanced Statistics	Advanced Statistics
	3	Breakthrough Strategy	Diagnostic Methods
3	1	Principles of Experiment Design	Full Factorial Designs
	2	Full Factorial Designs	Full Factorial Designs
	3	Fractional Factorial Designs	Advanced Topics in Experiment Design
4	1	Foundations of Process Control	Control Charts for Variables
	2	Control Charts for Variables	Control Charts for Variables
	3	Control Charts for Attributes	Planning Process Control

Exhibit 3.7 - Training Strategy

Six Sigma Black Belt Certification Program

The program delivery follows the Six Sigma Plan-Train-Apply-Review (PTAR) model. As should be apparent, such a model is founded upon the merits and benefits most commonly associated with a closed-loop feedback system.

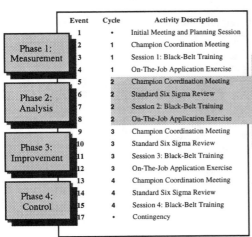

	Event	Cycle	Activity Description
	1	•	Initial Meeting and Planning Session
Phase 1: Measurement	2	1	Champion Coordination Meeting
	3	1	Session 1: Black-Belt Training
	4	1	On-The-Job Application Exercise
Phase 2: Analysis	5	2	Champion Coordination Meeting
	6	2	Standard Six Sigma Review
	7	2	Session 2: Black-Belt Training
	8	2	On-The-Job Application Exercise
Phase 3: Improvement	9	3	Champion Coordination Meeting
	10	3	Standard Six Sigma Review
	11	3	Session 3: Black-Belt Training
	12	3	On-The-Job Application Exercise
Phase 4: Control	13	4	Champion Coordination Meeting
	14	4	Standard Six Sigma Review
	15	4	Session 4: Black-Belt Training
	17	•	Contingency

Plan

Train

Apply

Review

Exhibit 3.8 - Session 1

Six Sigma Black Belt Certification Program

Core Six Sigma Concepts and Basic Statistics   *Session 1, Days 1 - 2*

Up front, the training will cover the basic tenants of Six Sigma in a non-technical manner and then proceed to a more technically oriented discussion on the topic of descriptive (basic) statistics. In turn, this knowledge provides the educational backdrop necessary for exposure to more advanced topics relating to the key Six Sigma methods, practices, and procedures. The target audience will be continually exposed to implementation considerations and constraints. In particular, deployment techniques will be highlighted. Specifically, the participants will discover:

- The Driving Need for Six Sigma Quality
- The Fundamental Objective of Six Sigma
- The Basic Tenants of Six Sigma Quality
- Key Business Conclusions Resulting From Global Benchmarking
- Six Sigma as a Target for Total Quality Management (TQM)
- The Analytical Tools for Achieving Six Sigma
- The Customer's Perspective of Six Sigma
- The Financial Impact of Six Sigma on the Bottom Line
- Strategies and Tactics for Implementing Six Sigma
- Typical Costs Associated with Implementation
- The Theory and Practical Application of Descriptive Statistics

Advanced Six Sigma Concepts   *Session 1, Day 3*

At this point in the curriculum, participants will begin to advance their knowledge of the Six Sigma principles and start to see first-hand how these principles apply to their respective businesses and related processes. In particular this portion of the training agenda will address:

- Advanced Six Sigma Concepts, Tools, and Methods
- The Impact of Product and Process Complexity on Quality
- The Impact of Six Sigma on Product Reliability
- The Impact of Six Sigma on Manufacturing Cycle-Time
- The Impact of Six Sigma on Inventory
- Developing Six Sigma Suppliers
- How to Create and Maintain Six Sigma Product Designs
- How to Create and Maintain Six Sigma Manufacturing Processes
- How to Create and Maintain Six Sigma Services

In addition, several "real life" case studies will be presented and thoroughly discussed. The case studies are from variety of companies. They are configured to illustrate many of the "how to's" with respect to selected Six Sigma methods and practices.

Exhibit 3.9 - Session 2

Six Sigma Black Belt Certification Program

Advanced Statistics

Session 2, Days 1 - 2

At this point, participants enter the domain of inferential statistics, the backbone of Six Sigma and performance breakthrough. Participants will learn the theory and application of commonly used sampling techniques. In addition, focus will be given to the most frequently used sampling distributions. From here, the discussion turns toward hypothesis testing and its vital link to diagnostic methods (DM), design-of-experiments (DOE), and statistical process control (SPC). In specific, the participants will learn how to construct statistical hypotheses and then how to test the hypotheses using well established methods, such as the t-test and analysis-of-variance (ANOVA). The knowledge gained from this portion of the curriculum is paramount to the effective use of performance metrics and indices of process capability. Through this training, the participant will gain tremendous insight into the logic and reasoning which underlies Six Sigma and process improvement.

The Breakthrough Strategy

Session 2, Day 3

Herein, participants will be presented a highly effective and time-proven strategy for realizing breakthrough. This strategy focuses on a deductive process for a) characterizing process performance, b) isolating leverage sources of variation, c) and systematically eliminating those variations over time. Furthermore, the participants will learn the science of planning a process characterization and optimization study in the context of breakthrough improvement. Emphasis will be placed on the standardized planning steps and how to properly sequence these steps for any given situation. Furthermore, a clear focus is given to the tactics necessary to support short-cycle implementation.

Diagnostic Methods

Session 2, Day 3

Once a process has been characterized, benchmarked and tagged for improvement, it is often desirable to diagnose the given performance metric. This is done so as to identify the dominant families of variation. In many instances, the simple application of a few diagnostic tools can preclude the need for exhaustive experimentation during the improvement phase of the breakthrough process. The participant will discover the analytical and statistical tools necessary for isolating critical sources of variation in terms of process centering and spread. The methods and techniques for statistically analyzing, describing, and graphing resultant data is given major emphasis. In particular, the participant will learn how to select the right variables and parameters for inclusion in a factorial experiment. The participant will also learn how to establish realistic process tolerances. From here, the discussion progresses to those tools which can be applied when operating under the constraint of discrete data. Furthermore, a clear focus is given to the tactics necessary to support short-cycle implementation. As with the other portions of the curriculum, reinforcement of major techniques and applications is realized through exercises, scenarios, and case studies.

Exhibit 3.10 - Sessions 3 & 4

Six Sigma Black Belt Certification Program

Improving Process Performance   *Session 3 Days 1 - 3*

The participants are now ready to gain great insight into the statistical tools and knowledge necessary for planning, conducting, and analyzing a wide array of statistically designed experiments. Through this portion of the curriculum, the participant will learn how to translate a practical problem into a statistical problem and then isolate complex cause and effect relationships which often remain undetected with traditional problem-solving methods. The participant will also learn how the application of a statistically designed experiment can identify optimum operating conditions for the critical process variables. The participant will also learn how to communicate and depict experimental results in down-to-earth language. Primary focus is given to design principles, data analysis, and graphical procedures. From here, the participant progresses on to a discussion related to the application of more advanced experiment designs. A heavy emphasis is given to the application of fractional factorial experiments as an economy measure when the availability of samples or the cost of sampling restricts the use of a full factorial experiment or when it is necessary to screen a large number of variables for subsequent detailed analysis. Furthermore, a clear focus is given to the tactics necessary to support short-cycle implementation. Reinforcement of major concepts, techniques, and applications is realized through exercises, scenarios, case studies, and field studies.

Controlling Process Performance   *Session 4, Days 1 - 3*

In particular, this part of the curriculum will provide the participant with the skills necessary for understanding the need for and application of process control tools. Emphasis is given to the methods associated with planning a control chart study, rational sampling, and computation. In addition, the participant will learn how to compute various indices of process capability as well as the fundamentals of statistical process control charts. From here, the participant progresses on to more advanced process control techniques and tools. Heavy emphasis is placed on the planning, organizing, constructing, implementing, and interpreting statistical process control charts for variables and attribute data. Insights are developed for applications to chronic process control problems. Primary emphasis is placed on construction methods and interpretation of variables and attribute control charts. In addition, participants will learn how to identify areas which can directly benefit from the use of control charts. In addition, the development of analytical philosophy and language serves to augment the existing skills of participants. Furthermore, a clear focus is given to the tactics necessary to support short-cycle implementation. Reinforcement of major concepts, techniques, and applications is realized through exercises, scenarios, case studies, and field studies.

Exhibit 3.11 - Session Topics

Six Sigma Black Belt Certification Program

Core Six Sigma Concepts

Understanding Customer Satisfaction
Linking Probability to Satisfaction
Understanding the Normal Distribution
Understanding the Standard Deviation
Understanding Mean Variation
Understanding Six Sigma Quality
Understanding Sources of Variation
Computing the Standard Deviation
Visualizing the Standard Deviation
Estimating Defect Probability
The Poisson Model
The Binomial Model
Indices of Capability
Rolled Throughput Yield
Defects-per-Unit Metric
Theory and Science of Benchmarking
Performance Benchmarking Results
Display of Benchmarking Results
Correlating Quality to Cycle Time
Cycle-Time Theory and Relationships
Cycle-Time Improvement Principles
Correlating Cycle Time to Inventory
Correlating Quality to Product Reliability
Correlating Quality to R.O.I.
Concurrent Engineering Principles and Practices
Quality Function Deployment
Keys for Implementing Six Sigma

Rationale for Performance Metrics
Components of a Performance Metric
Basis of Instantaneous Reproducibility
Computing Instantaneous Reproducibility
Basis of Sustained Resproducibility
Computing Sustained Resproducibility
The Role of Rational Subgroups
Understanding Static Mean Behavior
Understanding Dynamic Mean Behavior
Computing Equivalent Mean Shifts
The Performance Metrics
Graphing Performance Metrics
Establishing Performance Goals
Implementing Performance Metrics
Impact of Measurement Error

Basic Statistics

The Nature of Problems
Translating Practical Problems
Constructing Statistical Hypotheses
The Concept of Decision Error
Distribution of Averages
Central Limit Theorem
The Standard Error
The Impact of Sample Size
The t Distribution
Confidence Interval for the Mean
The Chi-Square Distribution
Confidence Interval for the Standard Deviation
Applications of the Confidence Intervals

Estimating Sample Size
The t Test
The F Test
One-Way Analysiss-of-Variance
Post-Hoc Comparisons

Understanding the Elements of Breakthrough
Common Strategic Mistakes
The Four Phase Strategy
The Step-Wise Roadmap
Translating Statistical Problems
The Role of Performance Measures

Reverse Planning Tactics
The Fundamental Tools
Data Reporting Issues
Roles and Responsibilities

Process and Data Mapping
Brainstorming
Fishbone Diagram
Cause and Effect Matrices
Data Collection Practices
Multivari Analysis
Graphical Correlation
Realistic Tolerancing
Cross-Tabulation
Chi-Square Analysis and Adaptations
Nonparametric Correlation Methods
Nonparametric Goodness-of-Fit Tests

Optimizing Process Performance

Experiment Design Principles
Experimentation Systems
Single Factor Experiments
2^2 Full Factorial Experiments
2^k Full Factorial Experiments
Multi Factor Multi Level Designs
Analysis of 2^2 Full Factorials
Yate's Algorithm
Analysis of 2^3 Full Factorials
Principles of Fractional Factorials
2^4-1 Fractional Design
2^5-1 Fractional Design
2^6-2 Fractional Design
2^k-p Fractional Designs

Response Surface Designs
Principles of Robust Design
Planning Experiments

Foundations of SPC

Control Charts for Attribute Data
Control Chart for Individuals
Xbar Chart (average)
R Chart (range)
S Chart (standard deviation)
NP Chart (number nonconforming)

U Chart (defects-per-unit chart)
EWMA Chart
Creating Customized SPC Charts
Planning Process Control
Implementing Control Charts

Exhibit 3.12 - Follow-On Topics

Six Sigma Black Belt Certification Program

Technical

Inferential Statistical Methods
Nonparametric Statistical Methods
Advanced Diagnostic Tools
Design and Analysis of Experiments
Statistical Process Control Charts

Technology and Human Behavior
Components of Management
Change as a Process
Analysis of Change
Strategic and Operations Planning
Implementation and Control of Change
Perception and Attitude Formation
Motivation and Human Behavior
namics of Group Behavior and Control
Effective Managerial Leadership
Synergistic Management Practices
Conflict Management
Decision Optimization
Effective Delegation
The Role and Use of Empowerment
Building High Performance Teams
Dynamics of Effective Communication
Formulating Organizational Success
Strategic Improvement Workshop
Results Oriented Marketing and Sales Skills
Effective Consulting Practices
Creating Management Sponsorship
Short Cycle Knowledge Transfer Process
Short Cycle Knowledge Transfer Tools

Organizational

Further Reading

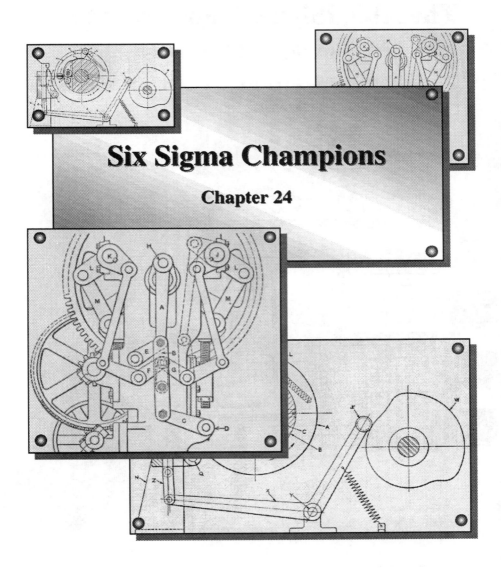

Six Sigma Champions

Chapter 24

The AlliedSignal Deployment Plan

Six Sigma Champions

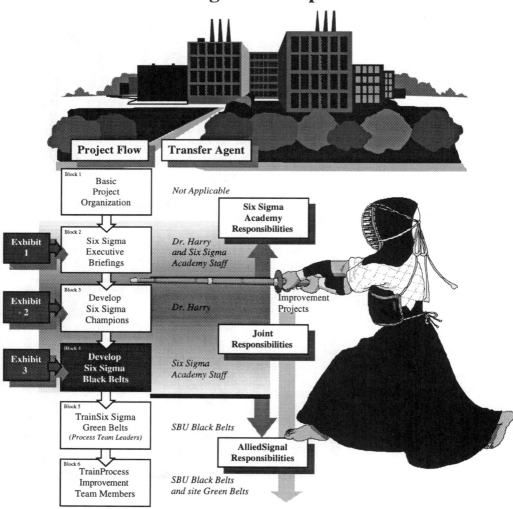

Project Flow	Transfer Agent	
Block 1 Basic Project Organization	*Not Applicable*	
		Six Sigma Academy Responsibilities
Exhibit 1 → **Block 2** Six Sigma Executive Briefings	*Dr. Harry and Six Sigma Academy Staff*	
Exhibit 2 → **Block 3** Develop Six Sigma Champions	*Dr. Harry*	Improvement Projects
		Joint Responsibilities
Exhibit 3 → **Block 4** Develop Six Sigma Black Belts	*Six Sigma Academy Staff*	
Block 5 TrainSix Sigma Green Belts *(Process Team Leaders)*	*SBU Black Belts*	
		AlliedSignal Responsibilities
Block 6 TrainProcess Improvement Team Members	*SBU Black Belts and site Green Belts*	

Roles of a Six Sigma Champion

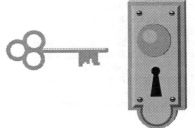

What the Champion Must Do

Create the Vision

Tool the Mind

Define the Path

Realize the Gains

Hold the Ground

How the Champion Must Do It

Technical	Process Mapping
Statistical	Presentation
Leadership	Managing Diversity
Coaching	Report Writing
Communications	Consulting
Instructional	Active Listening
Team Work	Software
Business Literacy	Computer Literacy
Mentoring	Negotiation
Empathy	Communication
Interpersonal	Sales
Problem Solving	Project Management
Facilitation	Organizational Skills
Motivation	Budgeting

Six Sigma Champion Overview

The customers that form the enormous base of today's world market are sending a clear and undeniable message -- produce higher quality products at lower costs with greater responsiveness. Numerous companies have heard this message and are visibly rising to the Six Sigma challenge. For many, the stalking of Six Sigma has led to the breakthrough improvement of business, engineering, manufacturing, service, and administrative processes. Of course, such a process-oriented focus leads to significant reduction in cost and cycle-time; however, the principal focus is always on the continuous improvement of customer satisfaction. To this end, the Six Sigma Champion Certification Program was conceived, designed, and developed.

The intent of this program of study is to provide key individuals with the managerial and technical knowledge necessary to facilitate the leadership, implementation, and deployment of Six Sigma. The instructional goal is to transfer and reinforce the fundamental Six Sigma strategies, tactics, and tools necessary for achieving breakthrough in key product designs, manufacturing processes, services, and administrative processes. To best support this focus, the program delivery has been structured into 2 self-contained segments which, when successfully completed, leads to certification. Naturally, the resulting certificate denotes and communicates a high level of executive commitment, dedication, competency, and leadership.

Each segment will concentrate on the underlying philosophy, supporting theory, conventional practices, and application dynamics related to the Six Sigma strategies, tactics, and tools. In addition, each segment will focus on the critical implementation issues and mechanics which surrounds the instructional material. Directly following each program session, the participants will synthesize the key points of instruction and then contribute to the progressive development of a model Six Sigma implementation plan aimed at their respective business. After contributing to the progressive implementation model, the participants will be provided an out-of-class assignment. Naturally, the objective of such an assignment is rooted in the belief that we "learn by doing." With this as a backdrop, knowledge is translated to action.

Through this program of study, the instructional material delivered within the classroom is smoothly blended into an implementation and deployment plan. In turn, such plans are translated to front-line practice within the targeted business. In this context, program delivery follows the Six Sigma Plan-Train-Apply-Review (PTAR) model. As should be apparent, such a model is founded upon the merits and benefits most commonly associated with a closed-loop feedback system.

Exhibit 2.0 - Program Description

Six Sigma Champion Certification Program

Description: The overall intent of this curriculum is to prepare and install a Six Sigma project leader within each Strategic Business Unit (SBU) of AlliedSignal Inc. Such an individual is referred to as the local "Six Sigma Champion." Through the *Six Sigma Champion Certification Program,* the candidate will learn how to successfully organize and effectively lead the deployment of Six Sigma across a large organization.

To achieve this aim, the program delivery has been structured into 2 instructional segments. The first segment is 5 days in duration and concentrates on the underlying philosophy, supporting theory, conventional practices, and application dynamics of Six Sigma. In addition, the training zeros in on the critical implementation issues and deployment mechanics. Directly following this segment of the program, each Champion develops a detailed Six Sigma implementation plan aimed at their respective SBU. In turn, the plan is reviewed and approved by the SBU management team and Dr. Harry.

Completion of the second segment is tied to participation in the given SBU's Black Belt Certification Program (see Exhibit 3.0). Upon successful completion of both segments, the candidate is certified. It must be recognized that the Champion is the primary key to successful implementation, deployment, and application of Six Sigma. Therefore, careful consideration must be given to selecting candidates for this position. In short, they must be Best-in-Class.

Target Population:	Senior managers with an operations, technical, and/or quality background.
Prerequisites:	Strong leadership skills and a keen interest in business improvement through process improvement
Instructor:	Dr. Mikel J. Harry
Location:	Phoenix, Arizona
Timing:	As per project schedule
Class Size:	Minimum of 10 participants required per session
Workbook:	*"The Vision of Six Sigma: A Roadmap for Breakthrough"*

Exhibit 3.1 - Black Belt Certificate

Six Sigma Black Belt Certification Program

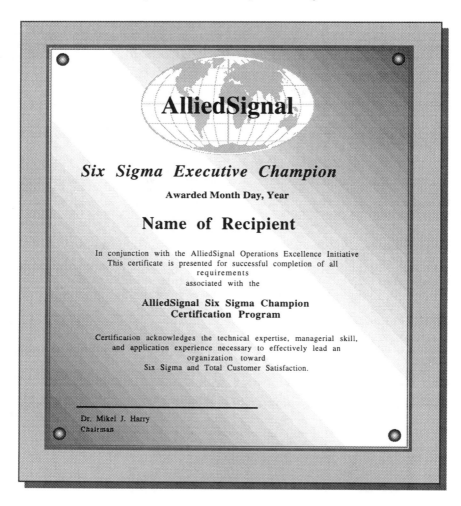

AlliedSignal

Six Sigma Executive Champion

Awarded Month Day, Year

Name of Recipient

In conjunction with the AlliedSignal Operations Excellence Initiative
This certificate is presented for successful completion of all
requirements
associated with the

**AlliedSignal Six Sigma Champion
Certification Program**

Certification acknowledges the technical expertise, managerial skill,
and application experience necessary to effectively lead an
organization toward
Six Sigma and Total Customer Satisfaction.

Dr. Mikel J. Harry
Chairman

Exhibit 2.2 - Certification Process

Six Sigma Champion Certification Program

Event	Description	Duration
1	Champion Mentoring and Training	**5 days**
2	Develop Deployment Plan	**14 days**
3	Complete Black Belt Process	**90 days**

Six Sigma Champion Certification Process: Once the key principles are accepted by the management, the task of implementation most often falls squarely on the shoulders of champions. They are the ones on the forward edge of the battlefield. Their technical and human relations skills can inspire and give people the motivation they need to "take the next step." This certification process is intended to develop executive level leaders who understand the underlying theories, principles, and practices of Six Sigma from a management and technical perspective. With this knowledge and skill set, the champion will be able to perform an organizational assessment, benchmark the organization's products and services, conduct a detailed gap analysis, create an operational vision, develop a cross-functional Six Sigma deployment plan, and provide technical and managerial leadership to the cadre of Six Sigma Black-Belts.

Exhibit 2.3 - Training Agenda

Six Sigma Champion Certification Program

Session	Day	AM	PM
1	1	Core Six Sigma Concepts	Basic Statistics
	2	Basic Statistics	Advanced Six Sigma Concepts
	3	Advanced Six Sigma Concepts	Advanced Statistics
	4	Breakthrough Strategy	Creating the Vision
	5	Strategic Planning	Deployment Planning
2		Reference Six Sigma Black Belt Certification Process (Exhibit 3.2)	

Note: Focus of the given agenda is on the strategies, tactics, and tools related to the Six Sigma initiative . Each topic will be treated from a technical point-of-view so as to gain a rudimentary understanding of the application strengths and weaknesses. Following this, the discussion will immediately center on the key implementation, deployment, management , and organizational dynamics surrounding the topic. From this perspective, it is easy to see that the mechanistic application of a statistical tool or method is one thing, but getting 2,000 people (at 15 locations around the world) using it is quite another. It is from the latter vantage point that the mentoring process will operate.

Exhibit 2.4 - Discussion Topics

Six Sigma Champion Certification Program

1 Company of the Past, Present, and Future
2 Understanding the Impact of Corporate Values
3 The Driving Need for Customer Focus and Six Sigma
4 The Fundamental Objective of Six Sigma
5 The Nature, Tenants, and Principles of Six Sigma
6 The Art and Science of Quantitiative Benchmarking
7 Key Business Conclusions Resulting From Global Benchmarking
8 Financial Impact of the Quality Gap
9 Six Sigma as a Target for Total Quality Management (TQM)
10 The Primary Tools for Achieving Six Sigma
11 The Customer's Perspective of Six Sigma
12 The Financial Impact of Six Sigma on the Bottom Line
13 The Impact of Product and Process Complexity on Quality
14 The Impact of Six Sigma on Product Reliability
15 The Impact of Six Sigma on Manufacturing Cycle-Time
16 The Impact of Six Sigma on Inventory
17 Advanced Six Sigma Concepts
18 The Tools for Diagnosing Process Performance
19 The Tools for Optimizing Process Performance
20 The Tools for Controlling Process Performance
21 Principles and Practices in Design-for-Manufacturability
22 How to Create and Maintain Six Sigma Product Designs
23 How to Create and Maintain Six Sigma Manufacturing Processes
24 How to Create and Maintain Six Sigma Services
25 How to Create and Maintain Six Sigma Suppliers
26 Six Sigma Risk Assessment and Financial Analysis
27 Motorola Case Study
28 Texas Instruments Case Study
29 Asea Brown Boveri Case Study
30 The Building-Block Implementation Model
31 The Role of Top Management and the Senior Quality Officer
32 Formulating and Leveraging a Quality Council
33 Creating and Benefiting from Business Metrics
34 The Need for a Quality System Review
35 The Six Sigma Black-Belt Infrastructure
36 Using Training and Education as a Vehicle for Change
37 The Vision Beyond Six Sigma

Exhibit 2.5 - Follow-On Topics

Six Sigma Champion Certification Program

Technical

Inferential Statistical Methods
Nonparametric Statistical Methods
Advanced Diagnostic Tools
Design and Analysis of Experiments
Statistical Process Control Charts
Technology and Human Behavior
Components of Management
Change as a Process
Analysis of Change
Strategic and Operations Planning
Implementation and Control of Change
Perception and Attitude Formation
Motivation and Human Behavior
namics of Group Behavior and Control
Effective Managerial Leadership
Synergistic Management Practices
Conflict Management
Decision Optimization
Effective Delegation
The Role and Use of Empowerment
Building High Performance Teams
Dynamics of Effective Communication
Formulating Organizational Success
Strategic Improvement Workshop
Results Oriented Marketing and Sales Skills
Effective Consulting Practices
Creating Management Sponsorship
Short Cycle Knowledge Transfer Process
Short Cycle Knowledge Transfer Tools

Further Reading

Organizational

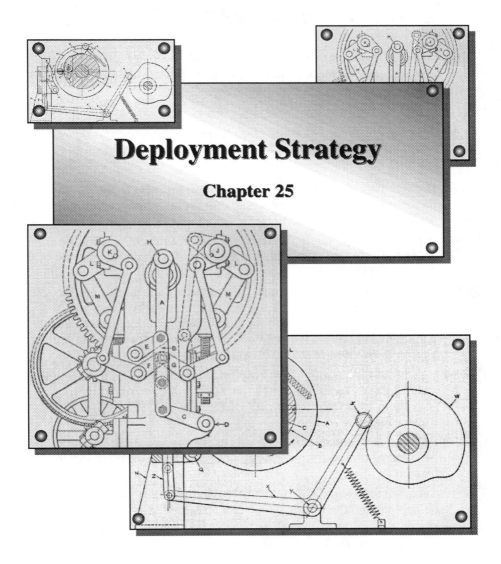

Deployment Strategy

Chapter 25

The Implementation Principles

Question: How can a business unit, regardless of size, product, service, production volume, or product mix, leapfrog its way to the Six Sigma goal in a relatively short period of time?

Answer: Experience has shown that successful implementation depends on an interaction between the following principles:

Highly visible top-down management commitment to the initiatives. People must perceive active leadership versus management-ship during the course of implementation.

A measurement system (metrics) to track the progress. This weaves accountability into the initiatives and provides a tangible picture of the organization's efforts.

Internal and external benchmarking of the organization's products, services, and processes. This information inevitably leads to a "significant emotional event" in that the organization can see and communicate its relative position. When this happens, the organization begins to gravitate toward a break-through philosophy.

Reach-out goal setting (10x, 100x, etc.). Such goals focuses people on changing the process by which the work gets done rather than "tweaking " the existing process. This leads to "leap-frog" rates of improvement.

Provision of education to all levels of the organization. Without the necessary mind-tools, people can not make break-through improvement happen.

Success stories which demonstrate how the tools of improvement can be applied and the results which can be achieved.

Champions and Black-Belts to promote the initiatives and provide the necessary planning , teaching, coaching, and consulting at all levels of the organization.

The Six Sigma Success Factors

Six Sigma Champions

Business Metrics

Common Process Metrics

Benchmarking

Stretch-Goals

Breakthrough Strategy

Six Sigma Black-Belts

Success Stories

Experiment Design & SPC

Quality and Time Focus

Design-for-Manufacturability Methods

Quality Policy and Deployment

Quality Council and Associate Membership

Empowered High-Performance Work Teams

The Aim of Deployment

○ **Strategy: Achieve World-Class Process Capability**

○ **Tactic: Quality Improvement**

○ **Measurement: Total-Defects-Per-Unit & Sigma Scale**

○ **Baseline: Current Performance Level**

○ **Immediate Goal: 1σ Improvement by End of the Second Year**

○ **Intermediate Goal: 2σ Improvement by End of the Fourth Year**

○ **Long-Range Goal: Be at 6σ by End of Sixth Year**

Taking the Initial Steps

Contact

The organization becomes aware of the Six Sigma concept and seeks additional information.

The executive briefing provides management insights on how Six Sigma can be implemented and applied within their business.

6σ

Briefing

6σ = \$

Decision

Management makes the decision to take the next step by selecting a key executive as their Six Sigma Champion.

Champion

Plan

6σ Deployment Plan

The deployment plan spells out the details of how Six Sigma will be implemented.

The Six Sigma Champion receives intensive training and is subsequently certified. This person oversees and guides the overall Six Sigma initiative. The Champion understands all of the implementation and application details associated with Six Sigma. During the training experience, the Champion develops a comprehensive deployment plan. Management reviews the plan and makes the decision to continue forward movement with Six Sigma.

Developing and Applying Resources

Black Belts

Black Belts are trained in the strategies, tactics, and application tools of Six Sigma. Once the training experience is complete, they are certified. Back on the job, they execute their normal activities; however, they also guide and assist Customer Focus Teams in pursuit of process improvement goals.

Customer Focus Teams are formed and then trained in the 7 basic tools of improvement by their Black Belt. In turn, they apply the tools within their respective line-of-sight process.

Teams

Step 1	Step 2	Output

Processes

Each CF team establishes and executes a Six Sigma process improvement project under the guidance of a Black Belt.

Measurement

Measurements are taken on the key product characteristics so as to establish process capability. In turn, this data is used to benchmark the product and process.

Analysis

If the process capability is substandard, the process is further diagnosed in an effort to find points of leverage using the basic tools of SPC. Such analyses are performed by the Black Belt and key members of the Customer Focus Team.

Improvement

Designed experiments are conducted to find the "vital few" process and material variables. Next, the optimum operating conditions are established. Finally, the key variables are controlled over time.

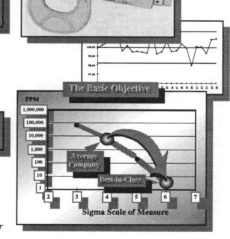

Creating High Performance Teams

. . . What do high performance teams do?

- ○ **Identify Customer Requirements**
- ○ **Measure Performance**
- ○ **Eliminate Causes of Variation**
- ○ **Design Work Systems**
- ○ **Provide Supplier Feedback**
- ○ **Analyze and Solve Problems**

Establishing the Roadmap

6σ
Deployment
Plan

Quality Council

- **Budget Process**
- **Deployment Strategy**
- **Quality Council**
- **Tools and Methods**
- **Measurement System**
- **Business Metrics**
- **Training Curriculum**
- **Cross-Functional Teams**
- **Black-Belt Infrastructure**
- **Reach-Out Goal Setting**
- **Vision and Mission Statement**
- **Quality Policy Process**
- **Benchmarking and Analysis**
- **Quality Data System**
- **Communication System**
- **Process Characterization**
- **Implementation Reviews**
- **Roles and Responsibilities**
- **Business System Integration**
- **Reward and Recognition**
- **Documents Publication**

The Deployment Milestones

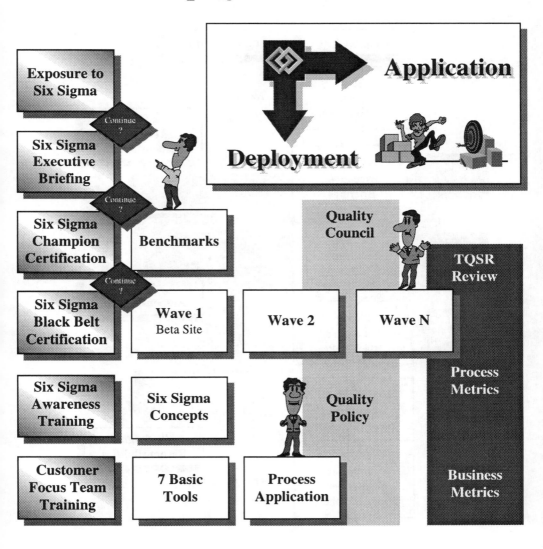

Exposure to Six Sigma

Continue?

Six Sigma Executive Briefing

Continue?

Six Sigma Champion Certification — Benchmarks

Continue?

Six Sigma Black Belt Certification — Wave 1 Beta Site

Application

Deployment

Quality Council

TQSR Review

Wave 2 — Wave N

Process Metrics

Six Sigma Awareness Training — Six Sigma Concepts — Quality Policy

Customer Focus Team Training — 7 Basic Tools — Process Application

Business Metrics

The AlliedSignal Deployment Plan

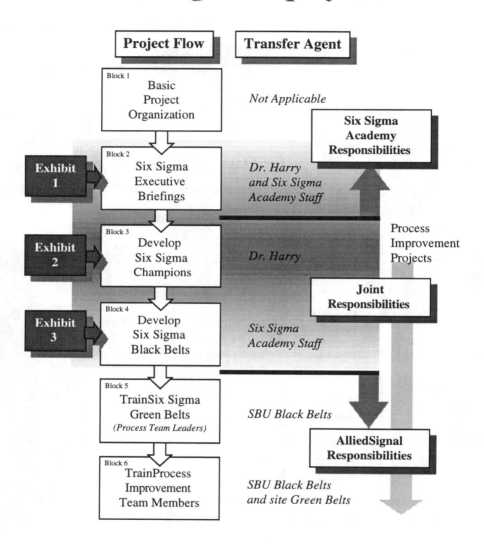

Project Flow	Transfer Agent

Block 1 — Basic Project Organization — *Not Applicable*

Six Sigma Academy Responsibilities

Exhibit 1 → **Block 2** — Six Sigma Executive Briefings — *Dr. Harry and Six Sigma Academy Staff*

Exhibit 2 → **Block 3** — Develop Six Sigma Champions — *Dr. Harry*

Process Improvement Projects

Joint Responsibilities

Exhibit 3 → **Block 4** — Develop Six Sigma Black Belts — *Six Sigma Academy Staff*

Block 5 — Train Six Sigma Green Belts *(Process Team Leaders)* — *SBU Black Belts*

AlliedSignal Responsibilities

Block 6 — Train Process Improvement Team Members — *SBU Black Belts and site Green Belts*

25 . 10

The AlliedSignal Timeline

n = minimum number of people committed to the given training event.

General Deployment Considerations

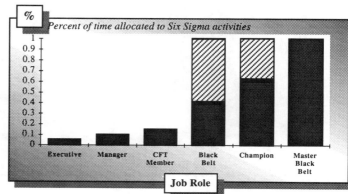

Depth of Six Sigma Deployment

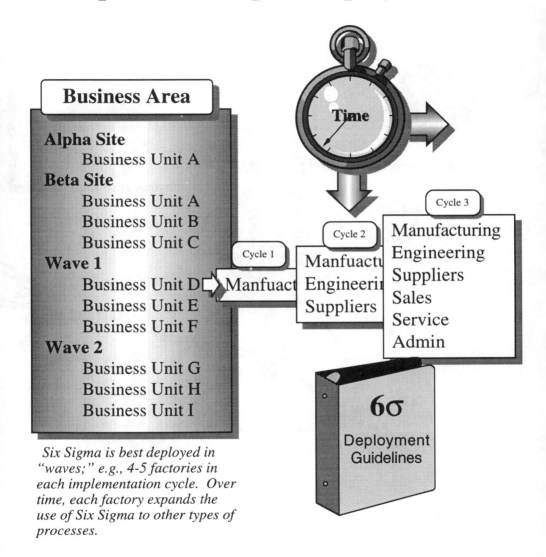

Business Area

Alpha Site
   Business Unit A
Beta Site
   Business Unit A
   Business Unit B
   Business Unit C
Wave 1
   Business Unit D
   Business Unit E
   Business Unit F
Wave 2
   Business Unit G
   Business Unit H
   Business Unit I

Time

Cycle 1
Manfuact

Cycle 2
Manfuactu
Engineeri
Suppliers

Cycle 3
Manufacturing
Engineering
Suppliers
Sales
Service
Admin

6σ
Deployment
Guidelines

Six Sigma is best deployed in "waves;" e.g., 4-5 factories in each implementation cycle. Over time, each factory expands the use of Six Sigma to other types of processes.

Scope of Six Sigma Deployment

Building the Infrastructure

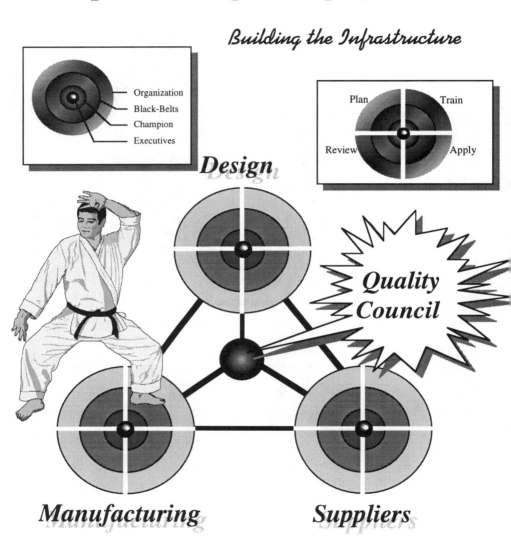

Organization
Black-Belts
Champion
Executives

Plan
Train
Review
Apply

Design

Quality Council

Manufacturing

Suppliers

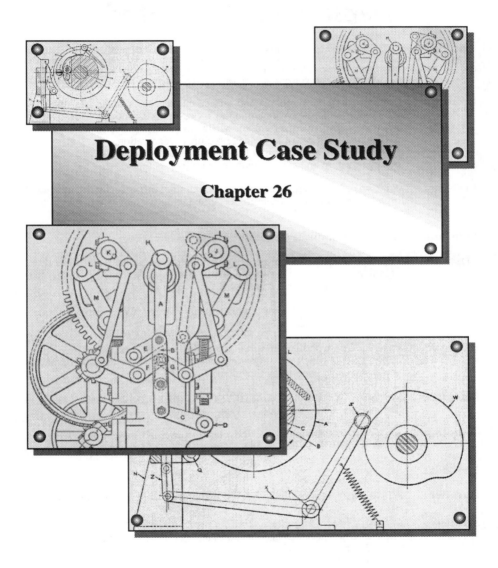

Deployment Case Study

Chapter 26

Deployment Case Study

Note: The purpose of this case study is to illustrate how one organization used the deployment principles and guidelines to initiate Six Sigma in their Business Area (BA). Of course, the step-wise progression presented in this case is specific to a certain business area; however, the general form will prevail across any type of business. In this sense, the case study appears quite generic and, as a consequence, can serve as a model for others to mold.

Belief:
1) Processes govern product and service quality, costs, and cycle-time
2) Breakthrough improvement in key processes is essential
3) People must have the right knowledge to make improvement happen
4) The mass transfer of knowledge requires organization
5) The uniform application of knowledge requires support
6) Organization and support requires an infrastructure

Problem: XYZ business area does not posses the required infrastructure to adequately organize or support a long-term Six Sigma initiative aimed at breakthrough process improvement

Solution: Establish and activate the necessary infrastructure

Mission: Primary - Establish an infrastructure which has the capacity and capability to organize, transfer, and network essential Six Sigma knowledge and tools within the human resource base of XYZ

Secondary - Provide the customers and suppliers of XYZ with Six Sigma knowledge and tools

Aim: Provide XYZ with the self-sustaining ability to realize process improvements which will ultimately lead to the attainment of Six Sigma performance, in everything they do

Clients: Primary - XYZ Business Area (BA) and internal organizations
Secondary - XYZ customers and suppliers

Training:
A) Six Sigma Champion — 2 cycles of 5 days + 1 on-site review
B) Six Sigma Black-Belt — 4 cycles of 3 days + 3 reviews + contingency

Method: Six Sigma PTAR cycle (plan, train, apply, and review)

Duration: Active engagement with the BA through Phase 5 (approximately 6 months)

Strategy:
Phase 1: Cluster Definition
Phase 2: Orientation, Decision, and Planning (at the BA level)
Phase 3: Champion Training
Phase 4: Wave 1 Black-Belt PTAR cycle (at the BA level)
Phase 5: Wave N Black-Belt PTAR cycle (at the BA level)

Deployment Case Study

Schedule:

Orientation and Planning	Week 1
Champion Training	Week 2 - 5
Champion Review	Week 6
Black-Belt Training (session 1, wave 1)	Week 7
Black-Belt Application (wave 1)	Week 8 - 10
Black-Belt Review (wave 1)	Week 11
Black-Belt Training (session 2, wave 1)	Week 11
Black-Belt Application (wave 1)	Week 12 - 14
Black-Belt Review (wave 1)	Week 15
Black-Belt Training (session 3, wave 1)	Week 15
Black-Belt Application (wave 1)	Week 16 - 18
Black-Belt Review (wave 1)	Week 19
Black-Belt Training (session 4, wave 1)	Week 19
Black-Belt Application (wave 1)	Week 20 - 22
Black-Belt Review (wave 1)	Week 23 - 24
Contingency	Week 22 - 24

Start-up: Reference FAX correspondence to Mr. Smith dated April 1, 1994

Process: Reference FAX correspondence to Mr. Smith dated April 1, 1994

Initiation: Upon formulation of a cluster (4 -5 factories)

Funding: FY94: Costs supported by Mr. Smith with charge-back to BA

Direction: Six Sigma Champion (supported by Quality Council)

Staffing: Pull system based on BA needs (project based)

Facilities: Arranged as required

Equipment: Provided by the BA as required

Deployment Case Study

Step 1:   **Make Initial Contact With BA Management**
Milestone: Agreement for Meeting
Timing: Completed by April 15

> Mr. Smith will make the initial contact with the selected BA. The purpose of this initial contact is to; a) establish that the respective BA is interested in pursuing Six Sigma, b) gain the concurrence for a constructive meeting between the Master Black Belt and the BA management and c) establish a single contact for future communication and correspondence. In general, one day should be dedicated for this meeting.

Step 2:   **Confirm Initial Meeting with the Candidate BA**
Milestone: Confirmation of the Meeting
Timing: Completed by May 3

> After the initial contact has been made, Mr. Smith will FAX to the Master Black Belt the name of the key contact for each candidate BA. Of course, we will need the full name, job title, address, phone number, and fax number of this person. In turn, the Master Black Belt will compose a letter of introduction, meeting conformation, and schedule of activity.

Step 3:   **Conduct Initial Meeting with the Candidate BA**
Milestone: Completion of the Meeting
Timing: Completed by May 20

The purpose of this meeting is to:
a) Assess the BA's current situation in terms of performance improvement.
b) Discover the BA's perceptions on what must be done to further improve.
c) Establish if Six Sigma can be used to facilitate the BA's long-term goals.
d) Determine how committed the BA is to long-term improvement.
e) Understand how Six Sigma can be integrated into the BA's business fabric.
f) Assess the BA's current practices and procedures from a Six Sigma viewpoint
g) Get a feel for how Six Sigma could best be implemented (long-term approach)

Agenda for the Meeting:
9:00 AM: Presentation by the BA concerning the nature of their:
     a) products, customers, and suppliers
     b) business philosophy, strategy, goals, and objectives
     c) historical actions to improve cost, time, performance, and quality
     d) current actions to make such improvements happen
     e) other information the BA believes to be relevant
11:00 AM: Tour of a representative factory (at or near the meeting location)
     a) the tour should focus on the key processes within the factory
     b) the tour to be lead by the operations manager and the quality officer
1:00 PM: "Vision, Application, and Implementation of Six Sigma" presentation
3:00 PM: Open forum for discussion
4:30 PM: Take decision to make the next step

Deployment Case Study

Step 4:   **Make Decision to Accept Candidate BA**
Milestone: Completion of the BA Six Sigma Assessment (Report)
Timing: Completed by June 20

Following the meeting, the Master Black Belt will compile the information which we collected. Based on the resulting data and information, the likelihood of successful implementation will be determined. This information will be documented in a standardized report. The Master Black Belt will assume responsibility for development and submission of this report. In turn, the summary report and correlated recommendations will be reviewed by Mr. Smith and subsequently released to the candidate BA. Assuming a satisfactory report, the candidate BA will be accepted for the Six Sigma implementation process. If it is determined there is an insurmountable problem with the candidate BA, Mr. Smith will select another for consideration.

Step 5:   **Start the Six Sigma Implementation Process**
Milestone: Completion of the Six Sigma Executive Briefing
Timing: Completed by August 1

So as to initiate the Six Sigma implementation process, the general managers (from each of the selected factories) and key BA staff members will attend the one day *"Six Sigma Executive Briefing"* presented by the Master Black Belt. The event will be scheduled at a location which is central to the participating managers. The purpose of this presentation is to provide a detailed orientation to Six Sigma; i.e., what it is, what it can do for their businesses, what it will cost, how it should be implemented, and how long it will take to implement, and how to sustain the gains. Following the briefing, the BA management takes the decision to take the next step toward implementation of Six Sigma. If the decision is favorable, then go to step 6; otherwise, Mr. Smith will identify another BA.

Step 6:   **Identify a BA Level Six Sigma Champion**
Milestone: Name of Champion Submitted to Mike Harry
Timing: Completed by August 15

The candidate BA must identify a champion to lead the initiative. In essence, the Six Sigma Champion is a senior BA manager. This person is the principal conduit for flowing Six Sigma into the BA, as well as the key contact for the Master Black Belt. This person is responsible for the planning and coordination of those activities associated with the implementation of Six Sigma. A letter of confirmation shall be prepared by the BA and directed to the Black Belt and Mr. Smith. In essence, the letter will confirm the BA's commitment to the Six Sigma process and specify the Six Sigma champion. At this point, all future communication and coordination concerning Six Sigma will be directed through the designated Six Sigma champion. Of course, the full name, job title, address, phone number, and fax number of this person must be provided.

Deployment Case Study

Step 7: **Conduct Six Sigma Training for the BA Champion**
Milestone: Program of Study Completed by the BA Champions
Timing: Completed by September 20

The BA Champion completes an intensive 2 week program of study in Phoenix Arizona. During this course of study, the champion will learn the strategies, tactics, and tools associated with the successful implementation and application of Six Sigma. In addition, the program of study will be focused on the development of a detailed implementation process, specific to the candidate BA. A high-level example of the "factory level" implementation process is as follows:

Step 1   Conduct Initial Six Sigma Management Meeting
Step 2   Conduct Six Sigma Executive Briefing
Step 3   Take Decision to Move Forward
Step 4   Conduct Six Sigma Champion Training
Step 5   Select First Cluster of Factories for Implementation
Step 6   Identify Black-Belts Candidates
Step 7   Conduct Six Sigma Black-Belt Training
Step 8   Conduct Standard Six Sigma Process Review
Step 9   Make Second Assessment of Implementation
Step 10 Take Decision to Move Forward
Step 11 Establish Six Sigma Deployment Guidelines
Step 12 Start General Deployment in Accordance to Guidelines

Naturally, the program of study and implementation process is highly synergistic, owing to the fact that the BA Champions interact with each other during the course of learning and planning. As a consequence of such interaction, they come to discover how to pool resources so as to achieve greater economy of scale and reduced implementation time. In essence, they come to see the "commonalties" of implementation and application.

Step 8: **Implement BA Level Action Plans**
Milestone: First Standard Six Sigma Implementation Review Completed
Timing: Completed by November 1

Following this training experience, each champion will return to their respective BA and begin execution of their customized implementation plan (see baseline implementation flow chart). The Master Black Belt will establish a schedule for conducting the Standard Six Sigma Implementation Reviews. The purpose of such reviews is to ensure a "parallel rate of progress" among the participating BA's. In this manner, "lessons learned" can be shared in a real-time environment. In addition, Black-Belt training activities can be mutually coordinated and pooled with other BA's; thereby, achieving shorter implementation time, greater economy of scale, and more efficient use of scarce resources. In addition, the Master Black Belt will provide application and implementation guidance to the BA Champions during such reviews. When appropriate, additional time will be dedicated for specialized training, as well as for guest speakers (from partnering organizations internal and external to XYZ).

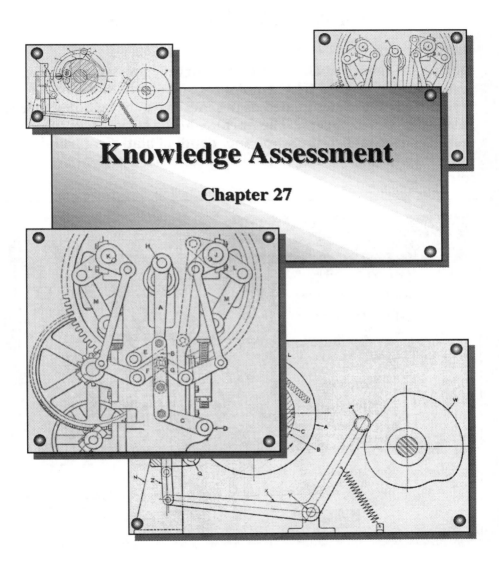

Knowledge Assessment

Chapter 27

The Survey Instrument

During the month of October 1988 a survey questionnaire was distributed to certain GEG employees , all of whom were recognized and/or designated as process characterization experts, sustainers, or managers. The purpose of the survey was to empirically establish the scope and depth of statistical training necessary for supporting a major process characterization initiative.

Rate the extent to which you would need help from someone else in order to:

	1	2	3	4
10. Add a series of numbers (22 + 34 + 45 = ?)	■	□	□	□
11. Subtract two numbers (67 - 43 = ?)	■	□	□	□
12. Multiply two numbers (897 x 58 = ?)	□	■	□	□

Survey Questions

Rating Scale

	1	2	3	4
55. Analyze the outcomes of a factorial experiment	□	□	■	□
56. Design a response surface experiment	□	□	□	■
57. Analyze the outcomes of a response surface experiment	□	□	□	■

1 = None   2 =Very Little   3 = Some   4 = A Lot

Comments on the Instrument

☞ Essentially, the survey instrument consists of three major sections. The first section (questions 1 and 2) consists of basic demographics. The second section (questions 3 through 9) classifies certain aspects of the respondent's job.

☞ It should be noted that questions 1 through 9 were not considered pertinent to the objectives of this particular survey; consequently, they were disregarded during data analysis.

☞ The third, and most important section relates to questions 10 through 57. This particular set of questions provides the basis for determining the existing scope and depth of any given respondent's knowledge with respect to quantitative data analysis methods.

☞ Finally, the fourth section relates to those forces which tend to restrain and drive the use of those skills specified in questions 10 through 57. As may be apparent, questions 58 through 86 provide a basis for management planning and organizational implementation.

The Statistics Survey Questions

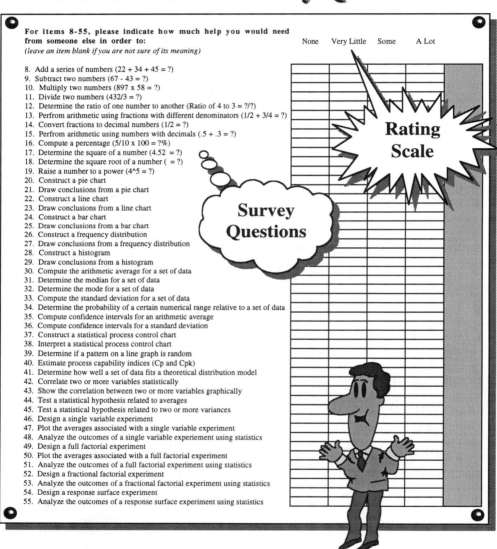

For items 8-55, please indicate how much help you would need from someone else in order to:

(leave an item blank if you are not sure of its meaning)

None   Very Little   Some   A Lot

8. Add a series of numbers (22 + 34 + 45 = ?)
9. Subtract two numbers (67 - 43 = ?)
10. Multiply two numbers (897 x 58 = ?)
11. Divide two numbers (432/3 = ?)
12. Determine the ratio of one number to another (Ratio of 4 to 3 = ?/?)
13. Perfrom arithmetic using fractions with different denominators (1/2 + 3/4 = ?)
14. Convert fractions to decimal numbers (1/2 = ?)
15. Perfrom arithmetic using numbers with decimals (.5 + .3 = ?)
16. Compute a percentage (5/10 x 100 = ?%)
17. Determine the square of a number (4.52 = ?)
18. Determine the square root of a number (= ?)
19. Raise a number to a power (4^5 = ?)
20. Construct a pie chart
21. Draw conclusions from a pie chart
22. Construct a line chart
23. Draw conclusions from a line chart
24. Construct a bar chart
25. Draw conclusions from a bar chart
26. Construct a frequency distribution
27. Draw conclusions from a frequency distribution
28. Construct a histogram
29. Draw conclusions from a histogram
30. Compute the arithmetic average for a set of data
31. Determine the median for a set of data
32. Determine the mode for a set of data
33. Compute the standard deviation for a set of data
34. Determine the probability of a certain numerical range relative to a set of data
35. Compute confidence intervals for an arithmetic average
36. Compute confidence intervals for a standard deviation
37. Construct a statistical process control chart
38. Interpret a statistical process control chart
39. Determine if a pattern on a line graph is random
40. Estimate process capability indices (Cp and Cpk)
41. Determine how well a set of data fits a theoretical distribution model
42. Correlate two or more variables statistically
43. Show the correlation between two or more variables graphically
44. Test a statistical hypothesis related to averages
45. Test a statistical hypothesis related to two or more variances
46. Design a single variable experiment
47. Plot the averages associated with a single variable experiment
48. Analyze the outcomes of a single variable experiement using statistics
49. Design a full factorial experiment
50. Plot the averages associated with a full factorial experiment
51. Analyze the outcomes of a full factorial experiment using statistics
52. Design a fractional factorial experiment
53. Analyze the outcomes of a fractional factorial experiment using statistics
54. Design a response surface experiment
55. Analyze the outcomes of a response surface experiment using statistics

Rating Scale

Survey Questions

The Statistics Survey Questions

For items 56 to 71, pick the top 3 items which you believe would tend to PROHIBIT you from using data analysis methods more often to help you with your job. Please rank each the 3 items you select by marking the appropriate box to the right of the item. *DO NOT MARK ANY OF THE ITEMS WHICH ARE NOT AMONG YOUR TOP 3. NO TIES, PLEASE.*

First   Second   Third

56. My unfamiliarity with data analysis methods
57. Not enough "hands-on" experience
58. Inadequate budget
59. Not enough time for me to use data analysis methods
60. Lack of numerical data to analyze
61. Unclear goals and objectives for the use of data
62. Accessiblity to data
63. Fear or uneasiness of math
64. Culture of the organization
65. Lack of planning by management
66. Availability of computers
67. Lack of leadership
68. Inadequate communication
69. Lack of confidence in analytical outcomes
70. Customers that do not allow the application of statistics
71. Other (please specify in the space provided below

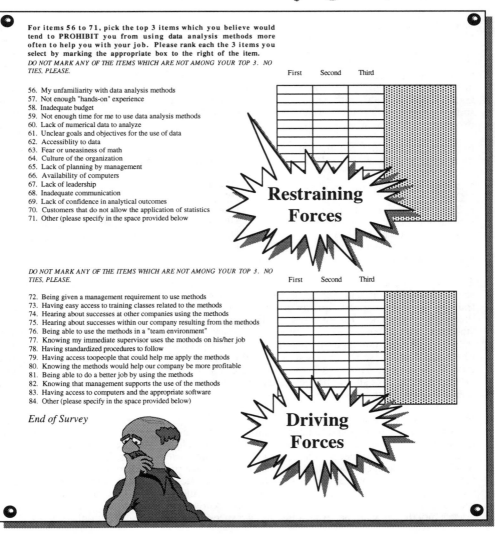

Restraining Forces

DO NOT MARK ANY OF THE ITEMS WHICH ARE NOT AMONG YOUR TOP 3. NO TIES, PLEASE.

First   Second   Third

72. Being given a management requirement to use methods
73. Having easy access to training classes related to the methods
74. Hearing about successes at other companies using the methods
75. Hearing about successes within our company resulting from the methods
76. Being able to use the methods in a "team environment"
77. Knowing my immediate supervisor uses the mothods on his/her job
78. Having standardized procedures to follow
79. Having access toopeople that could help me apply the methods
80. Knowing the methods would help our company be more profitable
81. Being able to do a better job by using the methods
82. Knowing that management supports the use of the methods
83. Having access to computers and the appropriate software
84. Other (please specify in the space provided below)

End of Survey

Driving Forces

Nature of the Items

When any given respondent's survey is considered, it is possible to show the degree of help he/she would "need from someone else" in order to execute the various analytical tasks specified in questions 10 through 57. Obviously, if the percentage of respondents indicating "some" or "a lot" is substantially high, there would be reason to believe that some form of training would be in order with respect to the skills under consideration. Interestingly, questions 10 through 57 are ordered in terms of conceptual difficulty; e.g., the initial questions address fundamental arithmetic operations while the latter questions transition to fairly sophisticated statistical methods and procedures which require a substantial amount of abstract reasoning and mathematical background.

It should be pointed out that questions 10 through 57 may be grouped into 7 distinct knowledge categories. Namely, in progressive order, those categories are:

• Arithmetic Operations	Q10-21
• Data Display	Q22-31
• Basic Descriptive Statistics	Q32-38
• Statistical Process Control (SPC)	Q39-42
• Basic Inferential Statistics	Q43-47
• Factorial Experimentation	Q48-55
• Optimization Experiments	Q56-57

Thus, when the survey data are summarized into the aforementioned knowledge categories, specific conclusions and various generalizations may be made with respect to a technical training curricula -- specific to any given strata of personnel. For example, if the data reveals that 20%-35% of the respondents need "some" or "a lot" of help with say, descriptive statistics, then this particular knowledge category should be included as "review" material within a technical training curricula. If 35%-50% respond as such, then it would be reasonable to conclude that descriptive statistics should be treated as introductory material rather than content for review. Finally, if more than 50% of the respondents indicate that they need help, descriptive statistics should be viewed as advanced material which would necessarily require one or more prerequisites.

Furthermore, when the restraining and driving forces are considered, the organization has a basis for better defining and understanding the issues surrounding implementation, training, and application. As a consequence, organizational change can be better managed. For example, if the respondents believe that there are no formal "goals for using the tools," it would be more than obvious that management must make provisions to remove this restraining force. While this may seem intuitively apparent, we often forget that such intuition assumes that we really know what the restraining forces are. Unless we ask (via such communication methods as questionnaires), how can we really know? When one has "heard it from the horse's mouth," they are better postured to take specific and meaningful action.

High Level Data Analysis

➥ Approximately **25%** of the respondents need some or a lot of help with basic descriptive statistics and SPC methods. This would tend to imply that the training curricula should emphasize these topics as review material.

➥ Approximately **50%** of the respondents need some or a lot of help with inferential statistics. This would tend to suggest that inferential statistics be the first substantive topic in a statistical training curricula.

➥ More than **60%** of the respondents need some or a lot of help with experiment design and analysis. Since such skills are an intrinsic part of process characterization, the data would tend to support the notion that experiment design and analysis be a major focal point of the statistical training curricula.

The Results for Items 10 - 57

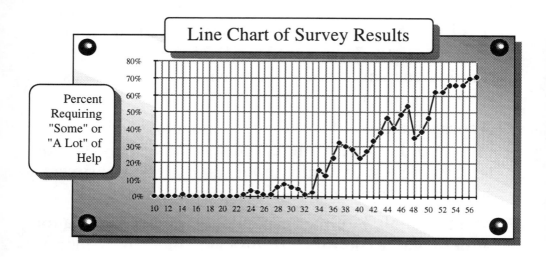

Line Chart of Survey Results

Percent Requiring "Some" or "A Lot" of Help

80% 70% 60% 50% 40% 30% 20% 10% 0%

10 12 14 16 18 20 22 24 26 28 30 32 34 36 38 40 42 44 46 48 50 52 54 56

A=Arithmetic Operations (Q10-21)

B=Data Display (Q22-31)

C=Descriptive Statistics (Q32-38)

D=Statistical Process Control (Q39-42)

D=Inferential Statistics (Q43-47)

E=Factorial Experiments (Q48-55)

F=Optimization Methods (Q56-57)

Driving and Restraining Forces

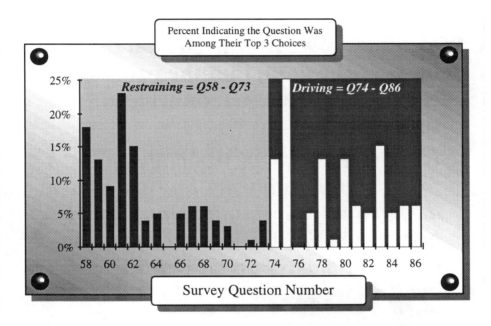

Percent Indicating the Question Was Among Their Top 3 Choices

Restraining = Q58 - Q73

Driving = Q74 - Q86

Survey Question Number

Top Restrainers	**Top Drivers**
1) Having easy access to training classes (Q75),	1) Not enough time to use the data analysis methods (Q61),
2) Being able to do a better job (Q83).	2) My unfamiliarity with data analysis methods (Q58),
3) Having standardized procedures to follow (Q80).	3) Lack of numerical data to analyze (Q62).

Summary and Conclusions

In summary, we may argue, on the basis of the data, that the process characterization personnel are saying:

Give me the cookbook training approach for inferential statistics and experiment design/analysis, show me how it will help me on the job, give me the time to do it, and make sure the data is avail̶e̶ ̶w̶h̶e̶n̶ it will all get done̶

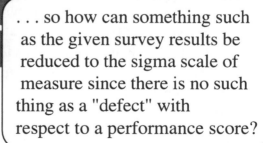

. . . so how can something such as the given survey results be reduced to the sigma scale of measure since there is no such thing as a "defect" with respect to a performance score?

Results of Australian Survey

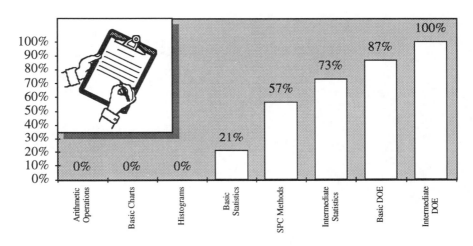

Line Chart of Survey Results

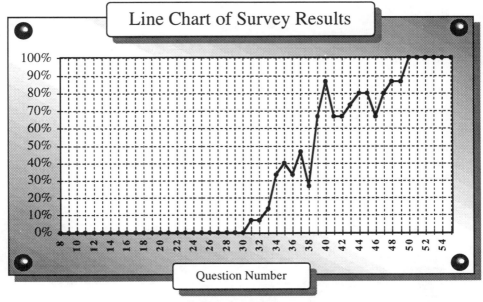

Question Number

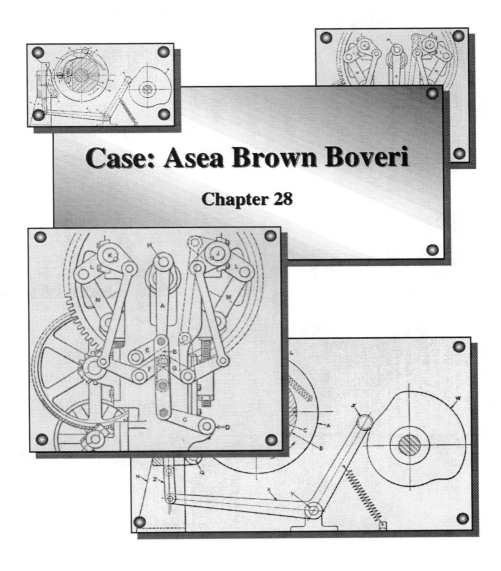

Case: Asea Brown Boveri

Chapter 28

Understanding the Product

Photo Courtesy
of Asea Brown
Boveri

Power
Transformer

History of Six Sigma in the TPT

★ Top Management of BA TPT Recognized Need for Change

★ Dr. Mikel Harry Joins ABB to Lead 6σ Project

★ Transformer BA Rises to the Six Sigma Challenge

★ Mr. Kjell Magnusson Creates and Leads Quality Council

★ BA TPT Benchmarking Reveals Quality State-of-Affairs

★ Six Sigma Executive Briefing given to TPT General Managers and Key Personnel in Frankfurt, Germany

★ Pilot Plants Identified (Sweden, Germany, Italy, US & Engineering)

★ Six Sigma Black-Belts Selected & Trained (n = 30)

★ BA Quality Council Identifies Target Project (Windings)

★ First Pass Measurements Reveal Process Control Problems

★ Advanced Six Sigma Training Conducted for Black-Belts

★ Top 30 Transformer Characteristics Identified and Measured

★ Second Pass Measurements Reveal Significant Opportunities

★ Standard Six Sigma Review Established & Implemented

★ Second Wave Black-Belt Training Initiated (Manuf. & Eng.)

State-of-Affairs as of June 1994

. . . From the notes of Mr. Kjell Magnusson, Vice President, Customer Focus, TPT.

✳ **Through the application of Six Sigma, we discovered there was is no internal "wizard" with all of the knowledge about transformers. We believed "someone" knew but, in a lot of instances, found out (through measurements) that no one knew.**

✳ **Six Sigma has been institutionalized at this point. Managers have set great hopes and engineers speak about it.**

✳ **The third wave of Black Belt training is overfilled with volunteers. Five plants have distributed Six Sigma leaflets to employees. Six Sigma has now been introduced to Supply Management.**

✳ **Four plants have now introduced Six Sigma awareness training to their workforce. The class ranges from 2 to 4 hours in duration.**

✳ **Six Sigma measurements have been taken in 9 plants around the globe. We have started to measure things that should have been measured a long time ago.**

✳ **We are planning a full scale quality information system (data base) in 3 factories (Geneva, Pomezia, and Ludvika).**

State-of-Affairs as of June 1994

✪ We have discovered and are applying the statistical tools which allow us to find new ways to derive improvement.

✪ Interesting Finding: The more senior Black Belts tend to prefer continuous data while the less senior display a preference for discrete data.

✪ Interesting Comment from Black Belts: "Management is our number one problem." "We think Six Sigma goes to slow, but management thinks it goes fine."

✪ Six Sigma is coordinated with the R&D groups for load losses and no load losses.

✪ Germany is lagging in implementation.

✪ For a mature business, cost reduction is not a "vital few" issue, but rather a trivial many.

✪ The Measure-Analyze-Improve-Control methodology works very well and is easily understood by all.

✪ One of the Black Belts has picked up on Six Sigma tolerance methods, prepared   materials, and is now teaching the methodolo   r design engineers.

The TPT Success Factors

Following are the factors which the TPT Business Area believe are among the "Vital Few" in terms of the successful implementation of Six Sigma:

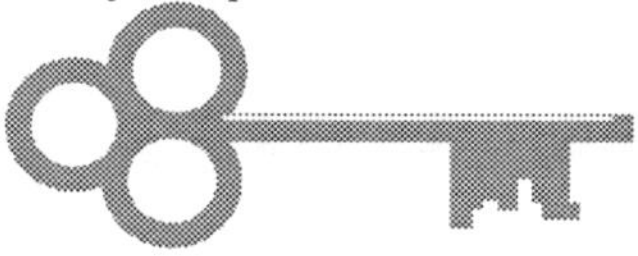

- ✰ **Set a vision**
- ✰ **Make your commitment highly visible**
- ✰ **Help middle management understand and support Six Sigma**
- ✰ **Inspire the Black Belts, personally**
- ✰ **Set goals**
- ✰ **Require project plans**
- ✰ **Require a monthly report, written**
- ✰ **Provide education to all levels**
- ✰ **Make success stories known, no matter how large or small**
- ✰ **Recognize that some people, regardless of position, will reject change**

The TPT Project Milestones

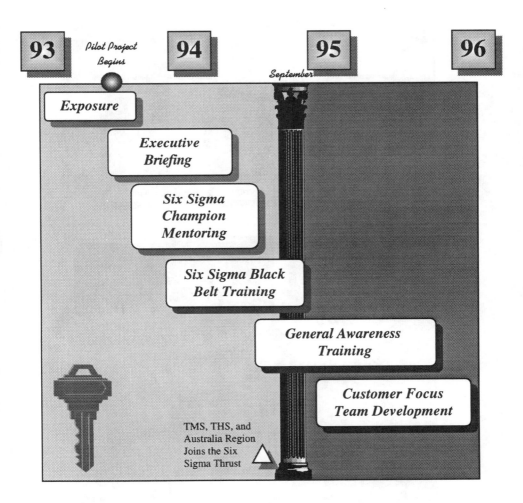

The Baseline of Quality

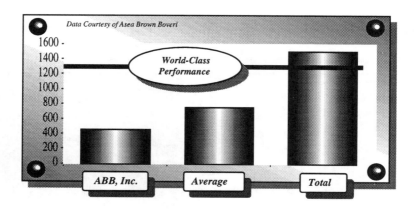

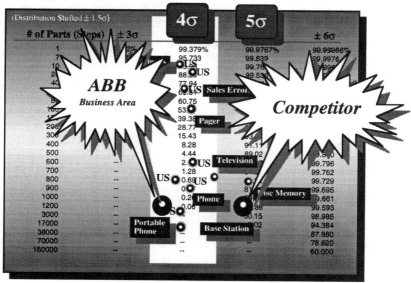

Data Courtesy of Asea Brown Boveri

Macro-Level Benchmarking

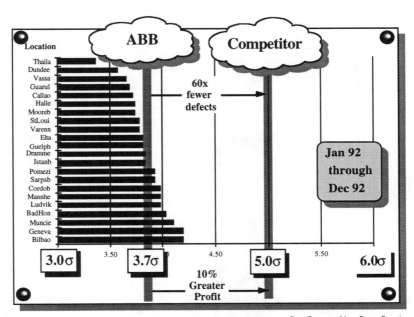

Data Courtesy of Asea Brown Boveri

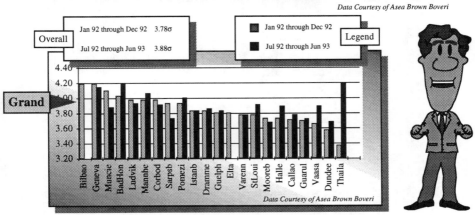

Data Courtesy of Asea Brown Boveri

Quality of Engineering Drawings

Report Name	Engineering Defects		Baseline Period	From	Dec'92	To	Dec'93
Organization	ABB Power T&D Ltd		Improvement Goal			To	
Project			Unit Definition				
Department	Power Engineering		Characteristic				
Deliverable			Units of Measure				
Deliverable ID			Upper Specification				
Process			Target Value				
Step			Lower Specification				
Machine ID			Default Shift	1.50			
Special Note	All Engineering Defects						

Line	Desp.	Contract	Description	D	U	OP	TOP	DPU	DPO	DPMO	Shift	Z.B
1	02-93	910019		2	1	659	659	2	0.0030	3,035	1.50	4.24
2	05-93	910062		8	1	544	544	8	0.0147	14,706	1.50	3.68
3	05-93	910063	Data Courtesy of Asea Brown Boveri	5	1	544	544	5	0.0092	9,191	1.50	3.86
4	07-93	910069		5	1	659	659	5	0.0076	7,587	1.50	3.93
5	03-93	910070		14	1	659	659	14	0.0212	21,244	1.50	3.53
6	06-92	910082		1	1	544	544	1	0.0018	1,838	1.50	4.41
7	09-92	910091		1	1	544	544	1	0.0018	1,838	1.50	4.41
8	01-93	910092		1	1	544	544	1	0.0018	1,838	1.50	4.41
9	01-93	910093		1	1	544	544	1	0.0018	1,838	1.50	4.41
10	01-93	910109		4	1	544	544	4	0.0074	7,353	1.50	3.94
11	04-93	920006		17	1	481	481	17	0.0353	35,343	1.50	3.31
12	04-93	920007		1	1	481	481	1	0.0021	2,079	1.50	4.37
13	12-92	920009		1	1	481	481	1	0.0021	2,079	1.50	4.37
14	07-93	920012		8	1	544	544	8	0.0147	14,706	1.50	3.68
15	07-93	920013		6	1	544	544	6	0.0110	11,029	1.50	3.79
16	04-93	920017		19	1	544	544	19	0.0349	34,926	1.50	3.31
17	07-93	920018		10	1	544	544	10	0.0184	18,382	1.50	3.59
18	02-93	920032		6	1	481	481	6	0.0125	12,474	1.50	3.74
19	02-93	920033		0	1	481	481	0	0.0000	0	1.50	6.00
20	04-93	920038		29	1	481	481	29	0.0603	60,291	1.50	3.05
21	12-93	920050		38	1	659	659	38	0.0577	57,663	1.50	3.08
22	09-93	920056		32	1	659	659	32	0.0486	48,558	1.50	3.16
23	09-93	920063		19	1	500	500	19	0.0380	38,000	1.50	3.27
24	09-93	920064		3	1	500	500	3	0.0060	6,000	1.50	4.01
25	02-93	920071		12	1	481	481	12	0.0249	24,948	1.50	3.46
26	06-93	920072		7	1	481	481	7	0.0146	14,553	1.50	3.68
27	09-93	920073		2	1	481	481	2	0.0042	4,158	1.50	4.14
28	03-93	920074		27	1	481	481	27	0.0561	56,133	1.50	3.09
29	03-93	920075		6	1	481	481	6	0.0125	12,474	1.50	3.74
30	05-93	920076		4	1	481	481	4	0.0083	8,316	1.50	3.90
31	11-93	920080		46	1	583	583	46	0.0789	78,902	1.50	2.91
32	11-93	920081		7	1	583	583	7	0.0120	12,007	1.50	3.76
33	11-93	920083		7	1	544	544	7	0.0129	12,868	1.50	3.73
34	10-93	920084		1	1	544	544	1	0.0018	1,838	1.50	4.41
35	06-93	920087		12	1	481	481	12	0.0249	24,948	1.50	3.46
36	11-93	920091		8	1	544	544	8	0.0147	14,706	1.50	3.68
37	12-93	920094		5	1	544	544	5	0.0092	9,191	1.50	3.86
38	02-94	920096		1	1	544	544	1	0.0018	1,838	1.50	4.41
39	09-93	920098		8	1	544	544	8	0.0147	14,706	1.50	3.68
40	11-93	920100		7	1	544	544	7	0.0129	12,868	1.50	3.73
41	07-93	920103		9	1	481	481	9	0.0187	18,711	1.50	3.58
42	11-93	920104		8	1	544	544	8	0.0147	14,706	1.50	3.68
43	11-93	920105		3	1	544	544	3	0.0055	5,515	1.50	4.04
44	11-93	920106		1	1	544	544	1	0.0018	1,838	1.50	4.41
45	05-93	920107		4	1	481	481	4	0.0083	8,316	1.50	3.90
46	09-93	920108		7	1	481	481	7	0.0146	14,553	1.50	3.68
47	05-93	920110		4	1	481	481	4	0.0083	8,316	1.50	3.90
48	11-93	920112		12	1	481	481	12	0.0249	24,948	1.50	3.46
49	07-93	920113		18	1	420	420	18	0.0429	42,857	1.50	3.22
50	10-93	920115		12	1	394	394	12	0.0305	30,457	1.50	3.37
51	10-93	930007		16	1	500	500	16	0.0320	32,000	1.50	3.35
52	10-93	930008		1	1	500	500	1	0.0020	2,000	1.50	4.38
53	11-93	930025		13	1	481	481	13	0.0270	27,027	1.50	3.43
54	10-93	930028		8	1	481	481	8	0.0166	16,632	1.50	3.63
55	10-93	930029		1	1	481	481	1	0.0021	2,079	1.50	4.37
56	10-93	930030		1	1	481	481	1	0.0021	2,079	1.50	4.37
57	11-93	930031		0	1	481	481	0	0.0000	0	1.50	6.00
58	10-93	930038		5	1	481	481	5	0.0104	10,395	1.50	3.81
59	12-93	930043		1	1	481	481	1	0.0021	2,079	1.50	4.37
60	12-93	930044		0	1	481	481	0	0.0000	0	1.50	6.00
61	12-93	930051		13	1	420	420	13	0.0310	30,952	1.50	3.37
62	12-93	930052		2	1	420	420	2	0.0048	4,762	1.50	4.09
63	12-93	930058		2	1	481	481	2	0.0042	4,158	1.50	4.14
			Grand = 532				32,526		0.0164	16,356	1.50	3.64

Overall 3.64σ

Quality of Engineering Drawings

Data Courtesy of Asea Brown Boveri

Sigma's for Production Planning

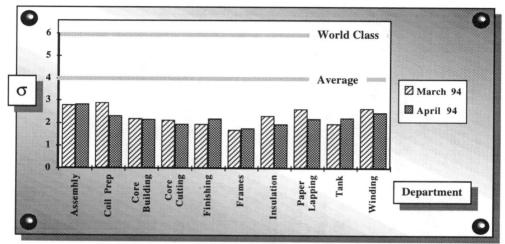

Data Courtesy of Asea Brown Boveri

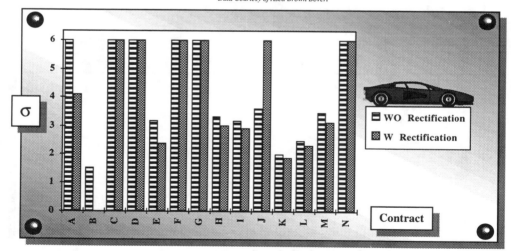

Sigma's for Supplier Performance

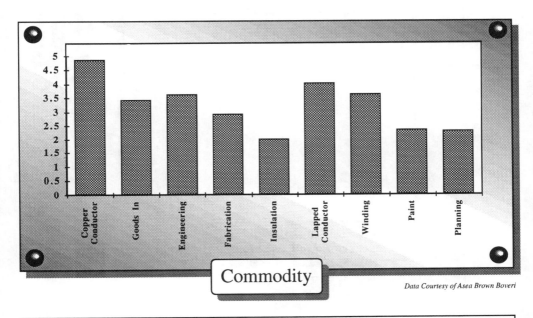

Data Courtesy of Asea Brown Boveri

Questioning Basic Beliefs

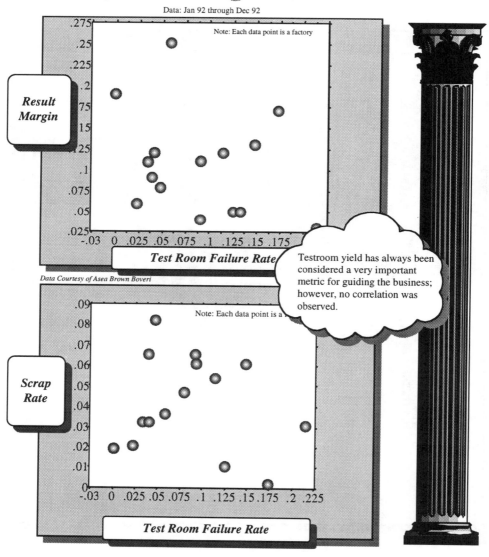

Data: Jan 92 through Dec 92

Note: Each data point is a factory

Result Margin

Test Room Failure Rate

Data Courtesy of Asea Brown Boveri

Note: Each data point is a

Testroom yield has always been considered a very important metric for guiding the business; however, no correlation was observed.

Scrap Rate

Test Room Failure Rate

28 . 14

Analysis of Historical Failures

Transformer Test Room Data

Data Courtesy of Asea Brown Boveri

Line	Class MVA	Reported Nonconf.	Test Results	Failure Mode	Actual MVA	Reported Nonconf.	Test: Pass = 0 Fail = 1
1	Medium	One or More	Fail	Flash	25	3	1
2	Medium	None	Pass	NA	25	0	0
3	Large	None	Pass	NA	1125	0	0
4	Large	None	Pass	NA	1125	0	0
5	Large	None	Pass	NA			
6	Large	None	Pass	NA			
7	Large	None	Pass	NA			
8	Large	One or More	Pass	NA			
9	Large	O					
10	Medium	O					
•	•						
•	•						
•	•						
20			Fail	Flash			
21			Pass	NA			

	Pass	Fail	Totals
None	113	1	114
One or More	87	14	101
Totals	200	15	215

Num. Missing	0
DF	1
Chi Square	13.911
Chi Square P-Value	.0002
G-Squared	16.050
G-Squared P-Value	<.0001
Contingency Coef.	.247
Phi	.254
or. Chi Square	11.983
or. P	05
s Ex	002

"Old Data"

Number of Defects

There is a strong correlation between the presence of nonconformity reports and the occurrence of transformer failures in the test room.

4.25
4
3.75
3.5
3.25
3
2.75
2.5
2.25
2

Fail   Pass

Test Result

28.15

Key Conclusions From Analysis

	MVA Class	Nonconform.	Test Results	Failure Type
MVA Class	●	●	●	●
Nonconform.	*Very Strong*	●	●	●
Test Results	*Moderate*	*Very Strong*	●	●
Failure Type	*Weak*	*Strong*	*Very Strong*	●

Note: Conclusions based on Chi-Square analysis and related measures of association such as Phi, Cramers V, Contingency Coefficient, etc.

• There is a positive correlation between the number of transformer nonconformity reports and transformer size; however, such a conclusion might be rendered invalid when the initial differences in transformer complexity is adjusted for.

• There is a positive correlation between the number of transformer nonconformity reports and final performance test results. This would suggest that Total-Defects-Per-Unit (TDPU) could serve as a primary tool for predicting the occurrence of test failures. In this sense, action could be taken early on in the manufacturing process so as to prevent the occurrence of test failures (i.e., flashover, etc.).

• Test Failures are Poisson Distributed, as confirmed by a Chi-Square Goodness-of-Fit test. Consequently, this would suggest that the underlying concepts of Six Sigma applies to transformer performance.

• There is a positive correlation between failure mode and transformer size; e.g., the size of a transformer is positively related to the likelihood of a test failure, where the failure is due to "flashover."

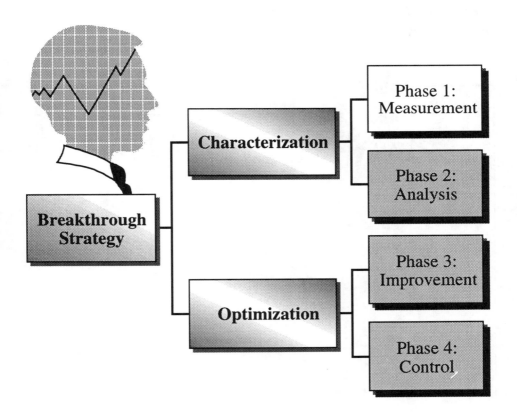

Getting Inside the Transformer

. . . The top 30 characteristics of a power transformer were selected for detailed measurement and subsequent benchmarking.

Photo Courtesy of Asea Brown Boveri

Using Six Sigma Control Cards

The scorecards are used by the BATPT to record various measurements related to the top 30 characteristics of a Power Transformer.

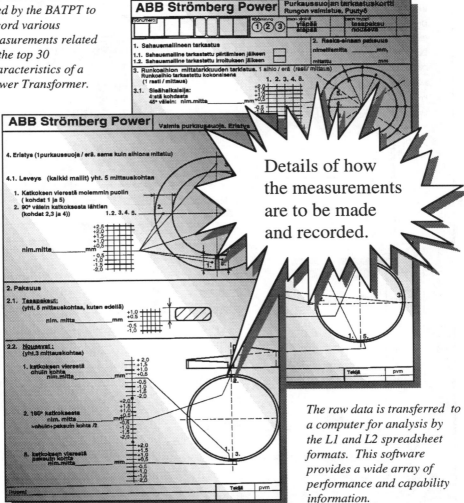

Details of how the measurements are to be made and recorded.

The raw data is transferred to a computer for analysis by the L1 and L2 spreadsheet formats. This software provides a wide array of performance and capability information.

Conducting the Six Sigma Analysis

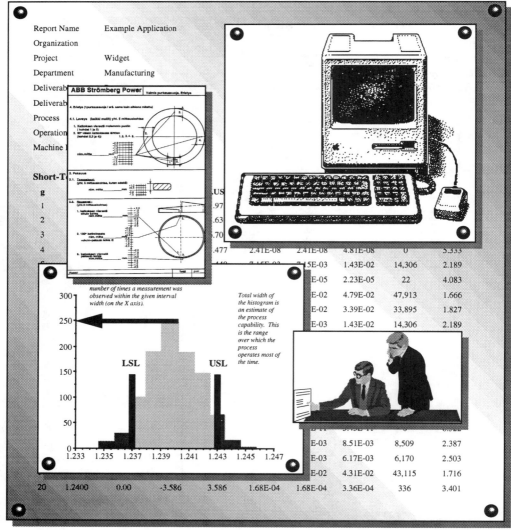

Report Name   Example Application

Organization

Project   Widget

Department   Manufacturing

number of times a measurement was observed within the given interval width (on the X axis).

Total width of the histogram is an estimate of the process capability. This is the range over which the process operates most of the time.

Data Courtesy of Asea Brown Boveri

Distribution of Process Capability

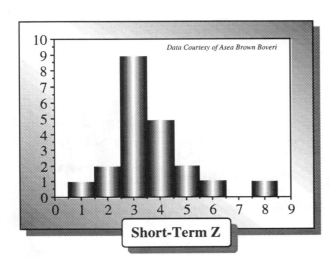

Short-Term Z

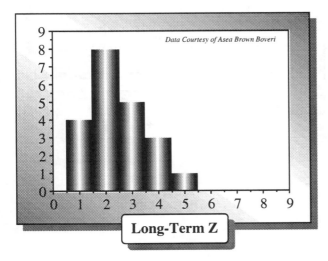

Long-Term Z

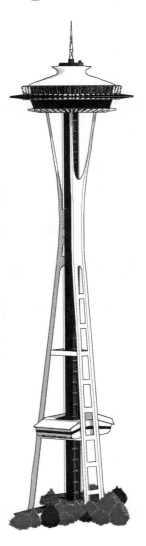

28 . 21

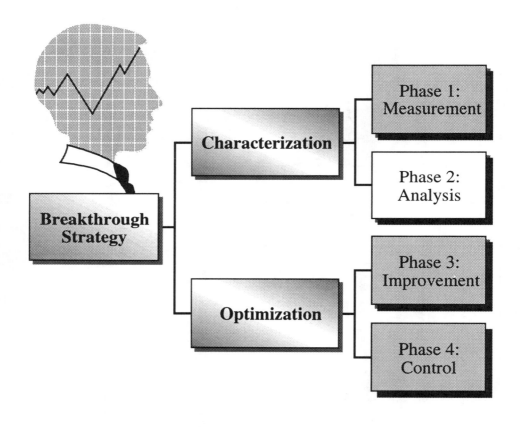

Benchmarking the Key Characteristics

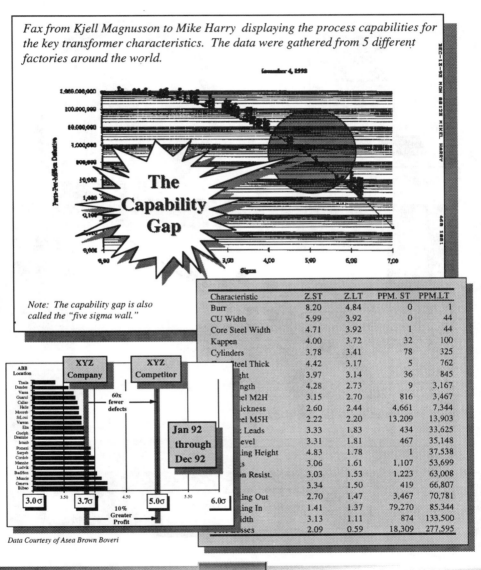

Fax from Kjell Magnusson to Mike Harry displaying the process capabilities for the key transformer characteristics. The data were gathered from 5 different factories around the world.

Note: The capability gap is also called the "five sigma wall."

Characteristic	Z.ST	Z.LT	PPM. ST	PPM.LT
Burr	8.20	4.84	0	1
CU Width	5.99	3.92	0	44
Core Steel Width	4.71	3.92	1	44
Kappen	4.00	3.72	32	100
Cylinders	3.78	3.41	78	325
Steel Thick	4.42	3.17	5	762
ght	3.97	3.14	36	845
ngth	4.28	2.73	9	3,167
eel M2H	3.15	2.70	816	3,467
ickness	2.60	2.44	4,661	7,344
eel MSH	2.22	2.20	13,209	13,903
Leads	3.33	1.83	434	33,625
evel	3.31	1.81	467	35,148
ing Height	4.83	1.78	1	37,538
s	3.06	1.61	1,107	53,699
n Resist.	3.03	1.53	1,223	63,008
	3.34	1.50	419	66,807
ing Out	2.70	1.47	3,467	70,781
ing In	1.41	1.37	79,270	85,344
idth	3.13	1.11	874	133,500
sses	2.09	0.59	18,309	277,595

Data Courtesy of Asea Brown Boveri

Diagnosing Process Performance

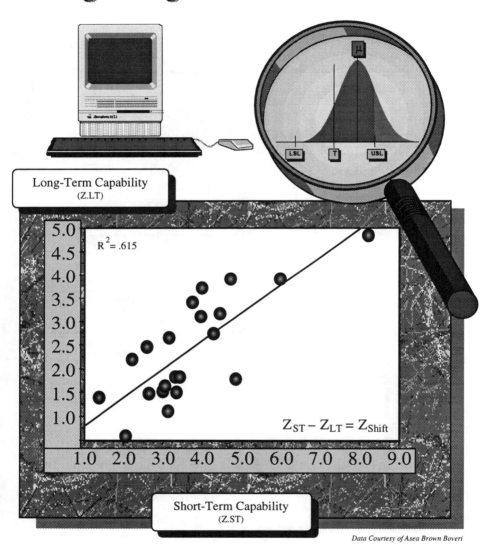

Long-Term Capability
(Z.LT)

$R^2 = .615$

$Z_{ST} - Z_{LT} = Z_{Shift}$

Short-Term Capability
(Z.ST)

Data Courtesy of Asea Brown Boveri

28 . 24

Establishing the Goal

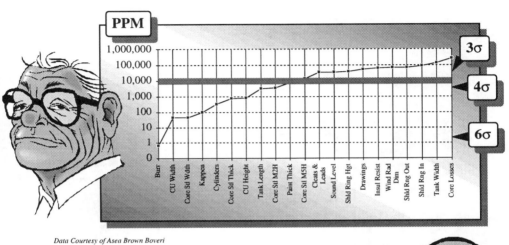

Data Courtesy of Asea Brown Boveri

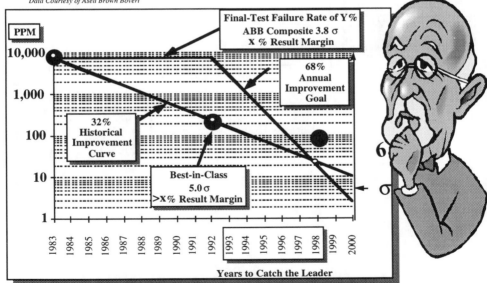

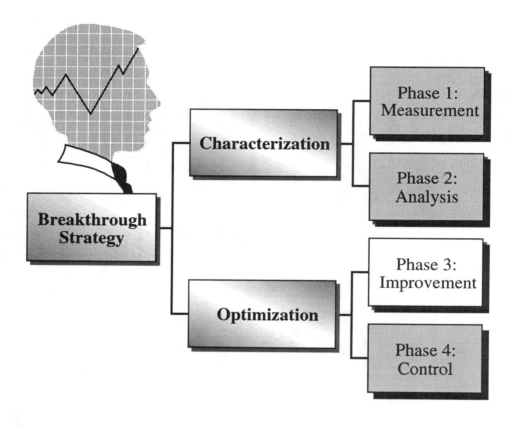

Improvement in Muncie, Indiana

US Transformer Facility

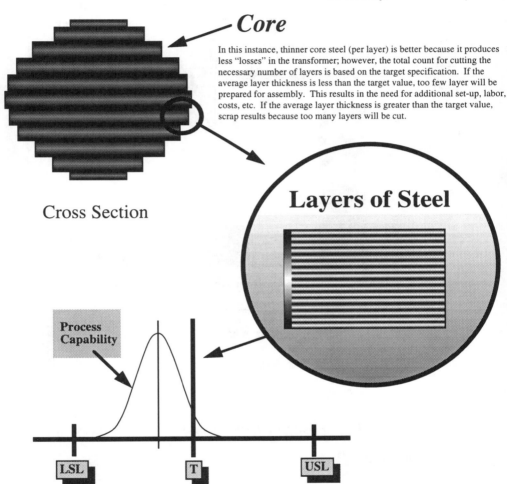

Core

In this instance, thinner core steel (per layer) is better because it produces less "losses" in the transformer; however, the total count for cutting the necessary number of layers is based on the target specification. If the average layer thickness is less than the target value, too few layer will be prepared for assembly. This results in the need for additional set-up, labor, costs, etc. If the average layer thickness is greater than the target value, scrap results because too many layers will be cut.

Cross Section

Layers of Steel

Process Capability

LSL   T   USL

Vendor not providing material at target value

Results of Muncie Application

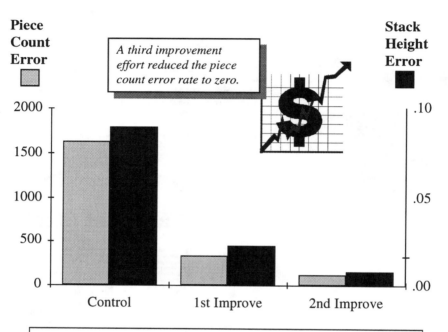

Piece Count Error

A third improvement effort reduced the piece count error rate to zero.

Stack Height Error

Reduced Measurement Equipment Error by 83%	$11,000
Reduced Piece Count Error From 8.3% to 1.3%	$31,000
No-Load Loss to Coil Within 2%	$400,000
Better Material Handling Based on Down-Time Analysis	$48,000
Achieved Quantifiable Comparison of Steel Suppliers	$285,000
Estimated Cost Avoidance =	$775,000

Data Courtesy of Asea Brown Boveri

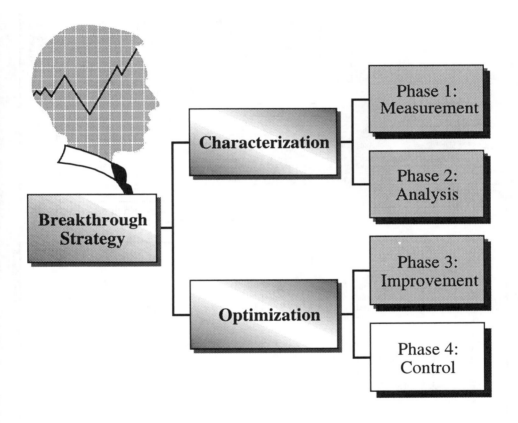

The Tool for Data Collection

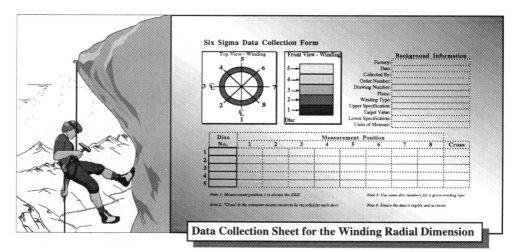

Data Collection Sheet for the Winding Radial Dimension

Data Courtesy of Asea Brown Boveri

Measurement Location

Phase	Disc	1	2	3	4	5	6	7	8
1	1	135.50	135.45	136.75	137.65	137.05	138.55	140.05	134.40
1	2	137.70	137.45	136.65	137.10	136.95	136.40	137.25	137.30
1	3	137.05	137.45	137.45	137.60	138.80	137.85	138.95	137.50
1	4	137.35	137.05	137.15	137.00	136.95	137.25	136.85	137.60
1	5	137.15	137.15	138.75	137.60	138.40	136.50	137.00	139.50
2	1	135.45	135.30	137.15	135.70	137.15	135.90	134.50	135.65
2	2	135.90	137.80	136.85	138.70	135.85	136.00	137.20	136.50
2	3	136.70	137.70	136.70	138.00	136.50	137.30	136.50	137.20
2	4	137.85	137.75	139.15	136.50	137.05	137.20	137.55	137.10
2	5	138.50	139.30	138.95	141.50	140.60	138.45	140.30	141.00
3	1	141.35	142.90	139.55	142.00	141.55	151.35	143.10	140.70
3	2	139.50	144.00	143.85	139.60	137.50	137.35	136.75	137.51
3	3	136.80	138.20	137.30	136.10	137.00	136.15	137.15	137.20
3	4	137.85	138.25	138.85	137.35	137.75	137.65	137.25	137.10
3	5	138.40	139.90	140.65	137.25	140.00	140.80	143.05	142.00

The Underlying Distribution

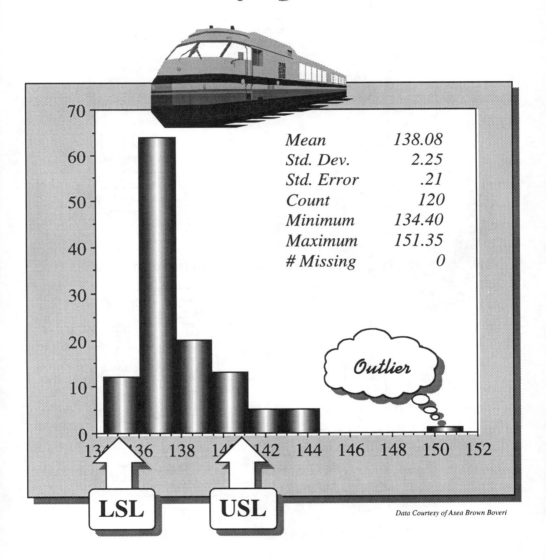

Mean	138.08
Std. Dev.	2.25
Std. Error	.21
Count	120
Minimum	134.40
Maximum	151.35
# Missing	0

Outlier

LSL

USL

Data Courtesy of Asea Brown Boveri

Applying Process Control Charts

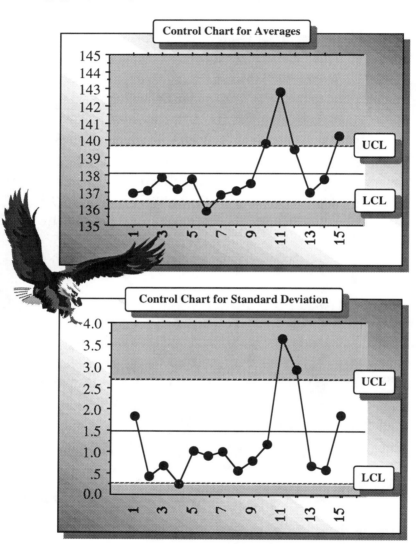

Control Chart for Averages

Control Chart for Standard Deviation

Data Courtesy of Asea Brown Boveri

The Macro Perspective

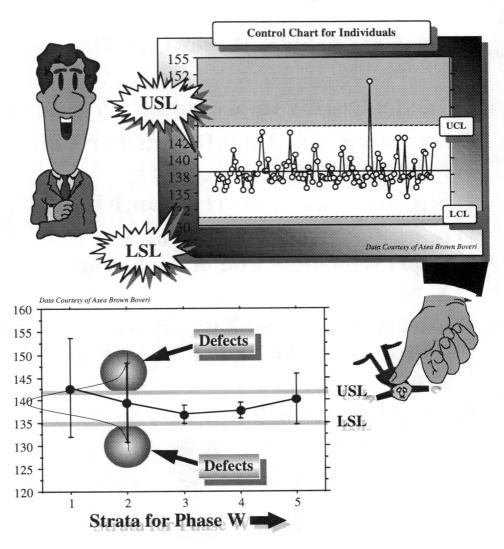

Control Chart for Individuals

155
152

USL

UCL

142
140
138
135
132
130

LSL

LCL

Data Courtesy of Asea Brown Boveri

Data Courtesy of Asea Brown Boveri

160
155
150
145
140
135
130
125
120

Defects

Defects

USL

LSL

1   2   3   4   5

Strata for Phase W ➡

A Vision for ABB Transformers

❶ Strategy: Achieve World-Class Process Capability

❷ Tactic: Quality Improvement

❸ Measurement: Total-Defects-Per-Unit & Sigma Scale

❹ Baseline: Current Performance Level

❺ Immediate Goal: One Sigma Improvement by End of the Second Year

❻ Intermediate Goal: Two Sigma Improvement by End of the Fourth Year

❼ Long-Range Goal: Be at Six Sigma by End of Sixth Year

Kjell Magnusson
Vice President
Customer Focus
ABB Transformer

28 . 34

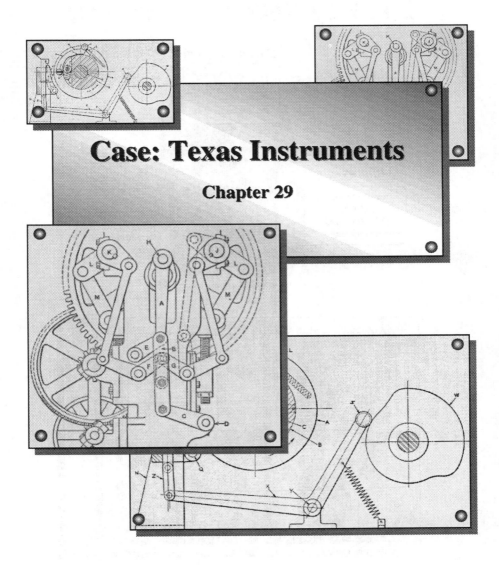

Case: Texas Instruments

Chapter 29

The Key Beliefs and Process

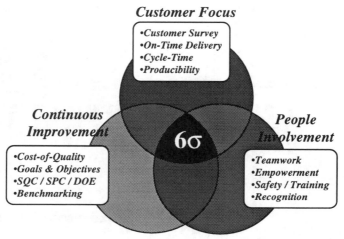

Framework for Customer Satisfaction

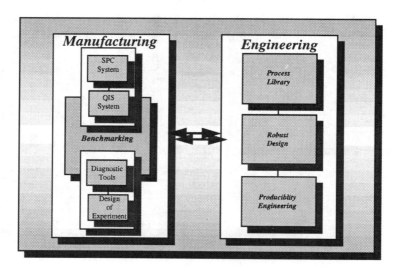

The Implementation Strategy

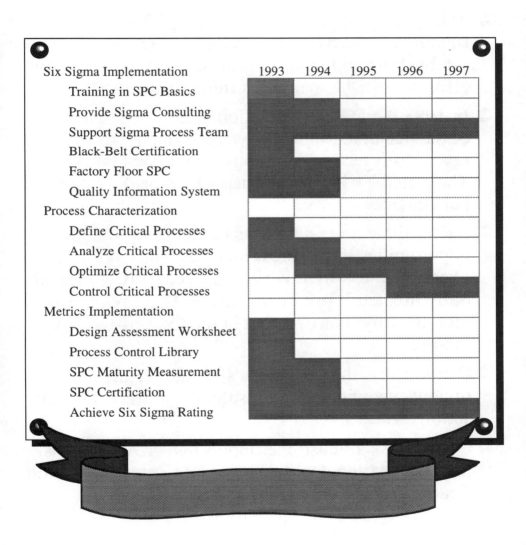

	1993	1994	1995	1996	1997
Six Sigma Implementation					
Training in SPC Basics					
Provide Sigma Consulting					
Support Sigma Process Team					
Black-Belt Certification					
Factory Floor SPC					
Quality Information System					
Process Characterization					
Define Critical Processes					
Analyze Critical Processes					
Optimize Critical Processes					
Control Critical Processes					
Metrics Implementation					
Design Assessment Worksheet					
Process Control Library					
SPC Maturity Measurement					
SPC Certification					
Achieve Six Sigma Rating					

Facts of the Case

➲ The Quality Improvement Team (QIT) is cross-functional by nature and is responsible for establishing and managing the quality improvement effort within the manufacturing organization.

➲ In 1988 the QIT investigation discovered that 30.1% of the manufacuring costs were attributed to scrap , rework, inspection, and non-value-added tasks. These items became the basis of the organization's performance metrics.

➲ Each Friday, the QIT meets to identify problems and opportunities for improvement, as well as to overview the Corrective Action Teams (CATs) and Self Directed Work Teams (SDWTs). Progress is measured by improvement in the Cost-of-Quality metric.

➲ Periodically, the QIT holds special meetings to review customer survey results and further the goal setting process.

➲ On the basis of customer inputs and COQ analysis, the QIT chartered and directed 52 Corrective Action Teams to solve critical problems

Fruits of the Labor

Issue	Before (1988)	After (1993)
Cost-Of-Quality	30.10%	7.40%
Defects-Per-Unit	0.104	0.009
Scrap	$3.0M	$0.3M
Lot Yield	92.0%	99.8%
Throughput Yield	84.3%	98.9%
Cycle-Time (weeks)	10.6	3.9
Warehouse Inventory	$3.9M	$1.1M

✔ As a result of the team's efforts, the cost of quality was reduced to 7.4%, resulting in a savings of $US12.7M.

✔ From 1988 to 1993 the Defects-Per-Unit (DPU) was reduced by 90%, from .104 to .009. This translated to a process capability of slightly greater than 5σ. With only 209 Defects-Per-Million-Opportunities (DPMO), the team now routinely reviews all quality incidents in a constructive and positive manner.

✔ In 1988 the annual scrap cost exceeded $US 3M in material and labor charges. Today, 96% of the cost due to scrap has been eliminated, resulting in a yearly improvement of $US 2.7M.

✔ Inspection costs were reduced by 31% while at the same time rework was reduced by 51.4%.

The Cost-Of-Quality Metric

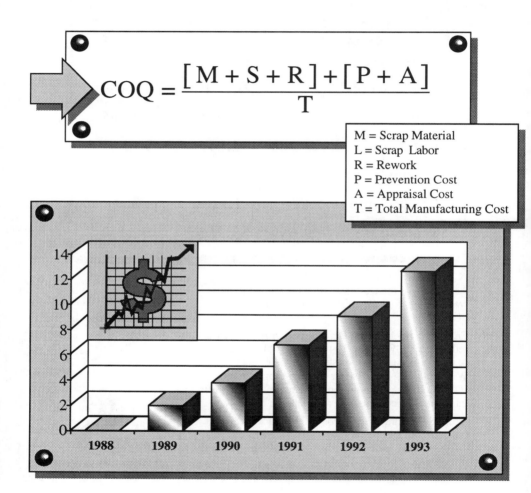

$$COQ = \frac{[M + S + R] + [P + A]}{T}$$

M = Scrap Material
L = Scrap Labor
R = Rework
P = Prevention Cost
A = Appraisal Cost
T = Total Manufacturing Cost

Measuring & Tracking Performance

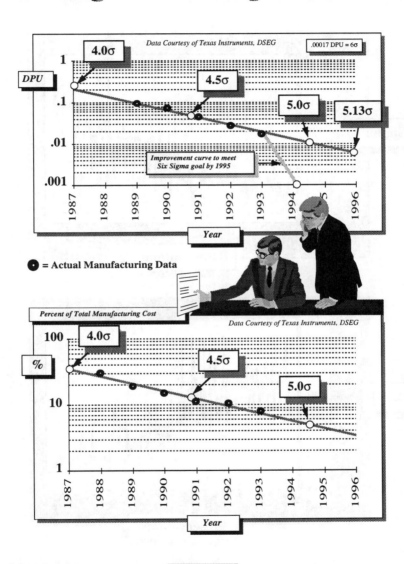

● = Actual Manufacturing Data

The Raw Data from 1989 - 1993

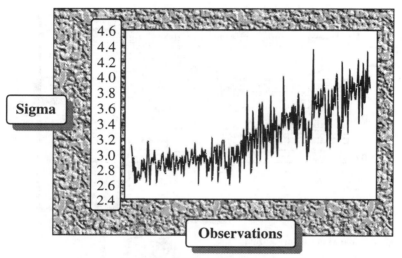

Data Courtesy of Texas Instruments, DSEG

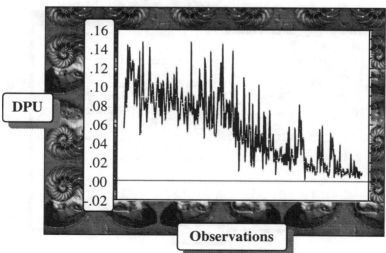

The Raw Data from 1989 - 1993

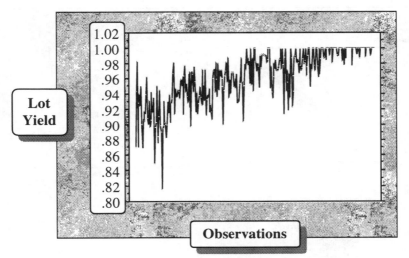

Lot Yield

Observations

Data Courtesy of Texas Instruments, DSEG

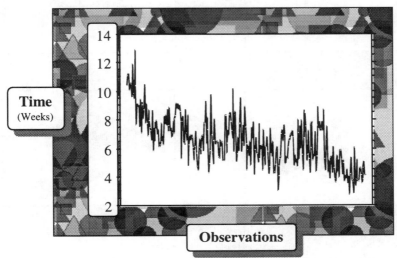

Time (Weeks)

Observations

The Diagnostic Analysis

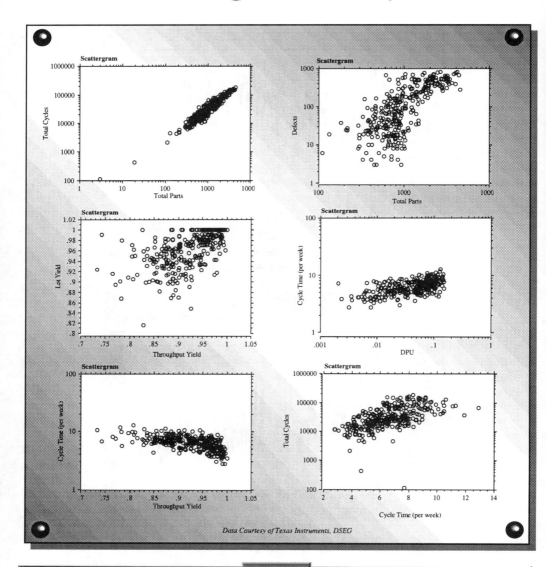

Data Courtesy of Texas Instruments, DSEG

29 . 10

Quality and Cycle Time Data

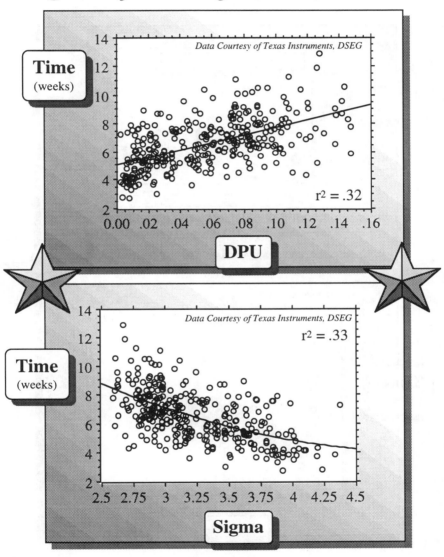

Time (weeks)

Data Courtesy of Texas Instruments, DSEG

$r^2 = .32$

DPU

Time (weeks)

Data Courtesy of Texas Instruments, DSEG

$r^2 = .33$

Sigma

Quality and Cycle Time Data

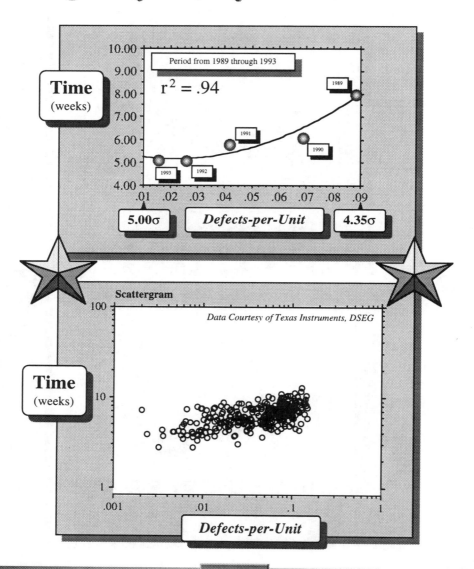

Quality and Manufacturing Costs

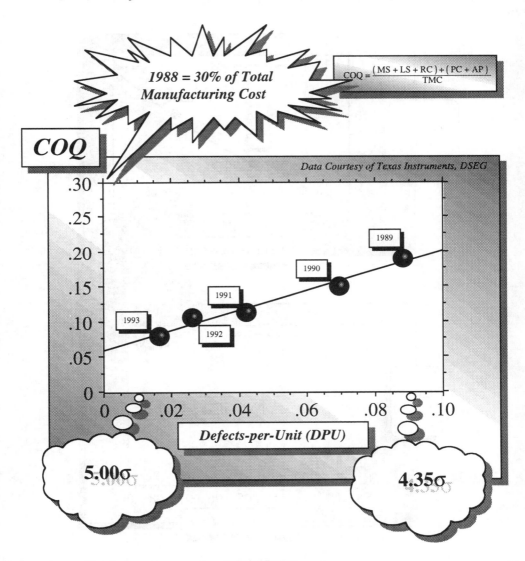

1988 = 30% of Total Manufacturing Cost

$$COQ = \frac{(MS + LS + RC) + (PC + AP)}{TMC}$$

COQ

Data Courtesy of Texas Instruments, DSEG

Defects-per-Unit (DPU)

1989
1990
1991
1993
1992

5.00σ

4.35σ

Quality-Material Correlation

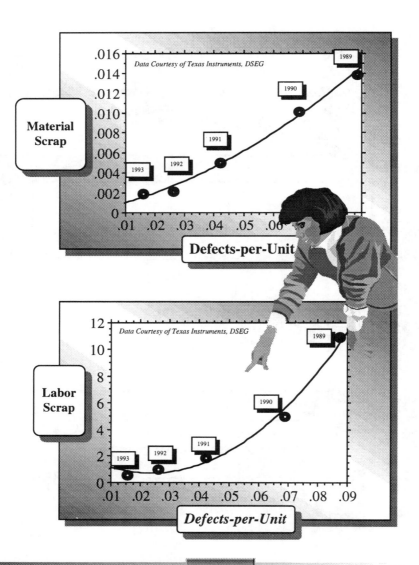

Lesson Learned at Texas Instruments

Extract from a paper entitled "Six Sigma -- Reaching Our Goal" Raymond L. Velasco

- Six Sigma is a new way of looking at familiar tools such as Statistical Process Control and Design of Experiments.

- Senior level management acceptance, commitment , and dedication is essential for successful deployment.

- Six Sigma can not be successfully deployed unless it has been captured in a dynamic and flexible plan.

- Management must clearly communicate their expectations regarding the use of Six Sigma.

- The use of a "Six Sigma Implementation Team" fell short of its expectation and goals.

- The use of a "Six Sigma Design Coordination Board" worked well to ensure continued propagation .

- Standardized reporting is essential to ensure continual focus on and resolution of problems by affected parties.

- The "Scorecard" concept worked very well.

- The completion of specialized training required a cadre of individuals and resources.

- To establish credibility, Six Sigma instructors must be respected individuals from their field of expertise.

- Implementation of training must be carefully coordinated across the board.

- Training should occur in a 'top down' manner.

- Producing a Six Sigma product requires the involvement of customers and suppliers.

- Some people, regardless of position, will reject change. Education is the principle tool to overcome this.

- Training dedicated in-house Six Sigma Consultants is very essential.

- The reinforcement and propagation of success stories is essential.

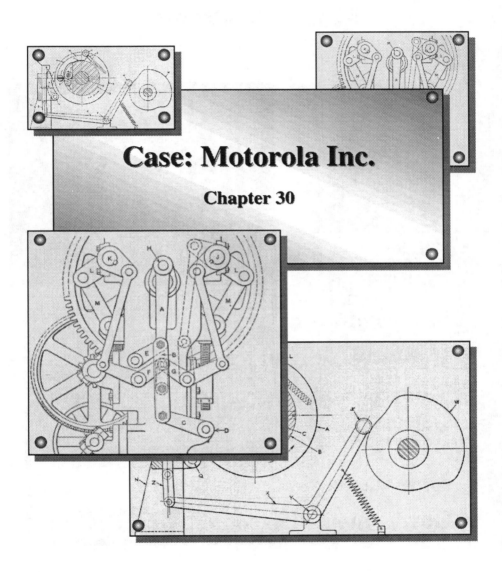

Case: Motorola Inc.

Chapter 30

Motorola Products

Photos Courtesy of Motorola

- **Pagers**
- **Cellular phones**
- **Semiconductors**
- **Two-way communications**
- **Modems and integrated management systems**
- **Automotive electronic modules and components**
- **Government electronics**

Basic Facts About Motorola

In 1990:

- **42nd in Fortune 500**
- **4th in electronic manufacturing (U.S.A.)**
- **14th in total U.S. exports**
- **3rd in U.S. electronics exports**
- **103,000 employees**

Data Courtesy of Motorola

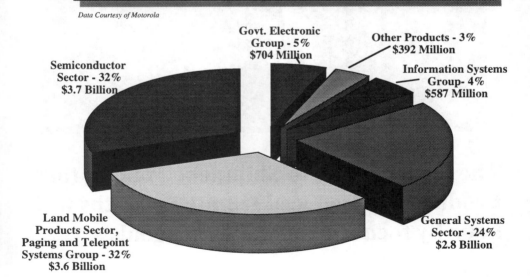

Govt. Electronic
Group - 5%
$704 Million

Other Products - 3%
$392 Million

Semiconductor
Sector - 32%
$3.7 Billion

Information Systems
Group- 4%
$587 Million

Land Mobile
Products Sector,
Paging and Telepoint
Systems Group - 32%
$3.6 Billion

General Systems
Sector - 24%
$2.8 Billion

30.3

A Major Success Story

Photos Courtesy of Motorola

The Order Entry to Shipment Time of this Product was Reduced from 1.5 months to 1 hour by focusing on Six Sigma goals

Key Benchmarking Data

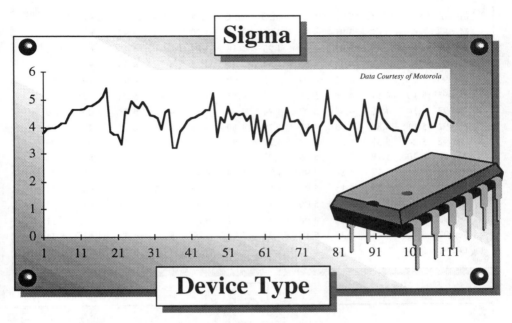

Source: Reliability and Quality Handbook: Motorola Semiconductor Products Sector (1987)

Improvement Over Time

Sigma	LMPS	PTSG	GSS	SPS	GEG	AIEG	CDX	UDS	CORP	INT	TOTAL
Mar-88	•	•	3.91	4.31	3.89	3.26	4.20	•	3.99	•	3.98
Dec-88	•	•	3.92	4.45	4.23	4.10	3.84	4.71	4.25	•	4.27
Dec-89	•	•	4.49	4.56	4.54	4.47	3.35	4.90	4.69	•	4.40
Dec-90	•	•	4.41	4.99	5.12	4.69	3.59	4.92	4.95	5.19	4.58
Dec-91	5.10	4.81	4.98	5.09	4.78	4.83	4.70	4.96	5.02	4.92	4.95
Jan-92	5.14	4.56	4.87	5.07	4.94	4.45	3.98	4.91	5.21	6.00	4.79
Feb-92	5.11	4.87	5.05	4.90	4.70	4.69	4.88	5.16	4.46	4.73	4.91
Mar-92	5.24	5.32	5.03	5.17	4.77	4.84	4.91	5.16	4.80	6.00	5.06
Apr-92	5.40	5.19	5.09	5.08	4.72	4.87	5.05	4.91	5.15	4.82	5.08
May-92	5.31	5.17	4.84	4.96	4.78	4.89	4.43	5.01	5.05	4.76	4.94
Jun-92	5.35	5.70	5.15	5.03	4.68	4.93	4.99	5.10	5.07	4.68	5.07
Jul-92	5.41	5.40	5.29	5.06	4.77	4.96	4.93	5.05	5.17	4.65	4.92
Aug-92	5.41	5.46	5.19	4.98	4.80	4.91	5.01	4.98	5.17	4.99	5.11
Sep-92	5.41	5.45	5.33	5.13	5.06	5.04	5.09	5.29	4.92	4.43	5.21
Oct-92	5.54	5.47	5.20	5.10	5.17	4.98	5.06	5.09	5.10	4.79	5.21

Data Courtesy of Motorola

σ

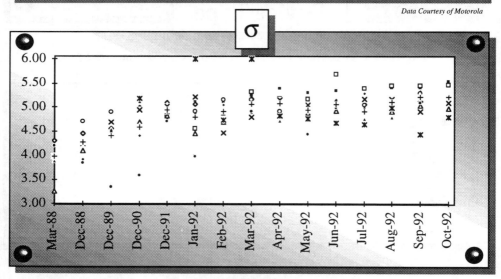

30.6

Sales per Employee

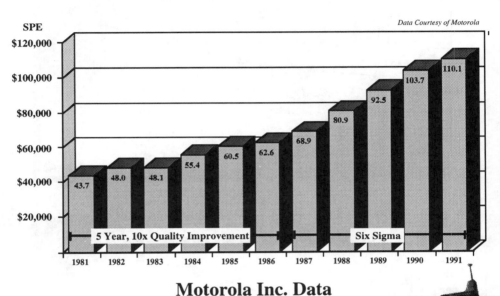

Data Courtesy of Motorola

SPE

$120,000 —

$100,000 —

$80,000 —

$60,000 —

$40,000 —

$20,000 —

43.7 | 48.0 | 48.1 | 55.4 | 60.5 | 62.6 | 68.9 | 80.9 | 92.5 | 103.7 | 110.1

5 Year, 10x Quality Improvement | Six Sigma

1981 | 1982 | 1983 | 1984 | 1985 | 1986 | 1987 | 1988 | 1989 | 1990 | 1991

Motorola Inc. Data

What Questions Should We Ask?

30 . 7

The Key Relationship

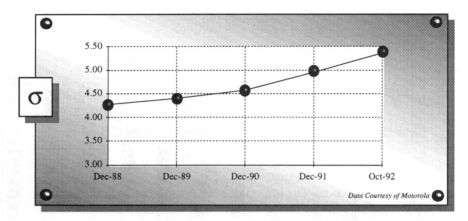

Data Courtesy of Motorola

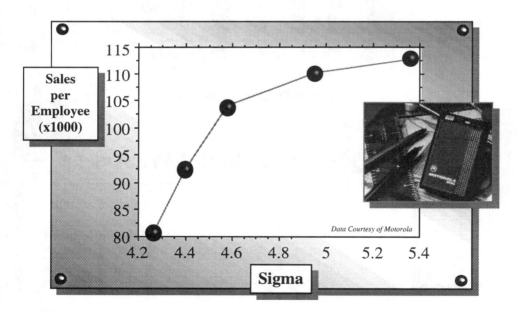

Data Courtesy of Motorola

Furthering the Insight

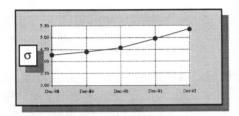

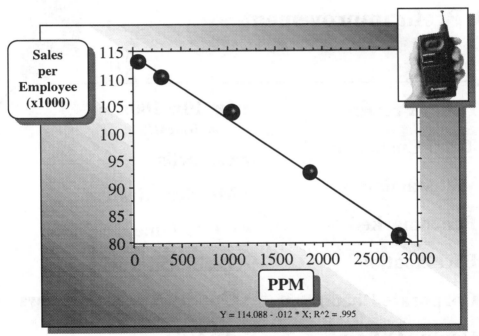

Sales per Employee (x1000)

PPM

$Y = 114.088 - .012 * X; R^2 = .995$

Data Courtesy of Motorola

The Driving Beliefs

✼ **Six Sigma Quality**

✼ **Total Cycle Time Reduction**

✼ **Product and Service Leadership**

✼ **Profit Improvement**

- **Policy Process**
- **Total Customer**

   Satisfaction
- **Benchmarked**
- **Participation**
- **Corporate Documents**
- **Quality Officer**

- **5x 10x 100x 6σ**
   Implement!
- **Councils**
- **Metrics - System**
- **Cycle Time**
- **Technical Reviews**
- **Quality System Reviews**
- **Award**

30 . 10

Key Leadership Points

Total Customer Satisfaction

    Fundamental Objective

    Drives all operations

Translated into:

    Key Beliefs

    Key Goals

    Key Initiatives

Cultural change begins at the top

10x by 1989, 100x by 1991, Six Sigma by 1992

Establish culture of quality

    Internal

        Quality policy deployment

        Common metrics

    External

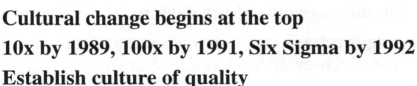

        Visits to key customers

        Visits to key suppliers

        Partnership for growth

CEO Quality Award

Focusing on the Customer

Total Customer Satisfaction

>   Drives all business planning

>   Translates into key goals and initiatives

>   Made concrete by quantitative goals

Customer satisfaction equates to business success

Constantly moving target, therefore continuous improvement is required

>   Listening to voice of the customer

>   Using mechanisms to translate customer requirements into product/service

>   Enforcing mechanisms to ensure defect-free production with lowest possible cycle time

>   Continual monitoring of performance

>   Continually resetting expectation levels to benchmark performance, or better

How the quality culture was established

>   Leadership from the top

>   Employee involvement and ownership

>   Training to support the initiatives

Quality Information and Analysis

Six Sigma Strategy

>**Universal**
>
>**Pro-active**
>
>**Iterative**

Identifying Customer Requirements

>**Direct customer contact**
>
>**Surveys, field return data, etc.**

Methodology for manufactured product

>**Defect-per-unit (dpu) targets for new designs**
>
>**Concurrent product/process design**
>
>**Tools for simulating performance**
>
>**Reducing variation in manufacturing**
>
>**Performance measures: dpu and cycle time**

Methodology for services and nonmanufacturing

>**Identifying work necessary to satisfy customer**
>
>**Identifying opportunities for error**
>
>**Performance measures: dpmo and cycle time**

Benchmarking to evaluate against best-in-class

Strategic Quality Planning Process

Total customer satisfaction drives quality planning

Key inputs: the customer and benchmarking

Six Sigma methodology for achieving quality goals

Utilization of defect budgets

> **Each new product must have ever-lower dpu**

> **Controls design and manufacturing**

Annual quality goal is decomposed to lower levels

Incentives keyed to achievement of goals

> **Six Sigma Quality**

> **Cycle time reduction**

Progress toward goals continuously monitored

The Results of Improvement

Six Sigma has shown that the Highest Quality Producer is the Lowest Cost Producer

Savings Over

$US 2.2 Billion

1987, 1988, 1989, 1990, 1991

Data Courtesy of Motorola

$1 Billion

Savings Potential in non-manufacturing costs

Some Landmark Events

1979 • "Our Quality Stinks."

1980 • Corporate Quality Officer named

1981 • Motorola Training Center established
5 year, 10x quality improvement goal set

• Benchmarking revealed 10 x not enough

1984 • Communications Sector staff meeting

1985 • Communications Sector begins total defect per
unit measurement July - Manufactured Products
November - Sales Orders

1986 • Chairman changes agenda of customer visits

1987 • Corporation adopts Six Sigma

• 4 year, 100x quality improvement, Six Sigma
goal set

1992 • 2 year, 10x continuous improvement goal set

Some Key Initiatives

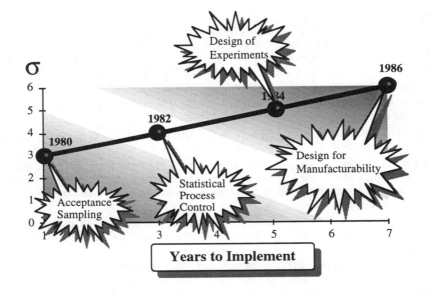

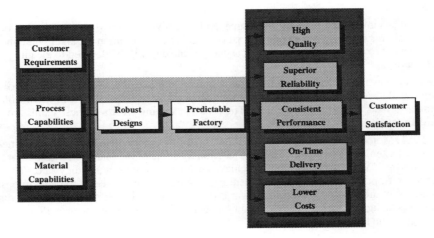

Motorola Case Study

Extract from a paper entitled "The Motorola Story" Bill Smith

- Motorola, Inc. is one of the world's leading manufacturers of electronic equipment, systems, and components produced for both United States and international markets. Motorola products include two-way radios, pagers, and cellular radiotelephones, other forms of electronic communications systems, integrated circuits and discrete semiconductors, defense and aerospace electronics, automotive and industrial electronics, data communications and information processing and handling equipment.

- Ranked among the United States' 100 largest industrial companies, Motorola has about 102,000 employees worldwide.

- The company's operations are highly decentralized, with business operations structured as sectors, groups, or divisions, depending on size.

- Motorola has major facilities in 10 states and Puerto Rico, and maintains more than 30 major facilities outside the U.S. Its employee population numbers more than 60,000 in the U.S., with the remainder found predominantly in Asia, Australia, Canada, Mexico, Europe and the Middle East.

- To know a company's people is to know the company. The task of creating a "quality culture" is much easier within a company that already has an existing culture based on people values.

- Bob Galvin recalled attending a retirement party held several years ago, where the retiree told him that he and his family had met the night before, and counted a total of 52 relatives who were either currently working for Motorola, or had worked for the company in the past.

- Motorolans greet each other by first name, and unless visitors are present, the dress code is informal, that is, men do not wear suit jackets. It is not uncommon for an engineering department to declare a "jeans" day, especially if the day will be devoted to cleaning up the laboratory.

- Teams are usually organized by function within an organization. Their purpose is to continually assess the process of performing their work, and to change it in ways which will reduce defects and reduce cycle time. The problem solving efforts of these teams are directly analogous to Quality Circles.

- In 1981, Motorola established, as one of its Top Ten Corporate Goals, the improvement of quality by ten times by 1986. The first reaction by some of the managers was that of skepticism. "We don't know how to achieve such an ambitious goal", they said. The response from the corporate management was, "We agree that it seems to be an impossible goal, but in the process of working towards that goal, we will find new ways to run our business at significantly improved quality levels. Each of these new ways will ultimately lead us to the ten times improvement."

Motorola Case Study

Extract from a paper entitled "The Motorola Story" Bill Smith

■ Concurrent with this understanding which has caused the integration of quality strategy into the day to day operations of the business, is a common measurement which directly correlates to customer satisfaction.

■ At Motorola, the quality culture is pervasive. The CEO formally restated our company objectives, beliefs, goals and key initiatives in 1987, and quality remained as a central theme. Total Customer Satisfaction is Motorola's fundamental objective. It is the overriding responsibility of everyone in the company, and the focus of all of our efforts.

■ The first of these is Six Sigma Quality. We intend that all products and services are to be at the Six Sigma level by 1992. This means designing products that will accept reasonable variation in component parts, and developing manufacturing processes that will produce minimum variation in the final output product. It also means analyzing all the services we provide, breaking them down into their component parts, and designing systems that will achieve Six Sigma performance. We are taking statistical technologies and making them a part of each and every employee's job, regardless of assignment. Measuring begins by recording the defects found in every function of our business, then relating them to a product or process by the number of opportunities to fabricate the product or carry out the process. We have converted our yield language to parts per million (ppm), and the Six Sigma goal is 3.4 ppm defect levels across the company. Despite the wide variety of products and services, the corporate goal is the same Six Sigma by 1992.

■ Our second key initiative, Total Cycle Time Reduction, is closely related to Six Sigma Quality. We define cycle time as the elapsed time from the moment a customer places an order for an existing product to the time we deliver it.

■ The third initiative, Product and Manufacturing Leadership, also emphasizes the need for product development and manufacturing disciplines to work together in an integrated world.

■ Our fourth initiative, Profit Improvement, is a long-term, customer-driven approach that shows us where to commit our resources to give customers what they need, thus improving long-term profits. It recognizes that investing in quality today will produce growth in the future.

■ The final initiative is Participative Management Within, and Cooperation Between Organizations. This approach is designed to achieve more synergy, greater efficiency and improved quality.

■ In 1986, Bob Galvin began a more formal program of customer visits. These visits traditionally had been less systematic and covered only specific topics. Under the new program, members of top management talk to customers at various levels of their business. They ask two basic questions: What do you like about Motorola, and what don't you like? After each visit, a detailed report with specific recommendations is submitted.

Motorola Case Study

Extract from a paper entitled "The Motorola Story" Bill Smith

- Management demonstrates its leadership in the quality initiative in many ways. The CEO chairs the Operating and Policy Committees in twice a quarter, all day meetings. The Chief Quality Officer of the corporation opens the meetings with an update on key initiatives of the Quality Program. This includes results of management visits to customers, results of Quality System Reviews (QSR's) of major parts of the company, cost of poor quality reports, supplier-Motorola activity, and a review of quality breakthroughs and shortfalls. This is followed by a report by a major business manager on the current status of his/her particular quality initiative. This covers progress against plans, successes, failures, and what he projects to do to close the gap on deficient results, all pointed at achieving Six Sigma capability by 1992. Discussion follows among the leaders concerning all of the above agenda items.

- Our focus on very specific numeric goals, i.e., 10X, 100X, and Six Sigma capability is unique in this country.

- Quality System Reviews are not a new technology, but we believe very few companies have utilized this system, and it has been successful.

- Cycle Time Management is a growing integral part of our programs, and in conjunction with Six Sigma, represents a very powerful and effective thrust.

- In our Six Sigma Quality Program, the key elements of data are the defects found, compared to the number of opportunities to make defects in the product or process. Throughout Motorola, we have changed our data systems to record defects, opportunities, and the means, variation and limits of both product and process . We direct corrective action through use of Pareto charts, histograms, scatter charts, Ishikawa diagrams, etc.

- Analytical techniques begin with the product design cycle, when circuits are analyzed for limit conditions and for Six Sigma distribution of characteristics.

- Defect per unit goals are established during the design phase of the product and verified through early prototype and pilot runs.

- Shipping takes place only when the budget is achieved for the defects per unit, and the unit successfully passes an Accelerated Life Test.

- Achieving an improvement rate of ten times in two years cannot be done by conventional corrective actions on current products. Such corrective actions must be taken, but they can only yield an evolutionary improvement rate.

- Thus, the cornerstone of our strategy for dramatic improvement is one that requires each new product to be introduced at a defect per unit level that is typically one-fourth to one-fifth of the product it will replace, or significantly less than similar products in current production.

Motorola Case Study

Extract from a paper entitled "The Motorola Story" Bill Smith

- We manage our quality improvement objectives just as we would new product introduction, technology and any other part of the company's activity.

- Coupled to these basic quality business goals are goal-directed incentives for both management and employees. These are the Motorola Executive Incentive Plan (MEIP) and the Participative Management Program (PMP).

- Finally, a large training and education university-like function (Motorola Training and Education Center, MTEC) provides training on quality at all levels, with specific emphasis on providing all employees the knowledge and skills necessary to achieve our quality goals.

- We have quantitatively benchmarked best-in-class companies worldwide, and as a result of these efforts, have driven many of our products and processes to best-in-class levels. Examples include soldering, surface-mounted chip component placement, and cycle time in the production of pagers and cellular mobile radiotelephones. This process allows us to constantly strive to be the best-in-class in all aspects with true measurements for our goal setting and results

- The mission of Motorola's training function is to provide the right training to the right people at the right time.

- On the average, we provide one million hours of training per year to our employees. In 1987, we spent $44 million on training. This represented 2.4% of the corporate payroll. Forty percent of the training is devoted to quality improvement processes, principles, technology, and objectives.

- During the past three years, over 150 hours of quality-related training have been developed, and are being delivered to assembly operators, technicians, engineers, support groups, and the management of these functions. "Course maps" help employees and their managers select programs which respond to individual needs as well as the key corporate initiative of Six Sigma Quality.

- Three important parts of our quality training are training, product/process-specific training, and special management training.

- Training programs in Statistical Process Control, Design for Manufacturability, and Understanding Six Sigma are helping us reach our ambitious goal of 100-fold improvement in four years. These courses provide a set of problem-solving strategies and tools for continuous improvement towards perfection in everything we do.

- To support our commitment to Total Customer Satisfaction through quality in all that we do, we have developed the Motorola Management Institute (MMI).

- MMI topics include customer-centered culture and marketing for world-class manufacturing and quality, designing for manfacturability, information systems, cycle time management, technology, and supply and change management.

Motorola Case Study

Extract from a paper entitled "The Motorola Story" Bill Smith

- The Senior Executive Program focused on the critical corporate objective of Total Customer Satisfaction.

- In 1970, Motorola formed the Science Advisory Board Associates (SABA). As the organization charter describes it, SABA is dedicated to identifying and rewarding exceptional creative engineering talent and contribution.

- The crown jewel of recognition awards at Motorola is the Chief Executive Office Quality Award. This prestigious award is presented, with appropriate ceremony, by the corporation's Chairman or Chief Executive Office or Chief Operating Officer.

- In 1987, a Chief Executive Office Award was given to product teams within the Government Electronics Group for providing over 900 space communication systems to the U.S. Government over the past ten years. None of this equipment has experienced a failure. All of the color photographs of the planets sent from Voyager and other deep space probes were sent to earth via Motorola communications equipment.

- Listening to the "Voice of the Customer", the process of assessing the customer's perception of the total quality of Motorola as a supplier, is accomplished by visits to customers by the Chairman, CEO, and other high level executives within the company.

- There are a number of examples of how Motorola and its customers have combined efforts to bring about a new solution in the marketplace [partnerships].

- Codex worked together with major international airlines in the definition of broad-based data communications networks and the special requirements of the airline industry.

- The Bandit pager program of Paging Division is notable, not only for its fully automated manufacturing capability, but for the extension of that automated system to include the order entry process, which in the future will be directly accessible to the customer.

- In the Communications Sector customer requirements for new products are captured in a contract book generated at the beginning of the development effort. The contract contains all features and requirements that the sales organization deems necessary to satisfy customer requirements.

- The new AIEG Detroit Application and System Engineering Center is an example of Motorola's dedication to enhancement of customer inputs to new product designs.

- SPS has made significant strides in providing design tools which are directly accessible to customers enabling them to perform the otherwise complicated task of designing complex functional devices for a special need.

- Motorola first earned the right to be a prime supplier in this prestigious Japanese market through the introduction of our highly reliable RC13 pager in 1982. This product was released at a proven reliability level 40% better than the standards then in existence in Japan for communication equipment.

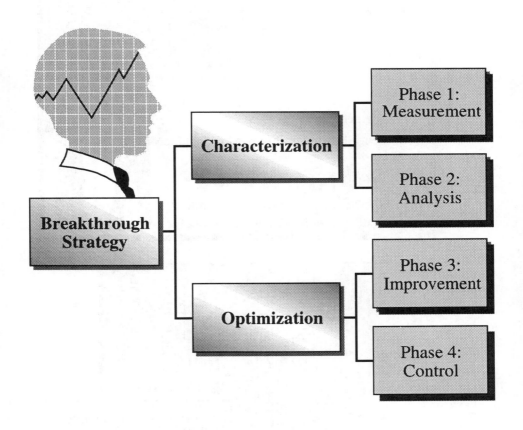

Nature of the Problem

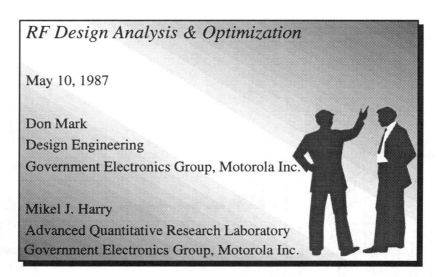

RF Design Analysis & Optimization

May 10, 1987

Don Mark
Design Engineering
Government Electronics Group, Motorola Inc.

Mikel J. Harry
Advanced Quantitative Research Laboratory
Government Electronics Group, Motorola Inc.

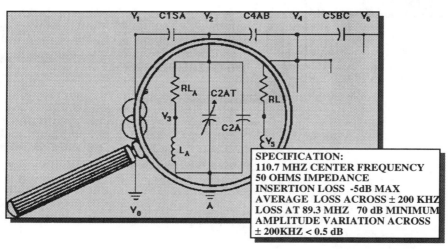

SPECIFICATION:
110.7 MHZ CENTER FREQUENCY
50 OHMS IMPEDANCE
INSERTION LOSS -5dB MAX
AVERAGE LOSS ACROSS ± 200 KHZ
LOSS AT 89.3 MHZ 70 dB MINIMUM
AMPLITUDE VARIATION ACROSS
± 200KHZ < 0.5 dB

The Improvement Strategy

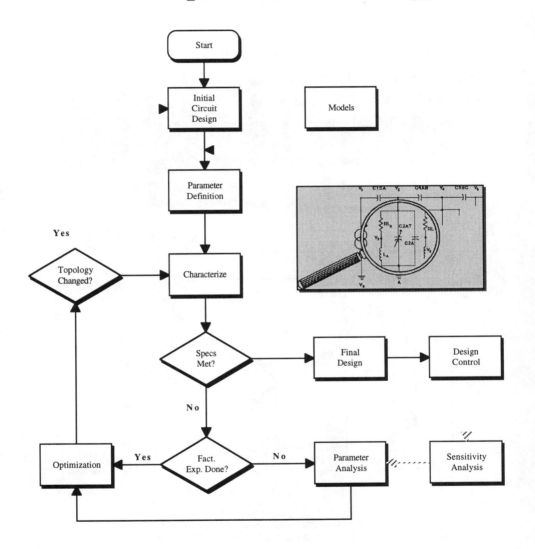

Conducting the Analysis

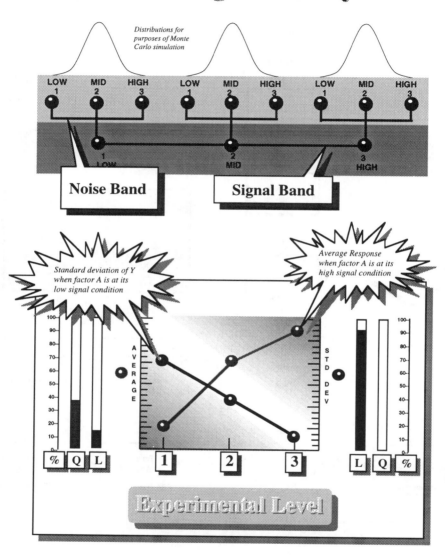

Interpreting the Results

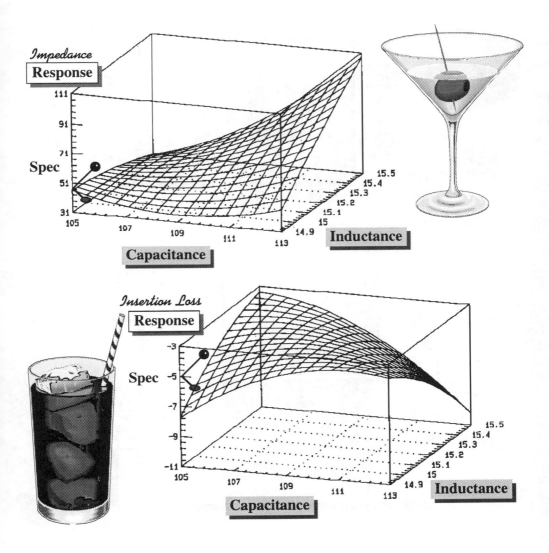

Impedance
Response

Spec

Inductance

Capacitance

Insertion Loss
Response

Spec

Inductance

Capacitance

Establishing Tolerances

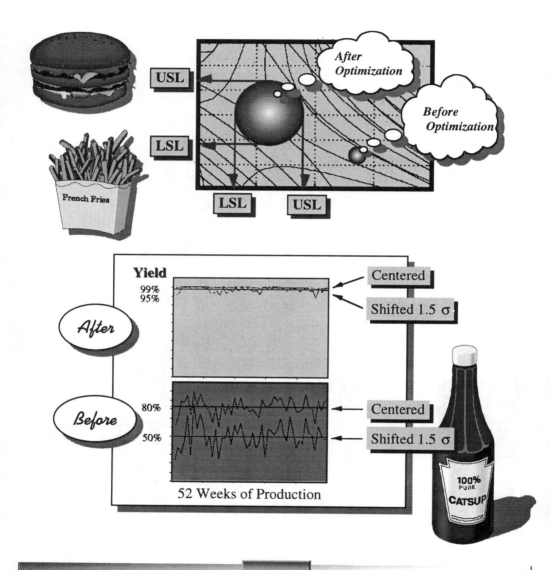

52 Weeks of Production

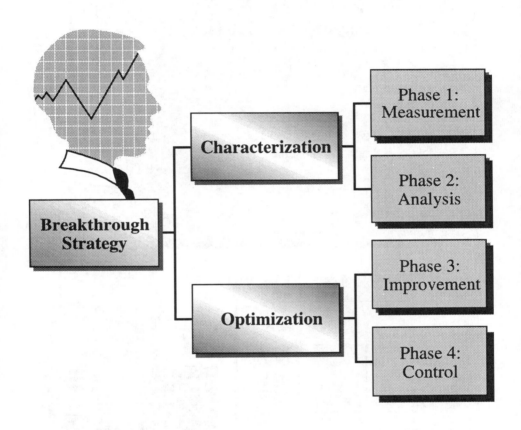

Nature of the Problem

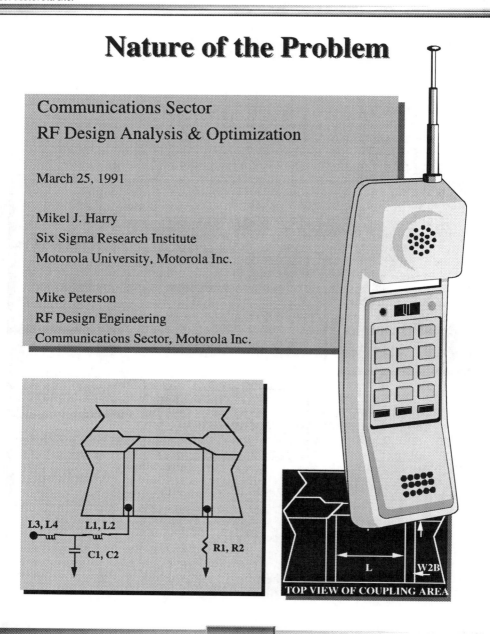

Communications Sector

RF Design Analysis & Optimization

March 25, 1991

Mikel J. Harry
Six Sigma Research Institute
Motorola University, Motorola Inc.

Mike Peterson
RF Design Engineering
Communications Sector, Motorola Inc.

L3, L4   L1, L2

C1, C2   R1, R2

L   W2B

TOP VIEW OF COUPLING AREA

Defining the Variables

High Directivity Multi-Layer Directional Coupler

Response Variables: *Response Frequencies*

S11	Input Return Loss	132 MHz
S21	Reflected Coupled Port	153 MHz
S31	Forward Coupled Port	174 MHz
S41	Insertion Loss	
D23	Directivity (S31 - S21)	

DESCRIPTION	NOMINAL	TOL (+/-)
DIELECTRIC CONSTANT	4.4	0.2
CONDUCTOR SPACING	0.010 IN	10%
CONDUCTOR-GROUND SPACING	0.047 IN	10%
COUPLED LINE WIDTH	0.023 IN	0.003 IN
STRIP T-LINE WIDTH	0.042 IN	0.003 IN
STRIP T-LINE WIDTH	0.042 IN	0.003 IN
COUPLED LINE LENGTH	0.720 IN	0.003 IN
TERMINATING RESISTOR	50 OHM	2%
TERMINATING RESISTOR	50 OHM	2%
INDUCTOR 1	39 nH	10%
INDUCTOR 2	39 nH	10%
INDUCTOR 3	39 nH	10%
INDUCTOR 4	39 nH	10%
CAPACITOR 1	39 pF	5%
CAPACITOR 2	39 pF	5%

The Sensitivity Analysis

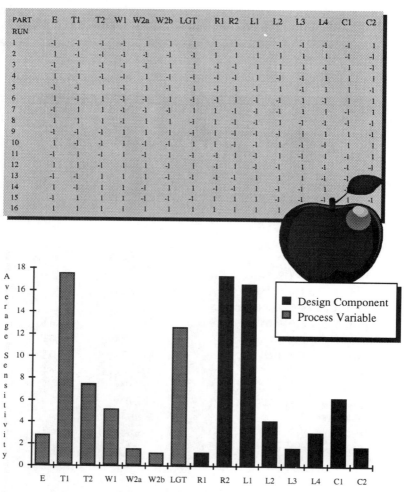

Note: Ordinate is the average sensitivity across all response characteristics

Second Order Analysis

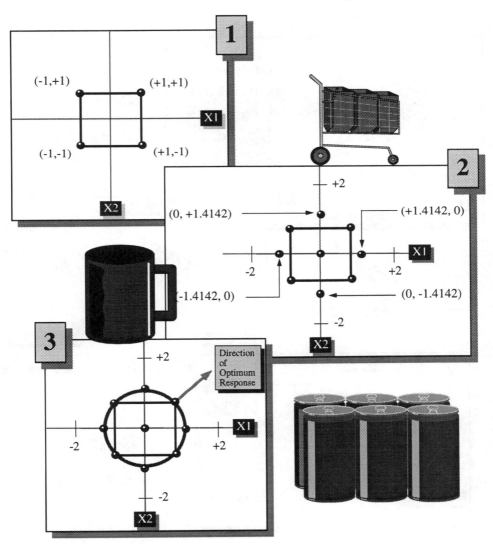

The Graphical Outcome

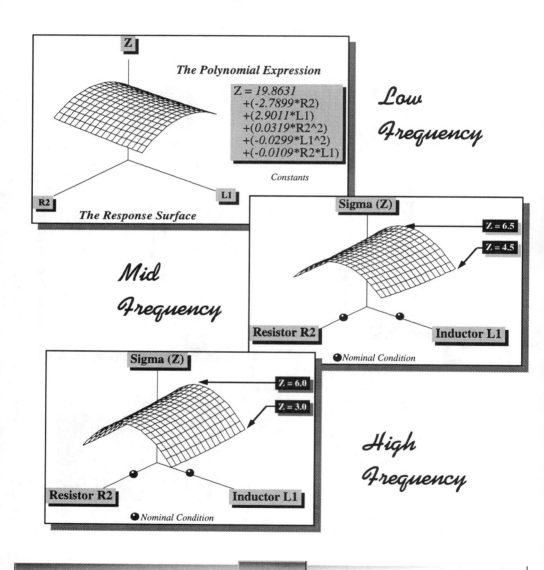

Establishing the Tolerances

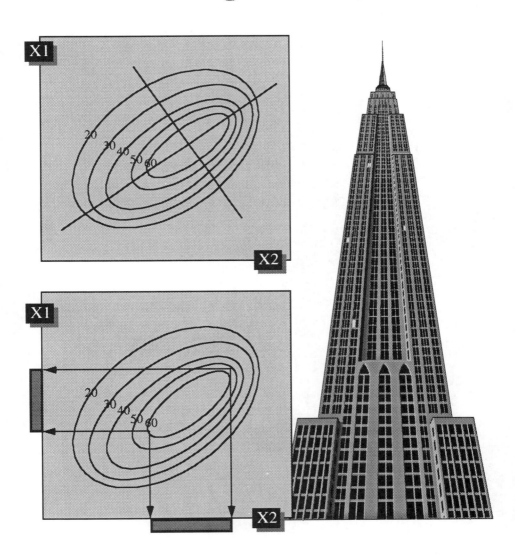

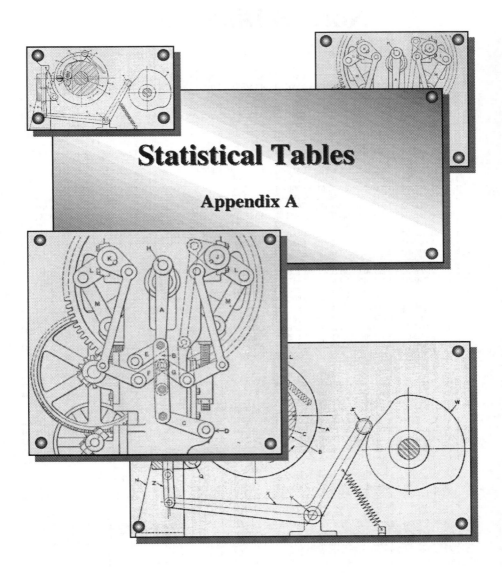

Statistical Tables

Appendix A

Normal Distribution

Z	0	0.01	0.02	0.03	0.04	0.05	0.06	0.07	0.08	0.09
0.0	5.00E-01	4.96E-01	4.92E-01	4.88E-01	4.84E-01	4.80E-01	4.76E-01	4.72E-01	4.68E-01	4.64E-01
0.1	4.60E-01	4.56E-01	4.52E-01	4.48E-01	4.44E-01	4.40E-01	4.36E-01	4.33E-01	4.29E-01	4.25E-01
0.2	4.21E-01	4.17E-01	4.13E-01	4.09E-01	4.05E-01	4.01E-01	3.97E-01	3.94E-01	3.90E-01	3.86E-01
0.3	3.82E-01	3.78E-01	3.75E-01	3.71E-01	3.67E-01	3.63E-01	3.59E-01	3.56E-01	3.52E-01	3.48E-01
0.4	3.45E-01	3.41E-01	3.37E-01	3.34E-01	3.30E-01	3.26E-01	3.23E-01	3.19E-01	3.16E-01	3.12E-01
0.5	3.09E-01	3.05E-01	3.02E-01	2.98E-01	2.95E-01	2.91E-01	2.88E-01	2.84E-01	2.81E-01	2.78E-01
0.6	2.74E-01	2.71E-01	2.68E-01	2.64E-01	2.61E-01	2.58E-01	2.55E-01	2.51E-01	2.48E-01	2.45E-01
0.7	2.42E-01	2.39E-01	2.36E-01	2.33E-01	2.30E-01	2.27E-01	2.24E-01	2.21E-01	2.18E-01	2.15E-01
0.8	2.12E-01	2.09E-01	2.06E-01	2.03E-01	2.01E-01	1.98E-01	1.95E-01	1.92E-01	1.89E-01	1.87E-01
0.9	1.84E-01	1.81E-01	1.79E-01	1.76E-01	1.74E-01	1.71E-01	1.69E-01	1.66E-01	1.64E-01	1.61E-01
1.0	1.59E-01	1.56E-01	1.5 39E01	1.52E-01	1.49E-01	1.47E-01	1.45E-01	1.42E-01	1.40E-01	1.38E-01
1.1	1.36E-01	1.34E-01	1.31E-01	1.29E-01	1.27E-01	1.25E-01	1.23E-01	1.21E-01	1.19E-01	1.17E-01
1.2	1.15E-01	1.13E-01	1.11E-01	1.09E-01	1.08E-01	1.06E-01	1.04E-01	1.02E-01	1.00E-01	9.85E-02
1.3	9.68E-02	9.51E-02	9.34E-02	9.18E-02	9.01E-02	8.85E-02	8.69E-02	8.53E-02	8.38E-02	8.23E-02
1.4	8.08E-02	7.93E-02	7.78E-02	7.64E-02	7.49E-02	7.35E-02	7.21E-02	7.08E-02	6.94E-02	6.81E-02
1.5	6.68E-02	6.55E-02	6.43E-02	6.30E-02	6.18E-02	6.06E-02	5.94E-02	5.82E-02	5.71E-02	5.59E-02
1.6	5.48E-02	5.37E-02	5.26E-02	5.16E-02	5.05E-02	4.95E-02	4.85E-02	4.75E-02	4.65E-02	4.55E-02
1.7	4.46E-02	4.36E-02	4.27E-02	4.18E-02	4.09E-02	4.01E-02	3.92E-02	3.84E-02	3.75E-02	3.67E-02
1.8	3.59E-02	3.52E-02	3.44E-02	3.36E-02	3.29E-02	3.22E-02	3.14E-02	3.07E-02	3.01E-02	2.94E-02
1.9	2.87E-02	2.81E-02	2.74E-02	2.68E-02	2.62E-02	2.56E-02	2.50E-02	2.44E-02	2.39E-02	2.33E-02
2.0	2.28E-02	2.22E-02	2.17E-02	2.12E-02	2.07E-02	2.02E-02	1.97E-02	1.92E-02	1.88E-02	1.83E-02
2.1	1.79E-02	1.74E-02	1.70E-02	1.66E-02	1.62E-02	1.58E-02	1.54E-02	1.50E-02	1.46E-02	1.43E-02
2.2	1.39E-02	1.36E-02	1.32E-02	1.29E-02	1.26E-02	1.22E-02	1.19E-02	1.16E-02	1.13E-02	1.10E-02
2.3	1.07E-02	1.04E-02	1.02E-02	9.90E-03	9.64E-03	9.39E-03	9.14E-03	8.89E-03	8.66E-03	8.42E-03
2.4	8.20E-03	7.98E-03	7.76E-03	7.55E-03	7.34E-03	7.14E-03	6.95E-03	6.76E-03	6.57E-03	6.39E-03
2.5	6.21E-03	6.04E-03	5.87E-03	5.70E-03	5.54E-03	5.39E-03	5.23E-03	5.09E-03	4.94E-03	4.80E-03
2.6	4.66E-03	4.53E-03	4.40E-03	4.27E-03	4.15E-03	4.02E-03	3.91E-03	3.79E-03	3.68E-03	3.57E-03
2.7	3.47E-03	3.36E-03	3.26E-03	3.17E-03	3.07E-03	2.98E-03	2.89E-03	2.80E-03	2.72E-03	2.64E-03
2.8	2.56E-03	2.48E-03	2.40E-03	2.33E-03	2.26E-03	2.19E-03	2.12E-03	2.05E-03	1.99E-03	1.93E-03
2.9	1.87E-03	1.81E-03	1.75E-03	1.70E-03	1.64E-03	1.59E-03	1.54E-03	1.49E-03	1.44E-03	1.40E-03
3.0	1.35E-03	1.31E-03	1.26E-03	1.22E-03	1.18E-03	1.14E-03	1.11E-03	1.07E-03	1.04E-03	1.00E-03
3.1	9.68E-04	9.35E-04	9.04E-04	8.74E-04	8.45E-04	8.16E-04	7.89E-04	7.62E-04	7.36E-04	7.11E-04
3.2	6.87E-04	6.64E-04	6.41E-04	6.19E-04	5.98E-04	5.77E-04	5.57E-04	5.38E-04	5.19E-04	5.01E-04
3.3	4.84E-04	4.67E-04	4.50E-04	4.34E-04	4.19E-04	4.04E-04	3.90E-04	3.76E-04	3.63E-04	3.50E-04
3.4	3.37E-04	3.25E-04	3.13E-04	3.02E-04	2.91E-04	2.80E-04	2.70E-04	2.60E-04	2.51E-04	2.42E-04
3.5	2.33E-04	2.24E-04	2.16E-04	2.08E-04	2.00E-04	1.93E-04	1.86E-04	1.79E-04	1.72E-04	1.66E-04
3.6	1.59E-04	1.53E-04	1.47E-04	1.42E-04	1.36E-04	1.31E-04	1.26E-04	1.21E-04	1.17E-04	1.12E-04
3.7	1.08E-04	1.04E-04	9.97E-05	9.59E-05	9.21E-05	8.86E-05	8.51E-05	8.18E-05	7.85E-05	7.55E-05
3.8	7.25E-05	6.96E-05	6.69E-05	6.42E-05	6.17E-05	5.92E-05	5.68E-05	5.46E-05	5.24E-05	5.03E-05
3.9	4.82E-05	4.63E-05	4.44E-05	4.26E-05	4.09E-05	3.92E-05	3.76E-05	3.61E-05	3.46E-05	3.32E-05
4.0	3.18E-05	3.05E-05	2.92E-05	2.80E-05	2.68E-05	2.57E-05	2.47E-05	2.36E-05	2.26E-05	2.17E-05
4.1	2.08E-05	1.99E-05	1.91E-05	1.82E-05	1.75E-05	1.67E-05	1.60E-05	1.53E-05	1.47E-05	1.40E-05
4.2	1.34E-05	1.29E-05	1.23E-05	1.18E-05	1.13E-05	1.08E-05	1.03E-05	9.86E-06	9.43E-06	9.01E-06
4.3	8.62E-06	8.24E-06	7.88E-06	7.53E-06	7.20E-06	6.88E-06	6.57E-06	6.28E-06	6.00E-06	5.73E-06
4.4	5.48E-06	5.23E-06	5.00E-06	4.77E-06	4.56E-06	4.35E-06	4.16E-06	3.97E-06	3.79E-06	3.62E-06
4.5	3.45E-06	3.29E-06	3.14E-06	3.00E-06	2.86E-06	2.73E-06	2.60E-06	2.48E-06	2.37E-06	2.26E-06
4.6	2.15E-06	2.05E-06	1.96E-06	1.87E-06	1.78E-06	1.70E-06	1.62E-06	1.54E-06	1.47E-06	1.40E-06
4.7	1.33E-06	1.27E-06	1.21E-06	1.15E-06	1.10E-06	1.05E-06	9.96E-07	9.48E-07	9.03E-07	8.59E-07
4.8	8.18E-07	7.79E-07	7.41E-07	7.05E-07	6.71E-07	6.39E-07	6.08E-07	5.78E-07	5.50E-07	5.23E-07
4.9	4.98E-07	4.73E-07	4.50E-07	4.28E-07	4.07E-07	3.87E-07	3.68E-07	3.50E-07	3.32E-07	3.16E-07

Normal Distribution

z	0	0.01	0.02	0.03	0.04	0.05	0.06	0.07	0.08	0.09
5.0	3.00E-07	2.85E-07	2.71E-07	2.58E-07	2.45E-07	2.32E-07	2.21E-07	2.10E-07	1.99E-07	1.89E-07
5.1	1.80E-07	1.71E-07	1.62E-07	1.54E-07	1.46E-07	1.39E-07	1.31E-07	1.25E-07	1.18E-07	1.12E-07
5.2	1.07E-07	1.01E-07	9.59E-08	9.10E-08	8.63E-08	8.18E-08	7.76E-08	7.36E-08	6.98E-08	6.62E-08
5.3	6.27E-08	5.95E-08	5.64E-08	5.34E-08	5.06E-08	4.80E-08	4.55E-08	4.31E-08	4.08E-08	3.87E-08
5.4	3.66E-08	3.47E-08	3.29E-08	3.11E-08	2.95E-08	2.79E-08	2.64E-08	2.50E-08	2.37E-08	2.24E-08
5.5	2.12E-08	2.01E-08	1.90E-08	1.80E-08	1.70E-08	1.61E-08	1.53E-08	1.44E-08	1.37E-08	1.29E-08
5.6	1.22E-08	1.16E-08	1.09E-08	1.03E-08	9.78E-09	9.24E-09	8.74E-09	8.26E-09	7.81E-09	7.39E-09
5.7	6.98E-09	6.60E-09	6.24E-09	5.89E-09	5.57E-09	5.26E-09	4.97E-09	4.70E-09	4.44E-09	4.19E-09
5.8	3.96E-09	3.74E-09	3.53E-09	3.34E-09	3.15E-09	2.97E-09	2.81E-09	2.65E-09	2.50E-09	2.36E-09
5.9	2.23E-09	2.11E-09	1.99E-09	1.88E-09	1.77E-09	1.67E-09	1.58E-09	1.49E-09	1.40E-09	1.32E-09
6.0	1.25E-09	1.18E-09	1.11E-09	1.05E-09	9.88E-10	9.31E-10	8.78E-10	8.28E-10	7.81E-10	7.36E-10
6.1	6.94E-10	6.54E-10	6.17E-10	5.81E-10	5.48E-10	5.16E-10	4.87E-10	4.59E-10	4.32E-10	4.07E-10
6.2	3.84E-10	3.61E-10	3.40E-10	3.21E-10	3.02E-10	2.84E-10	2.68E-10	2.52E-10	2.38E-10	2.24E-10
6.3	2.11E-10	1.98E-10	1.87E-10	1.76E-10	1.66E-10	1.56E-10	1.47E-10	1.38E-10	1.30E-10	1.22E-10
6.4	1.15E-10	1.08E-10	1.02E-10	9.59E-11	9.02E-11	8.49E-11	7.98E-11	7.51E-11	7.06E-11	6.65E-11
6.5	6.25E-11	5.88E-11	5.53E-11	5.20E-11	4.89E-11	4.60E-11	4.32E-11	4.07E-11	3.82E-11	3.59E-11
6.6	3.38E-11	3.18E-11	2.98E-11	2.81E-11	2.64E-11	2.48E-11	2.33E-11	2.19E-11	2.06E-11	1.93E-11
6.7	1.82E-11	1.71E-11	1.60E-11	1.51E-11	1.42E-11	1.33E-11	1.25E-11	1.17E-11	1.10E-11	1.04E-11
6.8	9.72E-12	9.13E-12	8.57E-12	8.05E-12	7.56E-12	7.10E-12	6.66E-12	6.26E-12	5.87E-12	5.52E-12
6.9	5.18E-12	4.86E-12	4.56E-12	4.28E-12	4.02E-12	3.77E-12	3.54E-12	3.32E-12	3.12E-12	2.93E-12
7.0	2.75E-12	2.58E-12	2.42E-12	2.27E-12	2.13E-12	2.00E-12	1.87E-12	1.76E-12	1.65E-12	1.55E-12
7.1	1.45E-12	1.36E-12	1.28E-12	1.20E-12	1.12E-12	1.05E-12	9.88E-13	9.26E-13	8.69E-13	8.15E-13
7.2	7.64E-13	7.16E-13	6.72E-13	6.30E-13	5.90E-13	5.54E-13	5.19E-13	4.86E-13	4.56E-13	4.28E-13
7.3	4.01E-13	3.76E-13	3.52E-13	3.30E-13	3.09E-13	2.90E-13	2.72E-13	2.55E-13	2.39E-13	2.24E-13
7.4	2.10E-13	1.96E-13	1.84E-13	1.72E-13	1.62E-13	1.51E-13	1.42E-13	1.33E-13	1.24E-13	1.17E-13
7.5	1.09E-13	1.02E-13	9.58E-14	8.98E-14	8.41E-14	7.87E-14	7.38E-14	6.91E-14	6.47E-14	6.06E-14
7.6	5.68E-14	5.32E-14	4.98E-14	4.66E-14	4.37E-14	4.09E-14	3.83E-14	3.58E-14	3.36E-14	3.14E-14
7.7	2.94E-14	2.76E-14	2.58E-14	2.42E-14	2.26E-14	2.12E-14	1.98E-14	1.86E-14	1.74E-14	1.63E-14
7.8	1.52E-14	1.42E-14	1.33E-14	1.25E-14	1.17E-14	1.09E-14	1.02E-14	9.58E-15	8.97E-15	8.39E-15
7.9	7.85E-15	7.35E-15	6.88E-15	6.44E-15	6.02E-15	5.64E-15	5.28E-15	4.94E-15	4.62E-15	4.32E-15
8.0	4.05E-15	3.79E-15	3.54E-15	3.31E-15	3.10E-15	2.90E-15	2.72E-15	2.54E-15	2.38E-15	2.22E-15
8.1	2.08E-15	1.95E-15	1.82E-15	1.70E-15	1.59E-15	1.49E-15	1.40E-15	1.31E-15	1.22E-15	1.14E-15
8.2	1.07E-15	9.99E-16	9.35E-16	8.74E-16	8.18E-16	7.65E-16	7.16E-16	6.69E-16	6.26E-16	5.86E-16
8 30	5.48E-16	5.12E-16	4.79E-16	4.48E-16	4.19E-16	3.92E-16	3.67E-16	3.43E-16	3.21E-16	3.00E-16
8.4	2.81E-16	2.62E-16	2.45E-16	2.30E-16	2.15E-16	2.01E-16	1.88E-16	1.76E-16	1.64E-16	1.54E-16
8.5	1.44E-16	1.34E-16	1.26E-16	1.17E-16	1.10E-16	1.03E-16	9.60E-17	8.98E-17	8.40E-17	7.85E-17
8.6	7.34E-17	6.87E-17	6.42E-17	6.00E-17	5.61E-17	5.25E-17	4.91E-17	4.59E-17	4.29E-17	4.01E-17
8.7	3.75E-17	3.51E-17	3.28E-17	3.07E-17	2.87E-17	2.68E-17	2.51E-17	2.35E-17	2.19E-17	2.05E-17
8.8	1.92E-17	1.79E-17	1.68E-17	1.57E-17	1.47E-17	1.37E-17	1.28E-17	1.20E-17	1.12E-17	1.05E-17
8.9	9.79E-18	9.16E-18	8.56E-18	8.00E-18	7.48E-18	7.00E-18	6.54E-18	6.12E-18	5.72E-18	5.35E-18
9.0	5.00E-18	4.68E-18	4.37E-18	4.09E-18	3.82E-18	3.57E-18	3.34E-18	3.13E-18	2.92E-18	2.73E-18
9.1	2.56E-18	2.39E-18	2.23E-18	2.09E-18	1.95E-18	1.83E-18	1.71E-18	1.60E-18	1.49E-18	1.40E-18
9.2	1.31E-18	1.22E-18	1.14E-18	1.07E-18	9.98E-19	9.33E-19	8.73E-19	8.16E-19	7.63E-19	7.14E-19
9.3	6.67E-19	6.24E-19	5.83E-19	5.46E-19	5.10E-19	4.77E-19	4.46E-19	4.17E-19	3.90E-19	3.65E-19
9.4	3.41E-19	3.19E-19	2.98E-19	2.79E-19	2.61E-19	2.44E-19	2.28E-19	2.14E-19	2.00E-19	1.87E-19
9.5	1.75E-19	1.63E-19	1.53E-19	1.43E-19	1.34E-19	1.25E-19	1.17E-19	1.09E-19	1.02E-19	9.56E-20
9.6	8.94E-20	8.37E-20	7.82E-20	7.32E-20	6.85E-20	6.40E-20	5.99E-20	5.60E-20	5.24E-20	4.90E-20
9.7	4.58E-20	4.29E-20	4.01E-20	3.75E-20	3.51E-20	3.28E-20	3.07E-20	2.87E-20	2.69E-20	2.52E-20
9.8	2.35E-20	2.20E-20	2.06E-20	1.93E-20	1.80E-20	1.69E-20	1.58E-20	1.48E-20	1.38E-20	1.29E-20
9.9	1.21E-20	1.13E-20	1.06E-20	9.90E-21	9.26E-21	8.67E-21	8.11E-21	7.59E-21	7.10E-21	6.64E-21
10.0	6.22E-21	5.82E-21	5.44E-21	5.09E-21	4.77E-21	4.46E-21	4.17E-21	3.91E-21	3.66E-21	3.42E-21

T-Distribution

	.600	.700	.800	.900	.950	.975	.990	.995
1	0.325	0.727	1.376	3.078	6.314	12.706	31.821	63.657
2	0.289	0.617	1.061	1.886	2.920	4.303	6.965	9.925
3	0.277	0.584	0.978	1.638	2.353	3.182	4.541	5.841
4	0.271	0.569	0.941	1.533	2.132	2.776	3.747	4.604
5	0.267	0.559	0.920	1.476	2.015	2.571	3.365	4.032
6	0.265	0.553	0.906	1.440	1.943	2.447	3.143	3.707
7	0.263	0.549	0.896	1.415	1.895	2.365	2.998	3.499
8	0.262	0.546	0.889	1.397	1.860	2.306	2.896	3.355
9	0.261	0.543	0.883	1.383	1.833	2.262	2.821	3.250
10	0.260	0.542	0.879	1.372	1.812	2.228	2.764	3.169
11	0.260	0.540	0.876	1.363	1.796	2.201	2.718	3.106
12	0.259	0.539	0.873	1.356	1.782	2.179	2.681	3.055
13	0.259	0.538	0.870	1.350	1.771	2.160	2.650	3.012
14	0.258	0.537	0.868	1.345	1.761	2.145	2.624	2.977
15	0.258	0.536	0.866	1.341	1.753	2.131	2.602	2.947
16	0.258	0.535	0.865	1.337	1.746	2.120	2.583	2.921
17	0.257	0.534	0.863	1.333	1.740	2.110	2.567	2.898
18	0.257	0.534	0.862	1.330	1.734	2.101	2.552	2.878
19	0.257	0.533	0.861	1.328	1.729	2.093	2.539	2.861
20	0.257	0.533	0.860	1.325	1.725	2.086	2.528	2.845
21	0.257	0.532	0.859	1.323	1.721	2.080	2.518	2.831
22	0.256	0.532	0.858	1.321	1.717	2.074	2.508	2.819
23	0.256	0.532	0.858	1.319	1.714	2.069	2.500	2.807
24	0.256	0.531	0.857	1.318	1.711	2.064	2.492	2.797
25	0.256	0.531	0.856	1.316	1.708	2.060	2.485	2.787
26	0.256	0.531	0.856	1.315	1.706	2.056	2.479	2.779
27	0.256	0.531	0.855	1.314	1.703	2.052	2.473	2.771
28	0.256	0.530	0.855	1.313	1.701	2.048	2.467	2.763
29	0.256	0.530	0.854	1.311	1.699	2.045	2.462	2.756
30	0.256	0.530	0.854	1.310	1.697	2.042	2.457	2.750
40	0.255	0.529	0.851	1.303	1.684	2.021	2.423	2.704
60	0.254	0.527	0.848	1.296	1.671	2.000	2.390	2.660
120	0.254	0.526	0.845	1.289	1.658	1.980	2.358	2.617
∞	0.253	0.524	0.842	1.282	1.645	1.960	2.326	2.576

F Distribution

Tabulated values for α = .05

D/N	1	2	3	4	5	6	7	8	9	10
1	161.40	199.50	215.70	224.60	230.20	234.00	236.80	238.90	240.50	241.90
2	18.51	19.00	19.16	19.25	19.30	19.33	19.35	19.37	19.38	19.40
3	10.13	9.55	9.28	9.12	9.01	8.94	8.89	8.85	8.81	8.79
4	7.71	6.94	6.59	6.39	6.26	6.16	6.09	6.04	6.00	5.96
5	6.61	5.79	5.41	5.19	5.05	4.95	4.88	4.82	4.77	4.74
6	5.99	5.14	4.76	4.53	4.39	4.28	4.21	4.15	4.10	4.06
7	5.59	4.74	4.35	4.12	3.97	3.87	3.79	3.73	3.68	3.64
8	5.32	4.46	4.07	3.84	3.69	3.58	3.50	3.44	3.39	3.35
9	5.12	4.26	3.86	3.63	3.48	3.37	3.29	3.23	3.18	3.14
10	4.96	4.10	3.71	3.48	3.33	3.22	3.14	3.07	3.02	2.98
11	4.84	3.98	3.59	3.36	3.20	3.09	3.01	2.95	2.90	2.85
12	4.75	3.89	3.49	3.26	3.11	3.00	2.91	2.85	2.80	2.75
13	4.67	3.81	3.41	3.18	3.03	2.92	2.83	2.77	2.71	2.67
14	4.60	3.74	3.34	3.11	2.96	2.85	2.76	2.70	2.65	2.60
15	4.54	3.68	3.29	3.06	2.90	2.79	2.71	2.64	2.59	2.54
16	4.49	3.63	3.24	3.01	2.85	2.74	2.66	2.59	2.54	2.49
17	4.45	3.59	3.20	2.96	2.81	2.70	2.61	2.55	2.49	2.45
18	4.41	3.55	3.16	2.93	2.77	2.66	2.58	2.51	2.46	2.41
19	4.38	3.52	3.13	2.90	2.74	2.63	2.54	2.48	2.42	2.38
20	4.35	3.49	3.10	2.87	2.71	2.60	2.51	2.45	2.39	2.35
21	4.32	3.47	3.07	2.84	2.68	2.57	2.49	2.42	2.37	2.32
22	4.30	3.44	3.05	2.82	2.66	2.55	2.46	2.40	2.34	2.30
23	4.28	3.42	3.03	2.80	2.64	2.53	2.44	2.37	2.32	2.27
24	4.26	3.40	3.01	2.78	2.62	2.51	2.42	2.36	2.30	2.25
25	4.24	3.39	2.99	2.76	2.60	2.49	2.40	2.34	2.28	2.24
26	4.23	3.37	2.98	2.74	2.59	2.47	2.39	2.32	2.27	2.22
27	4.21	3.35	2.96	2.73	2.57	2.46	2.37	2.31	2.25	2.20
28	4.20	3.34	2.95	2.71	2.56	2.45	2.36	2.29	2.24	2.19
29	4.18	3.33	2.93	2.70	2.55	2.43	2.35	2.28	2.22	2.18
30	4.17	3.32	2.92	2.69	2.53	2.42	2.33	2.27	2.21	2.16
40	4.08	3.23	2.84	2.61	2.45	2.34	2.25	2.18	2.12	2.08
60	4.00	3.15	2.76	2.53	2.37	2.25	2.17	2.10	2.04	1.99
120	3.92	3.07	2.68	2.45	2.29	2.17	2.09	2.02	1.96	1.91
∞	3.84	3.00	2.60	2.37	2.21	2.10	2.01	1.94	1.88	1.83

F Distribution

Tabulated values for α = .05

D/N	12	15	20	24	30	40	60	120	∞
1	243.90	245.90	248.00	249.10	250.10	251.10	252.20	253.30	254.30
2	19.41	19.43	19.45	19.45	19.46	19.47	19.48	19.49	19.50
3	8.74	8.70	8.66	8.64	8.62	8.59	8.57	8.55	8.53
4	5.91	5.86	5.80	5.77	5.75	5.72	5.69	5.66	5.63
5	4.68	4.62	4.56	4.53	4.50	4.46	4.43	4.40	4.36
6	4.00	3.94	3.87	3.84	3.81	3.77	3.74	3.70	3.67
7	3.57	3.51	3.44	3.41	3.38	3.34	3.30	3.27	3.23
8	3.28	3.22	3.15	3.12	3.08	3.04	3.01	2.97	2.93
9	3.07	3.01	2.94	2.90	2.86	2.83	2.79	2.75	2.71
10	2.91	2.85	2.77	2.74	2.70	2.66	2.62	2.58	2.54
11	2.79	2.72	2.65	2.61	2.57	2.53	2.49	2.45	2.40
12	2.69	2.62	2.54	2.51	2.47	2.43	2.38	2.34	2.30
13	2.60	2.53	2.46	2.42	2.38	2.34	2.30	2.25	2.21
14	2.53	2.46	2.39	2.35	2.31	2.27	2.22	2.18	2.13
15	2.48	2.40	2.33	2.29	2.25	2.20	2.16	2.11	2.07
16	2.42	2.35	2.28	2.24	2.19	2.15	2.11	2.06	2.01
17	2.38	2.31	2.23	2.19	2.15	2.10	2.06	2.01	1.96
18	2.34	2.27	2.19	2.15	2.11	2.06	2.02	1.97	1.92
19	2.31	2.23	2.16	2.11	2.07	2.03	1.98	1.93	1.88
20	2.28	2.20	2.12	2.08	2.04	1.99	1.95	1.90	1.84
21	2.25	2.18	2.10	2.05	2.01	1.96	1.92	1.87	1.81
22	2.23	2.15	2.07	2.03	1.98	1.94	1.89	1.84	1.78
23	2.20	2.13	2.05	2.01	1.96	1.91	1.86	1.81	1.76
24	2.18	2.11	2.03	1.98	1.94	1.89	1.84	1.79	1.73
25	2.16	2.09	2.01	1.96	1.92	1.87	1.82	1.77	1.71
26	2.15	2.07	1.99	1.95	1.90	1.85	1.80	1.75	1.69
27	2.13	2.06	1.97	1.93	1.88	1.84	1.79	1.73	1.67
28	2.12	2.04	1.96	1.91	1.87	1.82	1.77	1.71	1.65
29	2.10	2.03	1.94	1.90	1.85	1.81	1.75	1.70	1.64
30	2.09	2.01	1.93	1.89	1.84	1.79	1.74	1.68	1.62
40	2.00	1.92	1.84	1.79	1.74	1.69	1.64	1.58	1.51
60	1.92	1.84	1.75	1.70	1.65	1.59	1.53	1.47	1.39
120	1.83	1.75	1.66	1.61	1.55	1.50	1.43	1.35	1.25
∞	1.75	1.67	1.57	1.52	1.46	1.39	1.32	1.22	1.00

Chi-Square Distribution

df	.995	.990	.975	.950	.900	.750	.500
1	.000039	.000160	.000980	.003930	.015800	.101500	.455000
2	0.010	0.020	0.051	0.103	0.211	0.575	1.386
3	0.072	0.115	0.216	0.352	0.584	1.213	2.366
4	0.207	0.297	0.484	0.711	1.064	1.923	3.357
5	0.412	0.554	0.831	1.145	1.610	2.675	4.351
6	0.676	0.872	1.237	1.635	2.204	3.455	5.348
7	0.989	1.239	1.690	2.167	2.833	4.255	6.346
8	1.344	1.646	2.180	2.733	3.490	5.071	7.344
9	1.735	2.088	2.700	3.325	4.168	5.899	8.343
10	2.156	2.558	3.247	3.940	4.865	6.737	9.342
11	2.603	3.053	3.816	4.575	5.578	7.584	10.341
12	3.074	3.571	4.404	5.226	6.304	8.438	11.340
13	3.565	4.107	5.009	5.892	7.042	9.299	12.340
14	4.075	4.660	5.629	6.571	7.790	10.165	13.339
15	4.601	5.229	6.262	7.261	8.547	11.036	14.339
16	5.142	5.812	6.908	7.962	9.312	11.912	15.338
17	5.697	6.408	7.564	8.672	10.085	12.792	16.338
18	6.265	7.015	8.231	9.390	10.865	13.675	17.338
19	6.844	7.633	8.907	10.117	11.651	14.562	18.338
20	7.434	8.260	9.591	10.851	12.443	15.452	19.337
21	8.034	8.897	10.283	11.591	13.240	16.344	20.337
22	8.643	9.542	10.982	12.338	14.041	17.240	21.337
23	9.260	10.196	11.688	13.091	14.848	18.137	22.337
24	9.886	10.856	12.401	13.848	15.659	19.037	23.337
25	10.520	11.524	13.120	14.611	16.473	19.939	24.337
26	11.160	12.198	13.844	15.379	17.292	20.843	25.336
27	11.808	12.879	14.573	16.151	18.114	21.749	26.336
28	12.461	13.565	15.308	16.928	18.939	22.657	27.336
29	13.121	14.256	16.047	17.708	19.768	23.567	28.336
30	13.787	14.953	16.791	18.493	20.599	24.478	29.336
40	20.707	22.164	24.433	26.509	29.051	33.660	39.335
50	27.991	29.707	32.357	34.764	37.689	42.942	49.335
60	35.535	37.485	40.482	43.188	46.459	52.294	59.335
70	43.275	45.442	48.758	51.739	55.329	61.698	69.334
80	51.172	53.540	57.153	60.391	64.278	71.145	79.334
90	59.196	61.754	65.647	69.126	73.291	80.625	89.334
100	67.328	70.065	74.222	77.929	82.358	90.133	99.334

Chi-Square Distribution

df	.250	.100	.050	.025	.010	.005	.001
1	1.323	2.706	3.841	5.024	6.635	7.879	10.828
2	2.773	4.605	5.991	7.378	9.210	10.597	13.816
3	4.108	6.251	7.815	9.348	11.345	12.838	16.266
4	5.385	7.779	9.488	11.143	13.277	14.860	18.467
5	6.626	9.236	11.070	12.832	15.086	16.750	20.515
6	7.841	10.645	12.592	14.449	16.812	18.548	22.458
7	9.037	12.017	14.067	16.013	18.475	20.278	24.322
8	10.219	13.362	15.507	17.535	20.090	21.955	26.125
9	11.389	14.684	16.919	19.023	21.666	23.589	27.877
10	12.549	15.987	18.307	20.483	23.209	25.188	29.588
11	13.701	17.275	19.675	21.920	24.725	26.757	31.264
12	14.845	18.549	21.026	23.337	26.217	28.300	32.909
13	15.984	19.812	22.362	24.736	27.688	29.819	34.528
14	17.117	21.064	23.685	26.119	29.141	31.319	36.123
15	18.245	22.307	24.996	27.488	30.578	32.801	37.697
16	19.369	23.542	26.296	28.845	32.000	34.267	39.252
17	20.489	24.769	27.587	30.191	33.409	35.718	40.790
18	21.605	25.989	28.869	31.526	34.805	37.156	43.312
19	22.718	27.204	30.144	32.852	36.191	38.582	43.820
20	23.828	28.412	31.410	34.170	37.566	39.997	45.315
21	24.935	29.615	32.671	35.479	38.932	41.401	46.797
22	26.039	30.813	33.924	36.781	40.289	42.796	48.268
23	27.141	32.007	35.172	38.076	41.638	44.181	49.728
24	28.241	33.196	36.415	39.364	42.980	45.558	51.179
25	29.339	34.382	37.652	40.646	44.314	46.928	52.620
26	30.434	35.563	38.885	41.923	45.642	48.290	54.052
27	31.528	36.741	40.113	43.194	46.963	49.645	55.476
28	32.620	37.916	41.337	44.461	48.278	50.993	56.892
29	33.711	39.087	42.557	45.722	49.588	52.336	58.302
30	34.800	40.256	43.773	46.979	50.892	53.672	59.703
40	45.616	51.805	55.758	59.342	63.691	66.766	73.402
50	56.334	63.167	67.505	71.420	76.154	79.490	86.661
60	66.981	74.397	79.082	83.298	88.379	91.952	99.607
70	77.577	85.527	90.531	95.023	100.425	104.215	112.317
80	88.130	96.578	101.879	106.629	112.329	116.321	124.839
90	98.650	107.565	113.145	118.136	124.116	128.299	137.208
100	109.141	118.498	124.342	129.561	135.807	140.169	149.449

Sample Size

δ/σ	α = 20%				α = 10%				α = 5%				α = 1%				β
	20%	10%	5%	1%	20%	10%	5%	1%	20%	10%	5%	1%	20%	10%	5%	1%	
0.2	225	328	428	651	309	428	541	789	392	525	650	919	584	744	891	1202	
0.3	100	146	190	289	137	190	241	350	174	234	289	408	260	331	396	534	
0.4	56	82	107	163	77	107	135	197	98	131	162	230	146	186	223	300	
0.5	36	53	69	104	49	69	87	126	63	84	104	147	93	119	143	192	
0.6	25	36	48	72	34	48	60	88	44	58	72	102	65	83	99	134	
0.7	18	27	35	53	25	35	44	64	32	43	53	75	48	61	73	98	
0.8	14	21	27	41	19	27	34	49	25	33	41	57	36	46	56	75	
0.9	11	16	21	32	15	21	27	39	19	26	32	45	29	37	44	59	
1.0	9	13	17	26	12	17	22	32	16	21	26	37	23	30	36	48	
1.1	7	11	14	22	10	14	18	26	13	17	21	30	19	25	29	40	
1.2	6	9	12	18	9	12	15	22	11	15	18	26	16	21	25	33	
1.3	5	8	10	15	7	10	13	19	9	12	15	22	14	18	21	28	
1.4	5	7	9	13	6	9	11	16	8	11	13	19	12	15	18	25	
1.5	4	6	8	12	5	8	10	14	7	9	12	16	10	13	16	21	
1.6	4	5	7	10	5	7	8	12	6	8	10	14	9	12	14	19	
1.7	3	5	6	9	4	6	7	11	5	7	9	13	8	10	12	17	
1.8	3	4	5	8	4	5	7	10	5	6	8	11	7	9	11	15	
1.9	2	4	5	7	3	5	6	9	4	6	7	10	6	8	10	13	
2.0	2	3	4	7	3	4	5	8	4	5	6	9	6	7	9	12	
2.1	2	3	4	6	3	4	5	7	4	5	6	8	5	7	8	11	
2.2	2	3	4	5	3	4	4	7	3	4	5	8	5	6	7	10	
2.3	2	2	3	5	2	3	4	6	3	4	5	7	4	6	7	9	
2.4	2	2	3	5	2	3	4	5	3	4	5	6	4	5	6	8	
2.5	1	2	3	4	2	3	3	5	3	3	4	6	4	5	6	8	
2.6	1	2	3	4	2	3	3	5	2	3	4	5	3	4	5	7	
2.7	1	2	2	4	2	2	3	4	2	3	4	5	3	4	5	7	
2.8	1	2	2	3	2	2	3	4	2	3	3	5	3	4	5	6	
2.9	1	2	2	3	1	2	3	4	2	2	3	4	3	4	4	6	
3.0	1	1	2	3	1	2	2	4	2	2	3	4	3	3	4	5	
3.1	1	1	2	3	1	2	2	3	2	2	3	4	2	3	4	5	
3.2	1	1	2	3	1	2	2	3	2	2	3	4	2	3	3	5	
3.3	1	1	2	2	1	2	2	3	1	2	2	3	2	3	3	4	
3.4	1	1	1	2	1	1	2	3	1	2	2	3	2	3	3	4	
3.5	1	1	1	2	1	1	2	3	1	2	2	3	2	2	3	4	
3.6	1	1	1	2	1	1	2	2	1	2	2	3	2	2	3	4	
3.7	1	1	1	2	1	1	2	2	1	2	2	3	2	2	3	4	
3.8	1	1	1	2	1	1	1	2	1	1	2	3	2	2	2	3	
3.9	1	1	1	2	1	1	1	2	1	1	2	2	2	2	2	3	
4.0	1	1	1	2	1	1	1	2	1	1	2	2	1	1	2	3	

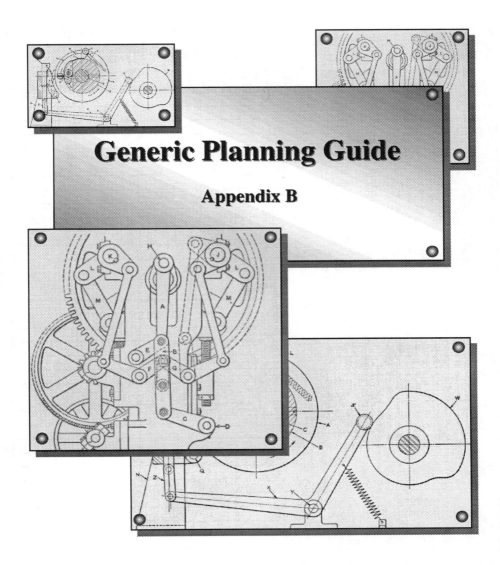

Generic Planning Guide

Appendix B

Breakthrough Phase

Block	Activity Description	Phase 1: Measurement	Phase 2: Analysis	Phase 3: Improvement	Phase 4: Control
	Organization				
1	Conduct Situation Analysis				
2	Conduct Literature Review				
3	Conduct Training Activities				
4	Synthesize and Focus				
	Variables				
5	Define Dependent Variables				
6	Define Independent Variables				
7	Define Control Variables				
	Measurement				
8	Identify Measurement System				
9	Identify Data Vehicle				
	Tools				
10	Design Measurement Validation Study				
11	Design Hierarchical Pareto Study				
12	Design Parameter Capability Study				
13	Design Multi-Vari Study				
14	Design Experimental Study				
15	Design Parameter Control Study				
	Data				
16	Develop Data Analysis System				
17	Develop Data Tracking System				
18	Develop Data Collection System				
19	Conduct Data Collection				
20	Conduct Data Analyses				
	Sampling				
21	Establish Sample Size				
22	Establish Sampling Methodology				
23	Design Test Vehicle				

1. CONDUCT SITUATION ANALYSIS

1.1. Form problem solving team if appropriate or required.
1.2. Conduct first problem solving team meeting
1.3. Review all available sources of information related to the situation
1.4. Define the historical state of the situation
1.5. Define the current situation in general terms
1.6. Establish the improvement objective(s) relative to the current situation
1.7. Identify all driving and restraining forces
1.8. Establish the nature of the information required to satisfy the objective(s)
1.9. Determine what type of performance measure meets the information needs
1.10. Select an appropriate index of variability for the given performance measure

2. CONDUCT LITERATURE REVIEW

2.1. Examine experimental objective
2.2. Examine dependent variable(s)
2.3 Examine measurement methodology
2.4. Examine experimental factor(s)
2.5. Examine blocking variables
2.6. Examine covariates
2.7. Evaluate author bias
2.8. Evaluate clarity of content
2.9. Evaluate recent references and bibliography
2.10. Evaluate assumptions of research methods and related activities
2.11. Study analytical methods
2.12. Study degree to which conclusions are supported by numerical evidence
2.13. Study sampling methodology
2.14. Assess referee status
2.15. Assess background of author
2.16. Consider text books
2.17. Consider journal articles
2.18. Consider periodicals
2.19. Consider white papers
2.20. Consider video tapes
2.21. Consider audio tapes
2.22. Consider seminar materials

3. CONDUCT TRAINING ACTIVITIES

3.1. Establish training and education need
3.2. Identify target population
3.3. Identify knowledge requirements
3.4. Identify skill requirements
3.5. Devise training and education action plan
3.6. Prepare initial cost estimate
3.7. Obtain management approval for further development
3.8. Develop training materials
3.9. Conduct necessary training

4. SYNTHESIZE AND FOCUS

4.1. Revise problem statement as necessary to reflect new information
4.2. Write technical report if appropriate or required
4.3. Write management report if appropriate or required
4.4. Disseminate reports and information to all concerned

4.5.   Prepare technical level presentation if appropriate or required
4.6.   Prepare management level presentation if appropriate or required
4.7.   Make presentation if appropriate or required
4.8.   Obtain management approval for continued investigation
4.9.   Prepare a preliminary agenda for next team meeting
4.10. Schedule next problem solving team meeting
4.11. Disseminate the preliminary agenda to team members and resource personnel
4.12. Conduct problem solving team meeting

5. DEFINE DEPENDENT VARIABLES
5.1.   Review carefully the phenomenon under investigation
5.2.   Identify potential response variable(s) to be studied
5.3   Describe the unique properties of each response variable
5.4   Describe the constraining properties of each variable
5.5.   Describes the desirable properties of each variable
5.6.   Select the most viable response variable for each phenomenon

6. DEFINE INDEPENDENT VARIABLES
6.1.   Construct a Cause and Effect matrix (C&E) for use during brainstorming
6.2.   Integrate literature search results into the C&E matrix
6.3.   Identify all individuals whom could make a contribution to brainstorming
6.4.   Prepare a working copy of the C&E matrix for each individual
6.5.   Distribute copies of the C&E matrix to all participating individuals
6.6.   Record respondent's C&E inputs as they are gathered
6.7.   Schedule first group level brainstorming session and notify all participants
6.8.   Conduct group level brainstorming session

7. DEFINE CONTROL VARIABLES
7.1.   Identify the key independent variable(s) to be controlled
7.2.   Define the control objectives for each variable
7.3.   Determine technical feasibility for controlling with SPC methods
7.4.   Prepare initial cost estimate
7.5.   Obtain management approval and support

8. IDENTIFY MEASUREMENT SYSTEM
8.1.   Brainstorm potential measurement scales for each response variable
8.2.   Establish a methodology for each measurement scale
8.3.   Identify all practical cost/time/resource constraints related to each scale
8.4.   Study data analysis implications of the various measurement scales
8.5.   Establish selection criteria
8.6.   Select the top rated measurement system based on the criteria

9. IDENTIFY DATA VEHICLE
9.1.   Define the primary objective of the data vehicle
9.2.   Identify all characteristics which the data vehicle must possess
9.3.   Review all data requirements in relation to the data vehicle characteristics
9.4.   Define all process performance specifications in relation to the data vehicle
9.5.   Devise final list of characteristics, requirements, and specifications
9.6.   Establish degree of compatibility between criteria and existing vehicle(s)
9.7.   Make engineering decision related to feasibility of using existing vehicle(s)

10. DESIGN MEASUREMENT VALIDATION STUDY
  10.1. Devise a test to study measurement sensitivity in relation to data vehicle
  10.2. Prepare initial cost estimate for the study
  10.3. Obtain management approval and funding for the study
  10.4. Develop measurement sensitivity test
  10.5. Study measurement sensitivity, validity, and reliability
  10.6. Modify the measurement methodology as required
  10.7. Document all pertinent information related to the methodology

11. DESIGN HIERARCHICAL PARETO STUDY
  11.1. Establish objectives related to study
  11.2. Review the product quality parameter(s) subject to study
  11.3. Devise defect/failure coding system if necessary
  11.4. Select the most appropriate type of format in which to display the data

12. DESIGN PARAMETER CAPABILITY STUDY
  12.1. Review the variables to be included in the study
  12.2. Identify the specification(s) related to the study
  12.3. Define operating limits of the specification
  12.4. Define model distribution parameters if appropriate or required
  12.5. Establish criterion capability indices if appropriate or required
  12.6. Identify all pertinent conditions to which the study is restricted
  12.7. Select representative personnel for participation in the study
  12.8. Make necessary administrative and logistical arrangements

13. DESIGN MULTI-VARI STUDY
  13.1. Establish objectives for the study
  13.2. Review the response characteristics to be investigated
  13.3. Define all major categories of variation worthy of investigation
  13.4. Design Multi-Vari chart format based on defined categories of variation
  13.5. Circulate MV format among colleagues for critical review
  13.6. Revise M,V chart format as necessary

14. DESIGN EXPERIMENTAL STUDY
  14.1. Define experimental objectives
  14.2. Establish the number of factors to be studied
  14.3. Make initial selection of factors based on the objective(s) and constraints
  14.4. Determine the degree of experimental confounding considered to be tolerable
  14.5. Define levels for the experimental factors to be used
  14.6. Revise system components
  14.7. Designate primary control variables
  14.8. Establish testing conditions for each primary control variable
  14.9. Revise system components
  14.10. Identify blocking variables
  14.11. Define how each blocking variable must be handled
  14.12. Revise system components
  14.13. Identify background variables which could contaminate experimental results
  14.14. Define how the effects of uncontrolled background variables must be handled
  14.15. Revise system components
  14.16. Finalize the list of experimental factors and related variables
  14.17. Construct an appropriate statistical model if appropriate
  14.18. Develop statistical hypotheses based on the model, objectives, and constraints

14.19. Define criteria for the selecting an appropriate experiment design
14.20. Select an appropriate experiment design
14.21. Evaluate rationality of all underlying assumptions related to the design
14.22. Revise system components
14.23. Prepare initial cost estimate for the experiment
14.24. Conduct a dry run of the experiment
14.25. Document all related aspects of the experiment design
14.26. Obtain management approval and support for continued investigation
14.27. Revise system components

15. DESIGN PARAMETER CONTROL STUDY
15.1. Review the system variables under consideration
15.2. Select the statistical parameters to be controlled relative to each variable
15.3. Establish the degree of sensitivity each variable parameter must display
15.4. Select appropriate types of charts based on parameters and sensitivity
15.5. Define an appropriate control chart format for each variable parameter
15.6. Determine type of centerline to be used for each parameter
15.7. Select the statistical control limits to be used on each chart
15.8. Establish basis for calculating control limits for each parameter
15.9. Evaluate all pertinent assumptions underlying the selected charts

16. DEVELOP DATA ANALYSIS SYSTEM
16.1. Define data analysis objectives
16.2. Establish the level of analytical precision required
16.3. Identify output format(s) which will satisfy the objectives
16.4. Identify specific methods which will drive the output format(s)
16.5. Select specific data analysis method(s) to be used
16.6. Study all assumptions underlying the selected method(s)
16.7. Devise plan to insure compliance with all relevant assumptions
16.8. Establish required test sensitivity and confidence/risk levels
16.9. Identify experimental error source if appropriate or required
16.10. Derive sample size based on appropriate equation(s) or tables
16.11. Identify practical constraints surrounding the sample size
16.12. Adjust risk and sensitivity parameters based on constraints
16.13. Revise sample size as necessary
16.14. Obtain management approval and support for continued investigation
16.15. Revise system components
16.16. Identify the most efficient computational strategy
16.17. Define hardware requirements
16.18. Define software requirements
16.19. Estimate costs related to the data analysis system
16.20. Obtain management funding
16.21. Conduct a complete dry run of the analytical system
16.22. Revise system components
16.23. Prepare all necessary written instructions

17. DEVELOP DATA TRACKING SYSTEM
17.1. Define tracking requirements
17.2. Establish data gates within the process
17.3. Devise sample coding/labeling system

17.4. Design tracking system
17.5. Estimate costs related to tracking system
17.6. Obtain management approval and funding
17.7. Conduct dry run of the tracking system
17.8. Revise system components
17.9. Document all related aspects of the tracking system

18. DEVELOP DATA COLLECTION SYSTEM

18.1. Establish a data format consistent with data analysis requirements
18.2. Identify all pertinent information which must be attached to the data
18.3. Devise method for establishing data accuracy and validity
18.4. Establish data collection points/gates within the process
18.5. Devise data collection form(s)
18.6. Provide for independent evaluation of data collection form(s)
18.7. Conduct dry run of the data collection devices and aids
18.8. Evaluate results of the dry run
18.9. Revise system components
18.10. Document all related aspects of the data collection system
18.11. Prepare cost estimates
18.12. Obtain management approval for continued development
18.13. Write detailed sample preparation instructions
18.14. Write detailed data collection instructions
18.15. Review instructions by appropriate persons
18.16. Revise data collection instructions as required
18.17. Document all related aspects of the data collection system

19. CONDUCT DATA COLLECTION

19.1. Insure that all required test and measurement apparatus are calibrated
19.2. Prepare sample in accordance to instructions
19.3. Subject samples to the process
19.4. Record response data on data collection form(s)
19.5. Verify accuracy of data recording

20. CONDUCT DATA ANALYSIS

20.1. Review data analysis plan
20.2. Construct data summary tables
20.3. Display data in accordance to the data analysis plan
20.4. Study data displays for potential distortion as a function of scale
20.5. Verify accuracy of the information
20.6. Interpret graphical outcomes
20.7. Compute defined summary indices
20.8. Compute defined statistics
20.9. Consider all pertinent underlying assumptions and test if necessary
20.10. Interpret statistical outcomes
20.11. Rationalize statistical outcomes against data display
20.12. Construct statistical summary table(s) if appropriate or required
20.13. Conduct secondary exploratory data analysis activities
20.14. Verify computational accuracy
20.15. Draw conclusions strictly based on the data
20.16. Establish implications based on the data and interpretations

20.17. Document conclusions and implications
20.18. Translate all analytical outcomes into costs and percentages
20.19. Construct technical level summary tables, charts, and graphs
20.20. Construct management level summary tables, charts, and graphs

21. ESTABLISH SAMPLE SIZE
21.1.   Establish sampling objectives
21.2.   Preliminary considerations
21.3.   Classify the response measurement scale
21.4.   Establish required test sensitivity (delta sigma)
21.5.   Establish type I error probability (alpha risk - producer's risk)
21.6.   Establish type II error probability (beta risk consumer's risk)
21.7.   Identify experimental error source (residual)
21.8.   Define number of required runs
21.9.   Establish the degree of replication necessary at each run
21.10. Identify practical constraints surrounding the sample size
21.11. Adjust risk and sensitivity parameters based on constraints
21.12. Revise system components
21.13. Document all related aspects of the sample size determination
21.14. Obtain management approval and support for continued investigation
21.15. Revise system components

22. ESTABLISH SAMPLING METHODOLOGY
22.1.   Random
22.2.   Sequential
22.3.   Systematic (based on specified classification variable)
22.4.   Time based
22.5.   Stratified sequential
22.6.   Stratified random
22.7.   Stratified systematic
22.8.   Establish sampling interval
22.9.   Rational subgrouping

23. DESIGN TEST VEHICLE
23.1.   Establish design criteria
23.2.   Conduct necessary design activities
23.3.   Prepare initial cost estimate
23.4.   Obtain management approval for further development
23.5.   Construct prototype test vehicle
23.6.   Verify test vehicle performance in relation to design criteria
23.7.   Revise test vehicle design as required
23.8.   Document all pertinent aspects of the test vehicle

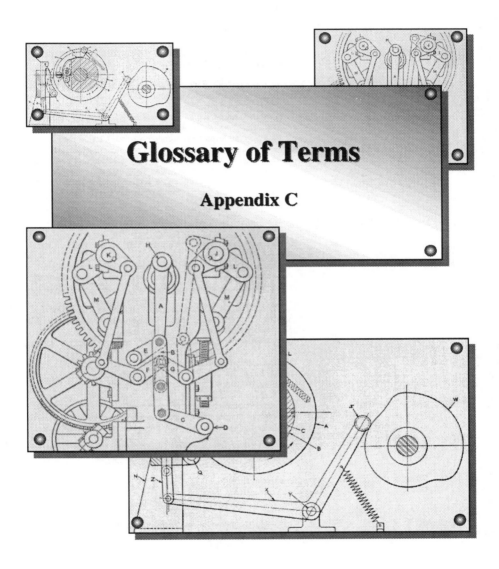

Glossary of Terms

Appendix C

ABSCISSA — The horizontal axis of a graph.

ACCEPTANCE REGION — The region of values for which the null hypothesis is accepted;

ALPHA RISK — The probability of accepting the alternate hypothesis when, in reality, the null hypothesis is true.

ALTERNATE HYPOTHESIS — A tentative explanation which indicates that an event does not follow a chance distribution; a contrast to the null hypothesis.

ASSIGNABLE CAUSE — A source of variation which is non-random; a change in the source ("VITAL FEW" variables) will produce a significant change of some magnitude in the response (dependent variable), e.g., a correlation exists; the change may be due to an intermittent in-phase effect or a constant cause system which may or may not be highly predictable; an assignable cause is often signaled by an excessive number of data points outside a control limit and/or a non-random pattern within the control limits; an unnatural source of variation; most often economical to eliminate.

ASSIGNABLE VARIATIONS — Variations in data which can be attributed to specific causes.

ATTRIBUTE — A characteristic that may take on only one value, e.g. 0 or 1.

ATTRIBUTE DATA — Numerical information at the nominal level; subdivision is not conceptually meaningful; data which represents the frequency of occurrence within some discrete category, e.g., 42 solder shorts.

BACKGROUND VARIABLES — Variables which are of no experimental interest and are not held constant. Their effects are often assumed insignificant or negligible, or they are randomized to ensure that contamination of the primary response does not occur.

BETA RISK — The probability of accepting the null hypothesis when, in reality, the alternate hypothesis is true.

BLOCKING VARIABLES — A relatively homogenous set of conditions within which different conditions of the primary variables are compared. Used to ensure that background variables do not contaminate the evaluation of primary variables.

CAUSALITY — The principle that every change implies the operation of a cause.

CAUSATIVE — Effective as a cause.

CAUSE — That which produces an effect or brings about a change.

C CHARTS — Charts which display the number of defects per sample.

CHARACTERISTIC | A definable or measurable feature of a process, product, or variable.

CENTRAL TENDENCY | Numerical average, e.g., mean, median, and mode; center line on a statistical process control chart.

CENTER LINE | The line on a statistical process control chart which represents the characteristic's central tendency.

CLASSIFICATION | Differentiation of variables.

COMMON CAUSE | See RANDOM CAUSE.

CONFIDENCE LEVEL | The probabiiity that a random variable x lies within a defined interval.

CONFIDENCE LIMITS | The two values that define the confidence interval.

CONFOUNDING | Allowing two or more variables to vary together so that it is impossible to separate their unique effects.

CONSUMERS RISK | Probability of accepting a lot when, in fact, the lot should have been rejected (see BETA RISK).

CONTINUOUS DATA | Numerical information at the interval of ratio level; subdivision is conceptually meaningful; can assume any number within an interval, e.g., 14.652 amps.

CONTINUOUS RANDOM VARIABLE | A random variable which can assume any value continuously in some specified interval.

CONTROL CHART | A graphical rendition of a characteristic's performance across time in relation to its natural limits and central tendency.

CONTROL SPECIFICATIONS | Specifications called for by the product being manufactured.

CUTOFF POINT | The point which partitions the acceptance region from the reject region.

DATA | Factual information used as a basis for reasoning, discussion, or calculation; often refers to quantitative information.

DEGREES OF FREEDOM | The number of independent measurements available for estimating a population parameter.

DENSITY FUNCTION | The function which yields the probability that a particular random variable takes on any one of its possible values.

DEPENDENT VARIABLE | A Response Variable; e.g., y is the dependent or "Response" variable where $Y=f(X_1 \ldots X_N)$ variable.

DISCRETE RANDOM VARIABLE   A random variable which can assume values only from a definite number of discrete values.

DISTRIBUTIONS   Tendency of large numbers of observations to group themselves around some central value with a certain amount of variation or "scatter" on either side.

EFFECT   That which was produced by a cause.

EXPERIMENT   A test under defined conditions to determine an unknown effect; to illustrate or verify a known law; to test or establish a hypothesis.

EXPERIMENTAL ERROR   Variation in observations made under identical test conditions. Also called residual error. The amount of variation which cannot be attributed to the variables included in the experiment.

FACTORS   Independent variables.

FIXED EFFECTS MODEL   Experimental treatments are specifically selected by the researcher. Conclusions only apply to the factor levels considered in the analysis. Inferences are restricted to the experimental levels.

FLUCTUATIONS   Variances in data which are caused by a large number of minute variations or differences.

FREQUENCY DISTRIBUTION   The pattern or shape formed by the group of measurements in a distribution.

HISTOGRAM   Vertical display of a population distribution in terms of frequencies; a formal method of plotting a frequency distribution.

HOMOGENEITY OF VARIANCE   The variances of the groups being contrasted are equal (as defined by statistical test of significant difference).

INDEPENDENT VARIABLE   A controlled variable; a variable whose value is independent of the value of another variable.

INTERACTION   When the effects of a factor A are not the same at all levels of another factor B.

INSTABILITY   Unnaturally large fluctuations in a pattern.

INTERACTION   The tendency of two or more variables to produce an effect in combination which neither variable would produce if acting alone.

INTERVAL   Numeric categories with equal units of measure but no absolute zero point, i.e., quality scale or index.

LINE CHARTS   Charts used to track the performance without relationship to process capability or control limits.

LOWER CONTROL LIMIT   A horizontal dotted line plotted on a control chart which represents the lower process limit capabilities of a process.

MIXED EFFECTS MODEL	Contains elements of both the fixed and random effects models.
NOMINAL	Unordered categories which indicate membership or nonmembership with no implication of quantity, i.e., assembly area number one, part numbers, etc.
NONCONFORMING UNIT	A unit which does not conform to one or more specifications, standards, and/or requirements.
NONCONFORMITY	A condition within a unit which does not conform to some specific specification, standard, and/or requirement; often referred to as a defect; any given nonconforming unit can have the potential for more than one nonconformity.
NORMAL DISTRIBUTION	A continuous, symmetrical density function characterized by a bell-shaped curve, e.g., distribution of sampling averages.
NULL HYPOTHESIS	A tentative explanation which indicates that a chance distribution is operating; a contrast to the null hypothesis.
ONE-SIDED ALTERNATIVE	The value of a parameter which has an upper bound or a lower bound, but not both.
ORDINAL	Ordered categories (ranking) with no information about distance between each category, i.e., rank ordering of several measurements of an output parameter.
ORDINATE	The vertical axis of a graph.
PARAMETER	A constant defining a particular property of the density function of a variable.
PARETO DIAGRAM	A chart which ranks, or places in order, common occurrences.
P CHARTS	Charts used to plot percent defectives in a sample.
PERTURBATION	A nonrandom disturbance.
POPULATION	A group of similar items from which a sample is drawn. Often referred to as the universe.
POWER OF AN EXPERIMENT	The probability of rejecting the null hypothesis when it is false and accepting the alternate hypothesis when it is true.
PREVENTION	The practice of eliminating unwanted variation a priori (before the fact), e.g., predicting a future condition from a control chart and then applying corrective action before the predicted event transpires.
PRIMARY CONTROL VARIABLES	The major independent variables used in the experiment.
PROBABILITY	The chance of something happening; the percent or number of occurrences over a large number of trials.
PROBABILITY OF AN EVENT	The number of successful events divided by the total number of trials.

PROBLEM	A deviation from a specified standard.
PROBLEM SOLVING	The process of solving problems; the isolation and control of those conditions which generate or facilitate the creation of undesirable symptoms.
PROCESS	A particular method of doing something, generally involving a number of steps or operations.
PROCESS AVERAGE	The central tendency of a given process characteristic across a given amount of time or at a specific point in time.
PROCESS CONTROL	See STATISTICAL PROCESS CONTROL.
PROCESS CONTROL CHART	Any of a number of various types of graphs upon which data are plotted against specific control limits.
PROCESS SPREAD	The range of values which a given process characteristic displays; this particular term most often applies to the range but may also encompass the variance. The spread may be based on a set of data collected at a specific point in time or may reflect the variability across a given amount of time.
PRODUCERS RISK	Probability of rejecting a lot when, in fact, the lot should have been accepted (see ALPHA RISK).
PROJECT	A problem, usually calling for planned action.
R CHARTS	Plot of the difference between the highest and lowest in a sample. Range control chart.
RANDOM	Selecting a sample so each item in the population has an equal chance of being selected; lack of predictability; without pattern.
RANDOM CAUSE	A source of variation which is random; a change in the source ("trivial many" variables) will not produce a highly predictable change in the response (dependent variable), e.g., a correlation does not exist; any individual source of variation results in a small amount of variation in the response; cannot be economically eliminated from a process; an inherent natural source of variation.
RANDOM EFFECTS MODEL	Experimental treatments are a random sample from a larger population of treatments. Conclusions can be extended to the population. Interferences are not restricted to the experimental levels.
POWER OF AN EXPERIMENT	The probability of rejecting the null hypothesis when it is false and accepting the alternate hypothesis when it is true.
PREVENTION	The practice of eliminating unwanted variation a priori (before the fact), e.g., predicting a future condition from a control chart and then applying corrective action before the predicted event transpires.
PRIMARY CONTROL VARIABLES	The major independent variables used in the experiment.

PROBABILITY	The chance of something happening; the percent or number of occurrences over a large number of trials.
PROBABILITY OF AN EVENT	The number of successful events divided by the total number of trials.
PROBLEM	A deviation from a specified standard.
PROBLEM SOLVING	The process of solving problems; the isolation and control of those conditions which generate or facilitate the creation of undesirable symptoms.
PROCESS	A particular method of doing something, generally involving a number of steps or operations.
PROCESS AVERAGE	The central tendency of a given process characteristic across a given amount of time or at a specific point in time.
PROCESS CONTROL	See STATISTICAL PROCESS CONTROL.
PROCESS CONTROL CHART	Any of a number of various types of graphs upon which data are plotted against specific control limits.
PROCESS SPREAD	The range of values which a given process characteristic displays; this particular term most often applies to the range but may also encompass the variance. The spread may be based on a set of data collected at a specific point in time or may reflect the variability across a given amount of time.
PRODUCERS RISK	Probability of rejecting a lot when, in fact, the lot should have been accepted (see ALPHA RISK).
PROJECT	A problem, usually calling for planned action.
R CHARTS	Plot of the difference between the highest and lowest in a sample. Range control chart.
RANDOM	Selecting a sample so each item in the population has an equal chance of being selected; lack of predictability; without pattern.
RANDOM CAUSE	A source of variation which is random; a change in the source ("trivial many" variables) will not produce a highly predictable change in the response (dependent variable), e.g., a correlation does not exist; any individual source of variation results in a small amount of variation in the response; cannot be economically eliminated from a process; an inherent natural source of variation.
RANDOM EFFECTS MODEL	Experimental treatments are a random sample from a larger population of treatments. Conclusions can be extended to the population. Interferences are not restricted to the experimental levels.
RANDOMNESS	A condition in which any individual event in a set of events has the same mathematical probability of occurrence as all other events within the specified set, i.e., individual events are not predictable even though they may collectively belong to a definable distribution.

RANDOM SAMPLE	One or more samples randomly selected from the universe (population).
RANDOM VARIABLE	A variable which can assume any value from a set of possible values.
RANDOM VARIATIONS	Variations in data which result from causes which cannot be pinpointed or controlled.
RANGE	The difference between the highest and lowest values in a set of values or "subgroup."
RANKS	Values assigned to items in a sample to determine their relative occurrence in a population.
RATIO	Numeric scale which has an absolute zero point and equal units of measure throughout, i.e., measurements of an output parameter, i.e., amps.
REJECT REGION	The region of values for which the alternate hypothesis is accepted.
REPLICATION	Observations made under identical test conditions.
ROBUST	The condition or state in which a response parameter exhibits hermeticity to external cause of a nonrandom nature; i.e., impervious to perturbing influence.
REPRESENTATIVE SAMPLE	A sample which accurately reflects a specific condition or set of conditions within the universe.
RESEARCH	Critical and exhaustive investigation or experimentation having for its aim the revision of accepted conclusions in the light of newly discovered facts.
RESIDUAL ERROR	See EXPERIMENTAL ERROR.
SAMPLE	One or more observations drawn from a larger collection of observations or universe (population).
SCATTER DIAGRAMS	Charts which allow the study of correlation, e.g., the relationship between two variables.
SPECIAL CAUSE	See ASSIGNABLE CAUSE.
STABLE PROCESS	A process which is free of assignable causes, e.g., in statistical control.
STANDARD DEVIATION	A statistical index of variability which describes the spread.
STATISTICAL CONTROL	A quantitative condition which describes a process that is free of assignable/special causes of variation, e.g., variation in the central tendency and variance. Such a condition is most often evidenced on a control chart, i.e., a control chart which displays an absence of nonrandom variation.
STATISTICAL PROCESS CONTROL	The application of statistical methods and procedures relative to a process and a given set of standards.

SUBGROUP	A logical grouping of objects or events which displays only random event-to-event variations, e.g., the objects or events are grouped to create homogenous groups free of assignable or special causes. By virtue of the minimum within group variability, any change in the central tendency or variance of the universe will be reflected in the "subgroup-to-subgroup" variability.
SYMPTOM	That which serves as evidence of something not seen.
SYSTEM	That which is connected according to a scheme.
SYSTEMATIC VARIABLES	A pattern which displays predictable tendencies.
THEORY	A plausible or scientifically acceptable general principle offered to explain phenomena.
TEST OF SIGNIFICANCE	A procedure to determine whether a quantity subjected to random variation differs from a postulated value by an amount greater than that due to random variation alone.
TWO-SIDED ALTERNATIVE	The values of a parameter which designate an upper and lower bound.
TYPE I ERROR	See ALPHA RISK.
TYPE II ERROR	See BETA RISK.
UNNATURAL PATTERN	Any pattern in which a significant number of the measurements do not group themselves around a center line; when the pattern is unnatural, it means that outside disturbances are present and are affecting the process.
UPPER CONTROL LIMIT	A horizontal line on a control chart (usually dotted) which represents the upper limits of process capability.
VARIABLE	A characteristic that may take on different values.
VARIABLES DATA	Numerical measurements made at the interval or ratio level; quantitative data, e.g., ohms, voltage, diameter; subdivisions of the measurement scale are conceptually meaningful, e.g., 1.6478 volts.
VARIATION	Any quantifiable difference between individual measurements; such differences can be classified as being due to common causes (random) or special causes (assignable).
VARIATION RESEARCH	Procedures, techniques, and methods used to isolate one type of variation from another (for example, separating product variation from test variation).
$\bar{x}$ & R CHARTS	A control chart which is a representation of process capability over time; displays the variability in the process average and range across time.

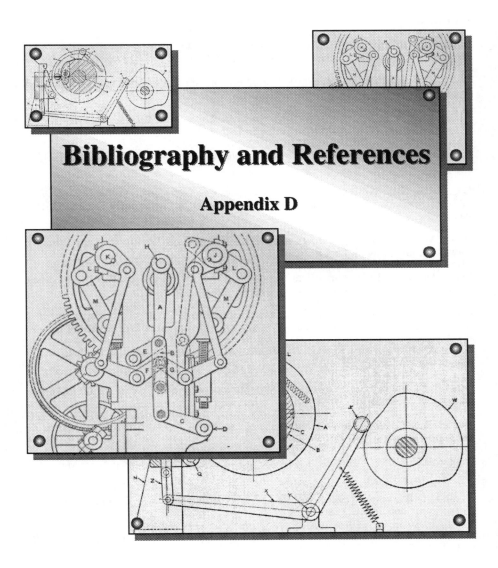

Bibliography and References

Appendix D

General

Bender, A. (1975). "Statistical Tolerancing as it Relates to Quality Control and the Designer." Automotive Division Newsletter of ASQC.

Bowker, A., and G. Lieberman. (1972). *Engineering Statistics.* New Jersey: McGraw-Hill Book Co.

Brownlee, K.A. (1965). *Statistical Theory and Methodology in Science and Engineering.* (Second Edition). New York: John Wiley and Sons, Inc.

Burr, I. (1953). *Engineering Statistics and Quality Control.* New York: McGraw-Hill Book Co.

Department of the Army Materials and Mechanics Research Center. (1984). *MIL-HDBK-727 Design Guidance for Producibility.* Washington, D.C.: Government Printing Office, April.

Dixon, W., and F. Massey. (1969). *Introduction To Statistical Analysis.* (Third Edition). New York: McGraw-Hill book Co.

Evans, David H. (1975). "Statistical Tolerancing: The State of the Art, Part III: Shifts and Drifts." *Journal of Quality and Technology;* 7(2), pp. 72-76.

Ford Motor Company. (1984). "Continuing Process Control and Process Capability Improvement." *Statistical Methods Office.* Operation Support Staffs, Ford Motor Co.

Gilson, J. (1951). *A New Approach to Engineering Tolerances.* London, England: Machinery Publishing Co. Ltd.

Grant, E.L., and R.S. Leavenworth. (1974). *Statistical Quality Control.* (Fifth Edition). New York: McGraw-Hill Book Co.

Gunter, B.H. (1989). "The Use and Abuse of Cpk, Part 2." *Quality Progress;* March, 1989, pp 108.

Gunter, B.H. (1989). "The Use and Abuse of Cpk, Part 3." *Quality Progress;* May, 1989, pp. 79.

Guralnk, D.B ., editor. (1986). *Webster' s New World Dictionary.* (Second Edition). New York: Simon and Schuster Inc.

Hald, A. (1952). *Statistical Theory with Engineering Applications.* New York: John Wiley and Sons.

Harry, M.J. (1989). "PCB Plated Through-Hole Optimization: A Case Study in SPC." *Circuit World;* 16, No. 1,1989, pp. 33-43.

Harry, M., and R. Stewart. (1988). Six *Sigma Mechanical Design Tolerancing.* Motorola, Inc.

Hillier, F.S., and G.J. Lieberman. (1980). *Operations Research.* (Second Edition). San Francisco: Holden Day, Inc.

Hillkirk, John, Editor. (1989). "Top Quality Is Behind Comeback." *USA Today.* Cover Story.

Juran, J.M., F.M. Gryna, and R.S. Bingham. (1979). *Quality Control Handbook.* New York: McGraw-Hill Book Co.

Kane, V.E. (1986). "Process Capability Indices." *Journal of Quality Technology;* 18(1), pp. 41-52.

Kelvin, W.T. (1891). *Popular Lectures and Addresses.*

Mendenhall, W., and R. Schaeffer. (1973). *Mathematical Statistics with Applications.* Massachusetts: Duxbury Press. pp. 185-188.

Motorola, Inc. (1986). *Design for Manufacturability: Eng 123 (Participant Guide).* Motorola Training and Education Center, Motorola, Inc., Illinois.

Nelson. (1988). "Control Charts: Rational Subgroups and Effective Applications." *Journal of Quality Technology;* 20(1), pp. 73-75.

Ott, L. (1977). *An Introduction.to Statistical Methods and Data Analysis.* Massachusetts: Duxbury Press.
Pearson, C. (1983). *Handbook of Applied Mathematics.* (Second Edition). New York: Van Nostrand Reinhold Co.

Shewhart, W.A. (1931). *Economic Control of Manufactured Product.* New Jersey: Van Nostrand Book Co.

Stoll, H., A. Kumar, and D. Maas. (Date Unknown). *Producibility Management: Key to the Design of Producible Products.* Industrial Technology Institute. Michigan: Unpublished.

Taylor. (1982). *An Introduction to Error Analysis - The Study of Uncertainties in Physical Measurements.* Califomia: University Science Books.

Webster's New Collegiate Dictionary. (1976). Massachusetts: Merriam-Webster.

Design Applications

Andreasen, M., S. Kahler, and T. Lund. (1983). *Design for Assembly.* IFS Publications, Ltd.

Bancroft, C. (1988). "Overlooked Aspects of Design for Manufacturability." *IEEE Circuits Devices Mag.* USA;Vol. 4, No. 6, Nov. pp. 15-19.

Barker, Paul A. (1989). "Design for Manufacturability." *Printed Circuit Design,* Vol. 6, No. 1, Jan. pp 37-38.

Battin, L. (1988). "Six Sigma Process by Design." *Design and Dimensions, a Publication of Group Mechanical Technology;* Vol. 1, No. 1, p. 4, Government Electronics Group, Motorola Inc.

Becker, David. (1988). "Flex Circuitry: Designing for Manufacturability." *Printed Circuit Design;* Vol. 5, No. 8, Aug. pp. 54-57.

Bender, A. (1962). "Benderizing Tolerances - A Simple Practical Probability Method of Handling Tolerances for Limit-Stack-Ups." *Graphic Science.* Dec.

Bender, A. (1968). "Statistical Tolerancing as it Relates to Quality Control and the Designer." *Society of Automotive Engineers;* SAE Paper No. 680490, May.

Boothroyd, Geoffrey, and Peter Dewhurst. (1983). *Design for Assembly: A Designer's Handbook.* Rhode Island: Boothroyd Dewhurst, Inc.

Boothroyd, G., and Dewhurst. (1986). *Product Design for Assembly.* Rhode Island: Boothroyd Dewhurst, Inc.

Box, G., and S. Bisgaard. (1988). "Statistical Tools for Improving Designs." *Mechanical Engineering,* Jan.

Bralla, J.G. (1986). *Handbook of Product Design for Manufacturing.* New York: McGraw-Hill Book Co.

Brayton, R.K., S.W. Director, and G.D. Hachtel. (1980). "Yield Maximization and Worst-Case Design with Arbitrary Statistical Distributions." *IEEE Transactions on Circuits and Systems;* Vol. 27, No. 9, pp. 756-764.

Burgess, John A. (1984). *Design Assurance for Engineers and Managers.* New York: Marcel Dekker, pp. 166-182.

Chase, K.W., and W.H. Greenwood. (1987). "Design Issues in Mechanical Tolerance Analysis." *ASME Conference Paper.* Winter Annual Meeting of the American Society of Mechanical Engineers. Dec. 13-18. pp. 11-26.

Cooke, et. al. (1984). *A Guide to Design for Production.* Institution of Production Engineers.

Dao-Thien, My. (1981). "Approach for Optimum Tolerancing of the Design Components." *CANCAM Proceedings.* Canadian Congress of Applied Mechanics 8th, Vol. 1, pp. 333-334.

DeVor, R.E. (1987). "Role of Parameter Design in the Simultaneous Engineering of Products and Processes." *American Society of Mechanical Engineers, Production Engineering Division.* New York: Vol. 27. pp 131-135.

Evans, David H. (1958). "Optimum Tolerance Assignment to Yield Minimum Manufacturing Cost." *Bell System Technical Journal;* 37(2).

Evans, David H. (1970). "Statistical Tolerancing Formulation." *Journal of Quality and Technology;* 2(4), pp. 226-231.

Evans, David H. (1972). "Application of Numerical Integration Techniques to Statistical Tolerancing - III." *Technometrics;* 14(1), pp. 23-35.

Evans, David H. (1974). "Statistical Tolerancing: The State of the Art, Part I: Background." *Journal of Quality and Technology;* 6(4), pp. 188-195.

Evans, David H. (1975). "Statistical Tolerancing: The State of the Art, Part II: Methods for Estimating Moments." *Journal of Quality and Technology;* 7(1), pp. I-12.

Greenwood, G. (1986). "Manufacturability and Testability Issues Increase Design Creativity." *Automated Design and Engineering for Electronics West.* Proceedings of the Technical Sessions, 209-11. 11-13 Mar., Illinois: Cahners Exposition Group.

Greenwood, W.H., and K.W. Chase. (1987). "A New Tolerance Analysis Method for Designers and Manufacturers." *Journal of Engineering for Industry;* Vol. 109, pp. 112-116.

Harry, M.J. (1987). *Electrical Engineering Application of the Taguchi Design Philosophy.* Government Electronics Group, Motorola, Inc.

Heath, H.H. (1979). "Statistical Tolerancing of Engineering Components: Is It Worth It?" *Precision Engineering;* 1(3), pp. 153-156.

Hunter, J.S. (1985). "Statistical Design Applied to Product Design." *Qual. Technol.;* Vol. 17, No. 4, Oct. 210(21).

Jones, S.W. (1973). *Product Design and Process Selection.* London, England: Butterworts.

Joshi, Dileep C. (1985). *Advantages of Simultaneous Design of Product and Processes.* Proceedings of the National Electronics Conference; Vol. 39, Professional Education Int. Inc. pp 650-657.

Kelly Sines, R. (1988). *Integrating Simultaneous Engineering Into New Product Introduction.* Sponsor: Troy Conferences; Boothroyd & Dewhurst. Proceedings of the 3rd International Conference on Product Design for Manufacture and Assembly. Michigan: Troy Conferences. 10 pp.

Knauer, Karl, and Hans Joerg Pfleiderer. (1982). "Yield Enhancement Realized for Analogue Integrated Filters by Design Techniques." *IEEE Proceedings, Part 1: Solid-State and Electron Devices;* 129(2), pp. 67-71.

Langford, T. (1986). "Design or Manufacturability-Cooperation+CAD+CIM." *Automated Design and Engineering for Electronics.* - East. Proceedings of the Technical Sessions, NCR, Corp; Illinois: Cahners Exposition Group, Sep.-Oct., pp. 45-54.

Mansoor, E.M. (1963). "The Application of Probability to Tolerances Used in Engineering Design." *Proceedings, Institute of Mechanical Engineering;* 1781(1).

Melander, Wes, and Kim Mast. (1986). "Design for Manufacturability: It's Not Just Design Rules Anymore." ATE East - E.I. Conference #10327, Hewlett-Packard Co., Massachusetts: MG Expositions Group. June, pp. IV 1 1-IV. 21.

Mercadante, M. (1986). "The Hewlett Packard Company's Approach to Design for Manufacturability." *Automated Design and Engineering for Electronics - East.* Proceedings of the Technical Sessions. Illinois: Cahners Exposition Group, Sep.-Oct., pp. 437.

Oh, H.L. (1987). "Variation Tolerant Design." *American Society of Mechanical Engineers - PED,* General Motors. New York: ASME. Vol. 27, pp. 137-146.

Olivera,R.(1988). *Sigma Fit Tolerance Analysis.* Communications Sector, Motorola, Inc., Illinois.

Phadke, Madhav S. (1986). "Design Optimization Case Studies." *AT&T Tech.* J., AT&T Bell lab. New Jersey: Vol. 65, No. 2, Mar.-Apr., pp. 51-68.

Pike, E.W., and T.R. Silverberg. (1953). "Assigning Tolerances for Maximum Economy." *Machine Design;* Sep. pp. 139-146.

Russell, G.A. (1985). "Design for Manufacturability of Printed Circuit Board Assemblies." *CIRP Annuals.* Berne, Switzerland: Technische Rundschau, Vol. 34, No. 1, Aug. pp. 37-40.

Shigley, Joseph E. (1972). *Mechanical Engineering Design.* (Second Edition). New York: McGraw-Hill Book Co.

Singhal, K., and J.F. Pinel. (1981). "Statistical Design Centering and Tolerancing Using Parametric Sampling." *IEEE Transactions on Circuits and Systems;* 28(7), pp. 692-701.

Starkey, John M., and Gregory J. Florin. (1986). " Design for Manufacturability." *American Society of Mechanical Engineers (Paper).* New York: ASME. Pap 86-DET-121, 6p.

Tietjen, Gary L., and Mark E. Johnson. (1979). "Exact Statistical Tolerance Limits for Sample Variances." *Technometrics;* 21(1), pp. 107-110.

Trucks, H.E. (1974). *Designing for Economical Production.* Michigan: Society of Manufacturing Engineers, 1974.

Wade, Oliver R. (1967). *Tolerance Control in Design and Manufacturing.* New York: Industrial Press, Inc.

Wallace, J.R., and J.L. Grant. (1977). "Least Squares Method for Computing Statistical Tolerance Limits." *Water Resources Research;* 13(5), pp. 819-823.

Computer-Aided Engineering

Afifi, A.A., and S.P. Azen. (1979). *Statistical Analysis. A Computer Oriented Approach.* (Second Edition), Academic Press.

Bohling, D.M., and L.A. O'Neill. (1970). "Interactive Computer Approach to Tolerance Analysis." *IEEE Trans Comput*; C-19(1), pp. 10-16.

Hennessey, Mike, and Gary Krutz. (1986). "Expert CAD System for Statistical Tolerancing Internal Hydraulic Components." *Proceedings of the National Conference on Fluid Power;* Annual Meeting 41st, pp. 115-120.

Ramalingam, Subbiah. (1985). "Expert Systems for Manufacturing: Examples of Tools to Assess Manufacturability." *SME;* 13th NAMRC Proceedings. Michigan: pp. 411-417.

Mathematical Statistics

Abramovitz, M., and Stegun, I.A., Editors. (1964). *Handbook of Mathematical Functions.* National Bureau of Standards Applied Mathematics Series 55, Washington, D.C., p. 955ff and references.

Box, G.E.P., W.G. Hunter, and J.S. Hunter. (1978). *Statistics for Experimenters.* New York: John Wiley and Sons, Inc.

Cowden, Dudley, J. (1957). *Statistical Methods in Quality Control.* New Jersey: Prentice-Hall.

Cramer, H. (1964). *Mathematical Methods of Statistics.* New Jersey: Princeton University Press.

Daniel, C. (1976). *Applications of Statistics To Industrial Experimentation.* New York: John Wiley and Sons.

Guenther, W. (1973). *Concepts of Statistical Interference.* New York: McGraw-Hill Book Co.

Hadley, G. (1967). *Introduction to Probability and Statistical Decision Theory.* California: Holden-Day, Inc.

Hahn, G., and S. Shapiro. (1967). *Statistical Models In Engineerings.* New York: John Wiley and Sons.

Hald, A. (1952). *Statistical Theory with Engineering Applications.* New York: John Wiley and Sons.

Hicks, T.G. (1972). *Standard Handbook of Engineering Calculations.* New York: McGraw-Hill Book Co.

Kendall, M.G., and A. Stuart. (1963). *The Advanced Theory of Statistics.* New York: Hafner Publishing Co.

King, James R. (1971). *Probability Charts for Decision Making.* New York: The Industrial Press.

Mendenhall, W., and R. Schaeffer. (1973). *Mathematical Statistics With Applications.* Massachusetts: Duxbury Press.

Miller, Irwin, and John E. Freund. (1965). *Probability and Statistics for Engineers.* New Jersey: Prentice-Hall, Inc.

Mood, A., and F. Graybill. (1963). *Introduction To The Theory of Statistics.*(Second Edition). New York: McGraw-Hill Book Co.

Moses, L.E. (1959). *Elementary Decision Theory.* New York: John Wiley and Sons.

Natrella,Mary G.(1963). *Experimental Statistics.* Washington, D.C.: National Bureau of Standards Handbook 91, Government Printing Office.

Neville, A.M., and J.B. Kennedy. (1964). *Basic Statistical Methods for Engineers and Scientists.* International Textbook Co.

Nie, N.N., C.H. Hull, J.G. Jenkins, K. Steinbrenner, and D.H. Bent. (1975). *Statistical Package for the Social Sciences.* (Second Edition). New York: McGraw-Hill Book Co.

Pearson, C. (1983). *Handbook of Applied Mathematics,* (Second Edition). New York: Van Nostrand Reinhold Co.

Pearson, E.S., and H.O. Hartley. (1972). *Biometrika Tables for Statisticians; Vol. 2.* Cambridge, Eng.: Cambridge University Press.

Snedecor, G.W., and W.G. Cochran (1967). *Statistical Methods.* (Sixth Edition). Iowa State University Press.

Spotts, M.F. (1978). "Fast Dimensional Checks With Statistics." *Machine Design;* Oct. pp. 171-173.

Wallis, W.A., and H.V. Roberts. (1956). *Statistics: A New Approach.* The Free Press.

Ward, J., and E. Jennings. (1973). *Introduction to Linear Models.* New Jersey: Prentice-Hall

Design of Experiments

Anderson, V.L., and R.A. McLean. (1974). *Design of Experiments.* New York: Marcel Dekker.

Cochran, W., and G. Cox. (1957). *Experimental Designs.* (Second Edition). New York: John Wiley and Sons.

Hicks, C.R. (1964). *Fundamental Concepts in the Design of Experiments.* New York: McGraw-Hill Book Co.

John, P.W.M. (1971). *Statistical Design and Analysis of Experiments.* New York: The MacMillan Company.

Kempthrone, O. (1952). *The Design and Analysis of Experiments.* New York.

Kwok-Leung, Tsui. (1988). "Strategies for Planning Experiments Using Orthogonal Arrays and Confounding Tables." *Qual. Reliab: Eng. Int.* AT&T Bell Lab., New Jersey (UK), Vol. 4, No. 2, Apr.-Jun. 113-22.

Lichtenberg, L.R., M. Sleiman, and M.J. Harry. (1986). "Statistics, Designed Experiments Assembly." *Circuit World Journal of the Institute of Circuit Technology;* 12(4), pp. 34-39.

Lipson, C., and N. Sheth. (1973). *Statistical Design and Analysis of Engineering Experiments.* New York: McGraw-Hill Book Co.

Montgomery, D.C. (1984). *Design and Analysis of Experiments.* (Second Edition). John Wiley and Sons.

Myers, R.H.(1971). *Response Surface Methodology.* Massachusetts: Allyn and Bacon, Inc.

Patel, M.S. (1962). "Group Screening with More Than Two Stages." *Technometrics;* 4(2), pp. 209-217.

Plackett, R.L., and J.P. Burman. (1946). "The Design of Optimum Multifactorial Experiments." *Biometrika;* Vol. 33, pp. 305-325.

Ryan, Thomas P. (1988). "Taguchi's Approach to Experimental Design: Some Concerns." *Quality Progress.* ABl/Inform. Vol. 21, No. 5, May, pp. 34-36.

Shoemaker, Anne C., and Raghu N. Kacker. (1988). "Methodology for Planning Experiments in Robust Product and Process Design." *Quality and Reliability Engineering Intn'l.* New Jersey: AT&T Bell lab. Vol. 4, No. 2, Apr.-Jun. pp. 95-103.

Watson, G.S. (1961). "A Study of the Group Screening Method." *Technometrics;* 3(3), pp. 371-388.

Wheeler, D.J., Ph.D. (1988). *Understanding Industrial Experimentation.* Tennessee: Statistical Process Control Inc.

Statistical Process Control

Duncan, Acheson, J. (1965). *Quality Control and Industrial Statistics.* (Third Edition). Illinois: Richard D. Irwin, Inc.

Grant, E.L., and R.S. Leavenworth. (1972). *Statistical Quality Control.* (Fourth Edition). New York: McGraw-Hill Book Co.

Johnson, L.G. (1964). *Theory and Techniques of Variation Research.* Elsevier Publishing Co.

Kackar, R.N. (1985). "Off Line Quality Control, Parameter Design, and the Taguchi Method." *Journal of Quality Technology;* 17(4), pp. 176-188.

Ott, Ellis R. (1975). *Process Quality Control.* New York: McGraw-Hill Book Co.

Shewhart, W.A. (1931). *Economic Control of Manufactured Product.* New Jersey: Van Nostrand Book Co.

Standard IPC-PC-90. (1989). *General Requirements for Implementation of Statistical Process Control.* Illinois: Institute for Interconnecting and Packaging Electronic Circuits.

Western Electric Company. (1956). *Statistical Quality Control Handbook.* Pennsylvania: Mack Printing Co.

Producibility

Billatos, Samir B. (1988). "Guidelines for Productivity and Manufacturability Strategy." *Manufacturing Review*, Univ. of Connecticut, Storrs, CT., Vol. 1, No. 3, Oct. pp. 164-167.

Boltz, Roger W. (1977). *Production Processes – The Producibility Handbook.* North Carolina: Conquest Publications.

Boothroyd, G., C. Poli, and L. Murch. (1982). *Automatic Assembly.* New York: Marcel Dekker, Inc.

Boyer, David E., and John W. Nazemetz. (1985). "Introducing Statistical Selective Assembly - A Means of Producing High Precision Assemblies from Low Precision Components." *Proceedings, American Institute of Industrial Engineers.* Annual Conference and Convention, pp. 562-570.

Brown, John O. (1987). "Producibility Problem Solving or the Supplier Quality Paradox - A Fix?" *Annual Quality Congress Transactions.* (Forty-First Edition). Wisconsin: ASQC.

Bunselmeyer, K. (1987). "Manufacturability Checklist for Printed Wiring Assemblies." *Printed Circuit Des.* Missouri: Manuf. Eng. Srvcs. Vol. 4, No. 6, Jun. pp. 23-4.

Deming, W. Edwards. (1982). *Quality, Productivity and Competitive Position.* Massachusetts Institute of Technology, Center for Advanced Engineering Study.

Dwivedi, Suren N., and Barry R. Klein. (1986). "Design for Manufacturability Makes Dollars and Sense." *CIM Rev; Vol.* 2, No. 3, pp. 53-59.

Fortini, E.T. (1967). *Dimensioning for Interchangeable Manufacture.* New York: Industrial Press.

Kackar, R.N., and A.C. Shoemaker. (1986). *Robust Design: A Cost-effective Method for Improving Manufacturing Processes.* New Jersey: AT&T Bell Labs. Vol. 65, No. 2, Mar.Apr. pp. 39-50.

King, Robert. (1987). "Listening to the Voice of the Customer: Using the Quality Function Deployment System." *National Productivity Review; Vol.* 6, No. 3, pp. 277-281.

Lewis, G.M. (1988). "Design for Manufacturability Applying the Methodology." *Proceedings of the 3rd International Conference on the Product Design for Manufacture and Assembly.* Michigan: Troy Conferences.

Lin, K.M., and R.N. Kacker. (1986). "Optimizing the Wave Soldering Process." *Packaging and Production;* Feb., pp. 108-1 15.

Maddoux, K.C., and S.C. Jain. (1986). "CAE for the Manufacturing Engineer: The Role of Process Simulation In Concurrent Engineering." *American Society of Mechanical Engineers. Production Engineering Division.* New York: ASME, Vol. 20, Dec. pp. 1-15.

McGregory, Jim, and Hal Conklin. (1986). "Analyzing Manufacturability and the Effects of Design Changes." *Printed Circuit Des.; Vol.* 3, No. 5, May, pp. 25-27, 31.

Phadke, M.S., and K. Dehnad. (1988). "Optimization of Product and Process Design for Quality and Cost." *Quality and Reliability Engineering International.* AT&T Bell Lab. New Jersey: Vol. 4, No. 2, Apr.-Jun. pp. 105-112.

Priest, J.W. (1988). *Engineering Design for Producibility and Reliability.* New York: Marcel Dekker.

Spotts, M.F. (1977). "Running the Risk of Interference Fits." *Machine Design;* 49(17), pp. 106-111.

Miscellaneous

Baldwin, L.V. (1983). "New Modes for Advanced Engineering Study." *Journal of Engineering Education; Vol.* 31, pp. 384-386.

Baumeister, T., and L.S. Marks. (1967). *Standard Handbook for Mechanical Engineers.* New York: McGraw-Hill Book

Charbonneau, Harvey C., and Gordon L. Webster. (1978). *Industrial Quality Control.* New Jersey: Prentice-Hall.

Coffman, Cathy. (1987). "Make Me A Match: Getting Design and Manufacturing Together - Simultaneously." *Automotive Industries;* Vol. 167, No. 12, Dec. pp 62-64.

Daetz, D. (1987). "The Effect of Product Design on Product Quality and Product Cost." *Manuf. Res. Center.* California: Hewlett-Packard Labs. Vol. 20, No. 6, 64(7), Jun.

DeGarmo, Paul. (1974). *Materials and Processes in Manufacturing.* (Fourth Edition). New York: MacMillan.

Department of the Navy. (1986). *Best Practices for Transitioning from Development to Production.* NAVSO P-607 1. Washington.

Doyle, L.E., C.A. Keyser, J.L. Leach, G.F. Schrader, and M.B. Singer. (1969). *Manufacturing Processes and Materials for Engineers.* New Jersey: Prentice-Hall, Inc.

Farag, M.M. (1979). *Materials and Process Selection in Engineering.* London, England: Applied Science Publishers Ltd.

Feigenbaum,A.V.(1961).*Total Quality Control.* New York: McGraw-Hill Book Co.

Gardiner, Paul, and Roy Rothwell. (1985). "Tough Customers: Good Designs." *Design Studies;* Vol. 6, No. 1, Jan. pp
7-17.

Harry, Mikel J. (1987). *The Nature of Six Sigma Quality.* Government Electronics Group, Motorola, Inc.

Ishikawa, Kaoru. (1976). *Guide to Quality Control.* Asian Productivity Organization, Revised Edition.

Juran, J.M., and Frank M. Gryna Jr. (1970). *Quality Planning and Analysis.* New York: McGraw-Hill Book Co.

Little, R.E. (1980). "Statistical Tolerance Limits for Censored Log-Normal Data (Tolerance Limit Computations: Fatigue Life Applications.)" *Journal of Testing and Evaluation;* 8(2), pp. 80-84.

Osborn, A. (1957). *Applied Imagination.* New York: Charles Scribner's Sons.

Parry, G.W., P. Shaw, and D.H. Worledge. (1981). "Statistical Tolerance in Safety Analysis." *Nuclear Safety;* 22(4), pp. 459-463.

Pignatiello, J.J., and J.S. Ramberg. (1985). "Discussion." *Journal of Quality Technology;* 17(4) pp. 198-206.

Notes